Eighteenth-Century British Fiction

THE CRITICAL COSMOS SERIES

Eighteenth-Century British Fiction

Edited and with an introduction
by *HAROLD BLOOM*
Sterling Professor of the Humanities
Yale University

CHELSEA HOUSE PUBLISHERS ◇ 1988
New York ◇ New Haven ◇ Philadelphia

© 1988 by Chelsea House Publishers, a division
of Chelsea House Educational Communications, Inc.
  95 Madison Avenue, New York, NY 10016
  345 Whitney Avenue, New Haven, CT 06511
  5068B West Chester Pike, Edgemont, PA 19028

Introduction © 1988 by Harold Bloom

Printed and bound in the United States of America

10 9 8 7 6 5 4 3 2 1

Library of Congress Cataloging-in-Publication Data
Eighteenth-century fiction.
  (The Critical cosmos series)
  Bibliography: p.
  Includes index.
  1. English fiction—18th century—History and
criticism.   I. Bloom, Harold. II. Series: Critical cosmos.
PR853.E44 1988   823'.5'09   87–8079
ISBN 0–87754–975–3 (alk. paper)

Contents

Editor's Note

This book gathers together a representative selection of the best criticism available upon the major writers of fiction in eighteenth-century Great Britain. It includes essays on Jonathan Swift and Dr. Johnson, who are only marginally authors of fictional narrative, since *Gulliver's Travels* and *Rasselas* cannot be neglected, as well as one on Jane Austen, who can be regarded as belonging to the Romantic era. Her *Mansfield Park* is treated here, however, from an eighteenth-century (feminist) perspective. I am grateful to Christina Büchmann for her erudition and judgment in helping me to edit this volume.

My introduction considers most of these writers as varied chroniclers of the vexed fortunes of the Protestant will. Martin Price reads Defoe's novels as the ebb and flow of creatures "of mixed and unstable motives," held within the literary context of the triumph of realism. Patrick Reilly considers Gulliver and Swift, both "displaced" persons attempting to cope with their environments.

The development of novelistic form from Defoe's *Moll Flanders* to Richardson's *Pamela* is examined by Ralph W. Rader. John J. Richetti analyzes the dramatic power of Richardson in *Clarissa*, while Mary Poovey contrasts the hope of heaven in *Clarissa* and *Tom Jones*.

Fielding's *Joseph Andrews* is seen by Mark Spilka as a resolution of major passions through benevolent humor, a view consonant with that of Ian Watt in his study of *Tom Jones*, which he judges to be the product of "a responsible wisdom about human affairs." A loving appreciation of *Rasselas* by a great Johnsonian, W. K. Wimsatt, is written very much in the spirit of Johnson's own tale.

Studying Romantic irony, Lilian R. Furst finds one of the instances of its triumph in *Tristram Shandy*, where it is "captured with bewildering brilliance." In a witty "digression" on *Tristram Shandy*, Leopold Damrosch,

Jr., insists that Sterne resists skepticism in the name of a movingly imperfect solipsism.

Smollett's balance of joyous play with the larger claims of existence is traced in his modification of the picaresque mode by Philip Stevick. Comparing Smollett to Richardson and Fielding, Jerry C. Beasley shows how each novelist revised private experience into public history. James H. Lehmann traces the effect of Bishop Lowth's secularized and "Orientalized" readings of the Hebrew Bible upon Goldsmith's use of the Book of Job as a model for his *Vicar of Wakefield*.

Fanny Burney's novels are examined by Edward W. Copeland in terms of the economic realities of middle-class women with fixed incomes in the concluding years of the eighteenth century. The Gothic mode in Horace Walpole, Mrs. Radcliffe, and Monk Lewis is analyzed by Howard Anderson through a consideration of its heroes, who attempt to transcend a past that encloses them. In this volume's concluding essay, Margaret Kirkham reads *Mansfield Park* as a work of early feminist irony, set gently but firmly against the dying world of late eighteenth-century England.

Introduction

Of his prayers and the like we take no account, since they are a source of pleasure to him, and he looks upon them as so much recreation.
                                            —KARL MARX on *Robinson Crusoe*

I got so tired of the very colors!
One day I dyed a baby goat bright red
with my berries, just to see
something a little different.
And then his mother wouldn't recognize him.
—ELIZABETH BISHOP, "Crusoe in England"

I

Had Karl Marx written *Robinson Crusoe,* it would have had even more moral vigor, but at the expense of the image of freedom it still provides for us. Had Elizabeth Bishop composed it, Defoe's narrative would have been enhanced as image and as impulse, but at the expense of its Puritan plainness, its persuasive search for some evidences of redemption. Certainly one of Defoe's novelistic virtues is precisely what Ian Watt and Martin Price have emphasized it to be; the puzzles of daily moral choice are omnipresent. Robinson Crusoe and Moll Flanders are human—all-too-human—and suffer what Calvin and Freud alike regarded as the economics of the spirit.

Defoe comes so early in the development of the modern novel as a literary form that there is always a temptation to historicize rather than to read him. But historicisms old and new are poor substitutes for reading, and I do not find it useful to place *Robinson Crusoe* and *Moll Flanders* in their contemporary context when I reread them, as I have just done. Ian Watt usefully remarked: "Defoe's heroes . . . keep us more fully informed of their present stocks of money and commodities than any other characters in fiction." I suspect that this had more to do with Defoe than with his age, and that Defoe would have been no less obsessed with economic motives if he had written in the era of Queen Victoria. He was a hard man who had led a hard life: raised as a Dissenter in the London of the Great Plague and the Great Fire; enduring Newgate prison and the pillory in bankrupt middle age; working as a secret agent and a scandalous journalist until imprisoned again for debt and treason. Defoe died old, and so may be accounted as a survivor, but he had endured a good share of reality, and his novels reflect that endurance.

Dr. Johnson once said that only three books ought to have been still longer than they were: *Don Quixote, The Pilgrim's Progress,* and *Robinson Crusoe.* Defoe has authentic affinities with Bunyan, but there is nothing quixotic about Robinson Crusoe or Moll Flanders. All of Defoe's protagonists are pragmatic and prudent, because they have to be; there is no play in the world as they know it.

II

I did not read *Robinson Crusoe* as a child, and so missed an experience that continues to be all but universal; it remains a book that cannot fail with children. Yet, as Dickens observed, it is also "the only instance of an universally popular book that could make no one laugh and could make no one cry." Crusoe's singular tone, his self-baffled affect, does not bother children, who appear to empathize with a near-perfect solipsist who nevertheless exhibits energy and inventiveness throughout a quarter-century of solitude. Perhaps Crusoe's survival argues implicitly against every child's fear of dependency and prophesies the longed-for individuality that is still to come. Or perhaps every child's loneliness is answered in Crusoe's remarkable strength at sustaining solitude.

Though the identification of Defoe with Crusoe is never wholly overt, the reader senses its prevalence throughout the narrative. Defoe seems to me the least ironic of writers, and yet Crusoe's story is informed by an overwhelming irony. A restless wanderer, driven to travel and adventure by forces that he (and the reader) cannot comprehend, Crusoe is confined to an isolation that ought to madden him by turning him toward an unbearable inwardness. Yet his sanity prevails, despite his apparent imprisonment. Defoe had borne much; Newgate and the pillory were nightmare experiences. Crusoe bears more, yet Defoe will not describe his hero's suffering as being psychic. As Virginia Woolf noted, Defoe "takes the opposite way from the psychologist's—he describes the effect of emotion on the body, not on the mind." Nowhere is this stronger than in Crusoe's agony as he views a shipwreck:

> Such certainly was the Case of these Men, of whom I could not so much as see room to suppose any of them were sav'd; nothing could make it rational, so much as to wish, or expect that they did not all perish there; except the Possibility only of their being taken up by another Ship in Company, and this was but meer Possibility indeed; for I saw not the least Signal or Appearance of any such Thing.
>
> I cannot explain by any possible Energy of Words what a strange longing or hankering of Desires I felt in my Soul upon this Sight; breaking out sometimes thus; O that there had been but one or two; nay, or but one Soul sav'd out of this Ship, to have escap'd to me, that I might but have had one Companion, one Fellow-

Creature to have spoken to me, and to have convers'd with! In all the Time of my solitary Life, I never felt so earnest, so strong a Desire after the Society of my Fellow-Creatures, or so deep a Regret at the want of it.

There are some secret moving Springs in the Affections, which when they are set a going by some Object in view; or be it some Object, though not in view, yet rendred present to the Mind by the Power of Imagination, that Motion carries out the Soul by its Impetuosity to such violent eager embracings of the Object, that the Absence of it is insupportable.

Such were these earnest Wishings, That but one Man had been sav'd! *O that it had been but One!* I believe I repeated the Words, *O that it had been but One!* a thousand Times; and the Desires were so mov'd by it, that when I spoke the Words, my Hands would clinch together, and my Fingers press the Palms of my Hands, that if I had had any soft Thing in my Hand, it would have crusht it involuntarily; and my Teeth in my Head wou'd strike together, and set against one another so strong, that for some time I cou'd not part them again.

These are the reactions of a compulsive craftsman who has found his freedom but cannot bear its full sublimity. Crusoe, himself the least sublime of personages, is embedded throughout in a sublime situation, best epitomized by the ghastly cannibal feasts he spies upon, and from which he rescues his man Friday. Against his superior technology and Puritan resolve, the cannibals offer almost no resistance, so that the rapid conversion of the cannibal Friday to Protestant theology and diet is not unconvincing. What may baffle the average rereader is Crusoe's comparative dearth of Protestant inwardness. It is not that Marx was accurate and that Crusoe becomes Protestant only upon the Sabbath, but rather that Defoe's God is himself a technocrat and an individualist, not much given to the nicer emotions. Defoe's God can be visualized as a giant tradesman, coping with the universe as Crusoe makes do on his island, but with teeming millions of adoring Fridays where Crusoe enjoys the devotion of just one.

III

With *Robinson Crusoe*, aesthetic judgment seems redundant; the book's status as popular myth is too permanent and so the critic must ground arms. *Moll Flanders* is another matter, and provokes a remarkably wide range of critical response, from the late poet-critic Allen Tate, who once told me it was a great novel of Tolstoyan intensity, to equally qualified readers who deny that it is a novel at all. The overpraisers include James Joyce, who spoke of "the unforgettable harlot Moll Flanders," and William Faulkner, who coupled *Moby-Dick* and *Moll Flanders* as works he would like to have written (together with one of Milne's Pooh books!). Rereading *Moll Flanders* leaves me a touch baffled, as I thought it had been better, it being one of those books that are much more vivid in parts than as a unit, so that the memory holds on to episodes and to impressions, investing them with an aura that much of the narrative does not possess. The status of the narrative is curiously wavering; one is not always certain one is reading a novel, rather than a colorful tract of the Puritan persuasion. Moll is a formidable person, who sustains our interest and our good will. But the story she tells seems alternately formed and formless, and frequently confuses the rival authorities of fiction and supposed fact.

Martin Price notes how little thematic unity Defoe imposes upon the stuff of existence that constitutes *Moll Flanders*. As a man who had suffered Newgate, Defoe gives us only one key indication of his novel's vision; Moll was born in Newgate and will do anything to avoid ending there. The quest for cash is simply her equivalent of Crusoe's literal quest to survive physically upon his island, except that Moll is more imaginative than the strangely compulsive Crusoe. He does only what he must, she does more, and we begin to see that her obsession has in it an actual taste for adventures. This taste surprises her, but then, as Price observes, she is always "surprised by herself and with herself." She learns by what she does, and almost everything she does is marked by gusto. Her vehemence is her most winning quality, but most of her qualities are attractive. Male readers are charmed by her, particularly male readers who both exalt and debase women, among whom Joyce and Faulkner remain the most prominent.

Puritan force, the drive for the soul's exuberant self-recognition, is as much exemplified by Moll as by Bunyan's protagonist. I suspect that was why William Hazlitt, the greatest literary critic to emerge from the tradition of Protestant Dissent, had so violent a negative reaction to *Moll Flanders*, which otherwise I would have expected him to admire. But, on some level, he evidently felt that she was a great discredit to Puritan sensibility. Charles Lamb greatly esteemed her, and understood how authentic the Puritan dialectic was in her, pointing to "the intervening flashes of religious visitation upon the rude and uninstructed soul," and judging this to "come near to the tenderness of Bunyan." Infuriated, Hazlitt responded: "Mr. Lamb admires *Moll Flanders*; would he marry Moll Flanders?" to which the only response a loyal Hazlittian could make is: "Would that Hazlitt had married a Moll Flanders, and been happy for once in a relationship with a woman." All proportion abandoned Hazlitt when he wrote about *Moll Flanders*:

> We . . . may, nevertheless, add, for the satisfaction of the inquisitive reader, that *Moll Flanders* is utterly vile and detestable: Mrs. Flanders was evidently born in sin. The best parts are the account of her childhood, which is pretty and affecting; the fluctuation of her feelings between remorse and hardened impenitence in

Newgate; and the incident of her leading off the horse from the inn-door, though she had no place to put it in after she had stolen it. This was carrying the love of thieving to an *ideal* pitch and making it perfectly disinterested and mechanical.

Hazlitt did not understand Moll, because he could not bear to see the Puritan impulse displaced into "carrying the love of thieving to an *ideal* pitch." Brilliant as the horse-stealing is, it is surpassed by Moll's famous second theft, the episode of the child's necklace:

Had I gone on here I had perhaps been a true Penitent; but I had an evil Counsellor within, and he was continually prompting me to relieve my self by the worst means; so one Evening he tempted me again by the same wicked Impulse that had said, *take that Bundle*, to go out again and seek for what might happen.

I went out now by Day-light, and wandred about I knew not whither, and in search of I knew not what, when the Devil put a Snare in my way of a dreadful Nature indeed, and such a one as I have never had before or since; going thro' *Aldersgate-street* there was a pretty little Child had been at a Dancing-School, and was going home, all alone, and my Prompter, like a true Devil, set me upon this innocent Creature; I talk'd to it, and it prattl'd to me again, and I took it by the Hand and led it a long till I came to a pav'd Alley that goes into *Bartholomew Close*, and I led it in there; the Child said that was not its way home; I said, yes, my Dear it is, I'll show you the way home; the Child had a little Necklace on of Gold Beads, and I had my Eye upon that, and in the dark of the Alley I stoop'd, pretending to mend the Child's Clog that was loose, and took off her Necklace and the Child never felt it, and so led the Child on again: Here, I say, the Devil put me upon killing the Child in the dark Alley, that it might not Cry; but the very thought frighted me so that I was ready to drop down, but I turn'd the Child about and bade it go back again, for that was not its way home; the Child said so she would, and I went thro' into *Bartholomew Close*, and then turn'd round to another Passage that goes into *Long-lane*, so away into *Charterhouse-Yard* and out into *St. John's-street*, then crossing into *Smithfield*, went down *Chick-lane* and into *Field-lane* to *Holbourn-bridge*, when mixing with the Crowd of People usually passing there, it was not possible to have been found out; and thus I enterpriz'd my second Sally into the World.

The thoughts of this Booty put out all the thoughts of the first, and the Reflections I had made wore quickly off; Poverty, as I have said, harden'd my Heart, and my own Necessities made me regardless of any thing: The last Affair left no great Concern upon me, for as I did the poor Child no harm, I only said to my self, I

had given the Parents a just Reproof for their Negligence in leaving
the poor little Lamb to come home by it self, and it would teach
them to take more Care of it another time.

This String of Beads was worth about Twelve or Fourteen
Pounds; I suppose it might have been formerly the Mother's, for
it was too big for the Child's wear, but that, perhaps, the Vanity
of the Mother to have her Child look Fine at the Dancing School,
had made her let the Child wear it; and no doubt the Child had
a Maid sent to take care of it, but she, like a careless Jade, was
taken up perhaps with some Fellow that had met her by the way,
and so the poor Baby wandred till it fell into my Hands.

However, I did the Child no harm; I did not so much as fright
it, for I had a great many tender Thoughts about me yet, and did
nothing but what, as I may say, meer Necessity drove me to.

The remarkable moment, which horrifies us and must have scandalized
Hazlitt, is when Moll says: "the Devil put me upon killing the Child in the
dark Alley, that it might not Cry; but the very thought frighted me so that
I was ready to drop down." We do not believe that Moll will slay the child,
but she frightens us, because of her capacity for surprising herself. We are
reminded that we do not understand Moll, *because Defoe does not understand
her.* This is his novel's most peculiar strength and its most peculiar weakness. Gide's Lafcadio, contemplating his own crime, murmurs that it is not
about events that he is curious, but only about himself. That is in the spirit
of Defoe's Moll. The Protestant sensibility stands back from itself, and
watches the spirits of good and of evil contend for it, with the detachment
of a certain estrangement, a certain wonder at the immense energies that
God has placed in one's soul.

IV

The terrible greatness of Jonathan Swift's *A Tale of a Tub* has much to do
with our sense of its excess, with its force being so exuberantly beyond its
form (or its calculated formlessness). *Gulliver's Travels*, the later and lesser
work, has survived for the common reader, whereas Swift's early masterpiece has not. Like its descendant, Carlyle's *Sartor Resartus, A Tale of a Tub*
demands too much of the reader, but it more than rewards those demands,
and it now seems unclear whether *Sartor Resartus* does or not. Gulliver's
first two voyages are loved by children (of all ages), while the third and
fourth voyages, being more clearly by the Swift who wrote *A Tale of a Tub,*
now make their appeal only to those who would benefit most from an
immersion in the *Tub.*

Gulliver himself is both the strength and the weakness of the book,
and his character is particularly ambiguous in the great fourth voyage, to
the country of the rational Houyhnhnms and the bestial Yahoos, who are

and are not, respectively, horses and humans. The inability to resist a societal perspectivism is at once Gulliver's true weakness, and his curious strength as an observer. Swift's barely concealed apprehension that the self is an abyss, that the ego is a fiction masking our fundamental nothingness, is exemplified by Gulliver, but on a level of commonplaceness far more bathetic than anything reductive in the Tale-teller. Poor Gulliver is a good enough man but almost devoid of imagination. One way of describing him might be to name him the least Nietzschean character ever to appear in any narrative. Though a ceaseless traveller, Gulliver lacks any desire to be elsewhere, or to be different. His pride is blind, and all too easily magnifies to pomposity, or declines to a self-contempt that is more truly a contempt for all other humans. If the Tale-teller is a Swiftian parody of one side of Swift, the anti-Cartesian, anti-Hobbesian, then Gulliver is a Swiftian parody of the great ironist's own misanthropy.

The reader of "A Voyage to Lilliput" is unlikely to forget the fatuity of Gulliver at the close of chapter 6:

> I am here obliged to vindicate the Reputation of an excellent Lady, who was an innocent Sufferer upon my Account. The Treasurer took a Fancy to be jealous of his Wife, from the Malice of some evil Tongues, who informed him that her Grace had taken a violent Affection for my Person; and the Court-Scandal ran for some Time that she once came privately to my Lodging. This I solemnly declare to be a most infamous Falshood, without any Grounds, farther than that her Grace was pleased to treat me with all innocent Marks of Freedom and Friendship. I own she came often to my House, but always publickly. . . . I should not have dwelt so long upon this Particular, if it had not been a Point wherein the Reputation of a great Lady is so nearly concerned, to say nothing of my own; although I had the Honour to be a *Nardac*, which the Treasurer himself is not; for all the World knows he is only a *Clumglum*, a Title inferior by one Degree, as that of a Marquess is to a Duke in *England*; yet I allow he preceded me in right of his Post.

The great Nardac has so fallen into the societal perspective of Lilliput, that he sublimely forgets he is twelve times the size of the Clumglum's virtuous wife, who therefore would have been quite safe with him were they naked and alone. Escaping back to England, Gulliver has learned nothing and sets forth on "A Voyage to Brobdingnag," land of the giants, where he learns less than nothing:

> The Learning of this People is very defective; consisting only in Morality, History, Poetry and Mathematicks; wherein they must be allowed to excel. But, the last of these is wholly applied to what may be useful in Life; to the Improvement of Agriculture and all

mechanical Arts; so that among us it would be little esteemed. And as to Ideas, Entities, Abstractions and Transcendentals, I could never drive the least Conception into their Heads.

No Law of that Country must exceed in Words the Number of Letters in their Alphabet; which consists only of two and twenty. But indeed, few of them extend even to that Length. They are expressed in the most plain and simple Terms, wherein those People are not Mercurial enough to discover above one Interpretation. And, to write a Comment upon any Law, is a capital Crime. As to the Decision of civil Causes, or Proceedings against Criminals, their Precedents are so few, that they have little Reason to boast of any extraordinary Skill in either.

Effective as this is, it seems too weak an irony for Swift, and we are pleased when the dull Gulliver abandons Brobdingnag behind him. The Third Voyage, more properly Swiftian, takes us first to Laputa, the floating island, at once a parody of a Platonic academy yet also a kind of science fiction punishment machine, always ready to crush earthlings who might assert liberty:

If any Town should engage in Rebellion or Mutiny, fall into violent Factions, or refuse to pay the usual Tribute; the King hath two Methods of reducing them to Obedience. The first and the mildest Course is by keeping the Island hovering over such a Town, and the Lands about it; whereby he can deprive them of the Benefit of the Sun and the Rain, and consequently afflict the Inhabitants with Dearth and Diseases. And if the Crime deserve it, they are at the same time pelted from above with great Stones, against which they have no Defence, but by creeping into Cellars or Caves, while the Roofs of their Houses are beaten to Pieces. But if they still continue obstinate, or offer to raise Insurrections; he proceeds to the last Remedy, by letting the Island drop directly upon their Heads, which makes a universal Destruction both of Houses and Men. However, this is an Extremity to which the Prince is seldom driven, neither indeed is he willing to put it in Execution; nor dare his Ministers advise him to an Action, which as it would render them odious to the People, so it would be a great Damage to their own Estates that lie all below; for the Island is the King's Demesn.

The maddening lack of affect on Gulliver's part begins to tell upon us here; the stolid narrator is absurdly inadequate to the grim force of his own recital, grimmer for us now even than it could have been for the prophetic Swift. Gulliver inexorably and blandly goes on to Lagado, where he observes the grand Academy of Projectors, Swift's famous spoof of the British Royal Society, but here the ironies go curiously flat, and I suspect we are left with the irony of irony, which wearies because by repetition it seems to become compulsive. Yet it may be that here, as subsequently with the immortal but senile and noxious Struldbruggs, the irony of irony is highly deliberate, in order to prepare Gulliver, and the battered reader, for the great shock of reversal that lies just ahead in the Country of the Houyhnhnms, which is also the land of the Yahoos, "a strange sort of Animal."

Critical reactions to Gulliver's fourth voyage have an astonishing range, from Thackeray calling its moral "horrible, shameful, unmanly, blasphemous," to T. S. Eliot regarding it as a grand triumph for the human spirit. Eliot's judgment seems to me as odd as Thackeray's, and presumably both writers believed that the Yahoos were intended as a just representation of the natural man, with Thackeray humanistically disagreeing, and the neo-Christian Eliot all too happy to concur. If that were the proper reading of Swift, we would have to conclude that the great satirist had drowned in his own misanthropy, and had suffered the terrible irony, after just evading becoming one with his Tale-teller, of joining himself to the uneducable Gulliver. Fit retribution perhaps, but it is unwise to underestimate the deep cunning of Swift.

Martin Price accurately reminds us that Swift's attitudes do not depend solely upon Christian morals but stem also from a traditional secular wisdom. Peace and decency are wholly compatible with Christian teaching but are secular virtues as well. Whatever the Yahoos represent, they are *not* a vision of secular humanity devoid of divine grace, since they offend the classical view of man quite as profoundly as they seem to suit an ascetic horror of our supposedly natural condition.

Clearly, it is the virtues of the Houyhnhnms, and not the squalors of the Yahoos, that constitute a burden for critics and for common readers. I myself agree with Price, when he remarks of the Houyhnhnms: "They are rational horses, neither ideal men nor a satire upon others' ideals for man." Certainly they cannot represent a human rational ideal, since none of us would wish to lack all impulse, or any imagination whatsoever. Nor do they seem a plausible satire upon the Deistic vision, a satire worthier of Blake than of Swift, and in any case contradicted by everything that truly is admirable about these cognitively advanced horses. A rational horse is a kind of oxymoron, and Swift's irony is therefore more difficult than ever to interpret:

> My Master heard me with great Appearances of Uneasiness in his Countenance; because *Doubting* or *not believing,* are so little known in this Country, that the Inhabitants cannot tell how to behave themselves under such Circumstances. And I remember in frequent Discourses with my Master concerning the Nature of Manhood, in other Parts of the World; having Occasion to talk of *Lying,* and *false Representation,* it was with much Difficulty that he comprehended what I meant; although he had otherwise a most acute

Judgment. For he argued thus; That the Use of Speech was to make us understand one another, and to receive Information of Facts; now if any one *said the Thing which was not,* these Ends were defeated; because I cannot properly be said to understand him; and I am so far from receiving Information, that he leaves me worse than in Ignorance; for I am led to believe a Thing *Black* when it is *White,* and *Short* when it is *Long.* And these were all the Notions he had concerning the Faculty of *Lying,* so perfectly well understood, and so universally practised among human Creatures.

Are we altogether to admire Gulliver's Master here, when that noble Houyhnhnm not only does not know how to react to the human propensity to say *the thing which was not* but lacks even the minimal imagination that might allow him to apprehend the human need for fictions, a "sickness not ignoble," as Keats observed in *The Fall of Hyperion*? Since the noble Houyhnhnm finds the notion "that the *Yahoos* were the only governing Animals" in Gulliver's country "altogether past his conception," are we again to admire him for an inability that would make it impossible for us to read *Gulliver's Travels* (or *King Lear,* for that matter)? The virtues of Swift's rational horses would not take us very far, if we imported them into our condition, but can that really be one of Swift's meanings? And what are we to do with Swiftian ironies that are too overt already, and become aesthetically intolerable if we take up the stance of the sublimely rational Houyhnhnm?

My Master likewise mentioned another Quality, which his Servants had discovered in several *Yahoos,* and to him was wholly unaccountable. He said, a Fancy would sometimes take a *Yahoo,* to retire into a Corner, to lie down and howl, and groan, and spurn away all that came near him, although he were young and fat, and wanted neither Food nor Water; nor did the Servants imagine what could possibly ail him. And the only Remedy they found was to set him to hard Work, after which he would infallibly come to himself. To this I was silent out of Partiality to my own Kind; yet here I could plainly discover the true Seeds of *Spleen,* which only seizeth on the *Lazy,* the *Luxurious,* and the *Rich;* who, if they were forced to undergo the *same Regimen,* I would undertake for the Cure.

His Honour had farther observed, that a Female-*Yahoo* would often stand behind a Bank or a Bush, to gaze on the young Males passing by, and then appear, and hide, using many antick Gestures and Grimaces; at which time it was observed, that she had a most *offensive Smell;* and when any of the Males advanced, would slowly retire, looking often back, and with a counterfeit Shew of Fear, run off into some convenient Place where she knew the Male would follow her.

Swift rather dubiously seems to want it every which way at once, so that the Yahoos both are and are not representations of ourselves, and the Houyhnhnms are and are not wholly admirable or ideal. Or is it the nature of irony itself, which must weary us, or finally make us long for a true sublime, even if it should turn out to be grotesque? Fearfully strong writer that he was, Swift as ironist resembles Kafka far more than, say, Orwell, among modern authors. We do not know precisely how to read "In the Penal Colony" or *The Trial*, and we certainly do not know exactly how to interpret Gulliver's fourth voyage. What most merits interpretation in Kafka is the extraordinary perversity of imagination with which he so deliberately makes himself uninterpretable. Is Swift a similar problem for the reader? What is the proper response to the dismaying conclusion of *Gulliver's Travels*?

> Having thus answered the *only* Objection that can be raised against me as a Traveller; I here take a final Leave of my Courteous Readers, and return to enjoy my own Speculations in my little Garden at *Redriff*; to apply those excellent Lessons of Virtue which I learned among the *Houyhnhnms*; to instruct the *Yahoos* of my own Family as far as I shall find them docible Animals; to behold my Figure often in a Glass, and thus if possible habituate my self by Time to tolerate the Sight of a human Creature: To lament the Brutality of *Houyhnhnms* in my own Country, but always treat their Persons with Respect, for the Sake of my noble Master, his Family, his Friends, and the whole *Houyhnhnm* Race, whom these of ours have the Honour to resemble in all their Lineaments, however their Intellectuals came to degenerate.
>
> I began last Week to permit my Wife to sit at Dinner with me, at the Farthest End of a long Table; and to answer (but with the utmost Brevity) the few Questions I ask her. Yet the Smell of a *Yahoo* continuing very offensive, I always keep my Nose well stopt with Rue, Lavender, or Tobacco-Leaves. And although it be hard for a Man late in Life to remove old Habits; I am not altogether out of Hopes in some Time to suffer a Neighbour *Yahoo* in my Company, without the Apprehensions I am yet under of his Teeth or his Claws.

Who are those "Courteous Readers" of whom Gulliver takes his final leave here? We pity the poor fellow, but we do not so much pity Mrs. Gulliver as wonder how she can tolerate the insufferable wretch. Yet the final paragraphs have a continued power that justifies their fame, even as we continue to see Gulliver as deranged:

> My Reconcilement to the *Yahoo*-kind in general might not be so difficult, if they would be content with those Vices and Follies only which Nature hath entitled them to. I am not in the least provoked

at the Sight of a Lawyer, a Pickpocket, a Colonel, a Fool, a Lord, a Gamester, a Politician, a Whoremunger, a Physician, an Evidence, a Suborner, an Attorney, a Traytor, or the like: This is all according to the due Course of Things: But, when I behold a Lump of Deformity, and Diseases both in Body and Mind, smitten with *Pride*, it immediately breaks all the Measures of my Patience; neither shall I be ever able to comprehend how such an Animal and such a Vice could tally together. The wise and virtuous *Houyhnhnms*, who abound in all Excellencies that can adorn a rational Creature, have no Name for this Vice in their Language, whereby they describe the detestable Qualities of their *Yahoos*; among which they were not able to distinguish this of Pride, for want of thoroughly understanding Human Nature, as it sheweth it self in other Countries, where that Animal presides. But I, who had more Experience, could plainly observe some Rudiments of it among the wild *Yahoos*.

But the *Houyhnhnms*, who live under the Government of Reason, are no more proud of the good Qualities they possess, than I should be for not wanting a Leg or an Arm, which no Man in his Wits would boast of, although he must be miserable without them. I dwell the longer upon this subject from the Desire I have to make the Society of an *English Yahoo* by any Means not insupportable; and therefore I here intreat those who have any Tincture of this absurd Vice, that they will not presume to appear in my Sight.

What takes precedence here, the palpable hit at the obscenity of false human pride, or the madness of Gulliver, who thinks he is a Yahoo, longs to be a Houyhnhnm, and could not bear to be convinced that he is neither? As in *A Tale of a Tub*, Swift audaciously plays at the farthest limits of irony, limits that make satire impossible, because no norm exists to which we might hope to return.

V

I first read *Clarissa* as a Cornell undergraduate in the late 1940s, under the skilled direction of my teacher William M. Sale, Jr., a fierce partisan of Richardson and a remarkable critic of fiction. Since I cannot read a novel other than the ways that Sale taught me, it is not surprising that forty years later I hold on fast to his canonical judgment that *Clarissa* is the finest novel in the English language. Rereading it through the years, I find it the only novel that can rival even Proust, despite Proust's evident advantages. The long and astonishing sequence that ends the novel, Clarissa's protracted death and its aftermath, is clearly at one of the limits of the novel as an art. I find myself fighting not to weep just before the moment of Clarissa's death, but as a critic I submit that these would be *cognitive* tears, and say little about me, but much about Richardson's extraordinary powers of representation. It remains a mystery that Richardson, with no strong novelistic precursors, should have been able to make Clarissa Harlowe the most persuasive instance of a kind of secular saint, a strong heroine, in the entire subsequent history of the Western novel.

Ian Watt, still our best historian of the rise of the novel, emphasizes that one of Richardson's major advances upon Defoe was in solving the problem of plot by centering it upon a single action: courtship between the sexes. That action necessarily entails Richardson's other grand innovation: the novelistic representation of the protagonists' inwardness, a mode of mimesis in which Richardson had only the one inevitable precursor, Shakespeare. If Jan Hendrik van den Berg is right, then historical psychology is essentially the study of the growing inner self, from Luther's "inner man" (1520) through Shakespeare's almost fully secularized tragic heroes on to Rousseau's and Wordsworth's solitary egos confronting, with ecstasy, the estrangement of things in a "sense of nature." *Clarissa* (1747–48) preceded all of Rousseau's publications, so that while Rousseau could have had something to tell Richardson about the sentiments and sensibility of inwardness, he did not teach the first great English novelist about the fictional representation of the inner life.

Whether anyone since has surpassed Richardson in this mimetic mode seems to me at least doubtful. George Eliot's Dorothea Brooke, Henry James's Isabel Archer, D. H. Lawrence's Ursula Brangwen, and even Virginia Woolf's Clarissa Dalloway, do not take us farther into the portrayal of a single consciousness than the original Clarissa brings us, and perhaps they all of them retreat to some degree from her full inwardness. Price remarks that "Richardson has transformed highly particularized characters so that their dense and familiar social setting fades away in the course of the slow disclosure of consequences." That transformation, in Clarissa and to some extent in Lovelace, replaces the social and historical context with a not less than tragic inwardness. If Clarissa is a saint and a martyr, then what she bears heroic witness to is not so much supernatural faith in Christ as it is natural faith in the heroic integrity of her own perpetually growing inner self.

VI

Richardson's power as a novelist centers in the wildly antithetical and fiercely ambivalent relationship between Clarissa and Lovelace, who destroy both themselves and one another, in what may be the most equivocal instance of a mutual passion in all of Western literature. I do not venture that assertion lightly, but no single love affair in Shakespeare, Tolstoy, or Proust seems comparable in its strength and complexity to the terrible agon that consumes Clarissa and Lovelace. We can no more speculate upon what a marriage between Richardson's protagonists might have been than we can visualize a world harmoniously ruled by a perpetually united Antony and Cleopatra. Lovelace and Clarissa are mighty opposites yet uncannily complementary, and it is Richardson's consummate art to have so created them that they must undo one another.

I begin with Lovelace, if only because his power of being, immense as it is, finally is eclipsed by the transcendental transformation of the gorgeously dying Clarissa. But that indeed is a finality; until Clarissa begins to die, the sheer force of her resistance to Lovelace compels her to become even more herself. Conversely, Lovelace's aggression greatly strengthens Clarissa, though the cost of her confirmation is her life. In the novel's most terrible irony, the slow dying of Clarissa directly causes a steady waning in Lovelace, a dwindling down from a heroic Satanist to a self-ruined libertine, drowning in remorse and confusion.

A. D. McKillop usefully traced Lovelace's literary ancestry to the libertine man-of-fashion in Restoration comedy and to the Herculean hero of Dryden's dramas, such as *Aureng-Zebe* and *The Conquest of Granada*. This lineage accounts both for some of Lovelace's obvious faults and for his few but authentic virtues: healthy disdain for societal appearances and for false morality, a curiously wistful longing for true virtue, and a brutal honesty. But a fusion of a Restoration witty rake and Herculean rhetorician is no more a match for Clarissa Harlowe than a Jacobean hero-villain would have been, and part of the novel's fascination is in watching Lovelace slowly realize that Clarissa is necessarily an apocalyptic defeat for him. The turning point is not the rape, but a moment late in Letter 266, when Lovelace suddenly apprehends the dialectical entrapment that he and Clarissa constitute for one another:

A horrid dear creature!—By my soul, she made me shudder! She had need, indeed, to talk of *her* unhappiness, in falling into the hands of the only *man* in the world who could have used her as I have used her! She is the only *woman* in the world who could have shocked and disturbed me as she has done—So we are upon a foot in that respect. And I think I have the *worst* of it by much. Since very little has been my joy; very much my trouble: and *her* punishment, as she calls it, is *over*: but when *mine* will, or what it *may be*, who can tell?

Here, only recapitulating (think, then, how I must be affected at the time), I was forced to leave off, and sing a song to myself. I aimed at a lively air; but I croaked rather than sung: and fell into the old dismal thirtieth of January strain. I hemmed up for a sprightlier note; but it would not do: and at last I ended, like a malefactor, in a dead psalm melody.

High-ho!—I gape like an unfledged kite in its nest, wanting to swallow a chicken, bobbed at its mouth by its marauding dam!—

What a devil ails me!—I can neither think nor write!—

Lie down, pen, for a moment!—

The devil that ails him is the beginning of his own end, his falling outwards and downwards from his last shreds of a libertine ideology into the dreadful inner space of his defeat by Clarissa, his enforced realization that self-willing and self-assertion are permanently over for him. Clarissa, a great Puritan withholder of esteem, will not accept him at his own evaluation, and he begins to know that pragmatically they have destroyed one another. His actual death is a release from the death-in-life he has suffered since Clarissa's death:

> He was delirious, at times, in the two last hours; and then several times cried out, Take her away! Take her away! but named nobody. And sometimes praised some lady (that Clarissa, I suppose, whom he had called upon when he received his death's wound) calling her, Sweet Excellence! Divine Creature! Fair Sufferer!—And once he said, Look down, blessed Spirit, look down!—And there stopped—his lips however moving.
>
> At nine in the morning, he was seized with convulsions, and fainted away; and it was a quarter of an hour before he came out of them.
>
> His few last words I must not omit, as they show an ultimate composure; which may administer some consolation to his honourable friends.
>
> *Blessed*—said he, addressing himself no doubt to Heaven; for his dying eyes were lifted up—a strong convulsion prevented him for a few moments saying more—But recovering, he again with great fervour (lifting up his eyes, and his spread hands) pronounced the word *Blessed*—Then, in a seeming ejaculation, he spoke inwardly so as not to be understood: at last, he distinctly pronounced these three words,

LET THIS EXPIATE!

> And then, his head sinking on his pillow, he expired; at about half an hour after ten.

Lovelace dies in his own acquired religion, which is the worship of the blessed Clarissa, whom he personally has converted into something considerably more than a saint or even an angel. Being himself pure will, and having been conquered by an even purer one, he worships his conqueror as God. Dying as a Clarissian rather than a Christian, as it were, Lovelace sustains his final pride, a peculiar sense of glory that has gone beyond remorse, and has little left in it of mere love. This is hardly expiation in any moral or spiritual sense whatsoever, as Richardson on some level must have known, but it is certainly an aesthetic expiation, worthy of Baudelaire or of Proust.

VII

Clarissa, as is radiantly appropriate, ends many trajectories beyond her lover's destination. I dissent from the entire critical tradition, from Watt and Price to my younger contemporaries, that has overemphasized Clarissa's supposed self-deceptions. Dr. Samuel Johnson first noted that Clarissa could not confront the truth of having fallen in love with Lovelace, but that hardly seems to me a duplicity in her, however unknowing. We cannot choose whom we are free to love, but Clarissa wars more strongly against every mode of overdetermination than any comparable character in secular fiction. What matters to her, and this is her greatness, is that her will cannot be violated, even by her own affections. *She refuses to see herself as anyone's victim*—whether Lovelace's, her family's, or her own turning against the self.

Lovelace becomes a wounded narcissist and so is aggressive down to the end. But Clarissa could honestly say, if she wanted to, that it is not her narcissism but her eros that has been crucified. If Lovelace indeed represented her desire for what she did not have and was not in herself, then her desire died, not so paradoxically, with the violation of her body. Lovelace becomes still more naturalistic after the rape, but she is transformed into a dualist, and begins the process of dying to the body of this life. The issue has nothing to do with society, and little to do with conventional reality. It is an aesthetic issue, the ancient agon of the Sublime mode, which always seeks to answer the triple question: more? equal to? less than? She was never less than Lovelace, hoped vainly he could be reformed into her equal, and knows now that she is far more than he is and more indeed than anyone else in her world. At that height of the Sublime, she can only commence dying.

If her will is to remain inviolate, then its independence and integrity must be manifested by a death that is anything but a revenge, whether it be against Lovelace, her family, herself, or even against time. Rather, *her* death is the true expiation, which can bring forgiveness upon everyone else involved, though I surmise that she is more interested in forgiving herself even as she forgives the bewildered Lovelace. A Puritan saint, as Shaw's St. Joan shows, is rather more interested in her own integrity than in anyone else's suffering. The cost for Clarissa or for Shaw's St. Joan is an absolute, inner isolation, but is that not the essence of Protestantism?

There is nothing like Clarissa's virtually endless death-scene in all of literature, and while no one would wish it longer, I do not wish it any shorter. Extraordinary as the actual moment of death is, in Letter 481, the most characteristic revelation of Clarissa's apotheosis is in Letter 475:

> Her breath being very short, she desired another pillow; and having two before, this made her in a manner sit up in her bed; and she spoke then with more distinctness; and seeing us greatly concerned, forgot her own sufferings to comfort us; and a charming

lecture she gave us, though a brief one, upon the happiness of a timely preparation and upon the hazards of a late repentance, when the mind, as she observed, was so much weakened, as well as the body, as to render a poor soul unable to contend with its own infirmities.

I beseech ye, my good friends, proceeded she, mourn not for one who mourns not, nor has cause to mourn, for herself. On the contrary, rejoice with me that all my worldly troubles are so near their end. Believe me, sirs, that I would not, if I might, choose to live, although the pleasantest part of my life were to come over again: and yet eighteen years of it, out of nineteen, have been *very* pleasant. To be so much exposed to temptation, and to be so liable to fail in the trial, who would not rejoice that all her dangers are over!—All I wished was pardon and blessing from my dear parents. Easy as my departure seems to promise to be, it would have been still easier had I had that pleasure. BUT GOD ALMIGHTY WOULD NOT LET ME DEPEND FOR COMFORT UPON ANY BUT HIMSELF.

This is certainly the purest Protestantism, and we might still be tempted to call this pride, particularly since Clarissa reminds us that she is all of nineteen years old. But we do Clarissa violence to name her total knowledge as a form of pride. The Protestant will by now has been blamed for practically everything that has gone wrong in our spiritual, intellectual, economic, and political life, as well as our sexual life, and the United States is the evening land of Protestantism and so the final stage for the travails of its will. Clarissa, as she dies, shows us the other side, the glory of the Protestant will. If God would not let Clarissa depend for comfort upon any but himself, then he gave her the ultimate accolade of the Protestant will: to accept esteem only where it chose to bestow esteem, and only on its own terms.

VIII

Martin Price remarks that "Fielding can reward his heroes because they do not seek a reward." As a critical observation, this is in Fielding's own spirit and tells us again what kind of a novel Fielding invented; a comic *Odyssey*, ancestor of Smollett and Dickens and of Joyce's *Ulysses*. My teacher Frederick W. Hilles liked to compare *Tom Jones* to *Ulysses*, while acknowledging that Fielding the narrator was neither invisible nor indifferent. Certainly Fielding was a fabulous artificer, which must be why he provoked so formidable a critical enemy as Dr. Samuel Johnson, who loved Alexander Pope while despising the most Popean of all novelists. Johnson vastly preferred Samuel Richardson to Fielding, a preference I myself share, though without prejudice to Fielding, since Richardson's *Clarissa* seems to me still the strongest novel in the language, surpassing even Austen's *Emma*, Eliot's *Middlemarch*, and James's *Portrait of a Lady*, all of them its descendants. *Tom*

Jones founds another line, the rival tradition that includes Dickens and Joyce, novelists as exuberant as Fielding, and metaphysically and psychologically more problematic.

Samuel Johnson evidently resented what he took to be Fielding's simplistic vision, a resentment understandable in a great moralist who believed that human life was everywhere a condition in which much was to be endured and little to be enjoyed. No one can match Johnson as a compelling moralist, but he necessarily undervalued Fielding's moral shrewdness. The true issue between Richardson and Fielding was in modes of representation, or different views of mimesis. It is as though Richardson and Fielding split Shakespeare between them, with Richardson absorbing the Shakespearean power to portray inwardness, while Fielding inherits Shakespeare's uncanny ease in depicting a romance world that becomes more real than reality.

Johnson told the protesting Boswell that "there is more knowledge of the heart in one letter of Richardson's, than in all *Tom Jones*." To Johnson, the personages in Fielding were "characters of manners," but in Richardson they were "characters of nature." This distinction is at least critical; one feels that many modern scholars who prefer Fielding to Richardson do so upon Coleridge's affective premises: "and how charming, how wholesome, Fielding always is! To take him up after Richardson is like emerging from a sick-room heated by stoves into an open lawn on a breezy day in May." That has the same persuasiveness as Richardson's explanation of why he would not read *Tom Jones:* "I was told, that it was a rambling Collection of Waking Dreams, in which Probability was not observed."

The seven volumes of *Clarissa* were published throughout the year from December 1747 through December 1748; *Tom Jones* came out in February 1749. Rivalry between the two novels was inevitable, and both seem to have sold very well. Between them, they established the modern novel, still the dominant literary form now, after two and a half centuries. Ian Watt, the definitive chronicler of *The Rise of the Novel* (1957), probably achieved the most balanced judgment on Fielding's crucial strengths and limitations:

> In his effort to infuse the new genre with something of the Shakespearean virtues Fielding departed too far from formal realism to initiate a viable tradition, but his work serves as a perpetual reminder that if the new genre was to challenge older literary forms it had to find a way of conveying not only a convincing impression but a wise assessment of life, an assessment that could only come from taking a much wider view than Defoe or Richardson of the affairs of mankind.

IX

What is Shakespearean about *Tom Jones?* The violent, daemonic, mindless energy of Squire Western, or the bodily ego rampant, is certainly part of the answer. Martin Price calls Western the finest English comic character after Falstaff, and the judgment seems indisputable. Yet here also a shadow falls. Falstaff, like his precursor, the Wife of Bath, is a heroic vitalist, raising vitalism, as she does, to the sublime of wit. Like Falstaff, the Wife is a great parodist, and a dangerously sophisticated Bible interpreter, as Talbot Donaldson demonstrates. But Western is energy without mind, and so is himself a living parody of vitalism. Fielding's genius nevertheless is so incarnated in Western that he breaks the limits of representation, and leaps out of the novel into that supermimetic domain where Falstaff and the Wife of Bath join Don Quixote and Sancho Panza. Western's simplicity is so exuberant and physical that it achieves a new kind of complexity, as in this astonishing comic reversal:

Western had been long impatient for the Event of this Conference, and was just now arrived at the Door to listen; when having heard the last Sentiments of his Daughter's Heart, he lost all Temper, and bursting open the Door in a Rage, cried out.—"It is a Lie. It is a d—n'd Lie. It is all owing to that d—n'd Rascal *Juones*; and if she could get at un, she'd ha un any Hour of the Day." Here *Allworthy* interposed, and addressing himself to the Squire with some Anger in his Look, he said, "Mr. *Western*, you have not kept your Word with me. You promised to abstain from all Violence."— "Why so I did," cries *Western*, "as long as it was possible; but to hear a Wench telling such confounded Lies.—Zounds! Doth she think if she can make Vools of other Volk, she can make one of me?—No, no, I know her better than thee dost." "I am sorry to tell you, Sir," answered *Allworthy*, "it doth not appear by your Behaviour to this young Lady, that you know her at all. I ask Pardon for what I say; but I think our Intimacy, your own Desires, and the Occasion justify me. She is your Daughter, Mr. *Western*, and I think she doth Honour to your Name. If I was capable of Envy, I should sooner envy you on this Account, than any other Man whatever."—"Odrabbit it," cries the Squire, "I wish she was thine with all my Heart—wouldst soon be glad to be rid of the Trouble o' her."—"Indeed, my good Friend," answered *Allworthy*, "you yourself are the Cause of all the Trouble you complain of. Place that Confidence in the young Lady which she so well deserves, and I am certain you will be the happiest Father on Earth."—"I Confidence in her!" cries the Squire.—"S'blood! what Confidence can I place in her, when she won't do as I wou'd ha her? Let her gi but her Consent to marry as I would ha her, and I'll place as much Confidence in her as wouldst ha me."—"You have no Right, Neighbour," answered *Allworthy*, "to insist on any such Consent. A negative Voice your Daughter allows you, and God and Nature have thought proper to allow you no more." "A negative Voice?" cries the Squire—"Ay! ay! I'll shew you what a negative Voice I ha.——Go along, go into your Chamber, go, you Stubborn."—"Indeed, Mr. *Western*," said *Allworthy*,—"Indeed, you use her cruelly—I cannot bear to see this—You shall, you must behave to her in a kinder Manner. She deserves the best of Treatment." "Yes, yes," said the Squire, "I know what she deserves: Now she's gone, I'll shew you what she deserves——See here, Sir, here is a Letter from my Cousin, my Lady *Bellaston*, in which she is so kind to gi me to understand, that the Fellow is got out of Prison again; and here she advises me to take all the Care I can o' the Wench. Odzookers! Neighbour *Allworthy*, you don't know what it is to govern a Daughter."

The Squire ended his Speech with some Compliments to his own Sagacity; and then *Allworthy*, after a formal Preface, acquainted him with the whole Discovery which he had made concerning *Jones*, with his Anger to *Blifil*, and with every Particular which hath been disclosed to the Reader in the preceding Chapters.

Men over-violent in their Dispositions, are, for the most Part, as changeable in them. No sooner then was *Western* informed of Mr. *Allworthy's* Intention to make *Jones* his Heir, than he joined heartily with the Uncle in every Commendation of the Nephew, and became as eager for her Marriage with *Jones*, as he had before been to couple her to *Blifil*.

Here Mr. *Allworthy* was again forced to interpose, and to relate what had passed between him and *Sophia*, at which he testified great Surprize.

The Squire was silent a Moment, and looked wild with Astonishment at this Account——At last he cried out, "Why what can be the Meaning of this, Neighbour *Allworthy?* Vond o un she was, that I'll be sworn to.—Odzookers! I have hit o't. As sure as a Gun I have hit o the very right o't. It's all along o Zister. The Girl hath got a Hankering after this Son of a Whore of a Lord. I vound'em together at my Cousin, my Lady *Bellaston's*. He hath turned the Head o' her that's certain—but d—n me if he shall ha her—I'll ha no Lords nor Courtiers in my Vamily."

Western is equally passionate, within moments, in swearing that Sophia shall *not* have Jones and that she *shall*. We are delighted by his stance either way, and most delighted at his childish ease in moving from one position to the other without pause, embarrassment, or reflection. A passionate infant, Squire Western is sublime on the page, or on the screen, where as played by Hugh Griffith he ran off with the Osborne-Richardson *Tom Jones*, but in mere reality he would be a monster. As a representation he is triumphant because like the much greater Falstaff he is free of the superego. We rejoice in Western because he is freedom gone wild, including freedom from nasty plotting, yet his mindlessness almost frightens us.

Price is accurate as ever when he observes that "Fielding controls his characters by limiting them," but Western is the grand exception, being out of control and extravagant, beyond all limits. No other eighteenth-century novel could accommodate Western, which is another indication of the power of *Tom Jones*. Something primeval in the mode of romance survives in Western the wild man, who hardly seems to belong to a post-Swiftian novel that still exalts the Augustan vision. Fielding, like Pope and Swift, joins the Enlightenment consciousness and ideas of order to an ongoing sense of the demands of energy. Johnson, who shared with Fielding the heritage of Pope and Swift, may have felt, obscurely but accurately, that Fielding like Swift gave too much away to the daemonic force of vitalism. "This kind of writing may be termed not improperly the Comedy of Romance," Johnson said of Fielding, thus relegating Fielding to the dark and enchanted ground not yet purified by reason. Johnson meant to condemn, perhaps, but guides us instead to Fielding's most surprising strength.

X

Sterne remarked in a letter that *Tristram Shandy* "was made and formed to baffle all criticism," but he probably knew better. Dr. Johnson, greatest of critics, insisted that *Tristram Shandy* would not last, a hopelessly wrong prophecy. Sterne gives the critic and reader everything to do, and can anyone resist, one wonders, a novel in which the hero-narrator declares (vol. 1, chap. 14) that: "I have been at it these six weeks, making all the speed I possibly could,—and am not yet born." Published in nine short volumes from 1759 to 1767, *Tristram Shandy* is the masterpiece of what Northrop Frye has taught us to call the Age of Sensibility, the era of Rousseau, and of a secularized, vernacular, "Orientalized" Bible, described by Bishop Lowth (*Lectures on the Sacred Poetry of the Hebrews*, 1753) as the true source of the "language of the passions." It is also the era of John Locke, much as we still live in the Age of Sigmund Freud. Johnson, who also opposed the poetry of Thomas Gray and of his own personal friend, William Collins, was quite consistent in setting himself against *Tristram Shandy*. Henry Fielding may have subverted novelistic forms, but Sterne subverts the entire Augustan mode of representation, and truly ends the cultural enterprise in which Pope triumphed.

It cannot be accidental that so many of the best contemporary Spanish-American novels are Shandean, whether or not the particular writer actually has read Sterne. One such distinguished novelist, when told by me how grand a fantasist he seemed, amiably assured me that his intentions were merely realistic. In the presence of extraordinary actuality, Wallace Stevens observed, consciousness could take the place of imagination. For Sterne, consciousness itself was the extraordinary actuality, so that sensibility became one with imagination. Dualism, Cartesian and Lockean, comes to us now mostly in Freudian guise. "Shandean guise" would do as well, since

Sterne is a thoroughgoing Freudian five generations before Freud. The fundamental Freudian frontier concepts—the drive, the bodily ego, the nonrepressive defenses of introjection and projection—are conceptually exemplified in *Tristram Shandy*, as is the central Freudian idea or trope of repression or defense. Most readers of Sterne see this at once, and many of his critics have reflected upon it. A Freudian exegesis of *Tristram Shandy* therefore becomes a redundancy. Far more vital is the question, What is Sterne trying to do for himself, as a novelist, by his dualistic, solipsistic, psychological emphasis?

That there is an aesthetic and moral program in the Shandean philosophy most critics agree, but phrasing it has led to some unfortunate banalities. You can sum up Pope's or Fielding's designs upon the reader rather more easily than you can express Sterne's. This is not simply a rhetorical dilemma; Sterne is a great ironist and parodist, but so are Pope and Fielding, while Swift excels even Sterne in such modes. But if all three of the great Augustans are cognitively subtle, Sterne is preternaturally subtle, to the point of being daemonic. Swift is ferocious, yet Sterne is uncanny; his artistry is indeed diabolic, as Martin Price comments, comparing it to the skill of Ionesco. The spirit of the comparison is right, but Ionesco hardly can work on Sterne's scale, which is both vast and minute. I prefer Richard Lanham's comparison of Sterne to Chaucer, who also is too wise to fall into an Arnoldian high seriousness. Like Chaucer and Cervantes, Sterne is very serious about play, but he is even more playful about form than they are.

XI

What is love, to an almost perfect solipsist? Can it be more than sex? Is sex all, and does every trembling hand make us squeak, like dolls, the wished-for word? Sterne is reductive enough to muse on the question, and to intimate an affirmative answer:

> I had escaped, continued the corporal, all that time from falling in love, and had gone on to the end of the chapter, had it not been predestined otherwise——there is no resisting our fate.
>
> It was on a *Sunday*, in the afternoon, as I told your honour——
>
> The old man and his wife had walked out——
>
> Every thing was still and hush as midnight about the house——
>
> There was not so much as a duck or a duckling about the yard——
>
> ——When the fair *Beguine* came in to see me.
>
> My wound was then in a fair way of doing well——the inflammation had been gone off for some time, but it was succeeded with an itching both above and below my knee, so insufferable, that I had not shut my eyes the whole night for it.

Let me see it, said she, kneeling down upon the ground parallel to my knee, and laying her hand upon the part below it——It only wants rubbing a little, said the *Beguine*; so covering it with the bed cloaths, she began with the forefinger of her right-hand to rub under my knee, guiding her fore-finger backwards and forwards by the edge of the flannel which kept on the dressing.

In five or six minutes I felt slightly the end of the second finger ——and presently it was laid flat with the other, and she continued rubbing in that way round and round for a good while; it then came into my head, that I should fall in love——I blush'd when I saw how white a hand she had——I shall never, an' please your honour, behold another hand so white whilst I live——

——Not in that place: said my uncle *Toby*——

Though it was the most serious despair in nature to the corporal——he could not forbear smiling.

The young *Beguine*, continued the corporal, perceiving it was of great service to me——from rubbing, for some time, with two fingers——proceeded to rub at length, with three——till by little and little she brought down the fourth, and then rubb'd with her whole hand: I will never say another word, an' please your honour, upon hands again——but it was softer than satin——

——Prithee, *Trim*, commend it as much as thou wilt, said my uncle *Toby*; I shall hear thy story with the more delight——The corporal thank'd his master most unfeignedly; but having nothing to say upon the *Beguine*'s hand, but the same over again——he proceeded to the effects of it.

The fair *Beguine*, said the corporal, continued rubbing with her whole hand under my knee——till I fear'd her zeal would weary her——"I would do a thousand times more," said she, "for the love of Christ"——In saying which she pass'd her hand across the flannel, to the part above my knee, which I had equally complained of, and rubb'd it also.

I perceived, then, I was beginning to be in love——

As she continued rub-rub-rubbing——I felt it spread from under her hand, an' please your honour, to every part of my frame——

The more she rubb'd, and the longer strokes she took——the more the fire kindled in my veins——till at length, by two or three strokes longer than the rest——my passion rose to the highest pitch——I seiz'd her hand——

——And then, thou clapped'st it to thy lips, *Trim*, said my uncle *Toby*——and madest a speech.

Whether the corporal's amour terminated precisely in the way my uncle *Toby* described it, is not material; it is enough that it contain'd in it the essence of all the love-romances which ever have been wrote since the beginning of the world.

To be in love is to be aroused; no more, no less. Sterne, something of an invalid, was abnormally sensitive, as W. B. C. Watkins remarked: "He was inevitably self-conscious physically to an abnormal degree. He was acutely aware of the very circulation of his blood and the beating of his heart." Much of Sterne's alleged prurience is actually his heightened vulnerability, cognitive and bodily, to sexual stimuli. The sense of "Sensibility" in Sterne is fully sexual, and aids us in seeing the true nature of the cultural term, both morally and aesthetically. A susceptibility to tender feelings, however fine (and whether one's own or those of others), becomes objectified as a quality or stance that turns away from the Stoic and Augustan ideal of reason in affective response. This is Sensibility or "the Sentimental" ideologically free from either right-wing celebration of bourgeois morality or left-wing idealization of proletarian or pastoral natural virtues. Its politics, though Whiggish in origin, diffuse into a universal and histrionic vision of the force and beauty of the habits of the heart. Martin Price terms it "a vehement, often defiant assertion of the value of man's feelings." Overtly self-conscious and dramatic, yet insisting upon its sincerity, the stance of Sensibility is a kind of sexualization of all the other effects, as Sterne most clearly knew, showed, and told. Richard Lanham sums this up when he writes: "For Sterne, we finally become not only insatiable pleasure-seekers but, by our nature, incurable poseurs."

All Shandeans have their favorite episodes, and I am tempted to cite all of volume 7, throughout which Tristram/Sterne flees from death by taking a Sentimental journey through France. One could vote for the story of Amandus and Amanda, or for the concluding country-dance with Nanette, two superb moments in volume 7. But, if we are pleasure-seeking poseurs, we cannot do better than chapter 15 of volume 8, which precedes the Widow Wadman's direct attempt to light Uncle Toby at both ends at once, in the sentry-box:

> It is a great pity——but 'tis certain from every day's observation of man, that he may be set on fire like a candle, at either end ——provided there is a sufficient wick standing out; if there is not ——there's an end of the affair; and if there is——by lighting it at the bottom, as the flame in that case has the misfortune generally to put out itself——there's an end of the affair again.
>
> For my part, could I always have the ordering of it which way I would be burnt myself——for I cannot bear the thoughts of being burnt like a beast——I would oblige a housewife constantly to light me at the top; for then I should burn down decently to the socket; that is, from my head to my heart, from my heart to my liver, from my liver to my bowels, and so on by the meseraick veins and arteries, through all the turns and lateral insertions of the intestines and their tunicles to the blind gut——
>
> ——I beseech you, doctor *Slop*, quoth my uncle *Toby*, inter-

rupting him as he mentioned the *blind gut*, in a discourse with my
father the night my mother was brought to bed of me——I beseech
you, quoth my uncle *Toby*, to tell me which is the blind gut; for,
old as I am, I vow I do not know to this day where it lies.

The *blind gut*, answered doctor *Slop*, lies betwixt the *Illion* and
Colon——

——In a man? said my father.

——'Tis precisely the same, cried doctor *Slop*, in a woman——
That's more than I know; quoth my father.

We confront again Sterne's marvelous sense of the dualistic perplexities
of human existence. Man is not exactly the Puritan candle of the Lord,
burning with a preternatural will-to-holiness, but a sexual candle altogether,
burning with the natural will-to-live. When Tristram/Sterne asks to be lit
at the top, presumably with a cognitive fire, then he asks also to "burn
down decently to the socket." Sterne's fierce metaphor rejects the Cartesian
ghost-in-the-machine (Gilbert Ryle's fine formulation) and desires instead
a conflagration of the mind through the senses. Though he is perhaps the
most satirical of all vitalists, Sterne's final affinities seem to be with Rabelais
and Blake, visionaries who sought to redeem us through an improvement
in sensual enjoyment.

XII

Despite the vigor and humor of *Humphry Clinker*, Smollett is currently the
most neglected of the major eighteenth-century British novelists. Since he
is not of the aesthetic eminence of Richardson, Fielding, and Sterne, one
would not expect him to provoke the intense critical interest that they
perpetually sustain. But *Humphry Clinker*, in my judgment, is a stronger
novel than Defoe's *Moll Flanders* or Goldsmith's *The Vicar of Wakefield*, and
compares favorably also with Fanny Burney's *Evelina*. Since it is now less
read and studied than any of those three, its eclipse perhaps indicates that
something in Smollett is not available to what is dominant in our current
sensibility. The era of Thomas Pynchon, apocalyptic and beyond the resources of any satiric vision, is not a time for accommodating Smollett's
rough tumble of an expedition toward a yearned-for health.

Smollett, a surgeon, probably knew he had not long to live even as he
composed *Humphry Clinker*. Resident in Italy from 1768 on for his health,
Smollett died there in 1771, just fifty, some three months after *Humphry
Clinker* was published. The expedition that is the novel, winding from Wales
up through the length of England well into Smollett's native Scotland, is
the author's long farewell to life, rendering Britain with a peculiar vividness
as he remembers it from abroad.

Why the novel is named for Humphry Clinker rather than for its central
figure Matthew Bramble, who clearly is Smollett's surrogate, never has

been clear to me, except that Clinker is a representative of the future and may be Smollett's wistful introjection of a life he would not survive to know. Clinker and Bramble rise together from the water, a natural son and the father he has saved from drowning, and both undergo a change of name into the same name: Matthew Loyd. This curious mutual baptism seems to have been a mythic transference for Smollett, since Matthew Loyd was Bramble's *former* name, and will be his son Humphry Clinker's *future* name. It is as though the slowly dying Smollett required a double vision of survival: as a Matthew Bramble largely purged of an irascibility close to madness, and as Humphry Clinker, a kindly and innocent youth restored to a lost heritage.

I have found that many of my friends and students, generally very good readers, shy away from *Humphry Clinker*, and from Smollett in general, because they are repelled by his mode, which at its strongest tends toward grotesque farce. The mode by definition is not pleasant, but, like the much greater Swift, Smollett is a master in this peculiar sub-genre. It is hardly accidental that Thomas Rowlandson illustrated Smollett in the early 1790s, because there is a profound affinity between the novelist and the carica-turist. Smollett's reality, at its most intense, is phantasmagoric, and there are moments early on in *Humphry Clinker* when the irritable (and well-named) Bramble seems close to madness. His speculations on the origins of the waters at Bath are not less than disgusting, and he is more than weary of mankind: "My curiosity is quite satisfied: I have done with the science of men, and must now endeavour to amuse myself with the novelty of things." Everywhere he finds only "food for spleen, and subject for ridicule."

Bramble satirizes everything he encounters, and is himself an instance of the mocker mocked or the satirist satirized. One can cultivate an amused affection for him, but he is not Don Quixote, and the vivid but unlikeable Lismahago, my favorite character in the book, is no Sancho Panza. Smollett evidently identifies with Bramble, but we cannot do so, and surely Smollett intended it that way. We may enjoy farce, but we do not wish to find ourselves acting in one as we stumble on in our lives. I think of my favorite farce in the language, Marlowe's *The Jew of Malta*. I have acted on stage just once in my life, playing Falstaff in an emergency, an amateur pressed into service, and played the witty knight more or less in the style of the late, great Zero Mostel playing Leopold Bloom in *Ulysses in Nighttown*. The one part I would love to play on stage is Barabas, bloody Jew of Malta, but in life obviously I would prefer being Falstaff to being Barabas.

When a novel conducts itself as realistic farce, which is Smollett's mode, we are denied the pleasures of introjection and identification. But a novel is wiser to forsake realism when it moves into farce. Sometimes I wish, reading Smollett, that he had been able to read the Evelyn Waugh of *Decline and Fall*, *Vile Bodies*, *A Handful of Dust*, because I think that Waugh would have been a good influence upon him. But that is to wish Smollett other than Smollett; one of his strengths is that he drives realistic representation almost beyond its proper limits, in order to extend the empire of farce. Perhaps his own fierce temperament required the extension, for he was more than a little mad, in this resembling certain elements of temperament in Swift, Sterne, and Dr. Samuel Johnson.

Sterne, in *A Sentimental Journey*, robustly satirizes Smollett as "the learned Smelfungus," who "set out with the spleen and jaundice, and every object he passed by was discoloured or distorted." Coming out of the Pantheon, Smelfungus comments: " 'Tis nothing but a huge cock pit," and all his travel adventures lead to similar judgments, provoking Sterne to a good retort: "I'll tell it, cried Smelfungus, to the world. You had better tell it, said I, to your physician." All of us would rather travel with Sterne than with Smollett, but reading Smollett remains a uniquely valuable experience. Let us take him at his most ferociously grotesque, in the account of the sufferings of Lismahago and the still more unfortunate Murphy at the horrid hands of the Miami Indians:

> By dint of her interrogations, however, we learned, that he and ensign Murphy had made their escape from the French hospital at Montreal, and taken to the woods, in hope of reaching some English settlement; but mistaking their route, they fell in with a party of Miamis, who carried them away in captivity. The intention of these Indians was to give one of them as an adopted son to a venerable sachem, who had lost his own in the course of the war, and to sacrifice the other according to the custom of the country. Murphy, as being the younger and handsomer of the two, was designed to fill the place of the deceased, not only as the son of the sachem, but as the spouse of a beautiful squaw, to whom his predecessor had been betrothed; but in passing through the different whigwhams or villages of the Miamis, poor Murphy was so mangled by the women and children, who have the privilege of torturing all prisoners in their passage, that, by the time they arrived at the place of the sachem's residence, he was rendered altogether unfit for the purposes of marriage: it was determined therefore, in the assembly of the warriors, that ensign Murphy should be brought to the stake, and that the lady should be given to lieutenant Lismahago, who had likewise received his share of torments, though they had not produced emasculation.—A joint of one finger had been cut, or rather sawed off with a rusty knife; one of his great toes was crushed into a mash betwixt two stones; some of his teeth were drawn, or dug out with a crooked nail; splintered reeds had been thrust up his nostrils and other tender parts; and the calves of his legs had been blown up with mines of gunpowder dug in the flesh with the sharp point of the tomahawk.

The Indians themselves allowed that Murphy died with great heroism, singing, as his death song, the *Drimmendoo*, in concert with Mr. Lismahago, who was present at the solemnity. After the warriors and the matrons had made a hearty meal upon the muscular flesh which they pared from the victim, and had applied a great variety of tortures, which he bore without flinching, an old lady, with a sharp knife, scooped out one of his eyes, and put a burning coal in the socket. The pain of this operation was so exquisite that he could not help bellowing, upon which the audience raised a shout of exultation, and one of the warriors stealing behind him, gave him the *coup de grace* with a hatchet.

Lismahago's bride, the squaw Squinkinacoosta, distinguished herself on this occasion.——She shewed a great superiority of genius in the tortures which she contrived and executed with her own hands.—She vied with the stoutest warrior in eating the flesh of the sacrifice; and after all the other females were fuddled with dram-drinking, she was not so intoxicated but that she was able to play the game of the platter with the conjuring sachem, and afterwards go through the ceremony of her own wedding, which was consummated that same evening. The captain had lived very happily with this accomplished squaw for two years, during which she bore him a son, who is now the representative of his mother's tribe; but, at length, to his unspeakable grief, she had died of a fever, occasioned by eating too much raw bear, which they had killed in a hunting excursion.

This is both dreadfully funny and funnily dreadful, and is quite marvelous writing, though evidently not to all tastes. If it were written by Mark Twain, we would know how to take it, but Smollett renders it with a dangerous relish, which makes us a little uncertain, since we do not wish to be quite as rancid as the learned Smelfungus, or even as the dreadful Lismahago for that matter. Reading Smollett is sometimes like eating too much raw bear, but that only acknowledges how authentic and strong his flavor is.

To have inspired Rowlandson and fostered Charles Dickens (who took his origins in a blend of Smollett and Ben Jonson) is enough merit for any one writer. Smollett is to Dickens what Marlowe was to Shakespeare, a forerunner so swallowed up by an enormous inheritor that the precursor sometimes seems a minnow devoured by a whale. But, considered in himself, Smollett has something of Marlowe's eminence. Each carried satirical farce and subversive melodrama to a new limit, and that too is merit enough.

XIII

Oliver Goldsmith, versatile and graceful in every genre, compels a critic to speculate upon the disproportion between the writer-as-person and the writer-as-writer. Some (not all) of the most accomplished writers I have known have been the most colorless of personalities, or if more vivid and interesting as people, then they have been remarkably unpleasant or foolish or merely mawkish. Goldsmith appears to have been a luckless individual, and even what Freud called a "moral masochist," a victim of his own death-drive at the age of forty-four. Indeed, Goldsmith is a fairly classic instance of many Freudian insights, and both *The Vicar of Wakefield* and *She Stoops to Conquer* sustain immediate illumination when Freudian categories are applied to them. What Freud termed "the most prevalent form of degradation in erotic life" is a clear guide to young Marlow's backwardness with well-born women, and exuberant aggressivity with inn barmaids, college bedmakers, and others of whom he remarks: "They are of *us* you know." And the lumpish Tony Lumpkin becomes an even more persuasive representation when his descent into the company of the alehouse is seen, again in Freudian guise, as a reaction-formation to his dreadful mother, Mrs. Hardcastle.

Goldsmith aped Johnson in most things, even to the copying of the critic's manner, according to Boswell. Johnson spoke the last word upon his friend and follower: "If nobody was suffered to abuse poor Goldy but those who could write as well, he would have few censors." Yet it is a curious sadness that the best lines in any poem by Goldsmith, the concluding passage of *The Deserted Village*, were written by Johnson himself:

> That trade's proud empire hastes to swift decay,
> As ocean sweeps the laboured mole away;
> While self-dependent power can time defy,
> As rocks resist the billows and the sky.

An ironical reading might interpret that humanly constructed breakwater, "the laboured mole," as Goldsmith's ego, in contrast to Johnsonian self-dependence, the great critic's rock-like ego. Still, Goldsmith's laboured breakwater has defied time also, though not quite with the massive Johnsonian force. Goldsmith's writing survives on its curious grace, curious both because it resists strict definition, and because it extends across the genres: from the Popean verse of *The Traveller*, through the Bunyanesque revision of the Book of Job in the sentimental novel *The Vicar of Wakefield*, on to the elegiac pastoralism of *The Deserted Village* and the permanently successful stage comedy *She Stoops to Conquer*, and the urbane good nature of the posthumously published poem *Retaliation*, a gentle satire upon the members of Dr. Johnson's Club.

The strongest case for Goldsmith was made by William Hazlitt, second only to Johnson, in my estimation, among all critics in the language:

> Goldsmith, both in verse and prose, was one of the most delightful writers in the language. . . . His ease is quite unconscious. Everything in him is spontaneous, unstudied, yet elegant, harmonious, graceful, nearly faultless.

A kind of natural or unconscious artist, Goldsmith prevails by disarming his reader. He seems the least tendentious of all authors, writing as though he had no design upon us. Even now, he has not lost his audience, although critics sometimes treat his works as period pieces. He is strangely close to popular literature, though he hardly can sustain comparison with the far more powerful Bunyan. Perhaps he moves us now primarily as an instance of our continuity with a past that we seem otherwise wholly to have abandoned.

XIV

The canonical status of *The Vicar of Wakefield* is beyond doubt, though I do not advise rereading it side by side with a rereading of Bunyan's far stronger *The Pilgrim's Progress*, as I have just done. But then, Bunyan is so powerful a visionary as to claim the company of Milton and Blake. Goldsmith gives us a gentle theodicy in the *Vicar*, and theodicy is hardly a gentle mode. Henry James, writing an introduction to the novel in 1900, called it "the spoiled child of our literature," a work so amiable that it seemed to him "happy in the manner in which a happy man is happy—a man, say, who has married an angel or been appointed to a sinecure."

Like the Book of Job, the *Vicar* brings a good man, here Dr. Primrose, into the power of Satan, here Squire Thornhill. Some recent revisionist readings of the *Vicar* have attempted to give us a Dr. Primrose who is more self-righteous than virtuous, more smugly egoistical than innocent. These seem to me weak misreadings, because they overlook Goldsmith's most surprising revision of the Book of Job. With singular audacity, Goldsmith makes his Job the narrator. Whatever you have Job do, you ought not to make him the hero of a first-person narrative. Consider the aesthetic and spiritual effect that even the opening would then have upon us:

> I was a man in the land of Uz, and my name was Job; I was perfect and upright, and I feared God, and eschewed evil.

No one proclaims his own virtues without alienating us, and no one recites his own sufferings without embarrassing us. The opening of *The Vicar of Wakefield* is not quite like that of a first-person Book of Job, but it is problematic enough:

> I was ever of opinion, that the honest man who married and brought up a large family, did more service than he who continued single and only talked of population. From this motive, I had scarce taken orders a year, before I began to think seriously of matrimony, and chose my wife, as she did her wedding-gown, not for a fine glossy surface, but such qualities as would wear well.

At best, poor Primrose sounds a pompous fool; at worst, a bore rampant. Why did Goldsmith take the risk? Was Primrose intended to be a satiric butt, and Burchell a reality instructor? Dickens evidently did not think so, and something of Primrose got into Mr. Pickwick. Unlike Goethe and Dickens, we do not find Primrose to be altogether comically lovable. However, we also ought not to fault him. Perhaps he does represent a secularization of the figure of Job, or a Johnsonian allegory of an education in true humility, but I suspect that he is primarily Goldsmith's introjection of Job. This is not to suggest a composite figure, Job Primrose-Goldsmith as it were, but to intimate that Primrose is a loving self-satire on Goldsmith's part, or an amiable Jobean parody directed against the feckless writer's own penchant for catastrophe.

Goldsmith takes the risk of first-person narration because he knows that the vicar Primrose is his own somewhat ironic self-portrait, and that his personal Jobean tribulations do not exactly achieve sublimity. Yet Goldsmith, in life, and the Vicar, in the novel, cannot refrain from self-praise, from a kind of snobbery of virtue, even as they are altogether the passive victims of fortune. Goldsmith, though an impossible personality, was a literary genius, but Dr. Primrose is simply not very clever. An unintelligent Job startles us, if only by reminding us what a formidable moral psychologist and reasoner the biblical Job was, so much so that he finally infuriated John Calvin, his greatest commentator. Calvin, in his sermons on the Book of Job, is finally provoked to cry out that God would have had to make new worlds, to satisfy Job. No one would say that God would have had to make new worlds to satisfy Dr. Primrose. Goldsmith himself, I suspect, was about half-way between Job and the Vicar in this regard.

XV

The oddest yet by no means inapt analogy to Jane Austen's art of representation is Shakespeare's—oddest, because she is so careful of limits, as classical as Ben Jonson in that regard, and Shakespeare transcends all limits. Austen's humor, her mode of rhetorical irony, is not particularly Shakespearean, and yet her precision and accuracy of representation is. Like Shakespeare, she gives us figures, major and minor, utterly consistent each in her or his own mode of speech and being, and utterly different from one another. Her heroines have firm selves, each molded with an individuality that continues to suggest Austen's reserve of power, her potential for creating an endless diversity. To recur to the metaphor of oddness, the highly deliberate limitation of social scale in Austen seems a paradoxical theater of mind in which so fecund a humanity could be fostered. Irony, the concern of most critics of Austen, seems more than a trope in her work, seems indeed to be the condition of her language, yet hardly accounts for the effect of moral and spiritual power that she so constantly conveys, however implicitly or obliquely.

Ian Watt, in his permanently useful *The Rise of the Novel*, portrays Austen as Fanny Burney's direct heir in the difficult art of combining the rival modes of Samuel Richardson and Henry Fielding. Like Burney, Austen is thus seen as following the Richardson of *Sir Charles Grandison* in a "minute presentation of daily life," while emulating Fielding "in adopting a more detached attitude to her narrative material, and in evaluating it from a comic and objective point of view." Watt goes further when he points out that Austen tells her stories in a discreet variant of Fielding's manner "as a confessed author," though her ironical juxtapositions are made to appear not those of "an intrusive author but rather of some august and impersonal spirit of social and psychological understanding."

And yet, as Watt knows, Austen truly is the daughter of Richardson and not of Fielding, just as she is the ancestor of George Eliot and Henry James rather than of Dickens and Thackeray. Her inwardness is an ironic revision of Richardson's extraordinary conversion of English Protestant sensibility into the figure of Clarissa Harlowe, and her own moral and spiritual concerns fuse in the crucial need of her heroines to sustain their individual integrities, a need so intense that it compels them to fall into those errors about life that are necessary for life (to adopt a Nietzschean formulation). In this too they follow, though in a comic register, the pattern of their tragic precursor, the magnificent but sublimely flawed Clarissa Harlowe.

Richardson's *Clarissa*, perhaps still the longest novel in the language, seems to me also still the greatest, despite the achievements of Austen, Dickens, George Eliot, Henry James, and Joyce. Austen's Elizabeth Bennet and Emma Woodhouse, Eliot's Dorothea Brooke and Gwendolen Harleth, James's Isabel Archer and Milly Theale—though all these are Clarissa Harlowe's direct descendants, they are not proportioned to her more sublime scale. David Copperfield and Leopold Bloom have her completeness; indeed Joyce's Bloom may be the most complete representation of a human being in all of literature. But they belong to the secular age; Clarissa Harlowe is poised upon the threshold that leads from the Protestant religion to a purely secular sainthood.

C. S. Lewis, who read Milton as though that fiercest of Protestant temperaments had been an orthodox Anglican, also seems to have read Jane Austen by listening for her echoings of the New Testament. Quite explicitly, Lewis named Austen as the daughter of Dr. Samuel Johnson, greatest of literary critics and rigorous Christian moralist:

> I feel . . . sure that she is the daughter of Dr. Johnson: she inherits his commonsense, his morality, even much of his style.

The Johnson of *Rasselas* and *The Rambler*, surely the essential Johnson, is something of a classical ironist, but we do not read Johnson for his ironies, or for his dramatic representations of fictive selves. Rather, we read him as we read Koheleth; he writes wisdom literature. That Jane Austen is a wise writer is indisputable, but we do not read *Pride and Prejudice* as though it were Ecclesiastes. Doubtless, Austen's religious ideas were as profound as Samuel Richardson's were shallow, but *Emma* and *Clarissa* are Protestant novels without being in any way religious. What is most original about the representation of Clarissa Harlowe is the magnificent intensity of her slowly described dying, which goes on for about the last third of Richardson's vast novel, in a Puritan ritual that celebrates the preternatural strength of her will. For that is Richardson's sublime concern: the self-reliant apotheosis of the Protestant will. What is tragedy in *Clarissa* becomes serious or moral comedy in *Pride and Prejudice* and *Emma*, and something just the other side of comedy in *Mansfield Park* and *Persuasion*.

XVI

Rereading *Pride and Prejudice* gives one a sense of Proustian ballet beautifully working itself through in the novel's formal centerpiece, the deferred but progressive mutual enlightenment of Elizabeth and Darcy in regard to the other's true nature. "Proper pride" is what they learn to recognize in one another; propriety scarcely needs definition in that phrase, but precisely what is the pride that allows amiability to flourish? Whatever it is in Darcy, to what extent is it an act of the will in Elizabeth Bennet? Consider the superb scene of Darcy's first and failed marriage proposal:

> While settling this point, she was suddenly roused by the sound of the door-bell, and her spirits were a little fluttered by the idea of its being Colonel Fitzwilliam himself, who had once before called late in the evening, and might now come to inquire particularly after her. But this idea was soon banished, and her spirits were very differently affected, when, to her utter amazement, she saw Mr. Darcy walk into the room. In an hurried manner he immediately began an inquiry after her health, imputing his visit to a wish of hearing that she were better. She answered him with cold civility. He sat down for a few moments, and then getting up, walked about the room. Elizabeth was surprised, but said not a word. After a silence of several minutes, he came towards her in an agitated manner, and thus began:
>
> "In vain have I struggled. It will not do. My feelings will not be repressed. You must allow me to tell you how ardently I admire and love you."
>
> Elizabeth's astonishment was beyond expression. She stared, coloured, doubted, and was silent. This he considered sufficient encouragement; and the avowal of all that he felt, and had long felt for her, immediately followed. He spoke well; but there were feelings besides those of the heart to be detailed, and he was not more eloquent on the subject of tenderness than of pride. His sense of her inferiority—of its being a degradation—of the family obstacles which judgment had always opposed to inclination,

were dwelt on with a warmth which seemed due to the consequence he was wounding, but was very unlikely to recommend his suit.

In spite of her deeply-rooted dislike, she could not be insensible to the compliment of such a man's affection, and though her intentions did not vary for an instant, she was at first sorry for the pain he was to receive; till, roused to resentment by his subsequent language, she lost all compassion in anger. She tried, however, to compose herself to answer him with patience, when he should have done. He concluded with representing to her the strength of that attachment which, in spite of all his endeavours, he had found impossible to conquer; and with expressing his hope that it would now be rewarded by her acceptance of his hand. As he said this, she could easily see that he had no doubt of a favourable answer. He *spoke* of apprehension and anxiety, but his countenance expressed real security. Such a circumstance could only exasperate farther, and, when he ceased, the colour rose into her cheeks, and she said:

"In such cases as this, it is, I believe, the established mode to express a sense of obligation for the sentiments avowed, however unequally they may be returned. It is natural that obligation should be felt, and if I could *feel* gratitude, I would now thank you. But I cannot—I have never desired your good opinion, and you have certainly bestowed it most unwillingly. I am sorry to have occasioned pain to anyone. It has been most unconsciously done, however, and I hope will be of short duration. The feelings which, you tell me, have long prevented the acknowledgment of your regard, can have little difficulty in overcoming it after this explanation."

Mr. Darcy, who was leaning against the mantelpiece with his eyes fixed on her face, seemed to catch her words with no less resentment than surprise. His complexion became pale with anger, and the disturbance of his mind was visible in every feature. He was struggling for the appearance of composure, and would not open his lips till he believed himself to have attained it. The pause was to Elizabeth's feelings dreadful. At length, in a voice of forced calmness, he said:

"And this is all the reply which I am to have the honour of expecting! I might, perhaps, wish to be informed why, with so little *endeavour* at civility, I am thus rejected. But it is of small importance."

Stuart M. Tave believes that both Darcy and Elizabeth become so changed by one another that their "happiness is deserved by a process of mortification begun early and ended late," mortification here being the wounding of pride. Tave's learning and insight are impressive, but I favor the judgment that Elizabeth and Darcy scarcely change, and learn rather that they complement each other's not wholly illegitimate pride. They come to see that their wills are naturally allied, since they have no differences upon the will. The will to what? Their will, Austen's, is neither the will to live nor the will to power. They wish to be esteemed precisely where they estimate value to be high, and neither can afford to make a fundamental error, which is both the anxiety and the comedy of the first proposal scene. Why after all does Darcy allow himself to be eloquent on the subject of his pride, to the extraordinary extent of conveying "with a warmth" what Austen grimly names as "his sense of her inferiority"?

As readers, we have learned already that Elizabeth is inferior to no one, whoever he is. Indeed, I sense as the novel closes (though nearly all Austen critics, and doubtless Austen herself, would disagree with me) that Darcy is her inferior, amiable and properly prideful as he is. I do not mean by this that Elizabeth is a clearer representation of Austenian values than Darcy ever could be; that is made finely obvious by Austen, and her critics have developed her ironic apprehension, which is that Elizabeth incarnates the standard of measurement in her cosmos. There is also a transcendent strength to Elizabeth's will that raises her above that cosmos, in a mode that returns us to Clarissa Harlowe's transcendence of her society, of Lovelace, and even of everything in herself that is not the will to a self-esteem that has also made an accurate estimate of every other will to pride it ever has encountered.

I am suggesting that Ralph Waldo Emerson (who to me is sacred) was mistaken when he rejected Austen as a "sterile" upholder of social conformities and social ironies, as an author who could not celebrate the soul's freedom from societal conventions. Austen's ultimate irony is that Elizabeth Bennet is inwardly so free that convention performs for her the ideal function it cannot perform for us: it liberates her will without tending to stifle her high individuality. But we ought to be wary of even the most distinguished of Austen's moral celebrants, Lionel Trilling, who in effect defended her against Emerson by seeing *Pride and Prejudice* as a triumph "of morality as style." If Emerson wanted to see a touch more Margaret Fuller in Elizabeth Bennet (sublimely ghastly notion!), Trilling wanted to forget the Emersonian law of Compensation, which is that nothing is got for nothing:

> The relation of Elizabeth Bennet to Darcy is real, is intense, but it expresses itself as a conflict and reconciliation of styles: a formal rhetoric, traditional and rigorous, must find a way to accommodate a female vivacity, which in turn must recognize the principled demands of the strict male syntax. The high moral import of the novel lies in the fact that the union of styles is accomplished without injury to either lover.

Yes and no, I would say. Yes, because the wills of both lovers work by similar dialectics, but also no, because Elizabeth's will is more intense and purer, and inevitably must be dimmed by her dwindling into a wife, even though Darcy may well be the best man that society could offer to her. Her pride has playfulness in it, a touch even of the Quixotic. Uncannily, she is both her father's daughter, and Samuel Richardson's daughter as well. Her wit is Mr. Bennet's, refined and elaborated, but her will, and her pride in her will, returns us to Clarissa's Puritan passion to maintain the power of the self to confer esteem, and to accept esteem only in response to its bestowal.

XVII

Sir Walter Scott, reviewing *Emma* in 1815, rather strangely compared Jane Austen to the masters of the Flemish school of painting, presumably because of her precision in representing her characters. The strangeness results from Scott's not seeing how English Austen was, though the Scots perspective may have entered into his estimate. To me, as an American critic, *Emma* seems the most English of English novels, and beyond question one of the very best. More than *Pride and Prejudice*, it is Austen's masterpiece, the largest triumph of her vigorous art. Her least accurate prophecy as to the fate of her fictions concerned *Emma*, whose heroine, she thought, "no one but myself will much like."

Aside from much else, Emma is immensely likable, because she is so extraordinarily imaginative, dangerous and misguided as her imagination frequently must appear to others and finally to herself. On the scale of being, Emma constitutes an answer to the immemorial questions of the Sublime: More? Equal to? Or less than? Like Clarissa Harlowe before her, and the strongest heroines of George Eliot and Henry James after her, Emma Woodhouse has a heroic will, and like them she risks identifying her will with her imagination. Socially considered, such identification is catastrophic, since the Protestant will has a tendency to bestow a ranking upon other selves, and such ranking may turn out to be a personal phantasmagoria. G. Armour Craig rather finely remarked that "society in *Emma* is not a ladder. It is a web of imputations that link feelings and conduct." Yet Emma herself, expansionist rather than reductionist in temperament, imputes more fiercely and freely than the web can sustain, and she threatens always, until she is enlightened, to dissolve the societal links, in and for others, that might allow some stability between feelings and conduct.

Armour Craig usefully added that: "*Emma* does not justify its heroine nor does it deride her." Rather it treats her with ironic love (not loving irony). Emma Woodhouse is dear to Jane Austen, because her errors are profoundly imaginative, and rise from the will's passion for autonomy of vision. The splendid Jane Fairfax is easier to admire, but I cannot agree with Wayne Booth's awarding the honors to her over Emma, though I admire the subtle balance of his formulation:

> Jane is superior to Emma in most respects except the stroke of good fortune that made Emma the heroine of the book. In matters of taste and ability, of head and of heart, she is Emma's superior.

Taste, ability, head, and heart are a formidable fourfold; the imagination and the will, working together, are an even more formidable twofold, and clearly may have their energies diverted to error and to mischief. Jane Fairfax is certainly more *amiable* even than Emma Woodhouse, but she is considerably less interesting. It is Emma who is meant to charm us, and who does charm us. Austen is not writing a tragedy of the will, like *Paradise Lost*, but a great comedy of the will, and her heroine must incarnate the full potential of the will, however misused for a time. Having rather too much her own way is certainly one of Emma's powers, and she does have a disposition to think a little too well of herself. When Austen says that these were "the real evils indeed of Emma's situation," we read "evils" as lightly as the author will let us, which is lightly enough.

Can we account for the qualities in Emma Woodhouse that make her worthy of comparison with George Eliot's Gwendolen Harleth and Henry James's Isabel Archer? The pure comedy of her context seems world enough for her; she evidently is not the heiress of all the ages. We are persuaded, by Austen's superb craft, that marriage to Mr. Knightley will more than suffice to fulfill totally the now perfectly amiable Emma. Or are we? It is James's genius to suggest that while Osmond's "beautiful mind" was a prison of the spirit for Isabel, no proper husband could exist anyway, since neither Touchett nor Goodwood was exactly a true match for her. Do we, presumably against Austen's promptings, not find Mr. Knightley something of a confinement also, benign and wise though he be?

I suspect that the heroine of the Protestant will, from Richardson's Clarissa Harlowe through to Virginia Woolf's Clarissa Dalloway, can never find a fit match because wills do not marry. The allegory or tragic irony of this dilemma is written large in *Clarissa*, since Lovelace, in strength of will and splendor of being, actually would have been the true husband for Clarissa (as he well knows) had he not been a moral squalor. His death-cry ("Let this expiate!") expiates nothing, and helps establish the long tradition of the Anglo-American novel in which the heroines of the will are fated to suffer either overt calamities or else happy unions with such good if unexciting men as Mr. Knightley or Will Ladislaw in *Middlemarch*. When George Eliot is reduced to having the fascinating Gwendolen Harleth fall hopelessly in love with the prince of prigs, Daniel Deronda, we sigh and resign ourselves to the sorrows of fictive overdetermination. Lovelace or Daniel Deronda? I myself do not know a high-spirited woman who would not prefer the first, though not for a husband!

Emma is replete with grand comic epiphanies, of which my favorite

comes in volume 3, chapter 11, when Emma receives the grave shock of
Harriet's disclosure that Mr. Knightley is the object of Harriet's hopeful
affections:

> When Harriet had closed her evidence, she appealed to her dear
> Miss Woodhouse, to say whether she had not good ground for
> hope.
> "I never should have presumed to think of it at first," said she,
> "but for you. You told me to observe him carefully, and let his
> behavior be the rule of mine—and so I have. But now I seem to
> feel that I may deserve him; and that if he does choose me, it will
> not be any thing so very wonderful."
> The bitter feelings occasioned by this speech, the many bitter
> feelings, made the utmost exertion necessary on Emma's side to
> enable her to say in reply,
> "Harriet, I will only venture to declare, that Mr. Knightley is
> the last man in the world, who would intentionally give any
> woman the idea of his feeling for her more than he really does."
> Harriet seemed ready to worship her friend for a sentence so
> satisfactory; and Emma was only saved from raptures and fond-
> ness, which at the moment would have been dreadful penance,
> by the sound of her father's footsteps. He was coming through
> the hall. Harriet was too much agitated to encounter him. "She
> could not compose herself—Mr. Woodhouse would be alarmed—
> she had better go;"—with most ready encouragement from her
> friend, therefore, she passed off through another door—and the
> moment she was gone, this was the spontaneous burst of Emma's
> feelings: "Oh God! that I had never seen her!"
> The rest of the day, the following night, were hardly enough
> for her thoughts.—She was bewildered amidst the confusion of
> all that had rushed on her within the last few hours. Every moment
> had brought a fresh surprise; and every surprise must be matter
> of humiliation to her.—How to understand it all! How to under-
> stand the deceptions she had been thus practising on herself, and
> living under!—The blunders, the blindness of her own head and
> heart!—she sat still, she walked about, she tried her own room,
> she tried the shrubbery—in every place, every posture, she per-
> ceived that she had acted most weakly; that she had been imposed
> on by others in a most mortifying degree; that she had been im-
> posing on herself in a degree yet more mortifying; that she was
> wretched, and should probably find this day but the beginning of
> wretchedness.

The acute aesthetic pleasure of this turns on the counterpoint between
Emma's spontaneous cry: "Oh God! that I had never seen her!" and the
exquisite comic touch of: "She sat still, she walked about, she tried her

own room, she tried the shrubbery—in every place, every posture, she perceived that she had acted most weakly." The acute humiliation of the will could not be better conveyed than by "she tried the shrubbery" and "every posture." Endlessly imaginative, Emma must now be compelled to endure the mortification of reducing herself to the postures and places of those driven into corners by the collapse of visions that have been exposed as delusions. Jane Austen, who seems to have identified herself with Emma, wisely chose to make this moment of ironic reversal a temporary purgatory, rather than an infernal discomfiture.

The Divided Heart: Defoe's Novels

Martin Price

The rise of the novel in the eighteenth century is the triumph of the particular, however we may explain the novel's coming into being. Two major tendencies feed into the central event. The mock heroic of Cervantes and his followers subjects the heroic image to the punishing presence of the commonplace. And the marvelous is naturalized as the saint's life, the rogue's picaresque career, the pilgrimage of the individual soul, are all enmeshed in the business of daily existence. The heroic may survive its punishment, but it takes on a new form. The allegorical translucency of the saint's life or of the pilgrim's progress may survive to some extent, but saint and pilgrim alike have now become first of all people with familiar names and addresses, with aunts and cousins, and the elaborate costume of a social existence. Saints become Clarissa Harlowes; pilgrims become Robinson Crusoes; and rogues become—instead of the resilient heroes of a hundred escapades—characters disclosed in the long, disorderly memoirs of Moll Flanders.

The triumph of the particular is the triumph of formal realism, a realism used to a different degree and for a different end by each of the great novelists of the century. The novel provides a spacious vehicle, with its slow rhythm of disclosure, its opportunities for dialogue, description, commentary. None of these is new in itself. They appear in epic, in romance, and in the genres of drama—but the mixture is new. The novel allows a rapid alternation between the character's internal thought and his action; between his view of himself and the author's view of him; between the intense scrutiny and the panoramic view. The novel gains fluidity by its prosiness. It sacrifices the concentration of poetic language for a new fusion

From *To the Palace of Wisdom: Studies in Order and Energy from Dryden to Blake.* © 1964 by Martin Price. Southern Illinois University Press, 1964.

of the poetic and the documentary, and for a more thoroughgoing involvement of the significant in the circumstances where it must find its life and from which it must wrest its values. The novel is the medium in which we can see the spirit of man in its most problematic form—not in lucid contests of principle but (in Lionel Trilling's words) "as it exists in the inescapable conditions which the actual and the trivial make for it" (*The Opposing Self*).

Defoe's novels—written late in a career given over to journalism and pamphleteering—have always been a puzzle to the critic. Defoe draws upon forms of autobiography as far apart as criminals' sensational narratives of their careers and Puritan preachers' records of their transactions with God and the devil, factual narratives of sea discoveries, and pious accounts of miraculous providences. Running through this compound is the troubled conscience of a Puritan tradesman, aware of the frequent conflict between the demands of commercial gain and those of spiritual salvation. It is this troubled conscience that gives his characters their depth. They are tremendously efficient and resourceful in meeting the difficulties of their "trade," and Defoe catches the excitement of their limited but genuine art. But they are also nagged by doubt and a sense of guilt, by an awareness of what they have ignored or put by in their single-minded commitment. These pangs are not, in most cases, very effectual, but they are none the less authentic. Defoe's characters participate, as often as not, in what Iris Murdoch calls the "dialectic of those who habitually succumb to temptation."

In the novels I shall consider Defoe gives us the great myth of the isolated man bringing order out of unfamiliar materials (the first part of *Robinson Crusoe*), the outlawry of a woman whose social isolation makes her a freebooter in the center of London (*Moll Flanders*), and the recovery of a man from the life of crime into which he is plunged as a child (*Colonel Jack*). All these characters aspire to some kind of morality; all have a glimpse of some idea of redemption. Without these aspirations, they would be near successors to the picaresque heroes of countless jestbooks, coming through dangerous scrapes with wily dexterity. If the aspirations had fuller control of their natures, they might become the heirs of those spiritual heroes who find their way at last from the City of Destruction to the Land of Beulah. But their lives remain curiously unresolved and open. As Ian Watt has said, "Defoe presents us with a narrative in which both 'high' and 'low' motives are treated with equal seriousness: the moral continuum of his novels is much closer than was that of any previous fiction to the complex combination of spiritual and material issues which moral choices in daily life customarily involve."

Defoe remains a puzzle because he imposes little thematic unity on his materials. Usually the writer who is content to give us the shape of the tale itself has a shapely tale to tell; a tale with its own logic, its awakening of tensions and expectations, its mounting repetition, its elaborate devices for forestalling too direct a resolution, and its satisfying—perhaps ingeniously surprising—way of tying all its threads in one great stroke. Such a tale need not leave those gaps in its narrative that are occasions for us to consider its meaning or theme. In Defoe's narratives the inconsistencies are such that we want to find a significant design, yet they hardly accommodate our wish.

Some critics have found consistent irony in a work like *Moll Flanders* by trimming away troublesome details, hardening the central character, and importing a moral stridency Defoe does not invite. Dorothy Van Ghent finds in Moll "the immense and seminal reality of an Earth Mother, pro-genetrix of the wasteland, sower of our harvests of technological skill, bombs, gadgets, and the platitudes and stereotypes and absurdities of a morality suitable to a wasteland world." This seems to me at once a great deal more fastidious and more vehement than the attitudes that underlie Defoe's conception of his heroine. The fact that Moll measures her success by money does not necessarily mean that money is her only object. Nor does Moll's indifference to the sensuousness and concrete texture of experience make her "monstrously abnormal."

Moll Flanders is the chronicle of a full life span, told by a woman in her seventieth year with wonder and acceptance. In one sense, she is the product of a Puritan society turned to worldly zeal. Hers is very much the world of the Peachums, and in it Moll is the supreme tradeswoman, always ready to draw up an account, to enter each experience in her ledger as profit or loss, bustling with incredible force in the marketplace of marriage, and finally turning to those bolder and franker forms of competitive enterprise, whoredom and theft. To an extent, she is the embodiment of thrift, good management, and industry. But she is also the perverse and savagely acquisitive outlaw, the once-dedicated servant of the Lord turned to the false worship of wealth, power, success.

Her drive is in part the inevitable quest for security, the island of property that will keep one above the waters of an individualistic, cruelly commercial society. Born in Newgate, left with no resources but her needle, she constantly seeks enough wealth or a wealthy enough husband to free her from the threat of poverty and the temptations of crime. But she finds herself fascinated by the quest itself, by the management of marriages, the danger of thievery. When she has more money than she needs, she is still disguising herself for new crimes, disdaining the humble trade of the seamstress. When she finally settles into respectability, it is with a gentleman, not a merchant; her husband is a rather pretentious, somewhat sentimental highwayman, who is not much good as a farmer but is a considerable sportsman. Moll is no simple middle-class mercantile figure; nor is she another Macheath. Yet she has elements of both.

There is still another dimension of Moll Flanders. Her constant moral resolutions, her efforts to reform, her doubts and remorse cannot be discounted as hypocrisy or even unrealistic self-deception. Moll is a daughter of Puritan thought, and her piety has all the troublesome ambiguities of the Puritan faith. Her religion and morality are not the rational and calculating hypocrisy of the simple canter—the Shimei of Dryden's *Absalom and Achitophel*, for example. They are essentially emotional. She has scruples against incest, but they take the form of nausea, physical revulsion. She intends virtuous behavior and is astonished to discover her hardness of heart. Moll's life is a career of self-discovery, of "herself surprised," surprised by herself and with herself. Just as for the earlier Puritan, the coming of grace might be unpredictable, terrifyingly sudden, and very possibly deceptive, so for Moll the ways of her heart are revealed to her by her conduct more than by her consciousness, and even her most earnest repentance arouses her own distrust until it can well up into an uncontrollable joy. Personality is not something created or earned; the self is not the stable essence the Stoic moralist might seek. It is something given, whether by God or the devil, always in process, eluding definition and slipping away from rational purpose. Even at her happiest, with the man she has long missed, and in the late autumn of her life, Moll can think of how pleasant life might still be without him. It is a wayward thought, a momentary inclination, as real as her devotion and no more real.

What we find in Moll Flanders is not an object lesson in Puritan avarice or in the misuse of divinely given talents. Moll has all the confusion of a life torn between worldliness and devotion, but what remains constant is the energy of life itself, the exuberant innocence that never learns from experience and meets each new event with surprise and force. Moll, like the secularized Puritanism she bespeaks, has the zeal that might found sects as well as amass booty, that might colonize a new world as readily as it robbed an old one. And the form of the old zeal, now turned into a secular world, needing the old faith at least intermittently as the new devotion to the world falters with failure, gives us a pattern of character that is one of the remarkable creations of fiction. Defoe, we are told, seems not to judge his material; Defoe must be a brilliant ironist. Both assertions imply a set of values thinner and more neatly ordered than Defoe can offer. He is aware of the tension between the adventurous spirit and the old piety; he can see the vitality of both religious zeal and worldly industry; the thrifty efficiency and the reckless outlawry that are both aspects of the middle-class adventure; the wonderful excitement of technology as well as its darker omens. And seeing all of this, he does not seem to see the need to reduce these tensions to a moral judgment. Like Mandeville, who struts much more in the role, he is one of the artists who make our moral judgments more difficult.

Ultimately, one might call Defoe a comic artist. The structure of *Moll Flanders* itself defies resolution. In giving us the life span, with its eager thrust from one experience to the next, Defoe robs life of its climactic structure. Does Moll face marriage to the brother of her seducer, a seducer she still loves? It is an impossible tragic dilemma. Yet the marriage takes place, the husband dies, the children are placed; and Moll is left taking stock as she enters the marriage market again. Does she face the dreadful fact of incest? This, too, passes away; she cannot reconcile herself to it, but she can make a settlement and depart in search of a new and illegal marriage. The commonplace inevitably recurs; we have parodies of tragic situations.

Moll herself is not contemptible in her insensitivity. She is magnificently unheroic; and yet there is a modest touch of heroism in her power of recuperation, her capacity for survival with decency. In her curiously meaningless life, there is a wonderful intensity of experience at a level where affection, inclination, impulse (both generous and cruel) generate all the motions that are usually governed, or perhaps simply accompanied, by a world of thought. We have Defoe's own account of this process in his *Serious Reflections of Robinson Crusoe:*

> There is an inconsiderate temper which reigns in our minds, that hurries us down the stream of our affections by a kind of involuntary agency, and makes us do a thousand things, in the doing of which we propose nothing to ourselves but an immediate subjection to our will, that is to say, our passion, even without the concurrence of our understandings, and of which we can give very little account after 'tis done.

This way of reading *Moll Flanders* imposes its own straitening on the untidy fullness of the book. Ian Watt has made a decisive case for the comparative artlessness of Defoe; there are too many wasted emphases, too many simple deficiencies of realization to make the case for deliberate irony tenable. But one can claim for Defoe a sensibility that admits more than it can fully articulate, that is particularly alert to unresolved paradoxes in human behavior. Watt dismisses in passing the parallel of a work like Joyce Cary's *Herself Surprised*. There is point in this dismissal, for Cary has raised to clear thematic emphasis what is left more reticent in Defoe. Yet the relationship is worth exploration. Few writers have been so fascinated as Cary with the ambiguities of the Protestant temper. In a great many characters—among them the statesman, Chester Nimmo, in the political trilogy and the evangelical faith-healer Preedy in the last novel, *The Captive and the Free*—Cary studied the shimmering iridescence with which motives seem, from different angles, dedicated service and the search for grace or the most opportunistic self-seeking. Cary was not interested in "rationalization" but in the peculiar power achieved by the coincidence of religious zeal and imperious egoism. Preedy, for example, seduces a young girl and makes her virtually his slave; but he is convinced that his power to win her love is a sign of grace—that a love so undemanding and undeserved as hers can only be a sign of God's love in turn. Preedy is monstrous in one aspect, terrifying but comprehensible in another; the difference lies in what we recognize to be his object.

Cary's effects are so adroit and so carefully repeated that we have no doubt about calling them ironic. Defoe's are less artful and less completely the point of his tale. Yet his awareness of them seems no less genuine. Defoe's characters have secularized old Puritan modes of thought. Moll Flanders is constantly taking inventory and casting up her accounts as she faces a new stage of her life. Crusoe, too, keeps an account book, and, more like the earlier Puritans, an account book of the soul. The doctrine of regeneration, we are told, caused the Puritans "to become experts in psychological dissection and connoisseurs of moods before it made them moralists. It forced them into solitude and meditation by requiring them continually to cast up their accounts" (Perry Miller, *The New England Mind*). In the diary, particularly, the Puritan might weigh each night what he had experienced of God's deliverance or of Satan's temptation during the day. "It was of the very essence of Puritan self-discipline that whatsoever thoughts and actions the old Adam within had most desire to keep hidden, the very worst abominations of the heart, one must when one retired to one's private chamber at night draw into the light of conscience. . . . Having thus balanced his spiritual books, he could go to bed with a good conscience, sleep sound and wake with courage" (William Haller, *The Rise of Puritanism*).

The "other-worldliness" of Puritan theology was, as Perry Miller puts it, "a recognition of the world, an awareness of a trait in human nature, a witness to the devious ways in which men can pervert the fruits of the earth and the creatures of the world and cause them to minister to their vices. Puritanism found the natural man invariably running into excess or imtemperance, and saw in such abuses an affront to God, who had made all things to be used according to their natures. Puritanism condemned not natural passions but inordinate passions."

This concern with the uses of things places emphasis not on their sensuous fullness but on their moral function and the seeming bleakness of Defoe's world of measurables derives in part from this. Characteristically, when Defoe in his *Tour* praises the countryside, it is for what man has made of it: "nothing can be more beautiful; here is a plain and pleasant country, a rich fertile soil, cultivated and enclosed to the utmost perfection of husbandry, then bespangled with villages; those villages filled with these houses, and the houses surrounded with gardens, walks, vistas, avenues, representing all the beauties of buildings, and all the pleasures of planting." So, too, the natural scene of Crusoe's island "appeals not for adoration, but for exploitation" (Ian Watt). It is not the things we care about but the motives or energies they bring into play: they may satisfy needs, or call forth technical ingenuity, or present temptations. The physical reality of sensual temptation need not be dwelt upon, for moral obliviousness or self-deception is Defoe's concern (as in the account of Moll's going to bed with the Bath gentleman). If Moll's inventories seem gross, they may also be seen as the balance of freedom against necessity; poverty is the inescapable temptation to crime. And her inventories are, in an oblique sense, still account books of the spirit.

What might once have served the cause of piety becomes a temptation to exploitation. This is the dialectic of which Perry Miller speaks: the natural passion insensibly turns into the inordinate passion. Each of Defoe's central characters at some point passes the boundary between need and acquisitiveness, between the search for subsistence and the love of outlawry. And it is only in the coolness of retrospect that they can see the transgression. Defoe does not play satirically upon their defections; he knows these to be inevitable, terrifying so long as they can be seen with moral clarity, but hard to keep in such clear focus. His characters live in a moral twilight, and this leads to Defoe as a writer of comedy.

We must also keep in mind the essential optimism of the Puritan creed. The Puritans could not, Perry Miller tells us, sustain the tragic sense of life. "They remembered their cosmic optimism in the midst of anguish, and they were too busy waging war against sin, too intoxicated with the exultation of the conflict to find occasional reversals, however costly, any cause for deep discouragement. . . . Far from making for tragedy, the necessity [for battle] produced exhilaration." The battle against sin is not, of course, the only battle in which Defoe's characters are involved, but the struggle in the world demands the same intense concentration and affords the same exhilaration. If there is any central motive in Defoe's novels, it is the pleasure in technical mastery: the fascination with how things get done, how Crusoe makes an earthenware pot or Moll Flanders dexterously makes off with a watch. The intensity of this concentration gives an almost allegorical cast to the operation, as if Crusoe's craftsmanship had the urgency of the art by which a man shapes his own soul. It is beside the point to complain that these operations are "merely" technical and practical; undoubtedly the man who invented the wheel had beside him a high-minded friend who reproached him with profaning the mystery of the circle by putting it to such menial uses. The delight in mastery and in problem-solving may be a lower and less liberal art than those we commonly admire, but it is a fundamental experience of men and a precious one.

Even more, the energy of spirit that is concentrated in these operations is a source of joy. One might wish that Moll Flanders had founded a garden suburb with the force she gave to robbing a child, and at moments she feels so too; but the strength she brings to the demands of life is at worst a perversion of the spiritual energy the Puritan seeks to keep alive. It is in doing that he finds himself and serves himself, and Moll Flanders reaches the lowest point of her life when she falls into the apathy of despair in Newgate: "I degenerated into stone, I turned first stupid and senseless, then brutish and thoughtless, and at last raving mad as any of them were; in short, I became as naturally pleased and easy with the place as if indeed I had been born there." She loses her sense of remorse:

A certain strange lethargy of soul possessed me; I had no trouble, no apprehensions, no sorrow about me, the first surprise was gone. . . . my senses, my reason, nay, my conscience, were all asleep.

In contrast is the recovered energy that comes with her repentance:

> I was covered with shame and tears for things past, and yet had at the same time a secret surprising joy at the prospect of being a true penitent . . . and so swift did thought circulate, and so high did the impressions they had made upon me run, that I thought I could freely have gone out that minute to execution, without any uneasiness at all, casting my soul entirely into the arms of infinite mercy as a penitent.

These moments of spiritual despair and joy have their counterparts in her secular life as well. After the death of her honest husband, she is left in poverty:

> I lived two years in this dismal condition, wasting that little I had, weeping continually over my dismal circumstances, and as it were only bleeding to death, without the least hope or prospect of help.

With the pressure of poverty and the temptation of the Devil, she commits her first theft and runs through a tortured circuit of streets:

> I felt not the ground I stepped on, and the farther I was out of danger, the faster I went. . . . I rested me a little and went on; my blood was all in a fire, my heart beat as if I was in sudden fright: in short, I was under such a surprise that I knew not whither I was going, or what to do.

This is the energy of fear, but it is a return to life; and before many pages have passed, Moll is speaking with pleasure of her new art.

The benign form of this energy is that of the honest tradesman whom Defoe always celebrates: "full of vigor, full of vitality, always striving and bustling, never idle, never sottish; his head and his heart are employed; he moves with a kind of velocity unknown to other men" (*Complete English Tradesman*). As R. H. Tawney has written, "a creed which transformed the acquisition of wealth from a drudgery or a temptation into a moral duty was the milk of lions" (*Religion and the Rise of Capitalism*). Yet, as Tawney recognizes, the older Puritan view of the evil of inordinate desires still survived. Defoe may call gain "the tradesman's life, the essence of his being," but gain makes it all the harder for a tradesman to be an honest man: "There are more snares, more obstructions in his way, and more allurements to him to turn knave, than in any employment. . . . [For] as getting money by all possible (fair) methods is his proper business, and what he opens his shop for . . . 'tis not the easiest thing in the world to distinguish between fair and foul, when 'tis against himself." This candid recognition of the traps of self-deception leads Defoe to a considerable degree of tolerance. He cites the Golden Rule, "a perfect and unexception-able rule" which "will hold for an unalterable law as long as there is a tradesman left in the world." But, he goes on, "it may be said, indeed, where is the man that acts thus? Where is the man whose spotless integrity reaches it?" He offers those tradesmen who "if they slip, are the first to reproach themselves with it; repent and re-assume their upright conduct; the general tenor of whose lives is to be honest and to do fair things. And this," he concludes, "is what we may be allowed to call *an honest man*; for as to perfection, we are not looking for it in life."

More fundamental is the "paradox of trade and morality" that Defoe recognizes as well as Mandeville: "the nation's prosperity is built on the ruins of the nation's morals"; or, more cogently, "It must be confessed, trade is almost universally founded upon crime." By this Defoe means what Mandeville means: "What a poor nation must we have been if we had been a sober, religious, temperate nation? . . . The wealth of the country is raised by its wickedness, and if it should be reformed it would be undone." Of luxury, Defoe could write "However it may be a vice in morals, [it] may at the same time be a virtue in trade." As Hans H. Anderson (from whose study I have drawn several of these quotations) points out, Defoe does not try to shock his readers as Mandeville does by insisting upon the irreducible paradox; he tends to abstract issues and to exclude "ethical considerations by the simple expedient of restricting his discussion to what he called the 'Language of Trade.' " But, although Defoe does not take pleasure in the difficulties he creates for the moralist, he shows a keen awareness of the difficulties his characters encounter.

When Robinson Crusoe voices his satisfaction with his island, he finds it a place where the dangerous paradox is happily resolved.

> I was removed from all the wickedness of the world here. . . . I had nothing to covet; for I had all that I was now capable of enjoying. . . . There were no rivals; I had no competitor. . . . But all I could make use of was all that was valuable. . . . The most covetous griping miser in the world would have been cured of the vice of covetousness, if he had been in my case; for I possessed infinitely more than I knew what to do with.

In short, Crusoe's island is the utopia of the Protestant Ethic (as Ian Watt puts it) in a double sense. It is a place where Crusoe holds undistracted to his work and where his work is rewarded; but it is a place, too, where his tradesmanlike energy remains innocent, with no danger of inordinate de-sires leading to dishonesty. Only in the overambitious project of the *periagua* does Crusoe exceed the limits of utility, and the only consequences are the futility of wasted effort.

All of Defoe's other major characters yearn at one time or another for this freedom from the "necessity" embodied in temptation. The only other character who comes close to Crusoe's freedom is Colonel Jack in his management of slaves. Jack is concerned with the exploitation of his fellow men. Jack's master, the slaveowner, must exact obedience in order to realize the value of his property, but he would prefer to win voluntary service. Jack introduces a policy of mercy that wins the obligation of gratitude from the slave, Mouchat, and thus Jack reconciles trade (or here expediency) with morality and eliminates cruelty:

> If they were used with compassion, they would serve with affec-
> tion as well as other servants . . . but never having been let taste
> what mercy is, they know not how to act from a principle of love.

Significantly, when Jack encounters a slave who will not learn this desirable lesson, he sells him off; he can achieve his reconciliation only within the limits of the plantation, as Crusoe can his only in the isolation of his island kingdom. Both these scenes are, in effect, islands of ideal social order.

Later, when Jack is instructed in religious matters, he is made to see how God's mercy acts upon all men just as his own mercy has worked upon the slaves. The sense of mercy "seizes all the passions and all the affections, and works a sincere unfeigned abhorrence of the crime as a crime, as an offence against our Benefactor, as an act of baseness and ingratitude to Him who has given us our life . . . and who has conquered us by continuing to do us good when He has been provoked to destroy us." The "scholar" who instructs Jack proposes, somewhat in the spirit of Shaftesbury, that if men could see with full clarity the nature of both heaven and hell, "the first would have a stronger and more powerful effect to reform the world than the latter." This conception of a grateful man rejoicing in a merciful God is an ideal vision that Defoe would like to sustain. "But," as Jack remarks as he leaves home to wander in the world, "man is a short-sighted creature at best, and in nothing more than in that of fixing his own felicity, or, as we may say, choosing for himself." We are back to Crusoe's "original sin" of leaving his father and the middle station of life, and in fact to all those expansive, restless efforts that are both the glory of the tradesman and the occasion for his temptations. The alternatives to this energy may be deadness of spirit or that serenity that at last confers "the leisure to repent." This leisure is given Defoe's characters intermittently in the course of their lives; only with age is it steadily achieved. Only after seventy-two years of a "life of infinite variety" does Crusoe fully "know the value of retirement, and the blessing of ending our days in peace."

Defoe's characters are all technicians, rational masters of their art, on one level, and creatures of impulse or obsession on another. When the young Robinson Crusoe hears his father's moving speech about the need to keep to the middle station of life, he is—as he tells us—"sincerely affected with this discourse . . . and I resolved not to think of going abroad any more, but to settle at home according to my father's wish." Then follows that verb that runs through Defoe's novels: "But alas! a few days wore it all off." When a year later he goes to Hull, it is done "casually, and without any purpose of making an elopement that time"; yet on a sudden prompting he finds himself on board a ship bound for London. After escaping a dreadful storm that reveals all the horror and dangers of a life at sea, Crusoe is divided: he cannot face the shame of returning home, but he is still vividly aware of his careèr as a Jonah:

> An irresistible reluctance continued to going home; and, as I stayed awhile, the remembrance of the distress I had been in wore off; and as that abated, the little motion I had in my desires to a return wore off with it, till at last I quite laid aside the thoughts of it, and looked out for a voyage.

This pattern is typical: the power of the impulse or obsession, the lack of clear decision; conflicts are settled in Crusoe or for him, not by him. Throughout his stay on the island, we see these fluctuations. Is the island a prison, or is it a deliverance from the sinful life he led in the world? Is the fate God has brought upon him an act of divine goodness, or is it fearfully inscrutable? All the trust he has achieved deserts him when he finds the footprint in the sand, and it is slowly regained. As he turns to Scripture and lights upon a telling verse, he finds comfort. "I thankfully laid down the book, and was no more sad," he tells us; and then adds, "at least, not on that occasion." There is always this note of reservation in Defoe's characters—as they prudently conceal some part of their fortune or story. It may be a note of mistrust, but, even more, it shows a sense, in the midst of joy or pleasure, that the mind of today need not be that of tomorrow, and perhaps cannot.

Moll Flanders, like Crusoe, is a creature of mixed and unstable motives. She goes to Bath, she tells us, "indeed in the view of taking what might offer; but I must do myself that justice as to protest I meant nothing but in an honest way, nor had any thoughts about me at first that looked the way which afterwards I suffered them to be guided." It is sincere enough, but the moral twilight is clear, too. She lodges in the house of a woman "who, though she did not keep an ill house, yet had none of the best principles in her self." When she has become the mistress of the gentleman she meets at Bath, she remarks that their living together was "the most undesigned thing in the world"; but in the next paragraph she adds: "It is true that from the first hour I began to converse with him I resolved to let him lie with me." The surprise has come in finding that what she had been prepared to accept through economic necessity, she has encouraged through "inclination."

Earlier in America, when Moll discovers that she is married to her brother and the disclosure drives him to attempt suicide, she casts about:

> In this distress I did not know what to do, as his life was apparently declining, and I might perhaps have married again there, very

much to my advantage, had it been my business to have stayed in the country; but my mind was restless too, I hankered after coming to England, and nothing would satisfy me without it.

Here, too, the motives are a wonderful mixture of concern, prudence, and impulse. What is most remarkable about Moll Flanders is her untroubled recognition of her motives, her readiness to set them forth with detachment, at least to the extent that she understands them. She recalls those Puritans who scrutinize their motives as if they were spectators beholding a mighty drama. When Moll robs a poor woman of the few goods that have survived a fire, she records:

I say, I confess the inhumanity of the action moved me very much, and made me relent exceedingly, and tears stood in my eyes upon that subject. But with all my sense of its being cruel and inhuman, I could never find it in my heart to make any restitution: the reflection wore off, and I quickly forgot the circumstances that attended it.

Fielding was to make something beautifully ironic of this kind of mixture of motives. Defoe uses it differently; candor disarms the moral judgment that irony would require. The stress is more upon the energy of impulse than upon its evil. And the energy is such that it can scarcely be contained by a single motive or be channeled long in a consistent course.

Gulliver's Travels:
The Displaced Person

Patrick Reilly

Gulliver travels to find himself. As much as *Oedipus* or *Der zerbrochene Krug* the action is a search for identity, its ultimate question as shocking as that posed by the twentieth-century death camps: not "where is God?" but, much more appallingly, "where is man?" In pursuit of this mystery, Swift employs throughout certain recurring images and themes—giants and girls, sexuality and vermin—as aids to identification.

The opening voyage, addressing a personal dilemma as well as universal concerns, is the most autobiographical; in the figure of the baffled giant, Swift investigates his own captivity in Lilliput. One of the most bitter sensations known to man is the consciousness of failure affixed to a conviction of ability. When the man is not merely talented but a genius, the agony of bewilderment, of unjustified self-reproach, is commensurately greater, and the mystery of defeat, forever soliciting explanation, can become a mode of diabolic torment. That Swift saw himself as both genius and failure we need not doubt, for his own word is the evidence. "What a genius I had when I wrote that book!" The note of elated discovery and gratified pride in his own belated tribute to the *Tale* only enhances and authenticates the sense of accomplishment he experienced in the rereading; and the reception of the *Travels* as recorded by Johnson—"It was received with such avidity that the price of the first edition was raised before the second could be made; it was read by the high and the low, the learned and illiterate. Criticism was for a while lost in wonder"—must surely have ratified in him the conviction of his old power. He had, in addition, other spectacular triumphs. The purpose of *The Conduct of the Allies*, says Johnson, was to persuade the nation to a peace, and never had pamphlet more

From *Jonathan Swift: The Brave Desponder*. © 1982 by Patrick Reilly. Manchester University Press, 1982.

success. In *The Drapier's Letters* he had, single-handed, defeated a government attempt to exploit Ireland—and, for Swift, saving the Irish was a labour that might have confounded Hercules himself.

The ordinary man shakes his head in perplexity on hearing such a life described as failure; what, he wonders, would Swift have accepted as success? Yet genius remains inconsolable; if there is one indisputable fact about Swift, it is his bitter, invincible conviction of defeat. We might pardonably exaggerate by describing him as a man programmed for defeat, and the great fish which he just missed catching as a boy was indeed, as he told Pope, to haunt his whole life as prophetic admonition, symbol of all those near things that darkened his career. The man whose pantheon of heroes was an assembly of spectacular failures—Brutus, Junius, Socrates, Epaminondas, Cato, More—was acutely sensitive to the obstacles cumbering the path of heroic virtue in a spiteful, petty, levelling world. He caustically supplies the one infallible test of a true genius: all the dunces are inveterately leagued against him. He provides the recipe to those seeking advancement through the power of the word:

> Write worse then if you can—be wise—
> Believe me 'tis the way to rise.

The pain of personal failure, the sense of wasted endeavour, of words marshalled to no creative purpose—doses prescribed for the dead, appeals to animals incapable of amendment, the charmer's skill squandered on deaf adders—all this hangs heavy over Swift's work, is indeed, paradoxically, the source of its greatness. No other writer of genius has so much made the foolish futility of words the master theme of his achievement, and it is this that partially justifies Leavis's pronouncement about great powers exhibited consistently in negation and rejection.

Failure is less tantalising when the great man falls through some excess or shortcoming, the tragedy of *hamartia* as defined by Hamlet, "the stamps of one defect" that pulls ruin upon a whole array of virtues. This helps to assuage whatever dismay we feel at Antony bested by Octavius or Coriolanus broken by the tribunes. Great men undoubtedly, but the reconciling pity is that greatness should be so lamentably vitiated. The reconciling element disappears, however, when heroism perishes with no *hamartia* to dull the edge of pain. The defeat of goodness is for Swift as nerve-jangling as Aristotle predicted, and we need only read Swift on More's fate at the hands of "Henry the Beast" to appreciate how unappeasably angry he could become at the spectacle of unmerited suffering—the greatest Englishman of all time murdered by the worst.

Swift reechoes the perplexed anguish of the Psalmist: how long, O God? Why does God forget his servant, hide in the seasons of distress? Why do the good fail, the wicked flourish? Why is the genius doomed to die like a poisoned rat in a Dublin hole while mediocrities monopolize power? Nor is it simply his own personal debacle that torments him. His friend Bolingbroke provides yet another confirmatory instance of the same perverse law that condemns great ability to impotence. In his poem "On the Death of Dr Swift" there is a footnote telling us that Bolingbroke "is reckoned the most universal genius in Europe," but that Walpole, dreading his gifts, has conspired with George I to keep him in the political doldrums. The mystery remains: how has an intellectual giant like Bolingbroke been outmanoeuvred and outsmarted by a commonplace rascal like Walpole? What is this strange moral equivalent of Gresham's Law which continually awards victory to Lilliputians, while the colossus, superior gifts notwithstanding, is lucky to escape with eyesight and life?

There is plausible internal evidence that Swift uses Lilliput to explore certain crises in his own life or in the lives of his friends; the giant's "eminent service" in extinguishing the blaze in the royal apartments which so offends the Empress that she declines ever again to enter the polluted palace, is an allegory of Queen Anne's outraged resolve never to advance the author of the *Tale*—or, alternatively, of the royal ingratitude towards Bolingbroke who had put the nation in his debt by concluding the Peace of Utrecht. Both book and treaty are giant achievements, maligned by pygmy malice. Gulliver, lodged in the profaned temple, desecrated some years before by an unnatural murder, recalls Swift's revulsion at the execution of Charles I, always for him, as his sermon on the royal martyr shows, the nadir of revolutionary evil. But, detailed interpretation apart, there is clearly something in the image of the bemused giant, curiously impotent despite enormous power, that holds intense personal interest for Swift. Not that Gulliver *is* Swift; on the contrary, he is in his role as wide-eyed ingénu laughably different from his sharp, knowing creator. The ropedancing and the crawling under sticks which so fascinate him as ceremonies unknown to the rest of the world are sickeningly familiar to Swift as the contemptible cantrips of power-seekers everywhere. But, however unlike in other ways, Gulliver as giant among pygmies is an apposite metaphor of Swift in his society, just as Gulliver's unavailing efforts to live decently and usefully, placing his great powers at the public service but forever frustrated by the envy of little men, is a thinly disguised rendition of his creator's unhappy fate.

Gulliver visits fantastic countries without ever leaving the real world. The veracity he is so touchy about is never really in doubt and his appeal to his long sojourn among the honest horses as verification of his story, is superfluous. Escapist is thoroughly inapplicable to a book which entraps us while pretending to visit exotic regions. Johnson's outrageous dismissal of the *Travels*—a mere matter of thinking of big men and little men with everything else at once falling into place—is unpardonable; what about flying islands and crazy academies, hideous immortals and sorcerers' realms, rational horses and Yahoos? Yet this perverse judgement is relevant to the first two voyages and can help us identify their salient characteristics: the only thing fantastic in Lilliput or Brobdingnag is Gulliver himself, so that it *is* finally nothing more remarkable than a question of relationships between big and little men.

These worlds are perfectly credible, totally recognizable—naturally enough, since they are both our own, diminished and magnified in powers of twelve. Gulliver impatiently waves away the printer's plea for changing the original text; how can he be prosecuted for what has happened so long ago and far away?—thus betraying these travels into remote nations as investigations of contemporary England. Kinship is established when Gulliver spots his first Lilliputian, a human creature not six inches high, with a bow and arrow in his hands and a quiver at his back, while he himself lies pinioned, sword at his side, pistols in his pocket. Unsurprisingly, Lilliput has the same dismal record of war and massacre as England—six feet or six inches, it is the same bellicose, destructive animals. Far from "remote," Lilliput's problems in warfare, political careerism, religious intolerance, are those of Europe. Not the country nor its customs and concerns but Gulliver's status within it—this creates the elements of fantasy and fairy tale, establishes it as the children's classic. Giants are a norm in fairy tale and "A Voyage to Lilliput" presents a metamorphosis as startling as any in Ovid or Kafka.

Gulliver changes. Shipwrecked an ordinary man on a Pacific beach, he loses consciousness and is reborn nine hours later a giant. Lest we miss the gestation symbolism, he tells us afterwards his stay in the new universe was just over nine months. How seems the world to someone who awakes to a twelvefold increase in stature? Swift supplies a comic analogue to Marlowe's Faustus, an examination of the benefits and perils of being suddenly raised far above ordinary mortals. Its picquancy is a function of Swift's own Olympian self-awareness linked to his sense of restriction and confinement, a fettered giant in his irksome Dublin exile. The dream of power is as old as the dream of immortality and the latest import from American comic books via television in the awesome figure of the Incredible Hulk, who uses his prodigious strength to right wrongs and foil villains, is testimony to the dream's staying-power, in however debased a form. The ordinary man fancies that, given giant power or eternal life, all things are possible, but just as in part 3 Swift destroys the dream of immortality by depicting it as a Struldbrugg nightmare, so in part 1 he explodes equally naïve expectations by showing that the giant Gulliver fares no better in Lilliput than his intellectual counterparts, Jonathan Swift and Henry St. John, do in eighteenth-century England. "A Voyage to Lilliput" scrutinises the fate of the giant in society by presenting him in certain representative guises: as Polyphemus, Hercules, Samson, and also as intellectual titan, bringer of new truth to ordinary men.

Irony is present from the start in the simultaneous recreation of Gulliver as giant and prisoner. His first impulse to resist as a match for their greatest army is followed by a prudential decision to submit, the linguistic problem circumvented by calling upon the sun as witness of the promise. The Lilliputians evince a similar capacity for prudential morality. They don't try to kill him while he sleeps, sensibly, since the aroused giant would have burst his bonds and caused a bloodbath. The initial relationship between giant and little people is a perfect *exemplum* of Swift's lifelong thesis that decency and commonsense, morality and reason, are ideal bedfellows, that men go to heaven with half the pains of the hellward journey.

The irony of Gulliver's dual status—giant and captive—is, however, soon matched in the ambivalent Lilliputian response. He is, clearly, a not-able acquisition; when he eats and drinks, they exhibit an ecstatic proprie-tary pride in the doer of these wonders. When, freed from the ropes but securely chained, he at last stands erect, they gasp with delighted aston-ishment. Their attitude to him is rather like Magwitch's to Pip: my gentle-man, our giant. But pride competes with other considerations. Like a modern nuclear reactor, Gulliver is both promise and threat, at once source of power and fear, and however gentle and obedient, he poses serious problems for his hosts' technology. What if he breaks loose, runs amok, causes famine or plague? Even if they manage to kill him, will not the stench of the monstrous carcass produce disastrous environmental pollu-tion? Can they afford so costly a luxury with the consequent strain upon their tiny resources?—he needs six hundred domestics and armies of crafts-men of all kinds from joiners to tailors, he consumes daily enough food to keep 1728 Lilliputians alive, the removal of his excreta requires a squad of labourers with wheelbarrows working a full shift.

His everyday acts are potential catastrophes: a man who extinguishes conflagrations simply by urinating might be welcome in London in 1666 or Chicago in 1871, but always there is the fear that he might just as easily drown the government as save the city. His mere presence is a peril in town or country. He must stick to the highways and stay out of the fields where a stroll would mean total devastation. Visiting the metropolis, he has to wear a short coat for fear of destroying buildings and there is a two hours' curfew to avoid a massacre of citizens. What if he sleepwalks? or sneezes? It's like living with a petrochemical complex on the doorstep. Every time he relieves himself, the health authorities face a major crisis in pollution disposal, the modern equivalent of a giant oil tanker wrecked daily on your coast. When he eats and drinks the spectacle is magnificent, but pride in his prowess and aesthetic delight are tempered by a frightened glance at the ravaged foodstore or the ledgers of a desperate exchequer. And yet the Lilliputians clearly find it a comfort to have a giant on their side and the high risks of his maintenance nag less when he puts on a fearsome display of the latest European weaponry; waving his scimitar or firing his pistols, he appeals to the same emotions, brings the same com-forting reassurance, as do the newest NATO missiles or the massive War-saw Pact armaments rolling through Red Square.

From the start he decides to be a "good" giant, earn his parole by contradicting the stereotype of the wicked ogre. His first conscious imper-sonation is of a mock Polyphemus. When the hooligans who stone him are delivered to him by the military for punishment, he puts them in his pocket and takes one out, like the Cyclops with the companions of Ulysses, as though he were about to eat him. The officers' dismay gives way to rejoicing when instead he uses his terrible knife to cut the culprits' bonds before gently setting them free—the ogre is really a genial giant, forever obliging and anxious not to disturb. He passes with full marks this clemency test and in a remarkable demonstration of power and magnanimity completely fulfills Isabella's injunction to the great ones of the world:

> O, 'tis excellent
> To have a giant's strength, but it is tyrannous
> To use it like a giant.

The policy of being a model prisoner seems to pay off when the Emperor, hearing of the incident, decides to give Gulliver a chance to prove himself "a useful servant." He becomes a kind of court entertainer or circus strongman, a Samson desperately eager to placate his captors by feats of strength and entertainments, using his handkerchief as exercise ground for the royal cavalry, straddling his legs to provide an imposing triumphal arch for the full military parade. Mildness reaches a charming apogee as the natives dance in his hand and the children play hide-and-seek in his hair—there could be no more striking proof that the passage from Polyphemus to lovable giant has been fully accomplished.

After such exemplary behaviour, it comes as no surprise when he at last obtains his freedom. With freedom, however, we have the first hint of something rotten in Lilliput. Gulliver is freed not as reward for good conduct but to frustrate an enemy invasion, and but for this emergency might have lain in chains for ever. Swift's own experience in securing the remission of firstfruits for the Church of Ireland taught him how sweet people seeking favours could be, how ungratefully curt after you had delivered. Gulliver, like Swift, delivers; he guarantees Lilliput against aggression by walking off with the enemy fleet, his spectacles a shield against arrows. Without the stir of one Lilliputian scientist, the nation acquires a new, stunningly invincible weapon that blows skyhigh the armaments parity with Blefuscu. But when the Lilliputian Emperor, insatiable for world empire, avid to become literally as well as panegyrically lord of the universe, spurns an advantageous peace, like the Whig hawks, and demands unconditional surrender, the reduction of Blefuscu to a colony, and universal dragooning into the Little Endian Church, the tool rebels, the weapon declines to be used: Gulliver, refusing to be an instrument for reducing a free people to servitude, withdraws his giant labour. The invasion threat over and Blefuscu, like Louis XIV at Utrecht, ready to treat, Gulliver declines to pulverise them into unconditional surrender. In response, forgetting all his debts to Gulliver, the Emperor begins plotting his death and the way is clear for Gulliver's two further impersonations of harassed, tormented titanism, Hercules and Samson.

Before this, however, we have the spectacle of Gulliver as intellectual giant, bringer of new, startling truth to little men and meeting the customary fate attending such giants ever since Plato's philosopher returned to the cave to enlighten its inhabitants about the world outside. The giant's flagrant capitulation to the petty follies of Lilliputian politics has already been noted. Certainly, Gulliver, in consequence of his ludicrous complaisancy, has only himself to blame if the little people treat him as a born Lilliputian with the full set of petty prejudices; but, at the same time, there is something absurdly egotistic in the easy assumption that whatever concerns a Lilliputian must also be of obsessive interest to a giant—a *drurr* may be crucial in Lilliput but Gulliver has to take it on trust. The very uncomplaisant god of "The Day of Judgement" surveys scornfully the petty wranglings of the odious vermin who dare to make him a party to their disputes before squashing them all underfoot.

It is therefore comically appropriate that smack in the middle of this display of egotism, Swift should insert a devastating critique of the Lilliputian reaction to Gulliver's news of the giant world. The little people credit only one world, that divided between their two great empires. They reject Gulliver's account of Europe on a priori grounds as incompatible with established truth, applying in the process pygmy reasoning and Lilliputian standards to the whole universe. Gulliver must have fallen out of the sky, from the moon or a star, since clearly a hundred such creatures would speedily eat the world to death—"world" is obviously a synonym for Lilliput. The logic is impeccable given the closed system of Lilliputian conditioning—and against the walls of this system Gulliver beats in vain in his attempt to persuade his hosts to a radical reappraisal of reality. There is no evidence in the text that he is exasperated by their resolve not to be enlightened, but this simply emphasizes the temperamental gulf between Swift and Gulliver, for similarly circumstanced the greatest single torment of Swift's life was his inability despite all his art and striving, to make people see.

If Gulliver as intellectual giant can be contemptuously ignored, Gulliver as good servant turned awkward is another matter, especially when his maintenance cost is remembered. Even a docile Gulliver comes dear; when refractory, the opportunity cost of his upkeep becomes totally unacceptable. Lilliputian vindictiveness gathers against the recalcitrant giant all the more readily when the budget is on the agenda. Gulliver's myopia is nowhere more humorously demonstrated than when, thinking he is honouring the royal host, he overeats scandalously, while the Treasurer Flimnap sourly looks on, thinking not only of his "faithless" wife but of the depleted exchequer. The Lilliputians by now want rid of him—what good is an intractable giant? But the dilemma is painful; exiled, he might cross to Blefuscu and take both fleets with him. The overriding priority is how safely to jettison this disobliging encumbrance, and in the context of the parallels already established between Lilliputian and European history, it is appropriate that the methods of elimination proposed should resemble closely the tragic ends of the two mightiest heroes in western mythology, Hercules and Samson.

It is fitting that the jealous treasurer should conceive a plan of strewing a poisonous juice on Gulliver's shirts to make him tear his flesh and die in torture: the shirt of Flimnap, Lilliputian replica of the shirt of Nessus, the device whereby Hercules, that other victim of love and jealousy, is untimely destroyed. The second, more merciful plan, proposed by Gulliver's friend, the Secretary Reldresal, looks back to Samson's treatment by the Philistines. Blinding the giant is in every sense the ideal solution: it will confirm "all the world" in its appreciation of imperial mercy, it will suitably acknowledge the giant's former services before he turned nasty, and it will make him totally dependent on his captors for the rest of his life. Strong as ever, he will be able to "see" only through his master's eyes; he will be braver than ever, for dangers unseen cannot deter, and he need fear no longer for his eyes, the one concern that almost frustrated the removal of the enemy fleet. The Emperor's decision is a compromise between death and blinding; Gulliver is to be blinded, then gradually starved to death—boring operations can begin in distant parts of the kingdom to find areas suitable for disposing of the noxious carcass to prevent atmospheric pollution.

Gulliver, to whom this plan is leaked through the loyalty of a high-placed friend (Philby in Lilliput), can now only react. He is being forced to his dismay into the role of Samson, and the always unstable relationship of guest and host has now clearly declined into that of captive and captor, victim and executioner. Propaganda about royal mercy notwithstanding, he recoils from the role of docile, tractable giant, eyeless in Lilliput at the mill with slaves, but equally he rejects with horror the part of heroic, defiant Samson, pelting the tiny metropolis to pieces with stones, pulling the whole guilty empire crashing down upon his puny enemies. Far from hero, Gulliver is comic as he desperately cudgels his brain trying to see the lenity of the imperial sentence or shrinks from harming the Lilliputians in grateful remembrance of that exalted title of Nardac so graciously bestowed upon him in happier days.

Salvation comes to him, ironically, by way of inexperience, his character as ingénu, young, rash, foolishly precipitate, as Swift supplies a delightfully comic instance of the advantages that sometimes accrue from being a fool among knaves. He simply decides to leave Lilliput and let the little people live as they did before he arrived. With greater maturity, deeper knowledge, a fuller acquaintance with the ways of princes, he would have seen the Emperor's unbelievable mercy, have embraced joyfully so mild a chastisement as mere blinding. He avoids it because, young and blessedly ignorant, he is still headstrong enough to disregard expert advice. The radical critique of habituation posing as knowledge, the merely provisional, relative and contingent claiming to be absolute and immutable, first seen in the offhand dismissal of Gulliver's European "fantasies" by the little people, is now redirected towards Gulliver himself as target as he confesses shamefacedly, on the basis of subsequent experience, what a fool he was in saving his eyes. Such "knowledge" as he has since then acquired is, Swift implies, as damaging as exposure to the stench of a dead giant, as fatal as radiation sickness, in the manner in which it weakens and finally deadens the instinctive human response, the intuitive moral reaction, to straight evil; adaptation to certain modes of experience is the disease that destroys humanity.

The international crisis sparked off by the flight to Blefuscu, which attains comic heights with the Emperor of Lilliput demanding in egotistic abandon the instant return of the defector in chains, is only defused when Gulliver finds a boat from the giant world. What better solution to the impasse than Gulliver's unimpeded departure? The Emperor of Blefuscu observes the conventions by politely asking him to stay on as *his* servant, but is mightily relieved when the Man-Mountain just as politely declines. Both empires are at last free "from so insupportable an encumbrance" and can cheerfully return to the mutual massacre that Gulliver's intervention threatens to end; Golding's officer sails away from the island, in Swift's version, and leaves the boys to Beelzebub. The little world has no place for giants who will not abet its corruption; it will always prefer Barabbas to Christ, Flimnap to Gulliver, Walpole to St. John.

Gulliver's leaving the world of the little people is the last ironical juxtaposition of Swift's giant with his own situation. Gulliver sails easily away from Lilliput, captivity ended, an innocent in the evil political world yet miraculously endowed with the power to leave it behind. Swift, shipped off to his Dublin exile, is still the captive giant, cruelly aware of the stink of political life, yet powerless, despite all his great powers, to master, amend or even escape it. Gulliver is liberated from Lilliput, Swift remains as agonizingly imprisoned among *his* little people as ever.

Gulliver leaves Lilliput to seek himself, for he is not at home with the little people. Swift's restless search, using travel as a metaphor, contrasts sharply with Pascal's recommended quietism. Pascal knows what ails us: an inability to sit quiet in one little room. Only on reaching that littlest room of all, the grave, is the frenzied hunt after distraction ended, the last unalterable identity assumed—eternal prisoner or heir to paradise. Swift avoids such otherwordly speculation, his preferred categories being reason and animalism rather than heaven and hell. He always resists committing himself unequivocally to what man cannot know; "if the way to Heaven be through piety, truth, justice, and charity, she is there." The search for comfort concerning his dead mother includes, characteristically, a scintilla of scepticism, a hint of doubt, if only in its mode of formulation; a conclusion is implied rather than affirmed and he and we together are left to hope that it is unchallengeable. Swift will assert only the empirically indisputable and his kingdom is very much of this world, what happens to men here and now his concern. Discussing heaven, he chooses predictably the negative mode; we know, not what goes on there, but what doesn't—neither marriage nor giving in marriage. It is what men do on earth—ropedancing in Lilliput, amassing shining stones in Yahooland, marrying and giving in marriage in England—that obsesses Swift. Where Pascal is interested only in the identity disclosed in the grave, the *Travels* pursues identity in this life and does so by forbidding in advance any pretended distinction between an alleged human nature (*animal rationale*, God's image, etc.) and the deeds of men. "Th'art the deed's creature": our deeds possess and define us, we think them ours but we are theirs, and we discover ourselves in the mirror of everyday life rather than in some final judgement after death. And so, against Pascal's advice, Gulliver is sent on his travels to gather the data enabling a final assessment of human nature to be made. The present aim is to show the part played by Gulliver's girls in reaching this verdict, the importance of sexual evidence in the *Travels* in defining human nature, how indeed at certain points in the text the sexual test assumes crucial significance not only thematically but as a structural principle in the book's organisation.

Gulliver travels because Swift needs evidence; only with the dossier complete and the prosecution case invincible, is he allowed to give up the sea and write his memoirs. To ask therefore why Gulliver returns from Lilliput is like asking why Hamlet doesn't kill Claudius in the prayer scene—the short answer is that there are three voyages and two acts to go. But this, undeniable if trite, refers to the needs of the artist rather than the demands of the art. To leave matters as shockingly obvious as this is to convict the writer of ineptitude or literary bad manners. Genius is the synchronization of external requirement with internal necessity so that what has been willed seems also inevitable: what Shakespeare and Swift want is what Hamlet and Gulliver decide. Thy will be done on earth as it is in heaven; *en la sua voluntade e nostra pace:* the words would be as appropriate in the mouths of Hamlet and Gulliver as in that of God's submissive subject. The Creator's world is a masterpiece ruined by characters who insist on doing their own thing.

Swift's literary strategy is of course very different from Shakespeare's; his gift is enlisted under satire and he never refines himself out of existence—behind the persona we suspect always a real presence and the guarded scepticism that made him, in the matter of Irish coinage, distrust the apparently honest Maculla as much as the rascally Wood, is equally evident in his relations with his own literary creations. From the narrator of the *Tale* to Gulliver, the Drapier and Modest Proposer, his characters are always delegates, never representatives; they say and do only what he wants. If we accept Keats's definition of the poet as having no character or identity, a chameleon forever "filling some other body," delighting as much in an Iago as an Imogen, then we must deny the title to Swift. Hack, Gulliver, Drapier, Proposer, do not relate to Swift as Timon, Lear, Antony to Shakespeare. Swift never set characters free in his sense because he never trusted anyone to speak for him—any persona who had tried anticipating Burke's line with the electors of Bristol would soon have got short shrift. Nevertheless, Swift is as aware as Shakespeare of art's exigencies; Gulliver's return from Lilliput, as much as Hamlet's delay, is motivated internally and not just because Swift is hankering for Brobdingnag. No more than Hamlet does Gulliver know that he's a fiction, at his creator's beck and call; the relationship is rather that identified by Augustine when discussing man's free will and divine foreknowledge: God knows *and* man is free. The artist, like the Creator, foresees what the character will choose.

Gulliver *is* needed for Brobdingnag but the internal justification is that giants cannot live with ordinary people without becoming their conquerors, tools or victims. Gulliver is no conqueror—never once in Lilliput does he use his giant strength to hurt anyone or even retaliate when attacked. He is willing to be a tool, but not to the degree required by pygmy megalomania, so the only part left him is that of victim. Even his complaisancy, however, does not extend to suicide or passive martyrdom. He cannot remain permanently in Lilliput; sooner or later, he will be killed or forced to kill in preemptive strike against his enemies. He is a displaced person, nowhere more strikingly revealed than in his sexual position. Reproduction is one of the chief characteristics by which we identify living organisms and the life of the ordinary man includes among its essential elements sex as well as sleep and food. Saints and the Dean of St. Patrick's may have different needs and priorities, but high on the average human agenda is the instinct to mate and procreate—and Gulliver is indisputably the ordinary, everyday representative of eighteenth-century English humanity. Swift's book is founded upon the fact that so unimaginatively banal a man could never have invented such fantastic places, and he is so manifestly not Scheherazade that the surest testimony of their existence is his telling us so—he is as incapable of such marvellous lies as the Houyhnhnms themselves.

His ordinariness is evident in the circumstances of his marriage, when, taking advice, he decides to alter his condition. He marries because everybody does; it is normal, almost routine, and he is the last man to challenge the prevailing orthodoxy, preferring, in sexual as in other matters, the human average. But in Lilliput he is barred from sexuality, fated to everlasting celibacy. The superb sexual equipment which excites the admiration of the soldiers marching between the bestrid legs of the colossus is, paradoxically, useless; big may be beautiful, but in Lilliput only at the sacrifice of utility value, at least as an organ of reproduction. As a fire extinguisher, he is priceless, as an object of aesthetic admiration, unique, but this very uniqueness certifies him unfit for Lilliput. The eunuchs who, in Yeats's graphic description, crowd round Don Juan as he enters hell, enviously contemplating his mighty thigh, are presumably right to be envious, hell being what it is, or are very foolish eunuchs indeed, but sexual envy is certainly the last thing to direct towards Gulliver in Lilliput.

The Man-Mountain, taker of fleets, invincible in war, is simultaneously not really a man at all, being forbidden full human participation. That Swift intends this is plain from the superb comedy of Gulliver hotly protesting his innocence of adultery in Lilliput, indignantly spurning the slanderous allegations of liaison with a court lady. So proud at having been made a Nardac, he is commensurately furious at being labelled adulterer, completely failing to see that in his position the honour is just as absurdly misplaced as the libel. A major irony of the *Travels* is Gulliver's susceptibility to brainwashing, his smooth accommodation to new environments. Swift's Olympian view sets him above such relativistic follies; Gulliver may think he's a Lilliputian but Swift knows better, and nowhere is the delusion more hilariously exposed than in these solemn protestations of sexual innocence. Gulliver returns from Lilliput not just because another voyage impends but because he has no future with the little people. They are, as he points out at the end of the *Travels*, not even worth conquering, and their final irrelevance to man as an abiding home is dramatised most vividly in terms of total sexual disparity. If you can't sleep with them, you can't live with them: it is, after all, the truism from which biology begins.

In Brobdingnag the total reversal of situation leaves the underlying constant unaffected—voluntary permanent residence is still unacceptable and for the same reason. The giants, unlike the Lilliputians, can of course keep him prisoner. The little people are relieved to see him go, for the miniature balance of power is disastrously upset—Gulliver is both misfit and menace in Lilliput because he is greater than man. In Brobdingnag he is misfit because his insignificance makes him the prey of rats, dogs and monkeys. Trifles, literal and culinary, threaten his existence: drowning in the soup, stifling in the cream, falling from the table, being pecked to death by birds or stung to death by bees; even reading a book is both strenuous and hazardous, like the regimen of an Olympic athlete. Glumdalclitch frets over little Grildrig as though he were an incubator baby, forever at risk. The forfeiture of manhood is again, though in a very different way, dramatised by exhibiting the stranger as complete sexual misfit. The contemptuous impudicity of the maids of honour torpedoes any claim to manhood he might make. His greatest uneasiness is that they use him with a total lack of ceremony, like a creature of complete inconsequence, stripping naked in his presence, uninhibitedly and insultingly, with no attempt at concealment.

It is a peeping Tom's dream and in Marlowe's *Faustus* Robin lasciviously loiters on thoughts of a life blessed with such magical powers as Gulliver possesses, but Gulliver, in his position of "privilege," far from being turned on, is disgusted and humiliated. The Brobdingnagian beauties, all blotches, moles and hairs, repel rather than tempt, are styptics to the erotic imagination as they urinate copiously and with blatant abandon in his presence—what a Brobdingnagian Strephon can only discover in foolhardy exploration is obligingly displayed to Gulliver's nauseated gaze. It is this casual, open indifference that he finds so humiliating, and his sense of shame is merely intensified when indifference modulates into deliberate stripteasing. It is, significantly, the handsomest of the girls, a lively sixteen-year-old, who takes the greatest liberties with the manikin, frolicsomely seating him, helpless and fuming, astride her nipple, "with many other tricks, wherein the reader will excuse me for not being over particular." But, as Swift well knows, the reader is not so easily fobbed off—his imagination has been triggered and he cannot help but be intrigued as to the kind of games they get up to in Brobdingnagian bedrooms.

The young lady is not some teenage erotomaniac; her conduct would doubtless be very different were a real man present and her first trick is in any case impossible with a male of her own species. Gulliver is, for her, simply not a man at all, just a little instrument for making fun or provoking sexual jokes (the more uproarious when set against his outraged expression), possessing finally no more dignity than a dildo. No wonder he persuades his nurses to contrive some excuse for not seeing that young lady any more, for nowhere else in Brobdingnag (and only once more in the whole of the *Travels*) is his sense of shame and degradation so forcibly impressed on him. Bad enough to be stroked condescendingly by the Giant King and called little Grildrig, so insulting to his humanity, but the obscene jests of the playful teenager strike at the very root of his manhood, emasculate him entirely. Helpless in the hands of the giantesses, writhing vainly against loathsome submission to the monstrously magnified flesh, Gulliver could serve as emblem to Spinoza's section of the *Ethics* dealing with the passions and entitled, significantly, "Of Human Bondage."

Gulliver naturally dreams of liberty amid such degradation. The Giant King, bent on keeping him, commands as overriding priority the acquisition of a female of Gulliver's race upon whom he can breed. Far from feeling grateful at this projected catering for his sexual needs, he sees this as the greatest insult of all and prefers death to "the disgrace of leaving a posterity to be kept in cages like canary birds, and perhaps in time sold about the kingdom to persons of quality for curiosities." He is now what the cattle of Lilliput were to him: a species of animal worth cultivating for its curiosity value but little else, and that the curiosity value may have a commercial spin-off leaves the intrinsic triviality unchanged. The envisaged sale of his descendants is the ultimate mortification; Gulliver shares the view, so superbly dramatized in the *Modest Proposal*, that the reduction of men to items of merchandise is the clinching denial of their humanity. The twin assumptions of the *Modest Proposal*—to be bought and sold is the sign of an object, to be kept for stud purposes the sign of an animal—are foreshadowed as Gulliver, anticipating the fate of the Irish poor, confronts both degradations in Brobdingnag, and the great bird that carries him out of the land of giants restores him to a society where his status as man will be renewed.

This claim to a unique human status is the central problem of the *Travels*. Swift was acutely aware of environment and custom in providing the standards by which we compare and judge: a great horse to a Welshman is a little one to a Fleming. The search for a basic human identity, some irrefutable constant infallibly certifying recognition, is pursued through all the voyages and it is intentionally mortifying that the only constants discovered are shameful. The relaxation of tension in the third voyage is attributable to Gulliver's ceasing to be an actor and becoming instead a detached observer. He surveys cynically the curious antics of Laputan ladies deceiving their starstruck husbands, a feat so easy that adultery becomes a yawn. He discovers that female perversity is the same the world over, a constant distinguishing all the daughters of Eve; he admits that the story of the great lady who deserts a loving, generous husband for an old deformed footman who beats her daily smacks more of Europe than Lagado— but "the caprices of womankind are not limited by any climate or nation, and . . . are much more uniform than can easily be imagined." Gulliver would doubtless have cited Emma Bovary, Anna Karenina and Connie Chatterley as further conformations of this judgement. But in part 3 sex is other people's problem, not Gulliver's.

In Lagado sexual vanity is exploited by a shrewd chancellor into an inland revenue dream; men pay taxes as sexual *conquistadores*, their own returns accepted as gospel truth. Women are assessed on their own declared beauty and skill in fashion, but "constancy, chastity, good sense and good nature were not rated, because they would not bear collecting." Glubbdubdrib reveals the filth behind history, the great European houses riddled with bastardy and syphilis. The standard route to high title and fortune is sodomy, incest or the selling of a wife or daughter. Gulliver's role as observer of sexual problems is nowhere more evident than in his introduction to the Struldbruggs. The Luggnaggians are not so sadistic as to condemn married Struldbruggs to everlasting misery; the union of two immortals is unchallengeable ground for divorce, the spots on the foreheads clear proof of irreparable breakdown. Gulliver's delusions of bliss eternal vanish when he sees the immortals—"the most mortifying sight I ever beheld, and the women more horrible than the men." Swift resumes the attack, begun in Brobdingnag, against the false, fleeting attractiveness of the female; the face that launched a thousand ships will seem shockingly different through a microscope or when Helen is a mass of wrinkles, and those romantics who talk glibly of loving for ever should wait till they see a Struldbrugg woman. Cumulatively, these unflattering observations throughout part 3 may signal the beginnings of a shift away from the affectionate husband of the first two parts, grieving over his lost wife and children, towards the alienated misogynist of the last voyage, returning from Houyhnhnmland with much the same view of woman as Young Goodman Brown brings back from the forest; but it seems more sensible to ascribe these general reflections to Gulliver's function within part 3 as observer rather than participant.

Certainly the satiric impact of part 4 derives from an opening in which Gulliver appears as loving husband and father. His home life, all those acid comments on women notwithstanding, is still normal—"I left my poor wife big with child." Conjugal rights and wedded love are clearly on a good footing and the narrator laments the decision to go seafaring again, leaving wife and children after five months of happiness, failing to learn the lesson of "knowing when I was well." What happens to transform him from loving husband to raging misogynist? As much as *Oedipus*, "A Voyage to the Houyhnhnms" charts a passage from unreflecting innocence to shocking awareness of pollution. Gulliver is initially as convinced as Oedipus that he is in no way related to the surrounding corruption. Disgust is his sole reaction, as stifled by the excremental onslaught he faces his Yahoo brethren. A more imaginative man might have afterwards recalled the problems his own animal nature had set the Lilliputians, but he experiences no hint of recollection or identity, no tremor of affinity, simply intense antipathy for the most revolting of all the creatures he has encountered. The Yahoo is for him completely other. It is the horses who first spot the resemblance; to his "everlasting mortification" they refer to him as Yahoo and later, when comparisons are made, he has to admit in his heart that the abominable creature beside him is "a perfect human figure." Only his clothes prevent the horses from making a total identification. Like a criminal overlooked in a lineup by a confused witness, he gains a temporary reprieve, but knowledge grows within and the rest of the book is an exercise in species identification, during which the evidence accumulates and drives him reluctantly towards admission of kinship. The long search for man's essence is almost over and the last, irrefutable proof of his Yahoo nature is the sexual test as irresistible criterion of species definition.

The evidence adduced is both negative and positive: the contrasting life-styles of Houyhnhnm and Yahoo, rational creature and brute; the methodology is that of the field scientist, anthropologist or ethologist—provisional, empirical, pragmatic. That a creature is truly rational should be as demonstrable from its sexual behaviour as from every other aspect of its life. The formal structure of the voyage is as logical as "To His Coy Mistress." The hypothesis of rationality is tested against Houyhnhnm practices and sustained. Their attitude to sex and marriage is clearly intended as exemplary, an intelligent combination of eugenics and population control, the rational power employed to tame the domain of libido. Procreation is the sole aim; once achieved, intercourse stops. They produce one offspring of each sex and only if a casualty occurs do "they meet again." They avoid the elaborate courtship and financial haggling inseparable from fashionable European marriage: "The young people meet and are joined, merely because it is the determination of their parents and friends; it is what they see done every day, and they look upon it as one of the necessary actions in a reasonable being."

There can be little doubt as to which side Swift would have favoured in the present debate within Britain's Indian community as to whether the traditional system of arranged marriage should prevail or give way to the western practice of individual choice determined by love. And the same justification urged by Indian conservatives in support of the ancient way is advanced by Swift in his eulogy of Houyhnhnm wedlock—marital violation is unknown among the horses, since the perfervid emotional atmosphere that spawns Medeas and Clytemnestras, Isoldes and Cleopatras, is simply not present. "The married pair pass their lives with the same friendship and mutual benevolence that they bear the others of the same species who come in their way; without jealousy, fondness, quarrelling, or discontent." It is the ban on fondness, the odd man out in a group of otherwise unopposedly bad qualities, that arrests attention as signifying a loss of control that disqualifies one as *animal rationale*. Female Houyhnhnms are properly educated—given, that is, the same education as males, so that they are not simply, as in Europe, viviparous animals. Taking all these as the characteristics of a rational species with regard to sexual activity, Swift challenges us to measure man against this proffered standard. The conclusion is negative: in every way man differs from the rational horses.

By contrast, Yahoo sexuality confirms the already frightening physical resemblance to man. With the aid of his Houyhnhnm tutor, Gulliver discovers the elementary biological truth that all members of a species look and behave alike in all important respects, that, even if similarities are not always immediately obvious, they soon become apparent once group characteristics are ascertained. He quickly perceives the blatant irrationalism of Yahoo sexuality. They are, he learns, uniquely disgusting in that the female will admit the male even after conception, an infamous brutality of which no other sensitive creature is guilty. They swing between "fondness" and "quarrelling," rampant copulation and a bitter intersexual strife found nowhere else in nature. Desire is unbridled and unregulated; the female will periodically lure the young male into the bushes while simultaneously counterfeiting fear, exuding at such times a "most offensive smell." Listening to the catalogue of their transgressions, Gulliver tremblingly awaits the revelation of the unnatural appetites of Europe, for surely here, as in all else, there is kinship too? But the horses know nothing of these perversions; men have, apparently, the edge in sophisticated depravity, "and these politer pleasures are entirely the production of art and reason on our side of the globe."

Throughout Swift's writing, from *The Mechanical Operation* onwards, there is a preoccupation, if not indeed fascination, with the dark irrationalism of sex. In Captain Creichton's memoirs there is the anecdote of the covenanting preacher who, on the run, hiding in a maidservant's bed while the soldiers seeking his life searched the house, nevertheless managed to get the girl pregnant; and Swift, clearly intrigued, recounts elsewhere a similar story of a nobleman, in the death cell to which treason had brought him, impregnating his wife shortly before his own execution. One easily imagines Swift shaking his head as he pondered these incongruities, divided between baffled amusement and scornful indignation. His sense of the rational is so patently offended by the discordance of a creature, for whom the grave yawns, pursuing sexual appetite, manifesting in so bizarre a fashion the irrational drives that rule him. Such incidents must have seemed to him too disturbingly akin to the situation of insects whose last living act is fertilising the female that devours them. Meditating on this, Swift foreshadows his compatriot Beckett: "They give birth astride of a grave, the light gleams an instant, then it's night once more."

The sexual identity of man and Yahoo is undeniable. Against all the evidence there is only man's verbal denial, supporting it his everyday conduct. The insistence on praxis, so crucial to Swift's life and work—as he wrote to Bolingbroke, "I renounce your whole Philosophy, because it is not your Practise"—is nowhere better exemplified than in the final voyage. Gulliver clings to the myth of his differentiation, but the Yahoos know better; when they see his naked arms and breast, they claim him as their own. The exposed beauties of Brobdingnag were no more exposed than he now. For the first time we see him as family man, holding an infant in his arms, the reality of Yahoo fatherhood emphasized when all his attempted tender ministrations end in the child soiling him, an occupational hazard of every father since Adam nursed Cain. Gulliver as Yahoo father textually precedes Gulliver as Yahoo lover, but the illogicality is artistically appropriate for the latter role is the book's climactic terminus.

When, bathing stark naked in the river, Gulliver so inflames the young female Yahoo that she leaps hungrily upon him, we have the last piece of the jigsaw, the ultimate, undeniable proof of kinship. Only the sorrel nag's timely intervention saves him, forcing her to withdraw: "she quitted her grasp with the utmost reluctancy" and "stood gazing and howling all the time I was putting on my clothes." The comedy incapsulates the grief of unrequited love, with the young Yahoo as desolate as Troilus looking towards the Greek camp where the lost Criseyde now lies. For the Houyhnhnms it's a great joke, but for Gulliver it's the end of the line, finis to self-deception; he must be a real Yahoo "since the females had a natural propensity to me as one of their own species." *Quod erat demonstrandum.* Reproduction will out.

It is so easy, in sharp contrast to Lilliput and Brobdingnag, for a family man from England to go on being so in Yahooland. Gulliver, who as a young man had been an avid reader of travellers' tales, must have read stories about sexual intercourse between African women and male apes—read and rejected them as contrary to nature, since breeding across species was regarded as incredible. He knows (it is what so unnerves him in the bathing incident) that the necessary characteristic of a species is a readiness to breed together. Here is identity at last, self-recognition with no possibility of error. When the Yahoo girl leaps upon him, she is really saying, with an irony Nathan never intended, thou art the man. *Ecce homo.*

With grim comedy Swift reveals Gulliver struggling from the hold of his would-be lover, aware, to his intense mortification, that in the deepest sense he can never escape her again, for he is hers by right and by nature. Who can argue with the sex glands? It is the shame of Brobdingnag carried to its furthest pitch; there he was helpless only because of a secondary, relative attribute, his size, now the humiliation is both primary and essential. After the blind alleys of Lilliput and Brobdingnag, he has found his proper niche, is at last sexually in the right place, a sexual equal, a possible mate, a Yahoo; like Antony, though in horror rather than delight, he can finally say, "Here is my space." It follows that the horrified rejection of the female Yahoo adumbrates the future repulse of her sister, Mary Gulliver; the crushing disappointment of the amorous Yahoo is given its appropriately refined form in Mary's complaint of neglect in the epistle Pope wrote for her:

> Welcome, thrice welcome to thy native Place!
> —What, touch me not? what, shun a Wife's Embrace?
> Have I for this thy tedious Absence born,
> And wak'd and wish'd whole Nights for thy Return?

In her chagrin at the unaccountable retreat to the stables, Mary even descends to sexual innuendo: "What mean those visits to the Sorrel Mare?" But, however understandable in a discarded wife, there is no call for the reader to find more in the text than Swift has made clear: *not* hippomania, a new set of perversions, but an admission by man of Yahoo guilt. Gulliver's "native Place" looks decidedly unattractive in a context of Yahoo parallelism and the erstwhile lover of mankind has at last truly seen himself, in a lake in Houyhnhnmland.

And what, after all, *is* his "native Place," where has Gulliver's sixteen-year search for man taken him? To *animal rationale*, glory of creation?—or to a species of animal incapable of amendment, a vicious *lusus naturae*? Corresponding to these warring definitions are two opposed versions of man's origins. The *Travels*, predictably, displaces the ancient myth of Genesis, of the child of God, made in his image but driven for sin from the Garden, with a new, naturalistic account of human beginnings from which any hint of a special relationship with a Creator is rigorously excluded. Houyhnhnm tradition has it that the Yahoos are not indigenous but that many ages ago two of these brutes appeared together upon a mountain, whether produced by the heat of the sun upon corrupted mud and slime, or from the ooze and froth of the sea, was never known; so prolific were they in breeding that within a short time they had overrun and infested the whole nation. The divine injunction to increase and multiply, with its accompanying promise of the earth as fief, is set aside for a view of human increase as the noisome proliferation of vermin. This degraded report of our first parents looks forward to Wilberforce's interpretation of Darwin or man's advent as described in Golding's *The Inheritors*, rather than backwards to Milton's noble pair, descending in tragic dignity after their ejection from Eden to the challenge of the world below. True, it is the unchristian Houyhnhnm who speaks, but where in the *Travels* is the proof that he is mistaken, that man is not brute but *imago Dei*? Can we seriously doubt on the evidence of his sexual behaviour to which category he belongs?

The origin of Yahoo man as stated in this Houyhnhnm anti-Genesis is the climactic scandal of a scandalous book. From its day of publication, amid the chorus of delighted acclamation, sounded an adversary voice that spoke for outraged humanism. The artistry, on such a view, only made the offence the more unpardonable. It was a "bad" book and Bolingbroke, reacting to his friend's masterpiece as Lord Longford to an inspired pornographer, tells us why: it was "a bad design to depreciate human nature," and if the design had been executed with the highest genius, so much the worse for its perverted motivation. The root of the offence is easy to find. More than a century before the traumatic scandal of Darwin, the *Travels* declines to distinguish man from the rest of the animal universe but instead decisively relegates him to the brutes. "If the book be true . . . religion is a lie . . . and men and women are only better beasts." This was a typical nineteenth-century reaction to Robert Chambers's *The Vestiges of Creation*, a rudimentary dry run for Darwin's epochal work. When *The Origin of Species* appeared, its deliberately mild and unprovocative tone did not save it from the fury of those who found there an appalling interpretation of the world. The superintending providence of God over nature and with it the uniquely privileged position of the human race as centre and *raison d'être* of creation seemed totally discredited. Even the docile Darwin could not refrain, if only in a private letter, from mocking his indignant critics: "Here is a pleasant genealogy for mankind."

The "better beasts" and "pleasant genealogy" have already surfaced, however unscientifically, in the *Travels*, with the man-Yahoo identification and the Houyhnhnm version of human evolution. The dismissal of Genesis and special creation, of the revered distinction between human and animal, anticipates the central Darwinian idea of an underlying unity in the development of life and it is no consolation to mortified man to find himself deposed as perfection of nature by a creature so patently unreal as a rational horse. Either man is *animal rationale* or there is no such thing. The scandal of the *Travels* is its apparent espousal of the latter alternative. Man, priding himself as star of the show, is demoted to a contemptible extra. No wonder that *vous autres*, the star's idolators—a party to which Gulliver as lover of mankind also belonged before his last voyage—were offended; they were meant to be. Even those, like Bolingbroke, who had broken with orthodox religion, still upheld, perhaps the more fiercely, a secularised version of man as *imago Dei*, creation's masterpiece. The eighteenth-century backlash of Deists and rationalists against the black legend of human nature promulgated by Augustinian Christianity and its naturalistic fellow traveller, Hobbesian psychology, helped boost the benevolent view of man. The standard homiletic denunciations of man as sink of iniquity, routine in seventeenth-century Calvinism, were becoming increasingly repugnant to rational philosophers of the Bolingbroke kind. Swift, with his mission to vex, surely welcomed the anger that his book would incite in such quarters.

Not just the Lilliputians but we, too, watch with puzzled consternation as, from the opening pages, Gulliver's animal attributes, gargantuanly enlarged, are thrust provocatively upon our attention. Swift was no Darwin; he set out to antagonize in a deliberate display of exhibitionist coattrailing designed to enrage the champions of human dignity. When Gulliver, lying bound on the beach, urinates, it is for the little people the equivalent of Niagara, a fearful torrent whose noise and violence stun them—one of the few occasions, significantly, when we look *with* the Lilliputians rather than *at* them. Later, Gulliver's home, the morally polluted temple, becomes literally so when, caught in the Swiftian dilemma between urgency and shame, the chained giant creeps inside to excrete.

Why does Swift drag such detail before us, domiciling us to a landscape of torrential urine and giant excrement, an effluent society where the body's prodigious waste can threaten plague or douse conflagrations? It is almost as though Gulliver, after his nine-hour sleep on the beach of Lilliput, has reverted to monstrous infancy, his bowel and bladder movements a matter of public concern and discussion—we must wait for Leopold Bloom before the hero's excretory functions are again assumed to be of significant interest to the reader. Gulliver justifies the exhibitionism in his self-exculpatory insistence that only once was he guilty of such uncleanliness, for afterwards he always defecated alfresco to make the removal of the offensive matter quick and relatively easy. He adduces this as proof of his personal hygiene, in indignant rebuttal of what detractors have nastily insinuated since his book was published. But if self-vindication is a plausible explanation of Gulliver's indiscreet disclosures, if he is driven by a commendable anxiety to be distinguished from lunatics like Jack in the *Tale* with his disgusting slogan, "he which is filthy, let him be filthy still," this nevertheless leaves undecided why Swift determinedly trumpets such goings-on.

It only becomes intelligible (as other than a personal hang-up) on the assumption that Swift attacks human pride by rubbing our faces in the mess we make and pretend not to notice. He solicits outrage with these baited revelations, banking on being accused, like Gulliver in his letter to Sympson, "of degrading human nature," for how else will he be able to launch that stinging parenthesis—"for so they have still the confidence to style it"? Bolingbroke, blundering into the trap, is answered even before he protests. The inventory of identification between man and beast is, accordingly, as exhaustive as possible, the mass of evidence exposing man's animalism piled high in a last bid to provoke the urgency of the rational response. Man, distressingly, blatantly animal, must prove his rational component, and when he arrogantly assumes the high, unearned title of *animal rationale*, Swift scornfully uncovers his sordid secrets, exhibiting them, like Gulliver's excreta, to full public view. Jack's antinomian plunge into brutality, his ardent capitulation to the inescapable filth, recurs as Gulliver unprotestingly endorses the sickening catalogue of human depravity—rape, mugging, perversion, murder—as "all according to the due course of things," beyond complaint and correction. Gulliver's modest proposal is that man continue, without recrimination, the incurable Yahoo he is, if only he desert the one astounding offence for which he can be faulted: pride. Let him cherish his natural defects but renounce his unnatural one— a renunciation the more feasible for Gulliver in his bafflement at how such an animal acquired such a vice. The privilege of filth claimed by Jack is insultingly tossed by Gulliver to Yahoo man.

It is, of course, dangerous to assume that Swift underwrites this easy relegation of man to Yahoo, no more accountable for his misdeeds than for the movement of his bowels or the pressure on his bladder. But neither can we complacently assume that Swift is ridiculing a glaring category-confusion in Gulliver's failure to distinguish between reprehensible because corrigible immorality and the ineluctable facts of being human. The relationship between guilt and responsibility is as central to Swift as to Kafka— and as puzzling to determine; our answer should emerge from a grappling with the text, not a prior assumption as to what he *must* have meant. From the guilt of being human under an extreme Calvinist dispensation to the guilt of being Jewish in Hitler's Europe, men have often been schooled to feel the iniquity of an imposed fate, condemned for what they cannot control.

Swift certainly claimed to have consistently observed in his satire the distinction between what is and what is not corrigible—only conceited ugliness and strutting folly are legitimate targets:

> His Satire points at no Defect
> But what all Mortals may correct.

To justify this claim, the troublesome prominence of man's animalism in the *Travels* must be seen as serving a reformative purpose; the brute facts, so long kept locked away, are turned loose to roam the streets so that man will have to take refuge in the house of reason. The mystery of Judas is explained by De Quincey as a desperate bid to force Jesus' hand, the betrayed messiah compelled to manifest his power. In a similar mood of moral *jusqu'au boutisme*, of vexation at the long unfulfilled pledge, Swift delivers man to his animal drives so that his very survival depends upon an analogous manifestation of reason. In each case, the ostensible hostility, the act of betrayal (Bolingbroke's "bad design")—prove you are the Son of God, prove you are *animal rationale*—mask a desperate longing for the "adversary's" triumph. The partnership of *animal* and *rationale* has, for Swift, hitherto been distressingly uneven, with the substantive having all its own way; it is long overdue for the adjective to stop being a sleeping partner and assert instead its rights as the major shareholder.

Hence the strategic emphasis on animalism, the menace made so frightening that reason, with back to the wall, must conquer or perish. Swift's "realism" is very different from Machiavelli's. *The Prince* presents political man as he is and must be, with no hint of shaming him into going and sinning no more. Swift, by contrast, is an undercover man, a double agent whose real allegiance is to morality. The *Travels* presents animal man, noisomely offensive, all according to the due course of things, but with a challenge to change what is alleged to be incorrigible. We are meant to protest the portrait's partiality, to demand, in addition to the undeniable animal, the rational being, the complementary and redeeming truth of human nature. Swift, that prince of trappers, entices us to make this crucial protest and then invites us to make good our claim. It will not be allowed on the near-miraculous exploits of a sprinkling of moral supermen like the Glubbdubdrib sextumvirate—no more than Milton will Swift let men be saved by a deputy or scramble into heaven on the coattails of heroes and saints; freeloading is strictly forbidden. Nobody pretends that Shakespeare and Newton are representative of man's ability in poetry and mathematics; why do we cheat by claiming that More and Brutus represent us morally? The everyday deeds of ordinary men are the only admissible evidence for judgement. Swift, meanwhile, strenuously devil's-advocating, will continue to present man as "perfect Yahoo" (despite his impertinent snobbery towards his brother brutes), dismissing *animal rationale* as merely a parvenu's pretext for cutting embarrassing relatives.

Man's vaunted uniqueness totters as Swift invades certain privileged areas—love, marriage, parenthood—where human beings have long thought themselves securely separate from the animal world, with a demand for the impostor's extradition. The myth of superiority is challenged. That Lilliputian ideas of the parent-child relationship differ so radically from our own is a consequence of their honest resolve to rank man with his animal brethren. They reject the attempt to refine sex into romantic love, seeing behind the sublimation only biological categories. For them the conjunction of male and female is founded upon the great law of nature which ensures the propagation and continuation of the species—men and women, like other animals, are joined together by motives of concupiscence.

In tiny detail as in sustained assault Swift challenges highfalutin romanticism, unceasingly reminding man and his mate of their animal lineage. Glancing at the Laputans' crazy obsession with music and mathematics, Gulliver casually remarks that when they want to praise the beauty of a woman "or any other animal," they do so in terms taken from these subjects. The derogatory linking is the more insulting in its unemphatic, throwaway context; Gulliver's innocent aside masks his creator's provocative malice, the relish which places "other" and "animal" in venomous conjunction. In Brobdingnag the magnified flesh so meticulously exhibited gives the manikin a sense of claustrophobic nausea; the monstrous breast of the wetnurse, its hideous nipple so minutely observed, achieves an effect antipodal to the pornographer's art. The Brobdingnagian beauties turn Gulliver's stomach, not his head. Swift's campaign to maim the erotic impulse—what led Aldous Huxley to protest that a poem like "A Beautiful Young Nymph Going to Bed" is worse than pornography—springs from his belief that man is much more animal than he admits. Hence the harshness of his onslaught on romantic delusion. Romanticism—interpreted by

Swift as a fatuous attempt to elevate unavoidable biological drives to a status higher than the rational, the flesh impudently presuming beyond its limits—is a major target in his work from youth onwards.

His first, false excursion along the road of eulogistic, exalted poetry (made, perhaps, with Temple's dislike of satire in mind) ends with a denunciation of the Duessa from whom he has broken free. The high poetic afflatus is brutally discarded as he turns to his true mate, verse satire, at once far more sensible and far less starstruck:

> There thy enchantment broke, and from this hour
> I here renounce thy visionary pow'r;
> And since thy essence on my breath depends,
> Thus with a puff the whole delusion ends.

Swift's decent muse, like a country virgin accosted by gallants or a young Houyhnhnm strayed among Yahoos, recoils disgusted from the "cattle she has got among" and departs as fast as she can. The delusion incorporates the fraud of romantic love as well as the phoney inspiration of romantic poetry. As trenchantly as Flaubert, Swift documents the disastrous consequences of romantic delusion, from the maidservant who causes the palace fire in Lilliput through dozing over a romance to the sordid heroine of "The Progress of Love," projecting herself as love's victim, as helpless as Racine's Phèdre: "*C'est Vénus toute entière à sa proie attachée.*" Phyllis justifies her shameful elopement with the butler on the eve of her wedding to another man, her family's choice, with the blasphemously threadbare appeal to love as heavenly dispensation:

> It was her Fate, must be forgiven,
> For Marriages are made in Heaven.

Swift prefers the Lilliputian view that marriages are of the earth, earthly, and comes, so contemptuous is he of Phyllis and her tribe, close to Iago's cynical reductionism—in her case, love *is* simply a lust of the blood and a permission of the will.

Swift's scornful intensity reflects his fear that so shameless an affront to self-restraint marks the fall into Yahoo bestiality, the point where the human definitively regresses into the zoological. Phyllis, rushing back to the zoo, is merely the sophisticated counterpart of the amorous she-Yahoo leaping upon the naked Gulliver, with the towering additional impudence that she dresses up her lust as the will of heaven. How much more decorous than this sordid imposture is the Houyhnhnm system of arranged marriage, how much superior eugenically in providing simultaneously for individual sex drives and the healthy perpetuation of the species, with no surrender to romantic folly. It would be misleading to say that in Houyhnhnmland eugenics prevails over love, for there is simply no contest. European women, by contrast, lamentably educated, woefully irrational, are "useless animals," good only for breeding—and for breeding badly. Love is, in

Swift's lexicon, a capitulation to sexual abandon that guarantees the deterioration of the species in a flagrant disregard of elementary eugenics. Far from translating man, as its devotees claim, to a higher plane, it simply takes him down to the "Old Blue Boar" at Staines, to a cat-and-dog existence interspersed with prostitution, pimping and gonorrhea—such is Swift's ironical vision of the "progress" of love. The progress of love is the regress of man.

Parental love suffers a corresponding dislodgement. Human beings cannot point to tenderness for their young as signalling a superiority, since the impulse, in both human and animal, proceeds from the same strictly natural principle. Swift anticipates Kant's insistence that a love dictated by nature can neither claim nor accept moral credit. Why should a child, any more than a kitten or a piglet, feel grateful to its parents for the alleged gift of life? How can a pair of animals humped in concupiscence, with no thought of benefitting a third party, in a "love-encounter" of sheer self-gratification, be a suitable target for gratitude? The sad discrepancy between Houyhnhnm reason and human irrationalism is highlighted in the vocabulary of their differing sexual codes. The Houyhnhnms "meet together" in a programme of planned procreation aimed at one offspring of each sex; wherever the desired balance is not achieved, they obligingly swap around until every family has its correct quota, after which intercourse ceases— they only "meet again" where casualties have occurred and the depletion has to be made good.

The whole business of sex and procreation among the virtuous horses is a disciplined, rational synchronization of needs and resources, like the x-efficiency dream of modern economic theorists. The contrast with Lilliputian (and human) messiness is glaringly exposed in the expression "love-encounters," hinting at the haphazard and casual, at something unpremeditated and adventitious in the sexual act; children come as by-product, the credit of an impersonal nature, with procreation apparently as without human control as the laws of science. Where a Houyhnhnm might therefore legitimately feel grateful to his parents for deliberately deciding to conceive him, similar emotion would be absurdly misplaced in a Lilliputian or European. The sole obligation stipulated in Lilliput is that of fathers towards children, the duty to support one's offspring, however inadvertently conceived. When Gulliver leaves on his second voyage, he shows how well he has absorbed this lesson by scrupulously providing for his family. The money he makes from exhibiting and then selling the tiny cattle guarantees the Gullivers from cadging public charity—if irresponsible as progenitor, he is commendably responsible as provider.

As well as challenging man's unique status in these hitherto privileged areas of love and parenthood, violating sanctuaries where humanity has long thought itself safe from pursuit, Swift also mercilessly erodes other traditional distinctions that have reassuringly fenced off man from beast: to be an object of merchandise or financial exploitation, to be part of the food chain, to be kept for breeding purposes. Gulliver's tiny cattle persuade his rescuers that he is not a madman but it is not just his moral credit they save—back home he displays them for cash and then sells them for a high profit. An identical fate awaits Gulliver in Brobdingnag where he switches from exploiter to exploited, worked almost to death in daylong exhibitions by the greedy farmer before being knocked down to the Queen.

Gulliver has difficulty in deciding which he resents more: this cruel exploitation, "the ignominy of being carried about for a monster" and shown for cash—an indignity which the King of Great Britain, similarly circumstanced, would have likewise had to thole; or Glumdalclitch's tearful resentment at her father for deceiving her yet again, as he had with the pet lamb, promised to her but sold to the butcher as soon as it was fat. Better, of course, to be the girl's pet than her father's freak attraction, but the insult to human dignity is equally mortifying. Gulliver's cold farewell to the exploiting farmer reveals his resentment, though he himself felt no qualms over the Lilliputian cattle—naturally enough, assuming the axiomatic gulf between man and beast fixed in Eden when God made Adam lord of creation, with dominion over all creatures, to use as he thinks fit. Man's cherished distinction, by contrast, is that he is not, on pain of forfeiting his unique dignity, exploitable; he is an end in himself, not to be used, otherwise his special status is denied and he becomes just another beast with a market value.

Even in Lilliput, though without knowing it till later, Gulliver is a valuable commodity, a hot property. Brought to the metropolis, he is as big a box-office draw as King Kong and the secretaries of state make a killing in ticket sales.

But in Brobdingnag the humiliation comes from seeing, but being powerless to stop, his own exploitation. The amused delight he provokes there stems from his amazing simulation to a human being, a rational creature—he is for the giants a charming forgery, a marvellously ingenious imitation, which the mind knows as such even while the eye is pleasingly deluded. Any claim to human status is straightaway denied when his giant captor sets the newly-found creature on all fours as its natural mode of locomotion. Stand up though he may, all his efforts to be accepted as *homo erectus* misfire. The Houyhnhnm master is similarly perplexed at the gentle Yahoo's strange folly in going around on his rear legs—cannot he see the advantages that accrue from his brother brutes' sensible decision to stay foursquare on the earth? Why go perversely against nature and one's animal lineage for the sake of so futile an affectation? But whatever the direction of the attack, whether from giants who see him as an ingenious clockwork device or *lusus naturae*, or from horses puzzling over this curious Yahoo, it is always Gulliver's human status that is in question; big or small, commodity or freak, target of marvel or derision, Gulliver is throughout his travels stripped of dignity, reduced to the level of a Lilliputian sheep or a dancing bear or a Bedlamite in his cell with the day-trippers bent on diversion enjoying his antics.

The animal's vulnerability is most obvious in the ease with which it becomes some other creature's dinner, whether bred to that end by man himself or falling victim to a superior predator. Returning from Lilliput, Gulliver loses a sheep to the ship's rats and later finds its bones picked clean. The incongruity of a live sheep carried off and eaten by rats becomes nightmare in Brobdingnag when European man fights for his life against the giant rats and narrowly escapes, thanks to his sword, the fate of his tiny sheep. No more vivid illustration of man as animal—as extremely vulnerable animal—is conceivable than Gulliver desperately parrying the rat attack, the lord of creation a whisker away from being a rodent's lunch.

The terror of being eaten alive modulates into the shame of being kept as a stud animal. The gravest affront to Gulliver as human being, paralleling the more specific onslaught on his male dignity at the hands of the Brobdingnagian women, comes with the Giant King's direction that a female be found upon whom the manikin can breed and so perpetuate his species. Gulliver, on such a view, is significantly no different from the Lilliputian cattle he tries to encourage in England. On the assumption of his unique status as man, he takes this as the greatest of insults, but just as validly, his giant captors, on *their* assumptions, would reject his claim with derision. The giant rats see him as a meal, the giant people as a pet, to be treated kindly but never as an equal. Gulliver in Brobdingnag is handled with the same easy disdain as he himself has already shown towards inferior creatures—what he has done unto others is now done unto him until separate identity becomes blurred as man merges with beast.

There are two key moments in Brobdingnag which anticipate the final damning identification with the Yahoo. The first is when the monkey kidnaps Gulliver in the conviction that he is a young one of the species and tries to feed him, cramming its partly-digested filth into his mouth, and, with true paternal solicitude, "patting me when I would not eat." The monkey claiming Gulliver as child, the female Yahoo seeking her mate, are each offering, in these crucial areas of rearing and breeding, clues to the real identity beneath the pose. The second is when the Giant King delivers judgement on European man as little odious vermin crawling on the earth's surface (Epicurus's chosen home), and, recalling the giant lice rooting through the beggars' rags, we realize, appalled, that these are what he has in mind. Louse and Yahoo represent the nadir of Swift's meditations on man's bestiality, the lowest stages in the regression from human to zoological existence charted throughout the *Travels*. Man slides dismayingly down the life-chain, from human to animal to noisome pest, starting off as rational, ending as fit only for extermination.

The difference between animal and pest is the difference between *A Modest Proposal* and "A Voyage to the Houyhnhnms." Gulliver as animal anticipates the shock of the children of the Irish poor suddenly becoming items on a butcher's price list or courses on a menu. "A child just dropt from its dam" is indistinguishable from a newly littered piglet, save that in Ireland the piglet is better cared for—one of the proposal's merits is that its implementation may persuade Irish husbands to treat their pregnant wives at least as well as their livestock. What an advance it would be, what a breakthrough in solving the Irish question, if the Irish were somehow *raised* to animal level and managed to pass themselves off as two-footed cattle, beasts in all else save this strange habit of walking erect. That this is the destiny against which Gulliver in Brobdingnag rebels as the worst of degradations—to be tended and bred like an animal—simply proves that the Irish poor are far worse off than little Grildrig among the giants; and it is a measure of Ireland's plight that the only solution is a grateful sur-render of human dignity.

A Modest Proposal presents the Irish as animals but not vermin, a useful addition to the food supply, comparable to the cows of Lilliput rather than the lice of Brobdingnag. Fit for human consumption: it is a kind of com-pliment and the extreme remedy of converting infants into meat to solve a population problem is no more inhumane and far more rational than reliance on starvation and infanticide. It is, after all, only this doomed surplus who end up in the kitchens; are cleavers any worse than the deaths to which we at present equally condemn them? A problem basically eco-nomic evokes a solution unchallengeably rational, given that the creatures in question do not differ significantly from other cattle. There are simply too many Irish for the needs of a healthy economy, so why not manage the Irish poor as we already manage Irish pigs—so many for stock, for breeding, for the slaughterhouse, as the market requires? The market rules and if we dislike the idea of people bred to its demands, we had better find a feasible alternative, for the surplus dies daily in any case. The frisson comes from hearing people discussed in terms of cattle control, units in a process that ignores all values but economic.

The Yahoo, by contrast, like the Jew under Hitler, is a problem in pest control, sanitary rather than economic, the cleansing of the world, not the regulation of the market. The Modest Proposer seeks the optimum number of Irish, not their extermination; but even *one* Jew or Yahoo left alive is an affront, a breeding pair a menace, to the sanitationists of Houyhnhnmland and the Reich—the aim *is* genocide. How to eliminate the Yahoo is the one debate in Houyhnhnmland and, ironically, the sole lesson his masters think worth learning from their gentle Yahoo is the castration technique that will extirpate his species forever without recourse to wholesale massacre. Did not the Emperor of Lilliput favour blinding and castration to summary execution as a gentler method of destroying the awkward giant? Imagine the unexceptionable zest with which the Nazi extermination apparatus would have been welcomed by the horses in solving *their* sanitation prob-lem. The Irish are fit for food, the Yahoos only for extermination.

Swift's exasperation in Ireland is real enough. Every section of society is condemned for its lavish contribution to the nation's ruin: a drunken, improvident poor; a middle class sottishly selfish; a leadership venal and afraid. The note of bitter elation sounding through *A Modest Proposal* is sustained by a conviction that a guilty nation is getting its deserts. Ireland was made for Swift, catalyst for his pedagogic despair, confirming in him a wider application of the verdict he once passed on the people of Leicester: "a parcel of wretched fools." Even the basic sagacity and will to self-preservation of the animal seemed lacking among the Irish; the national totem was the Gadarene swine and Dublin was Swift's Ephesus, where, like St. Paul, he was conscious of fighting with beasts.

Nevertheless, we detect a contrary impulse in Swift that made him champion as well as chastiser of this people. Ireland's unforgivable failure to help herself notwithstanding—and Swift's own twelve-year campaign to promote reform from within shows how much could have been done— the system imposed upon her from abroad was unjust and vindictive. Foolish accomplices in their own ruin, the Irish are also victims, as hampered and misgoverned as the wretched citizens of Balnibarbi. London rule is at least partly responsible for Irish distress, whereas we have no ground for believing that the Houyhnhnm have made the Yahoos any worse than nature created them; on the contrary, but for the efficient policing of the horses, the Yahoos would run ungovernably wild, destroying themselves and everything else. Certainly, a major target of the proposal is the Irish themselves—Swift is furious at fools who connive at their own destruction; but equally undeniable, in however oblique and qualified a form, it is also a defence of an exploited people against rapacious predators. There is no such competing or balancing element in Swift's attitude to the Yahoo, no rage at the exploiter to temper contempt for the victim nor pity for the oppressed to mitigate anger at the fool. In contrast to the double face of the Irish—villain and victim—the Yahoo appears as singly, irredeemably vermin; there can be nothing but relief and satisfaction at his suppression or even extermination, however achieved.

The events attending the expulsion from Houyhnhnmland make this vividly clear. Gulliver's leave-takings of the different countries he visits are dramatically appropriate, matching his role during residence. At the opening of the final chapter of part 1 he finds "a real boat" and the Lilliputian adventure is over. Resuming real manhood, he ends the petty predicaments of Lilliput by simply leaving them—the Man-Mountain deciding to go, where is the power to stop him? He is, contrastingly, carried out of Brobdingnag by the giant bird, as helplessly subject to superior force as throughout a sojourn in which things are forever being done *to* him, whether by monkeys or maids-of-honour. He is taken leisurely to Japan, like the tourist he is throughout the third voyage, in a ship assigned him by the King of Luggnagg, but his vital involvement in the action of part 4 is reflected in the climactic expulsion that ironically echoes the leaving of Lilliput—ironically, because the surface similarity of single-handedly preparing his own departures from Lilliput and Houyhnhnmland masks crucial differences.

Outward preparation is similar but inward disposition is transformed. That he leaves Lilliput with relief, Houyhnhnmland with dread, dramatises the transition from lover of mankind to misanthrope, and the metamorphosis is visible in his preparations for departure. In Lilliput he greases the boat, which so opportunely floats his way, with the tallow of three hundred tiny cows. We accept this unblinkingly as being, among other things, what cows are for—to be used by men as men see fit, in accordance with God's promise in the Garden. But the attitude of the Houyhnhnm and their disciple Gulliver towards the Yahoo intentionally causes the reader discomfort. The easy brutality, the untroubled assumption that no treatment is too bad for them, that vermin have no rights and scruples are absurd, are all part of the book's provocation.

Before the catastrophe, Gulliver unexcitedly relates how he did his shoe repairs with the skins of Yahoos dried in the sun and collected birds' feathers with springes made of Yahoo hair; sentenced to expulsion, he casually describes how he built his canoe, covered with Yahoo skins, its chinks sealed with their tallow to keep out the sea. One last twist is given with the information that, the older animals being unsuitable, he made the sail from the skins of the youngest Yahoos. Old scores are settled, old insults wiped out, as Gulliver, with vengeful relish, perhaps reflects that the boy who soiled, the girl who attacked him, have ended up in his sail. The casual callousness is underscored by the tearful farewell to the revered Houyhnhnm and the last solicitous exhortations of the sorrel nag. It is the same strange amalgam of tears and extermination, emotion and brutality, sentiment and atrocity, as appears in many of those who manned the death camps and the key in both cases is identical—pity is absurd when exterminating vermin.

But, as Swift well knows, this is no longer a matter of Lilliputian cows and he manipulates a significant shift in our response, a vague unease, a half-stifled disapproval trembling towards articulation. Old, reassuring distinctions between man and beast are now so darkened that the ground gives beneath us and we are left stateless in a realm where brute and human promiscuously merge—Orwell is never more Swift's pupil than at the end of *Animal Farm*. Discomfort is intensified by Houyhnhnm attitudes: that the Yahoos cannot help what they are does not make the horses more tolerant and their one recurring debate is merely procedural—a massacre of the pests in one genocidal swoop or the milder policy of male castration and gradual extinction. The reader's unease (deepened by a recollection of the Emperor of Lilliput's similar interpretation of mildness) testifies to the deadly accuracy of Swift's aim in part 4; driven throughout towards unwilling alliance with the Yahoos, we are now much too close for comfort. While the cows of Lilliput left us totally untroubled, the Yahoos of Houyhnhnmland, lacking only our clothes and the jabber we call language, are our kinsmen, however unwelcome, and we are meant to feel a twinge of fearful resentment at their treatment—blood *is* thicker than water, more precious than tallow. Their fate and Houyhnhnm callousness alike disturb us and there is no need for Redriff to see how thoroughly Gulliver detests his own kind—the material sealing his canoe is proof enough. The question of sadism does not arise; rather, Gulliver's attitude anticipates and intensifies that of the Modest Proposer towards the Irish: an untroubled assumption that the creatures in question are either animal or vermin. Even in *A Modest Proposal* the door is not closed on *Endlösung;* it needs only one more step from man as animal to man as pest in "A Voyage to the Houyhnhnm."

Defoe, Richardson, and the Concept of Form in the Novel

Ralph W. Rader

We experience literary works as inherently meaningful and beautiful. This not very challenging statement raises a troubling question: if literary works do in fact have an inherent structure of meaning and value which is the ground of our response to them, how is it possible for us to disagree and even flatly contradict one another as we do in our conceptions of what their meaning and value are? Let us put the question more usefully: what must the objective basis of our intuitive experience of literary works be like for us to misunderstand and disagree about them as we do?

A theory developed to answer this question would have to begin with the assumption that it is in fact just the intrinsic meaning and value of literary works which makes us respond to them as literature, and it would accordingly have to describe all such works as possessing forms which could present themselves to intuition as self-intelligible and self-justifying, that is, as forms the act of understanding which could be experienced as its own justification. The theory would have to elaborate a kind of grammar of the natural imagination which could spell out the general and particular ways in which works might differ from each other in their self-justifying intelligibility and do this clearly and distinctly enough so that we could understand how our ideas about our experience of them, singly and together, might have come to be confused and contradictory.

I want to develop an example of the kind of critical procedure such a theory might entail by posing and attempting to resolve some especially confusing problems raised by the contemporary controversy concerning the form of *Moll Flanders* as related to the form of *Pamela* and the standard

From *Autobiography, Biography, and the Novel: Papers Read at a Clark Library Seminar* (13 May 1972), coauthored by William Matthews. © 1973 by the William Andrews Clark Memorial Library.

novel. . . . My attempt will be to define all the particular forms involved in such a way as to offer a solution to the specific problems associated with each, but to do this as just indicated within a single controlling theoretical perspective which can be seen to relate them coherently to each other and to clarify our overall conception of the nature and history of the novel form.

I begin by pointing out that there are, generally speaking, two current views of *Moll Flanders*. On the one hand, the book is seen as a work which achieves that realism held to be characteristic of the novel form but which lacks plot and a coherent dimension of moral judgment; and, on the other, it is seen as an ironic masterpiece similar in structure and quality to twentieth-century forms. Opposed as these views are, they nevertheless attempt to measure *Moll* in terms of the same general formal conception: the first sees it as an example of failure in a simple version of the realism-plot-judgment form, the second sees it as an example of success in what is in effect a complex version of the same form.

The ubiquity of something like the realism-plot-judgment concept in novel criticism suggests to me that there is indeed an intuitively recognized class of works to which it refers. But the very fact that *Moll* itself is ambiguously perceived in relation to the class would seem to imply that *Moll* is not a member of it. We can of course say that *Moll* is a deficient member of the class, but if the basis of classification is an intuitive recognition that its members in fact share a common principle of self-justifying intelligibility, then this would mean that *Moll* was deficient in those very qualities which render the class as a whole meaningful and valuable to readers, and any such conclusion is adequately contradicted by the book's enduring popularity and interest. When we find two critics as careful but as divergent in their theoretical outlook as Ian Watt and Sheldon Sacks both declaring that, measured against their conceptions, *Moll Flanders* is an incomplete or incoherent member of a class of which *Pamela* is a complete and coherent member, and when we find that both believe their classification to be based on just those features of the class which render it inherently coherent and significant, than I believe that the logic of the situation instructs us to tighten up our conceptions in a way that will at the same time more clearly define the common class and exclude *Moll Flanders* from membership in it. It would also instruct us then to develop a concept of another principle of form which account for the independent intelligibility and significance of *Moll Flanders* and which would describe also the ambiguities which cause it to be confused in the first place with works written on principles different from its own.

I want now to develop some concepts of form that in my view satisfy these conditions. I will offer first a highly specific conception of the realism-plot-judgment form from which I will develop a concept of *Pamela*. I will call this conception and others to be developed later *models*, in order to emphasize their hypothetical character and their function as artificial similitudes of independently cognitive form. The model is a revision of the

R. S. Crane-Sheldon Sacks concept of represented action designed to make it meet clearly the condition just mentioned, namely to define the principle of the realism-plot-judgment class and to exclude *Moll Flanders*. I should say that the models are deductive models; that is, they are meant to define the most general differentiating principle of a work's form in such a way that its more particular aspects can be rigorously deduced from it.

The general action model, as I shall call it, is meant to indicate the form common to all those works that make up our idea of the standard novel and to permit a unique model to be drawn up within it for every particular standard novel. The cumbersome definition is necessary for explanatory adequacy. I shall simplify it for convenience after I give the full definition. Let us say than that the general action model specifies works of fiction designed to develop and maximize concern for a character (or characters) along a line of development in which the ground of concern is a dynamically shifting contrast between the reader's sense of the immediate and ultimate fate of the character (or characters) as compared with his (or their) immediate and ultimate desert, and to resolve this concern by a surprising but probable extension of the means used to raise it, so as to give the reader the greatest satisfaction in the ultimate fate of the character (or characters). To put it more simply, the author pits our induced sense of what will happen to a character against our induced sense of what we want to happen to him, our hopes against our fears, in order to give the greatest pleasure appropriate to their resolution.

The action model describes a work which the reader at some level of consciousness must know from the outset is being shaped beneath its realistic surface to meet the created requirements of desire. It has therefore the character of an objective fantasy, not such a fantasy as makes a reader the passive victim of a process hidden from his consciousness, but a deliberate, determinate, conscious, controlled fantasy identical with the cognitive structure of the book. I emphasize that the description is not pejorative. If it suggests the simple wish-fulfillment of shallow novels, it also suggests the possibility in serious novels of cathartically working out the shape of desire against the resistance of our ideals on the one hand and the objective conditions of experience on the other.

A particular model of *Pamela* would specify that the reader is meant to feel for Pamela a serious fear, which can be defined by saying that her merit and fate develop along a line of branching alternatives, where one branch, always closed by circumstance or choice, leads to an ethically acceptable but materially undesirable safety, while the other leads overtly and immediately to greater danger but covertly and ultimately to the most desirable resolution of her difficulties. "Overtly" here means that of which Pamela herself is aware, "covertly" means that of which only the reader is aware.

Notice that the model locates at once and insists upon the sources of the most common critical complaints about *Pamela*—the quality that Ian

Watt calls its "immitigable vulgarity of . . . moral texture" and the ambiguity of Pamela's status as heroine-hypocrite. The model also clearly explicates the difficulties. It says that it was no part of Richardson's intention that Pamela should be judged as a hypocrite but that it was likely, given the form, that a reader might react to her as one. We can see this more clearly if we consider that the first-person report of the narrative was, on the one hand, necessary to bring the reader close to Pamela's own fears and uncertainty about the future and to provide that inner account of her motives essential to the reader's admiration of her, but that, on the other hand, the choice involved the necessity of creating through Pamela as narrator the covert sense of potential prosperity so necessary to the special fantasy pleasure objectified in the form but which, as a condition of that pleasure, must not be attributed to Pamela. She must remain immune to the pressure of those material desires which the reader is nonetheless solicited to indulge actively on her behalf. (The formal situation is neatly epitomized in Pamela's exclamatory description of one of the early rape attempts: "O dreadful!" she says, "out rushed my master in a rich silk and silver morning gown." The danger-in-reward notation of the emblems of Mr. B.'s wealth is not to be taken as specially characterizing Pamela's consciousness but as part of the objective content of the scene. (In a cinematic version the camera would show the richness of the morning gown, with Pamela the image of uncalculating terror; but since Pamela herself is Richardson's only available camera, the notation must be potentially ambiguous.) We conclude, then, as a solution to our critical difficulties, that Pamela may appear at times to be a hypocrite in accidental consequence of an inner necessity of the form, whereas the tawdry moral effect of the novel, such as it is, is clearly the intended consequence of the form.

I will now very briefly indicate how the matter of an action novel is generated from the necessities imposed by its inner core and at the same time illustrate the specific explanatory capacity of the abstract model by asking it to explain the traits and actions of two characters in the novel— Mrs. Jewkes and Mr. Williams—and in particular to explain why Mrs. Jewkes is sensual and repulsively fat and why Mr. Williams is a clergyman.

The model directs an answer somewhat as follows: Richardson's chief problem in the novel is the need his form imposes to make Mr. B. both a villain and a hero. B. must threaten Pamela and threaten her increasingly, else our sense of her danger and the merit which develops from her response to danger will not increase, as the form requires, along lines that make her ultimate reward possible; but the more directly and villainously he does threaten her, the less acceptable he will appear as an ultimate and satisfactory reward for her, something that the form requires also. Richardson's attempt to face and minimize this paradox is implicit in almost every aspect of the book, but let us consider the problem only as it relates to Jewkes and Williams.

First of all, B.'s abduction of Pamela to Lincolnshire in general allows

Pamela's danger to increase in respect to B. but in such a way that B.'s direct culpability is minimized. Mrs. Jewkes becomes Pamela's direct oppressor, with ambiguous authority from B., while B. himself remains in the wings temporarily safe from blame but a real and increasing threat as, one by one, the possibilities of Pamela's escape are cut off. It was an ingenious solution to Richardson's problem except for one thing: B.'s physical absence removes the basis of the sexual fear which is a chief element in the reader's continuing concern for Pamela. And here we can see why Mrs. Jewkes is sensual and fat. Her repulsive fleshiness, especially as conjoined with her tendency to fondle Pamela, keeps the idea of B.'s sexual threat constantly before the reader's imagination, while Jewkes's often manifested physical strength makes her prospective cooperation with Mr. B. seem certain to result in successful rape. Yet upon reflection we see that Mrs. Jewkes is gross and repulsive very much in excess of B.'s actual threat, and we may be puzzled by this until the complex demands of the model force the recognition that she must not only condition our sense of Pamela's immediate danger but contribute also to our sense of her ultimate fate. Then we see that she is designed to be so repulsive that B. will seem actually attractive in contrast; in comparison with her he is seen to stand well within the outer limits of sensual sinfulness.

Mr. Williams is the last of a series of secure but unsatisfactory escape routes that are opened and closed for Pamela in her Lincolnshire imprisonment, as she waits trembling for B.'s arrival. Respectable and well-intentioned, Williams in his admiration for Pamela and willingness to help and marry her increases our developing sense of Pamela's social worth and thus the probability of her eventual marriage to B. At the same time, Williams's strength and merit must be sharply limited. If he were stronger and more morally forceful than he is, the reader's sense of Pamela's isolated danger and resourcefulness would decrease and his feeling that Pamela could and should escape would increase. As it is, Pamela consistently appears to be morally and prudentially the superior of the bumbling, somewhat timorous Williams. Both her danger and her merit are heightened, as just remarked, but more importantly the reader is made to feel an active desire that Pamela *not* run away with Williams and marry him—the potentially safe out becomes unacceptable. The reader feels the clear superiority of B. as a potential husband for Pamela, and so the as yet remote happy ending is built up as desirable, probable, and deserved.

But why specifically is Williams a clergyman? We see, on the one hand, that he must be a virtuous gentleman genuinely concerned for Pamela or he cannot contribute adequately to our sense of her moral and social merit. However, a gentleman willing to help Pamela would almost by definition be able to thwart Mrs. Jewkes effectively and take Pamela away, something that Richardson cannot allow to happen. Williams must therefore be a dependent gentleman, a contradiction in terms which can only be resolved if he is a clergyman in the service of Mr. B. His clerical capacity also has a further rationale in Richardson's need to use him to give retrospective sanction to B.'s outré behavior.

With a little work we can get the model to answer all sorts of interesting formal questions—Why should the good Mrs. Jervis at times be morally ambiguous? Why does the novel not end with the marriage? etc.—but perhaps enough has been said to establish tentatively the important general conclusion that in works of the action model kind the objective characters and events of the story are all at some level functions of the underlying fantasy structure. (I will only remark further that a slight change in the *Pamela* model—separating rather than joining merit and reward in the line of alternatives—produces a model that can be used to provide a precise account of *Clarissa* in its contrasting moral grandeur, one which enables us to see clearly how Richardson constructed *Clarissa* out of the same psychic materials as *Pamela* but with an intention now to separate in sharp moral austerity the moral and material goods which he had been accused in *Pamela* of joining with hypocritical ease.)

Moving now to *Moll Flanders*, I will say at once that if we test any version of the general action model against *Moll*, the results are absolutely negative; the model rejects *Moll* and *Moll* rejects the model. Either Defoe was not writing a work on the action model as here specified, or else he was doing such an impossibly bad job of it that the result could not be called even a deficient example of the form.

I will not seek to demonstrate the point further, because it should become incontestable later. I proceed then to build a new model for *Moll* on a different principle of natural intelligibility and inherent significance.

Let us say what has often been said but never fully understood: *Moll Flanders* is an imitation of a real autobiography. The implications of this fact begin to be clear when we realize that *Moll* is an imitation of real autobiography in a sense totally different from that in which *Pamela* is an imitation of real letters, though the difference is not easily perceived by those who think of realism as involving a single kind of imaginative relationship to the natural world. The "real documents" of *Pamela* cannot, as our model tells us, be like natural letters at all in the sense that they must at every point tell us Richardson's "once upon a time" story clearly and powerfully while they only seem to tell Pamela's story to her parents. In fact, the dramatic vividness of the letters (and the events they relate) is not the result of their likeness to real letters (and real events) but of their unlikeness to them, though, of course, the minimal signs of likeness given are a necessary condition of the illusion. Everyone will agree that the letters are the author's device, but I will say further that every reader of the work intuitively knows they are, in the midst of and as a condition of the illusion. He knows just as he knows in "once upon a time," as a natural condition of the fantasy.

Now the primary formal fact about *Moll Flanders* is that its form does not within itself convey the information that *Moll* is not the real agent of the story. To the contrary, it may be said to be an obviously positive feature of the form to make Moll seem the real author of the story but not of the events of the story—to make the work seem, in a word, literally true. This formal argument is entirely confirmed by the external historical fact that many sophisticated readers have mistaken Defoe's unidentified fictions for fact, as Donald Stauffer in 1941 mistook *Robert Drury's Journal*, whereas not even an unsophisticated reader could so mistake Richardson's fictions.

The point can be made more clear if we think of three figures: an angry man, a man acting the part of an angry man, and a man pretending to be angry. The first has the appearance he does because he is really angry: his outside expresses his inside. The second has an appearance quite different from his internal state, and the audience knows this, else it could not take pleasure in his performance, since it would not know that it was a performance. The third man—the pretender—has the appearance of the first—the angry man—and, as long as we do not see behind the appearance, we react to him so. When we do see behind the appearance, we understand that we have been deceived. Notice, for later use, that we cannot actively think of him as angry and know that we are deceived at the same time. Now *Pamela* is clearly analogous to the second instance—the actor—and *Moll* is clearly analogous to the third instance—the pretender.

If we take seriously the idea that an intention to make *Moll* seem like a real story is the whole principle of the book, then it follows directly that, as a matter of positive artistic principle, it would display neither of those features called plot and judgment, the desert/fate curve of the action model. To do so, we see, would have revealed at once the immanent presence of the real agent behind the apparent agent and destroyed the principle of the form. Simple and inevitable as this conclusion is, Defoe's critics have time and again noticed that Defoe was writing in imitation of real documents and gone on to say that he did not know how to make plots or that he failed to judge his characters. Part of the reason for this is the difficulty of seeing what the full positive principle of the form of *Moll Flanders* is.

We can begin to understand the principle if we think a bit about the form of true stories. We should note first that we react to true stories as true not primarily because we know them to be so in an objective, referential sense but because they require us to do so hypothetically in order to understand them. The true story invites us to believe it as an account of fact and makes sense only if we do think of it as referring beyond itself to what its author did not create; it presents itself as true—reality referring—and our assumption that it is true governs our entire imaginative participation in its meaning and value, so that if we do discover, for instance, that a fascinating true story is false, we do not think that we have been entertained with a good fiction, we think we have been told a lie. Both the intelligibility and the effect of the true story, then, depend on its factuality considered merely as form, quite independent of the actual connection with external reality which the form of course implies.

Now Defoe's aim was to simulate both the intelligibility and effect of a true story. But what kind of true story? A kind of story that I would call a naïve incoherent autobiography, a story really told by a real person like Moll. There are no well-known examples of the genre, because such works are by definition deficient in art. They depend for such interest as they have on the extraordinary, as does all factual literature, but in the special sense of the naturally improbable or bizarre. "Man bites dog" or "truth is stranger than fiction" hits it exactly.

Moll Flanders can be understood very well as an imitation of a work of this kind designed to maximize the effects possible to the form. When we sit down by woeful chance with the talkative lady on the bus, we can ordinarily expect to be bored, but occasionally it may turn out that she has led an interesting life—has been hostess of a speakeasy, say, a carnival shill, and a pickpocket—so that her wandering and formless tale, thanks not to her art but to her material, including her naïve self, turns out to be worthy of our interest.

The maker of the simulated naïve incoherent autobiography, however, would make very sure that his story was *not* boring, however wandering and apparently artless. How would an author proceed if he were going to write *Moll Flanders*? He would, first of all, need a good many extraordinary, even sensational incidents: a kidnapping by gypsies, for instance; a strange love triangle; a marriage based on mutual deception; an incident of clairvoyance; a case of accidental incest; a varied career in crime, replete with many small but interesting episodes; a capture and trial; a conversion in the face of execution; a reunion with a long-lost lover; and a happy establishment after all. Described and listed thus, the events clearly manifest Defoe's intention, as they do not in the story, where they are intermixed with many minor events, pieces of the unsensational ordinary made interesting by means which I shall discuss in a moment. In presenting both kinds of material, the author—Defoe—might well refine the crude procedures of earlier factual stories. In a work like Francis Kirkman's *The Counterfeit Lady*, for instance, the writer assumes the reader's belief in the actuality of the story and milks it for sensational effect, but Defoe reverses this emphasis, using a constructed sense of unsensational reality to produce imaginative belief, which is itself the effect. He does this by systematically crossing the lines of expected effect. On the one hand, he makes the inherently sensational incidents seem real by submerging sensation in the sense of the normal and probable. When, for instance, Moll discovers that she is married to her brother, she does not tear out her eyes but keeps her uneasy peace for three years. On the other hand, he makes the minor incidents seem oddly real by pointing up the unexpected and improbable, after the "man bites dog" principle. Thus Moll sleeps with her gentleman friend for months, but in complete innocence; a maid is offered a bribe of £100—many times her annual wages—and for no specified reason refuses; Moll standing in the street is given a horse to hold, and, on impulse, just walks away with it. Thus, the usual is moved away from the expected toward the unusual, and the unusual is moved away from the expected toward the usual. Everything is counter-sensational. What is the reason for telling me these odd things? the reader asks himself. Because they happened, is the only answer; they would not be told thus, otherwise. But since they *did* happen, then, how curious! how full of the strangeness of life! And Defoe has his effect.

Since the detailed story is to be taken as true, all the events will have to be fitted into the range of one life and narrated autobiographically. This is the first rule of Defoe's pseudo-factual stories, a rule which could have been used long ago to solve the problem of "The Apparition of Mrs. Veal," thought at first to be fiction and discovered to be fact. Since that story is narrated in the third-person, it was almost certain to be true (that is, genuinely factual) a priori. In Moll, the first-person report will have to be bland, unemotional, and matter of fact so as not to call attention to the unnatural succession of the natural extraordinary. For style, the tone of rambling speech will do—perfectly clear in its apparent naïve lack of clarity, a little repetitious, but, most of all, without apparent design.

As far as overall form goes, in a pseudo-natural story a pseudo-natural form will do, the apparent form of incoherent natural life. Life, someone has said, is just one damn thing after another, and the tortuous progress of Moll Flanders will violate no reader's sense of life (unless he were an analytical sort inclined to remember forgotten children and notice how conveniently husbands die when the run of incident needs freshening). Even then we might, as a last touch, give the life a little shape in its shapelessness, a semi-coherent natural shape familiar from the popular literature of spiritual autobiography and therefore presumptively real; but we would have to be careful not to give the shape any determinate homiletic or sentimental force, to avoid any sense of plottedness. (The incident of conversion would serve furthermore as an effective bridge form one improbable incident—the last-minute deliverance from execution—to another, the transportation to New World safety. The last incident itself would do nicely to end, an undeserved good fate but not wholly good. Moll does not quite live happily ever after.)

I have so far emphasized Moll as almost a device to hold the material events together, and this is quite proper, I think, for Defoe mainly wanted to maximize the episode-by-episode interest and believability of the story. In Defoe's weaker pseudo-factual stories—*The King of the Pirates*, for instance—we can see clearly how secondary his interest in his protagonists actually is, but it is an obvious virtue in such stories to give the narrator himself or herself as much interest as the matter of the story will allow. Since she is so much engaged in questionable activities, it is easy to give Moll a great deal of psychological and moral interest and even to have her comment on her activities in a morally interesting way. What must be avoided at all costs is a sense of full consistency either of psychological portraiture or implicit ethical judgment. Everything about Moll must be left ultimately a little skew and incoherent, as a real person seems when presenting himself naïvely. The image of himself which a natural person projects to others expresses his inner unity only tacitly; the self which expresses the image is not itself expressed. An artist attempting to simulate the image projected by another from within will not really be able to do so, since, if he achieves his purpose, the image will be informed by his explicit purposiveness and be, therefore, unlike the actual image; and if he leaves it unachieved, the partial incoherence will only superficially *seem* to replicate the tacit unity of the actual. The only solution is for the artist to project his own tacitness into the image, in which case the image becomes in its inner essence the image not of another but of himself. . . . The point here is, though, not that Defoe tried and failed to make Moll coherent; he didn't really care if she was or not, only that the reader should interpret her incoherence as that puzzling surface complexity of the real which betokens its underlying unity.

And so we return to the paradox at the heart of *Moll Flanders*. Fictional artists are supposed to show and not tell, but Defoe "shows" most effectively not by showing but by not telling, as when we feel through Moll's glancing reference the horror of the pickpocket's lynching at the hands of the street mob. The reason for this is that the form of the book forces our imagination to construe its matter as real. A reader who inspects his reaction to the story closely will discover that he gives Defoe the creative artist very little credit because he has in fact thought of the incidents as if they were not invented but merely reported.

But the hidden substance of the real to which we respond isn't there. When Moll tells us that she discovered the fact of her incest when her mother-in-law mother mentions her early name, and when later Moll tells us that she convinced her mother of the relationship "by such other tokens as she could not deny," we accept the complete vagueness as correlated with the truth of the facts alleged. It is told so because it was so, whereas in fiction the causal line for such a coincidence would have to be fully established (compare *Oedipus Rex* and *Tom Jones*). If our attention is then directed to Moll's earlier story that her first memory is of being left by gypsies at Colchester, we should infer—from a logical point of view, we cannot help but infer—that she can know nothing of her mother and so cannot recognize her by any tokens at all. But we are not able to infer this within our imaginative participation in the story, because to do so contradicts the assumption we have made in order to understand the story. If we infer the contradiction, the story disappears. My point here is difficult to grasp just because it forces us to turn in so sharply on our mental processes. We are likely to think that just because we know *Moll* to be made up, we are free to react to it as fiction, especially since its deceit is not referential, not forgery; but we aren't. We aren't free, just as in our original analogy we aren't free to perceive the pretender as if he were acting.

Moll, like the pretender, can be seen from only one perspective at a time. The pseudo-factual story does not turn itself into a workable fiction because of our knowledge but remains a story which the imagination must construe as real and cannot therefore fully interpret. When we are most caught up in the intended effect of the work, we cannot be conscious within the illusion that it is a work of art, and when we are most fully aware of it as a work of art, we cannot within that consciousness feel the effect. The wholeness of the work can be understood but not experienced because it affirms an imaginative contradiction.

If this is an accurate description of the form it is possible to see where twentieth-century critical difficulties with the book come from. Knowing it to be fiction in *fact*, critics try to understand it as if it were a fiction in *form*. Since a fiction is always created within the consciousness of an implied author, to use Wayne Booth's term, and since there are many obscure signs in *Moll* that someone other than Moll wrote it, critics then assume that Defoe is formally present in his fiction. But the *signs* are just that—inadvertent traces of his role that Defoe did not or could not avoid; they are not *signals*. All the signals in the book say that Moll wrote the book, that Defoe isn't there except as a kind of editor. But when the work is interpreted as fiction when the signs are taken as signals, they are seen to have no clear or consistent meaning, and the critics are left to say, on the one hand, that Defoe is "failing" to judge his material or, on the other hand, that he is judging it in ironic detachment. As Ian Watt neatly puts it, there seem to be only two possibilities, neither completely satisfactory: one that *Moll Flanders* is a work of irony, the other that it is an ironic object. But we need not choose between these alternatives. I am persuaded that anyone who examines his experience of the book closely from the perspective I have offered will come to see that it is neither a work of irony nor an ironic object but an ambiguous object in a sense that no work of any other well-known author is.

Understood in this way, *Moll Flanders* and Defoe's other stories of the pseudo-factual type fit cleanly into literary history. We see why the standard novel is usually not thought of as springing from Defoe, and why it was Richardson, rather, who was perceived by contemporaries as founding a new way of writing. Defoe, whom studies have shown to have ancestors but no posterity, is the last and most perfect artist in a tradition of works designed to exploit the interest naturally attaching to true stories. Richardson, with an ample posterity but not real ancestors, begins a new line of action-model fictions. The twenty-year gap between their stories is the dead space between two traditions.

Richardson's Dramatic Art in *Clarissa*

John J. Richetti

Samuel Richardson gave *Clarissa* a completely conventional subtitle, *The History of a Young Lady*, thereby linking his narrative for contemporary readers with any number of books that used the term *history* on their title pages to advertise the more or less domestic and contemporary events within. From the first, however, Richardson had unconventional aims, and he warned readers in his preface that his book was designed for more than amusement and would "probably be . . . tedious to all such as dip into it, expecting a light novel, or transitory romance." In due course, he claimed an overarching dramatic conception for his work, and in his "Postscript" in defense of the book against those who wished it happier or shorter than it was, he described it as a sort of revisionist Christian tragedy. There, he invoked Aristotle (by way of Addison) and Rapin to justify *Clarissa*'s unhappy ending as an occasion for morally improving pathos and the book itself as a divine comedy in which pathos is crowned by a "consideration of the doctrine of future rewards; which is everywhere strongly enforced in the history of Clarissa." The serious and thoughtful reader Richardson wished for encounters a drama in which his own involvement is transformed from the pleasures of pity and terror into moral-religious satisfaction that is intended as far superior to the poetic justice some of his readers demanded for his heroine. The book remains a "history," since there was no literary classification available to do justice to it, but Richardson groped toward a more exact label when he referred to himself as the "author of the history (or rather dramatic narrative) of Clarissa." Much of the most discerning praise of *Clarissa* since then has focused on that parenthesis, and Richardson's achievement as pioneer and perfecter of the psychological

From *British Theatre and the Other Arts, 1660–1800*, edited by Shirley Strum Kenny. © 1984 by Associated University Presses, Inc.

novel can perhaps be accounted for by his merging of drama and prose narrative.

Such hybridization seems to come naturally to prose fiction, and many of the novels we identify with the beginnings of modern narrative are intertwinings of different and sometimes conflicting literary modes. *Don Quixote* is an ironic blending of picaresque, pastoral, and romance, and this Cervantic mixture is what animates *Joseph Andrews* and *Tom Jones*. Defoe's novels work by combining the secular energies of picaresque and criminal biography with a moral introspection and devotional pattern that make them strangely profound. At first glance, the literary lineage of *Clarissa* is much simpler than these narrative hybrids. Richardson's story is the staple of numerous popular amatory narratives of the first forty years of the century, and in common with them it has a tendency to a theatricality of theme and style. The amatory novella as practiced expertly by Eliza Haywood, for example, tends toward erotic and pathetic moments featuring broad rhetorical flourishes and equally broadly rendered themes of love and honor, innocence, and betrayal. So, too, *Clarissa* is a dramatic narrative because on one rather obvious level it tends toward those large theatrical moments and allows some of its characters an occasional operatic grandeur of speech and gesture. *Clarissa* is dramatic, moreover, because these theatrics support a simple and intense set of conflicts. As the story unfolds, the main characters come to occupy clearly defined and radically opposing moral-cultural positions, and *Clarissa* turns into a dramatic spectacle in which it is easy for the reader to become, as it were, a spectator.

To be sure, Richardson is much better at this sort of importation of theatrical themes and styles than were hard-pressed hacks such as Mrs. Haywood. Modern literary history has shown in detail how *Clarissa* is specifically an integration of those themes and styles into Richardson's narrative, and how behind "each of Richardson's main protagonists there lies a stage tradition," as Mark Kinkead-Weekes has put it. But what every critic who has explored the dramatic and theatrical matrix of *Clarissa* necessarily adds is that Richardson transforms his materials and uses them for his own purposes, that is, for a moral and psychological realism beyond the capacities of his dramatic models.

The catalyst in that transformation was, of course, the epistolary convention as hugely expanded and intensified by Richardson. Such a convention provides opportunity for soliloquy and dialogue in which character and theme can aspire to that independence and objectivity of presentation associated with the dramatic mode. But again, these are merely external features of drama, and soliloquy and dialogue in themselves hardly guarantee dramtic achievement. It is, rather, Richardson's enormous powers of concentration and identification with his characters that validate these dramatic externalities. Richardson did not simply manage to efface himself in *Clarissa*. By virtue of an involvement in his correspondents probably without parallel in narrative literature, he disappeared from the text in more than the literal sense enforced by the letter convention. As he boasted to Lady Bradshaigh, his immersion in his characters was much more than ventriloquial animation: "Here I sit down to form characters. One I intend to be all Goodness; All Goodness he is; Another I intend to be all Gravity; All Gravity he is. Another Lady G——ish; all Lady G——ish is she. I am all the while absorbed in the character. It is not fair to say—I, identically I, am any-where, while I keep within the character." Richardson's claims involve a psychological participation in character that is an implicit revision of eighteenth-century theatrical practice, focused as that was on matters of external rhetorical effectiveness (or he aspires to the achievement of an old theatrical ideal of total identification with character).

Richardson's description of his method (or rather the effect on himself of an antimethod) leads to an internalizing revision of any literary means for imagining and presenting character. What matters is not really the validity of his claim, since we cannot know "where" he stood as he spoke for Clarissa or Lovelace. It is, rather, the effect of Richardson's example as author for his characters that is of interest. Just as he claims to be doing much more than speaking lines and reproducing the convincing external-ities of dramatis personae, his characters seem to be doing something more than speaking lines or writing letters. Lovelace and Clarissa, in different ways, are observed by the reader in acts of self-presentation and even of highly self-conscious dramatization, and those acts derive in many cases from the dramatic repertory and the theatrical conventions of the time. Ultimately, what makes that process supremely absorbing is that *Clarissa* produces an awareness of the imposed or invented theatricality of such acts, of their arbitrary and inessential nature. To put the case at its formalist extreme, the epistolary convention as Richardson enlarged it creates a sit-uation in which the reader is made conscious of the fundamental instru-mentality of the text as it is manipulated by the main correspondents. Viewed this way, *Clarissa* implies a self somewhere within or beyond the text, a self exploiting the text to express itself but somehow not wholly contained by the text, even though it has nothing to assert itself with except the text.

Now to some extent, any letter writer or any text is open to such charges and is full of these instabilities and paradoxes. The presumed spontaneity of experience and the authenticity of the self are, moreover, naturally com-promised by their insertion in so formalized a convention as eighteenth-century correspondence. What Richardson narrates in *Clarissa* is the inev-itability of self-dramatization, and what the book may be said to seek for its main characters is a way out of that circularity and implicit inauthenticity. Thus, what John Traugott acutely describes as Richardson's manipulation of theatricality is only the beginning of a description of his achievement. Traugott calls him "a master of realism who has a sense of how and why human beings need to be theatrical, need to put themselves on stage to voice their fantasies. Clarissa's 'she-tragedy' histrionics are what Lovelace wants to match his 'smart cock' charades." Richardson's realism involves the elaboration of a situation in which his protagonists try to develop ways to control or understand or even to discard what Traugott calls their theatrical needs. The nature or the location of the self that has these needs of which Traugott speaks so confidently is precisely what is at stake, since its reality and independence are compromised by those needs. The moral and psychological realism for which Richardson is justly praised is inseparable from his exploration of his characters' attempts to locate that self and to establish a stable relationship between the self and the stylistic and generic means by which it dramatizes or externalizes itself. The effort, in short, is to dramatize the limits of dramatization, to call a halt to self-presentation and present a self.

Such reflexive literary activity is an occasional possibility on stage, even in so manifestly artificial a location as the Restoration heroic play. Eric Rothstein has argued [in *Restoration Tragedy: Form and the Process of Change*] that heroic rant may sometimes be seen in the context of a play as being expressive of a character's failure with language or with himself. Rothstein says that a character such as Lee's Massinissa both identifies and undermines himself with his explosive rant; the character's language thus expresses an impossibly unstable personality. In *Clarissa* that failure is a constant possibility, as the continuous rush of language the novel requires from its two protagonists forces them and us to scrutinize their language for impropriety, that is, for uncontrolled significances where characterization passes out of the hands of the writer and the audience interprets and completes what is being said.

All the characters in *Clarissa* constitute themselves as characters, first and obviously by identifying themselves in the imagined world of the narrative, and secondly by expressing a self through a particular way of speaking, a style. But style is here much more than a decoration of language or an apt choice of forceful figures for emotional moments. For Lovelace and Clarissa, who are granted the large stretches of expression necessary for such things, style is a cumulative manner of self-presentation and a way of understanding self and others. Both of them are from the first preoccupied with asserting a particular self and establishing a particular kind of world; both of them make themselves present by an insistent literary revision of the normal and ordinary discourse all around them. Their development of appropriate styles is a matter of resisting in opposing ways the limitations and compulsions that language and literary occasion contain. Neither of them wishes to be like Lee's Massinissa, and each develops a distinct strategy for handling language so that it does not betray the self that lies (in some difficult sense) behind it.

This wary attitude to language may be what constitutes the special narrative discourse associated with the novel. It may be that this self-conscious withdrawal from language (or a bracketing of its formulations) is especially visible in *Clarissa* because of the dramatic matrix of the book.

That is to say, Richardson's protagonists take their opposing stances by developing different relationships between themselves and readily available dramatic modes of action and understanding; and insofar as both of them achieve self-consciousness about their projects, they are presenting different novelistic alternatives to those simpler dramatic modes.

Some thirty letters are exchanged before Lovelace's first letter is printed, and twenty-four of these are from Clarissa to Anna Howe. In these letters Clarissa is consistently aware of the necessity of self-control, and what she outlines to her friend is a delicate balance between resistance and submission to the demands of her family. Her asides during her narration of negotiations with her family show her to be clearly aware of the need to maintain an appearance of submission rather than to challenge her family's plans overtly. At the same time, she manages by suggestion and analysis (a sort of literalness and accuracy of observation and memory) to project in their presence a version of herself that refuses to compromise and that defends her resolution not to marry Solmes. Clarissa establishes herself as a character whose self-presentation insists upon a complexity that is very difficult to dramatize and even to articulate very clearly. Indeed, her prolixity and that of the novel itself are obvious effects of the complexity of character Richardson seems to be after.

Anna Howe functions as a moral and stylistic variation on Clarissa. In the crucial opening letters her sensible grasp of reality is just to the comic side of Clarissa's gathering seriousness. Her apt generalization about the Harlowes—"You are all too rich to be happy, child"—involves a confident irony about social and moral determinants that Clarissa carefully avoids. Anna writes with an ironic vivacity proper to worldly-wise heroines such as Congreve's Millamant and Angelica. Her amused skepticism when Clarissa tells her that she would not be in love with Lovelace displays an epigrammatic view of feminine instabilities that is at home in comic drama: "Well but, if you have not the throbs and glows, you have not; and are not in love; good reason why—because you would not be in love, and there's no more to be said; only, my dear, I shall keep a good look out upon you; and so I hope you will upon yourself; for it is no manner of argument that because you would not be in love, you therefore are not." After all, Anna is an onlooker, and she reminds Clarissa here that "a stander-by is often a better judge of the game than those that play." As an observer, she takes naturally to the dramatic metaphor; the advice she subsequently offers is no longer comic, but it is still structured in terms of simple dramatic transformations.

Anna proposes legal action, the simple and direct step of "resuming" the fortune left to Clarissa by her grandfather, a fortune she has put in her family's control. Anna's recommendation is plain and forceful: "You will say, you cannot do it while you are with them. I don't know that. Do you think they can use you worse than they do? And is it not your *right?* And do they not make use of your own generosity to oppress you? Your Uncle

Harlowe is one trustee, your Cousin Morden is the other: insist upon your right to your uncle; and write to your Cousin Morden about it. This, I dare say, will make them alter their behaviour to you." This advice is a mixture of briefly rendered scenes built around rhetorical questions, resolved by simple facts and legal inevitabilities; it constitutes a simple scenario for Clarissa, an outline for a proto-feminist play, one is tempted to say.

But it is addressed to a Clarissa whose mode of perception is deferential to circumstances, attuned to historical complications, exquisitely analytical and argumentative in the face of the brutally simple commands of her family—resistant, in short, to any kind of dramatic simplicity, Anna's or her family's. For example, Clarissa attempts to argue with her mother, who warns her that "this won't do somewhere else. You *know* it won't." That is a fearful reference to the dreaded paternal presence, who will hardly bear explicit naming, never mind being "thus dialogued with," as Mrs. Harlowe puts it. Indeed, when Mr. Harlowe condescends to speak a few pages later, Clarissa trembles at the "sterness in his looks" and notes that he speaks only to his silent wife: "My dear, you are long absent. Dinner is near ready. What you had to say lay in a very little compass. Surely, you have nothing to do but to declare *your* will, and *my* will—but perhaps you may be talking of the preparations." Simple and silent obedience is all that Mr. Harlowe's speeches, such as they are, call for, and his gouty generalized presence as "A JUSTLY-ENRAGED FATHER" (as he signs himself a bit later) is a literary self-dramatization quite opposed to the literary-moral manner his daughter is attempting to develop in this opening phase of her story. For Clarissa is more than the dutiful daughter she signs herself as at times. In this opening sequence she is what deserves to be called a novelistic sensibility in the sense that she is out to explore an untenable necessity and to find a way through and around it. As the pressures mount and she becomes more and more constricted by a tightening family circle drawn around her, she searches for reasons, meditates on the complexities of her situation, refuses the simple (and in several senses dramatic) solutions of obedience and defiance held out by others, and rejects tragic submission, domestic pathos, or feminist comedy.

She thus achieves, I think, an impressive self-understanding. Shortly before the "elopement" with Lovelace she mediates on the sources of her moral-intellectual habits and on the origins and consequences of the necessity that she has slowly clarified:

> I should have been very little the better for the *conversation-visits* which the good Dr. Lewen used to honour me with, and for the principles *wrought* (as I may say) into my earliest mind by my pious Mrs. Norton, founded on her reverend father's experience, as well as on her own, if I could not thus retrospect and argue, in such a strange situation as we are in. *Strange* I may well call it; for don't you see, my dear, that we seem all to be *impelled*, as it

were, by a perverse fate which none of us is able to resist? And yet all arising (with a strong appearance of self-punishment) from ourselves? Do not my parents see the hopeful children, from whom they expected a perpetuity of worldly happiness to their branching family, now grown up to answer the *till* now distant hope, setting their angry faces against each other, pulling up by the roots, as I may say, that hope which was ready to be carried into a probable certainty?

Your partial love will be ready to acquit me of *capital* and *intentional* faults: but oh, my dear! my calamities have humbled me enough, to make me turn my gaudy eye inward; to make me look into myself! And what have I discovered there? Why, my dear friend, more *secret* pride and vanity than I could have thought had lain in my unexamined heart.

This extraction of the psychological and historical background of her dilemma substitutes understanding for action, indeed makes understanding a form of action as Clarissa balances external circumstances and internal will. This passage is both meditative deference and aggressive exercise of the self; it represents a perfect form of displaced self-dramatization. Such balancing of external fate and internal will as Clarissa articulates here and elsewhere is the highest form of Christian moral understanding and, as such, a form of moral action.

In formal terms, Clarissa's character is described by making the alterations that occur in this manner of self-preservation and in its accompanying implicit understanding of the world. For much of the first two volumes or so, that understanding is a matter of deference to a tangle of moral, psychological, social, and even legal circumstances. Much of Clarissa's writing before the elopement constitutes a complicating revision of the positive and negative simplifications of her personality, as she insists that she is neither the self-willed egotist most of her family accuses her of being nor the legendary paragon of her grandfather's will. Such consistent self-effacement is easily seen as disingenuous, and Clarissa's denial of her very evident powers is in truth open to those charges of bad faith leveled against it from different perspectives by Lovelace and the Harlowes. And it is precisely that opposition and misunderstanding that make the term *novelistic* appropriate for Clarissa's stylistic identity, and in fact provoke or generate that mode.

Bella, James, and the rest claim to inhabit a psychological universe in which the individual is in full control of his will and totally aware of his motives. In place of the limiting tangle of circumstances and self Clarissa offers, they feel free to substitute a clear stage on which the individual can perform actions and make choices. The Harlowe scenario for Clarissa and for the family is both grand and simple—financial accumulation and social mobility. What they require of her is simple assent, an uncomplicated role in the drama of their emerging dynasty. Clarissa's refusal is novelistic pre-cisely because a good part of what she does is to substitute complicated case histories for that simple plot. Her analysis exposes problems by means of an essentially retrospective historical intelligence. She understands Ar-abella's jealousy in terms of the family history and Lovelace's withdrawn proposal; she places James's resentment exactly in its social and psycho-logical context; and perhaps most impressively, she locates her own prob-lem squarely in the history of her parents' marriage: "My MOTHER has never thought fit to oppose my FATHER'S will when once he has declared himself determined. My UNCLES, stiff, unbroken, highly-prosperous bach-elors, give me leave to say (though very worthy persons in the main), have as high notions of a child's duty as of a wife's obedience, in the *last* of which, my mother's meekness has confirmed them, and given them greater reason to expect the *first*."

Powerful as the Harlowes are, they represent the dramatic mode at a rather elementary level, and Clarissa has little trouble coming to a full understanding of their determining circumstances (hence the special kind of fear, rage, and frustration she excites in them). To be sure, there are times when Clarissa is forced to drop her controlling novelistic discourse and under the pressure of the moment turn to a form of resistance that involves the broadest kind of theatrical speech and gesture. For example, after Mr. Harlowe has "ordered patterns of the richest silks to be sent from London" for the marriage with Solmes, Clarissa turns "silent for some time" and then tells Anna how she ran through in her mind the circumstances gathering to push her toward Solmes. "All these reflections crowding upon my remembrance; I would, madam, said I, folding my hands, with an earnestness in which my whole heart was engaged, bear the cruellest tor-tures, bear loss of limb, and even of life to give *you* peace. But this man, every moment I would, at your command, think of him with favour, is the more my aversion. You cannot, indeed you cannot, think how my whole soul resists him! And to talk of contracts concluded upon; of patterns; of short day! Save me, save me, O my dearest mamma, save your child from this heavy, from this insupportable evil!" But we notice that even in so extreme a rhetorical moment Clarissa is scrupulously accurate in surround-ing that externality with a psychological interiority that is its effective cause. She is an instinctive novelist of her situation because she places even the broadest verbal moments in the context of their psychological determinants. The silence Clarissa summarizes so completely is full of "reflections" that trigger this outburst, and she is an honest recorder of her own feelings to give the odious Solmes a central place in these reflections: "and then Mr. Solmes's disagreeable person; still more disagreeable manners; his low un-derstanding." We are in a position to account for the violence of Clarissa's outburst even more exactly than she, since we can catch the disgust and sexual fear that she expresses thereby. She, by the way, does not really deny her sexual fear and disgust for Solmes, as modern critics like to think (although she is restricted to a genteel and prudish idiom). That repugnance is part of her self-characterization, and she uses it as an important element in the complex and, to her mind, convincing argument against the insultingly simple role her family wishes her to assume.

A swelling scene such as this one looks forward, of course, to the encounters with Lovelace later on, for he provokes Clarissa far more effectively than the Harlowes and succeeds more completely in making her lose control of her discourse. He is her antagonist for any number of interesting psychological and social reasons familiar to any reader of the book: he is sexually attracted by her difficult virtue and seems to sense what we can call the sadomasochistic possibilities of their relationship, he hates the smug bourgeois perfection she represents, and so on. It is important to insist that such a description of his desires is not a reader's extrapolation but a close paraphrase of Lovelace's own analysis of the situation. He is, as many have noted, a splendidly dramatic character, a self-consciously histrionic sensibility who not only imagines himself and others in the actions and postures of an actual eighteenth-century stage but also sees himself as a powerful directorial self with the omniscient perspective of the dramatist, able to view human action as ironically recurrent and predictable. His radically dramatized personality includes a radical self-consciousness. He is much more than the traditional literary rake, and we have objective testimony from other characters right at the beginning of the book that he is a man of moral and social parts in many respects. Indeed, as Robert D. Hume has demonstrated, the theatrical rake hardly exists as a simple or "a single, definable type," but even on stage represents a set of amusing or shocking attitudes that playwrights can vary and that characters can assume within a more complicated dramatic personality.

Throughout the long opening section of the novel, Lovelace does not appear in person, although he is spoken of and even quoted in the letters. Clarissa in her increasing confinement marvels at his freedom; "This man, somehow or other, knows everything that passes in our family. My confinement; Hannah's dismission; and more of the resentments and resolutions of my father, uncles, and brother that [than?] I can possibly know, and almost as soon as the things happen which he tells me of. He cannot come at these intelligences fairly." She's right, of course, since Lovelace is employing a very theatrical expedient—a domestic spy. When Lovelace's first letter appears shortly after this, his vivacity and clarity cut through the complexities Clarissa has so painfully rendered. More is at stake in the contrast offered to the reader than the stylistic playfulness in Lovelace's "Roman Style" (as Richardson identifies it in a footnote), for his style is characterized here and throughout the book by a manic dramatizing of the moment. Quite transparently when he writes to Belford and more insidiously in his conversations with Clarissa, Lovelace constructs literary moments in which he plays all the roles or anticipates all the lines and moves of others. Here, his first letter turns into energetic soliloquizing: "But is it not a confounded thing to be in love with one who is the daughter, the sister, the niece of a family I must eternally despise? And, the devil of it, that love increasing, with her—what shall I call it?—'tis not scorn: 'tis not pride: 'tis not the insolence of an adored beauty—but 'tis to *virtue,* it seems, that my difficulties are owing; and I pay for not being a sly sinner, an hypocrite; for being regardless of my reputation; for permitting slander to open its mouth against me. But is it necessary for such a one as I, who have been used to carry all before me, upon my own terms—I, who never inspired a fear, that had not a discernibly predominant mixture of love in it; to be an hypocrite?"

Belford is little more than an excuse for Lovelace's self-dramatization. Clarissa pointedly speaks and writes to others and shuns this sort of verbal excess. Richardson is obviously anxious to show the reader just this particular difference between the two. At the end of the letter that precedes Lovelace's she falls into a series of melodramatic exclamations: "O that they did but know my heart! It shall sooner burst, than voluntarily, uncompelled, undriven, dictate a measure that shall cast a slur either upon them, or upon my sex." Quickly, however, she drops that manner and asks Anna to excuse "these grave *soliloquies,* as I may call them." While Clarissa is out to efface herself and explore circumstances, to persuade others to moral accommodation, Lovelace treats the moment as an excuse for self-display and uses language as a means of self-assertion. His sensibility is defined by the denial of that complex necessity that Clarissa explores and the rejection of the deferential modes of analysis and expression that she seeks to exemplify. His theatrical models are clearly visible in his discourse, and he always places those models within the ironic brackets of his own self-consciousness about them. "I love," he says to Belford, "when I dig a pit, to have my prey tumble in with secure feet and open eyes; then a man can look down upon her, with an *O-ho, charmer, how came you there?"* One could multiply examples of Loveleace's formulations of his freedom. This one exemplifies his tendency for dramatic structure, in this case a simple comic scene that is the generic opposite for Clarissa's meditative complication of events in which she always stays, as it were, within the circumstances she presents and tries to avoid controlling imagery such as Lovelace's.

And yet for all his dramatic virtuosity, Lovelace always seems to understand that the attraction between him and Clarissa is grounded in the problematical and the contradictory, rooted in psychosocial factors that he is well aware of and that resist the simplifications of the heroic drama and the romantic wit-comedy that are his models. "Thou knowest my heart, if any man living does," he writes in that first letter to Belford. "As far as I know it myself, thou knowest it. But 'tis a cursed deceiver; for it has many and many a time imposed upon its master—*master,* did I say? That am I not now; nor have I been from the moment I beheld this angel of a woman." Lovelace goes so far as to construct in this letter an elaborate psychological theory to account for his obsession. Whether or not he is telling the truth about that "quality-jilt" who has driven him from his early manhood "to revenge upon as many of the sex as shall come into [his] power" is immaterial, for what results in the letter is his backing away from introspection and self-analysis into self-dramatization. Lovelace's dramatic imagination operates consistently as a means of organizing his own contradictions and instability. His opening letter turns into soliloquy and resorts to a series of vignettes with him at the center of each. If Clarissa's analytic intelligence is her way of resisting the simple Harlowe scenario and of revising her own dangerously simplified legend as moral paragon, then Lovelace's histrionics are a means of resisting the discoveries of his own formidably analytic mind. Both of them display, in short, capacities for dramatic and novelistic self-understanding, and they are the results of those choices of emphasis and style (in the broadest sense) that enforce their identities. In the beginning, the formal structure of the book at its simplest is an opposition between Clarissa's novelistic meditations and Lovelace's dramatic manipulations. As the book progresses, that structure grows more complex and involves a transformation of these terms into a new opposition.

The long, slow pivot of the book deserves, I think, to be called a dialectical transformation of Clarissa and Lovelace in terms of the interaction between the novelistic and the dramtic modes. "Dialectical" is appropriate in this case, since these characters and the modes they choose for their self-presentation collide and simultaneously repel and interpenetrate, each revealing the presence of a form of itself in the other, discovering itself in a new and transformed manner in the process, and transforming the other even as it transforms itself. We end with two new terms (characters in this case), each of which has been crucially modified by an interaction with the other in which it has discovered a truth about itself. This dialectic in *Clarissa* has a specifically literary form, and the transformations the characters undergo are properly described by the transformations in the literary modes they employ.

Clarissa's attempt to arbitrate between personal will and external circumstance is interrupted by Lovelace literally shifting the scene and altering the dominant tone of the discourse. The elopement itself, of course, is deliberately staged—a Lovelace production right down to the props and the imaginary actors. Clarissa perceives it in retrospect as the result of her tactical error in meeting Lovelace alone, but she experiences it and renders it for Anna as a mixture of spontaneous compulsion and neatly arranged dramatic tableau. "Now behind me, now before me, now on this side, now on that, turned I my affrighted face in the same moment; expecting a furious brother here, armed servants there, an enraged sister screaming, and a father armed with terror in his countenance more dreadful than even the drawn sword which I saw, or those I apprehended. I ran as fast as he; yet knew not that I ran; my fears adding wings to my feet, at the same time that they took all power of thinking from me." This passage marks a crucial shift in tone. Till now, Clarissa has negotiated in a carefully univocal and quasi-legal style, much given to citing precedents and cross-examining the discourse of others. She is also forced into other styles, including that of the tragic heroine, but she is always in some kind of control of those styles, even if only in retrospective narration to Anna. When James attacks her on stylistic grounds for what he calls her "whining vocatives" and infuriates her by his condescending pedantry, Clarissa declares in her answer that she writes "in a style different from my usual, and different from what I wished to have occasion to write." The result is, overall, an eloquence and moral reason that her family fears. As her Uncle John says, "There is no standing against your looks and language. . . . For my part, I could not read your letter to me, without being unmanned. How can you be so unmoved yourself, yet be so able to move everybody else?" In this scene, Lovelace tricks her into entering a world of action and movement where precisely those dramatic simplifications that she has been avoiding appear with a force that she cannot resist. Instead of thinking, she imagines and visualizes in an instant what she has been refining and sifting at great length.

In this scene and in their many encounters thereafter, Clarissa struggles against the spontaneity and loss of stylistic control that Lovelace's machinations seek to induce in her. The heated and heightened language of some of their exchanges is essentially Lovelace's discourse, and while she still has her reason Clarissa charges him repeatedly with a falsifying "volubility." The accusation is apt, since Lovelace is master of many accents and styles, from the jocular conspiratorial manner of his letters to Belford, to the smooth manners he displays as outraged man of honor and deferential suitor in his early dealings with the Harlowes, to the charming self-justifier with Lord M. and his aunts, to the impassioned imperial amorist of the love duets with Clarissa. While she suspends final judgment of him partly because of this variability and notes his "impenetrableness," Lovelace sees Clarissa in wholly conventionalized roles as a female character, refusing to grant her the directorial self-consciousness of roles, types, and styles that he possesses. For him she is an embodiment (a lovely one) of generalized and essentially literary female types, tragic and comic.

In an important sense, Lovelace is right about Clarissa. She is not "acting" the way he is. As Kinkead-Weekes observes, Clarissa's stylistic lapses are governed by her invariable "moral currency" and by "the kind of integrity that makes Clarissa Clarissa." Ironically, however (and dialectically), the dramatic universe forced upon her by Lovelace turns Clarissa to the divine comedy of her staged demise and transforms her at last into an icon who transcends the female types he has tried to impose or to extract. His plots and manipulations reduce the complex psychosocial world Clarissa begins with to fake situations and locations such as Mrs. Sinclair's and the elaborate Captain Tomlinson ruse. Meaningful moral analysis and accommodation to establish the novelistic mode of understanding are necessarily impossible in these artificial settings where a comic necessity controlled by Lovelace the dramatist hangs over all action and utterance. The incessant psychosexual pressure that Lovelace thus applies denies Clarissa the opportunity for revision and mediation that she enjoyed when facing her far less subtle family. Clarissa is kidnapped out of the real world, in effect, and stranded in Lovelace's formal world, given a choice only between the plots of romantic comedy and she-tragedy.

All of this happens very gradually. Initially Clarissa is well able to defend herself verbally, retaining traces of her characteristically analytic style. Lovelace's theatrical style of self-presentation is easily parried and even mocked by a Clarissa who listens to his summaries of what he has endured for her sake and remarks: "Can't you go on, sir? You see I have patience to hear you. Can't you go on, sir?" As Lovelace takes this bait and dramatizes what he has already overdramatized in an earlier letter, Clarissa's talents as a literary and moral intelligence are wonderfully evident:

> Menaces every day and defiances put into every one's mouth against me! Forced to creep about in disguises—and to watch *all hours*—And in *all weathers*, I suppose, sir—that, I remember, was once your grievance! *In all weathers*, sir! And all these hardships arising from yourself, not imposed by me.

She follows with a long and exact rebuttal of Lovelace's self-justifying speeches, modulating from irony ("O sir, sir! What sufferings have yours been!") to specific criticism of his verbal devices, exposing the shallow egotism behind them:

> So that all that followed of my treatment, and your redundant *onlys*, I might thank you for principally,as you may yourself for all your *sufferings*, your *mighty* sufferings! And if, voluble sir, you have founded any merit upon them, be so good as to revoke it; and look upon *me*, with my forfeited reputation, as the only sufferer.

Lovelace's final reaction to this irrefutable analysis, this exposure of his literary unsoundness, is an outburst of passion: "Darkness, light; light, darkness; by my soul!—just as you please to have it. O charmer of my heart . . . take me, take me to yourself; mould me as you please; I am wax in your hands; give me your own impression, and seal me for ever yours." Such rant seems to be provoked by the literary dead end into which Clarissa has driven Lovelace, and its only effect is to make her "perfectly frighted," wishing herself "a thousand miles distant from him." In Lovelace's own account of the scene to Belford, he qualifies the spontaneity of his outburst, giving it in retrospect an outrageous theatricality. "There was, I believe, a kind of frenzy in my manner which threw her into a panic like that of Semele perhaps, when the Thunderer, in all his majesty, surrounded with ten thousand celestial burning-glasses, was about to scorch her into a cinder." But in the same letter he also admits that the was carried away almost too far: "It is exceedingly difficult, thou seest, for an honest man to act in disguises; as the poet says, *Thurst Nature back with a pitchfork, it will return*." Lovelace's dramatization has been thrown slightly out of control, and his rapture has been the result of Clarissa's masterful elimination of his other verbal resources. What he tries to revise in retrospect as a Jovian erotic tableau and then as a self-justifying and exemplary moral-emotional moment (complete with Horatian tag!) is in fact the first of Clarissa's verbal triumphs. He is driven to react passionately, out of his projected dramatic sequence; he loses some of his control and becomes what Clarissa's novelistic intelligence and verbal talent show him to be rather than the overseeing dramatist he wishes to be.

But in the long struggle that ensues, Lovelace does manage to have things his own way—albeit by slow oscillations that repeat with many variations the interactions of this scene. Clarissa's moral-stylistic integrity is kept intact: she not only resists Lovelace's various scenarios but exercises her powers of analysis and maintains a scrupulous record of herself that is moral and religious in motive and documentary and novelistic in effect. For Lovelace, writing is a dramatic opportunity; for Clarissa it continues to be a process for self-discovery and a means of steadying a world that she readily admits is marked by psychological instabilities. She writes down "everything of moment that befalls me; and of all I *think*, and of all I *do*, that may be of future use to me; for beside that this helps to form one to a style, and opens and expands the ductile mind, every one will find that many a good thought evaporates in thinking; many a good resolution goes off, driven out of memory perhaps by some other not so good." She records not just herself but others as well with fairness and accuracy, sensing an unsoundness in the women at Mrs. Sinclair's and seeing directly through such lesser rakes as Mowbray, Belton, and Tourville. But Lovelace's compulsive stage-managing works to undermine that acuity and render it irrelevant. Clarissa is not only driven to escape, and act of shocking directness for her contemplative sensibility, but to other melodramatic and theatrical actions.

Writing to Anna from Hampstead after the escape, Clarissa shows traces of her situation in the instability of her discourse. It begins here with demonic imagery and shades off into a moralizing and hopeful allegory:

> Oh, why was the great fiend of all unchained, and permitted to assume so specious a form, and yet allowed to conceal his feet and his talons, till with the one he was ready to trample upon my honour, and to strike the other into my heart! . . .
>
> And is it not in my own power still, by the divine favour, to secure the great stake of all? And who knows but that this very path into which my inconsideration has thrown me, strewed as it is with briers and thorns which tear in pieces my gaudier trap-

pings, may not be the right path to lead me into the great road to my future happiness; which might have been endangered by evil communication?

Such imagery comes easily to a pious reader such as Clarissa, and she has turned to it before; but it is Lovelace who has provoked its new intensity and frequency. The transformation of experience by moral allegory is Clarissa's literary defense against him. When Lovelace finds her shortly after this, his comic metamorphosis from "a cursed crabbed old wretch" into "a lively gay young fellow" is a secular revision of her images. Even here, however, there is a marvelous literary complexity to the scene. Since Clarissa recognizes him, Lovelace is forced to reveal himself. She in fact metamorphoses him, and he is drawn into a literary comparison that follows his source as it both glorifies and degrades him: "I threw open my great-coat, and, like the devil in Milton [an odd comparison, though!] 'I started up in my own form divine / Touch'd by the beam of her celestial eye, / More potent than Ithuriel's spear!' " Even as he reaches for that parallel (or has it forced on him), Lovelace finds that nothing can describe Clarissa. He admits his literary failure: "Now, Belford, for a similitude—now for a likeness to illustrate the surprising scene, and the effect it had upon my charmer, and the gentlewoman!—But nothing *was* like it, or equal to it. The plain fact can only describe it, and set it off—thus then take it."

Lovelace finds that Clarissa inhabits his dramatic universe in unexpected ways, defying his powers of representation as in the previous scene and at other times enacting with a sincerity and moral eloquence what he had hoped would be merely sexually stimulating distress. After the rape, Clarissa's disordered pages point to a scattering of her literary powers; these moving fragments are a discarded and incoherent anthology of literary possibilities for understanding a self no longer whole and encompassing those forms that Clarissa has used up to now: moral allegory, prophetic denunciation, apt quotation, and retrospective analysis (which breaks off and turns to confused self-pity). She recovers from that breakdown by appropriating Lovelace's histrionics, stealing his dramatic thunder and transforming it by sincere reenactment.

That transition can be illustrated briefly by two scenes in which Clarissa dominates and surprises Lovelace by employing two radically different methods of self-dramatization. What enforces the moral superiority and irresistible pathos she now commands is a literary contest that Lovelace identifies quite specifically as a stylistic achievement that reduces him to incoherent babble. He repeats her speeches shortly after the rape and especially notes their oratorical adjuncts: "her eyes neither fierce nor mild, but very earnest; and a fixed sedateness in her whole aspect, which seemed to be the effect of deep contemplation: and thus she accosted me, with an air and action that I never saw equalled." Her performance here is exactly the clear and forceful opposite of what Lovelace's psychodramatic theory of behavior expected, and his summary of the scene is full of admiration for her oratorical and emotional control:

> As I told thee, I had prepared myself for high passions, raving, flying, tearing execration: these transient violences, the workings of sudden grief, and shame, and vengeance, would have set us upon a par with each other, and quitted scores. These have I been accustomed to; and, as nothing violent is lasting, with these I could have wished to encounter. But such a majestic composure—seeking me—whom yet, it is plain, by her attempt to get away, she would have avoided seeing—no Lucretia-like vengeance upon herself in her thought—yet swallowed up, her whole mind swallowed up, as I may say, by a grief so heavy, as, in her own words, to be beyond the power of speech to express—and to be able, discomposed as she was to the very morning, to put such a home question to me, as if she had penetrated my future view—how could I avoid looking like a fool, and answering, as before, in broken sentences, and confusion?
>
> What—what-a—what has been done—I, I, I—cannot but say— must own—must confess—hem—hem. . . .
>
> O Belford! Belford! whose the triumph now! HERS, or MINE?

Like all his moods, Lovelace's admiration is temporary, and Clarissa's moral oratory and compelling gestures have to give way. But when they do, it is to an intensified tragic idiom that is equally unanswerable.

Lovelace arranges to find Clarissa's "promissory note" to Dorcas, thereby involving her in a new escape scene; he prepares to confront her with feigned anger. Clarissa emerges from her room with a full tragic dignity that collapses Lovelace's farce (her term) and substitutes a dramatic authenticity that frightens Lovelace and his whores: "The infamous mother whispered me that it were better to *make terms* with this *strange* lady, and let her go." "Every tongue silent, every eye awed, every heart quaking, mine, in a particular manner, sunk, throbless, and twice below its usual region. . . . Such the glorious power of innocence exerted at that awful moment." The generality Lovelace grants to Clarissa here is quite different from the demeaning female roles he has tried to assign, and, as so often in the book, Lovelace is moved against his will. Here, he watches as his dramatic project is transformed with uncanny exactness. Clarissa not only speaks in the highest tragic style, but carries a penknife held at her breast. The suicide she threatens reenacts Lovelace's reenactment of the Richard III gesture in the garden just before the elopement but with obvious differences in authenticity.

What has happened is that Lovelace has slowly managed to shift the dominant discourse, to accomplish his ends by modulating the generic and stylistic emphasis toward the comedy-melodrama of seduction. But the interaction of personalities and the styles that accompany them complicate matters. Instead of simply succumbing according to one of Lovelace's lively plots, Clarissa in due course constructs a slow, massive drama of submission to fate and substitutes an eroticized religiosity for his ever-varying sexual tableaux. Deprived of the possibility of the limited freedom the novelistic mode can discover if given the chance, Clarissa's sensibility can only operate in the context of an inescapable necessity that is the negative pole of the novelistic project. Given her own compelling circumstances as a woman and as a Christian (circumstances that Lovelace's dramatic theory can only understand in self-serving or comically mechanistic terms), she may be said to reject Lovelace's literary models as ways of dealing with such facts. Instead, she diverts them into a religious spectacle of holy dying in which a stark providential pattern replaces the tangled circumstances uncovered by the novelistic mode. Clarissa passes over eventually into Lovelace's dramatic universe, but that sphere is crucially modified by the transformed remnant of her novelistic style and sensibility. Thus, she substitutes deference and submission for his assertion and manipulation, extracting the determinism implicit in the dramatic mode by replacing Lovelace, the omniscient dramatist, and his repertory of secular texts with God (the ultimate dramatist) and the Bible and other religious texts. In the dynamic of the dialectic, moreover, her sensibility has itself been redirected toward a new version of Lovelace's dramaturgy in which Clarissa is the stage manager of a spectacle but one consistent with her experience and chosen as fitting and fateful rather than invented for self-display. That is to say, Clarissa resolves matters by a death play founded on stylized gesture and movement, on scriptural quotation and religious allegory rather than on the secular models that Lovelace has obsessively in mind and that feature improvisation of gesture and language and strictly limited comic meanings.

The accomplishment of this transformation proceeds slowly through the last third or so of the novel, and it is marked by an obvious withdrawal of Clarissa from normal correspondence. More and more, she is written about by others, notably by Belford, and is thereby objectified, assuming in his reverential evocations an iconlike stillness and significance: "Up then raised the charming sufferer her lovely face; but with such a significance of woe overspreading it that I could not, for the soul of me, help being visibly affected." When she speaks and writes, Clarissa now tends to a brevity that contrasts with her earlier prolixity, and those cryptic utterances are thoroughly informed by Biblical echo and quotation. Clarissa is, of course, physically weak and emotionally drained, but she is also turning away stylistically from the personal and the psychological to the archetypal. Her discourse is pared down to pious aphorism, and she speaks in homilies that are deliberately impersonal, homilies that constitute a rejection of personal complication. For example, after a heartless and unforgiving letter from Arabella, Clarissa writes to her mother and begs forgiveness with self-depreciating self-dramatization: "No self-convicted criminal ever approached her angry and just judge with greater awe, nor with a truer contrition, than I do you by these lines." She then passes to self-justification, but even there she is true to the dramatic attitude struck at the beginning of the letter. This summary is a deposition, a sworn statement couched in a mode that turns impersonal:

> And this you will be readier believe, if the creature who never, to the best of her remembrance, told her mamma a wilful falsehood, may be credited, when she declares, as she does, in the most solemn manner, that she met the seducer with a determination not to go off with him.

What she finally asks (on her knees like Lovelace in the woods, but with what a difference!) is a blessing in one sentence that will become her "passport to Heaven": *"Lost, unhappy wretch, I forgive you! and may God bless you! This is all!* Let me, on a blessed scrap of paper, but see one sentence to this effect under your dear hand." The entire letter is a quasi-legal document, but Clarissa is the prisoner in the dock rather than the moral investigator of the early volumes. Legal language and dramatic spectacle are now joined, and this letter's imaginings look forward to the reading of Clarissa's will, which is really a series of moral dramatizations in which the legend of St. Clarissa is memorialized. The most striking of these scenes is a final dramatic reversal very much in Lovelace's manner: if Lovelace insists upon viewing my corpse, she writes,

> Let him behold and triumph over the wretched remains of one who has been made a victim to his barbarous perfidy: but let some good person, as by my desire, give him a paper, whilst he is viewing the ghastly spectacle, containing these few words only: "Gay, cruel heart! behold here the remains of the once ruined, yet now happy, Clarissa Harlowe! See what thou thyself must quickly be;—and REPENT!"

For his part, Lovelace is subject to the transformations within the dialectic. His dramatic discourse is gradually undermined for us (and for Clarissa and Belford), as readers of his letters, by the accumulating insight that its theatricality is an inevitable expression of his personality and history rather than simply the self-conscious role that he has freely chosen. After Clarissa escapes for good and begins her protracted death scene, Lovelace attempts to reassert his controlling grasp of the dominant discourse, imagining various resolutions—some comic, like marriage, others extravagant, like keeping Clarissa's preserved body by his side. But the comic inventiveness is gone, and in time Lovelace's persona turns into a mere person. He finds that his devices become his compulsions. In one scene after another, Lovelace's dramatic supervision is eroded, and he is surprised by emotions and pushed into language that he cannot wholly control. Quite early on, Clarissa's novelistic intelligence had placed him as a sadly predictable social and moral-psychological type, and what Lovelace thinks is his inventiveness and irrepressible freedom become by the end of the book the grim necessity appropriate to the aristocratic rake and megalomaniac. Just as he forces Clarissa into a synthesis in which the dramatic mode reinterprets and transforms her novelistic self-understanding, Lovelace stands exposed in the latter half of *Clarissa* as a novelistic character—that is, as a prey to social and psychological determinisms, a man forced to act out his grief, rage, and even his death with a theatricality no longer self-consciously assumed but imposed by that interplay of self and circumstances which is made central by the novelistic understanding. And just as Clarissa redefines the dramatic mode, negating its negation by turning it from the secular parody of divine arrangement that it is for Lovelace into an austere religious rite of submission that leads to liberation and transcendence, so, too, Lovelace in his career redefines the novelistic and makes it in the course of the novel the discovery of a theatrically rendered necessity rather than a study of the possibility of a modest freedom that Clarissa embarked upon at the beginning.

Journeys from this World to the Next: The Providential Promise in *Clarissa* and *Tom Jones*

Mary Poovey

Despite at least one recent attempt to discover substantive similarities between the novels of Richardson and Fielding, Dr. Johnson's initial impulse
to discriminate still seems essential. "There is all the difference in the
world," asserted Johnson, "between characters of nature and characters of
manners, and *there* is the difference between the characters of Fielding and
those of Richardson. Characters of manners are very entertaining; but they
are to be understood by a more superficial observation than characters of
nature, where a man must dive into the recesses of the human heart." As
usual, beneath the prejudicial language, Johnson strikes the kernel of truth,
but what he does not consider is that character is not required to bear the
same burden in the novels of Fielding as in those of Richardson, or that
the observation of superficials may yield an entirely different kind of truth
from what scrutiny of the heart discloses. Prior to considerations of taste
there must be delineation of design, for only through a definition of the
intended provinces of the two novelists will their relationship be clarified.
Clarissa and *Tom Jones*, the two colossal pillars of eighteenth-century fiction,
are the mature expressions of their authors' imaginations; the profound
dissimilarities between these two Augustan novels reveal differences not
in talent but in didactic conceptions of art and the world.

Both *Clarissa* and *Tom Jones* are fictional expressions of the Christian
epic. This pattern, based on the design of providence with its attendant
promise of reward, is necessarily fictionalized as romance. What is at issue,
then, is not the outcome of the plot but the way of conceptualizing and
expressing the relationship between the absolute world, from which the
guarantee proceeds, and the temporal world, in which the promise must

From *ELH* 43, no. 3 (Fall 1976). © 1976 by The Johns Hopkins University Press, Baltimore/
London.

be earned. Whereas Clarissa's reunion with her Father occurs only in an absolute context and necessitates exile from her fallen family, Tom's acquisition of redemptive wisdom is expressed metaphorically through his discovery of paternity and marriage with Sophia. Richardson's conception of the two realms as contiguous but incompatible dictates different fictional strategies from those permitted by Fielding's assumption that the absolute can be perceived through temporal realities. These different conceptions also determine focus, for while Richardson concentrates on individual spiritual development, Fielding is concerned with ethics. Richardson's absorbing interest in the development of spiritual perfection paradoxically emerges from a context of realism; Fielding's concern with social behavior necessitates metaphorical expression of the providential pattern in quotidian terms.

Richardson's fictionalization of the Christian epic depends upon his depiction of Clarissa as a model of Christian perfection. As John A. Dussinger has convincingly demonstrated, the course of Clarissa's development faithfully mirrors the pattern of Christ's mortification, atonement, and redemption. Consistent with the emphasis on the importance of imitating Christ of such divines as John Tillotson, Robert South, and Isaac Barrow, Clarissa's rape, submission, and apotheosis chart the course of salvation. According to Dussinger: "In creating a parable illustrating the fundamental doctrine of the cross, Richardson attempted to portray the nature of sin and guilt under the operations of conscience and to represent in his heroine the ultimate refinement of sensibility as the condition of salvation."

But *Clarissa* cannot be described adequately as a parable, for the accessibility of the solution she enacts depends upon Richardson's relation of the absolute perfection she attains to the temporal reality from which she emerges. The initial circumstancing of Clarissa in the mundane world and the tracing of the spiritual development that ejects her from this world is a function of detail. Serving first to clarify Clarissa's physical and emotional dilemma and then to emphasize the growing discrepancy between spiritual and physical realms, the details of formal realism index the emergence of the absolute from the quotidian.

In roughly the first half of the novel detail functions to engage the reader's sympathy, to particularize Clarissa's terror and torture. Clarissa's initial interview with Mr. Solmes highlights the threat she faces.

> The man stalked in. His usual walk is by pauses, as if (from the same vacuity of thought which made Dryden's clown whistle) he was telling his steps: he first paid his clumsy respects to my mother; then to my sister; next to me; as if I were already his wife, and therefore to be last in his notice; and sitting down by me, told us in general what weather it was. Very cold, he made it; but I was warm enough. Then addressing himself to me; and how do *you* find it, miss? was his question; and would have taken my hand.

I withdrew it, I believe with disdain enough. My mother frowned. My sister bit her lip.

I could not contain myself: I never was so bold in my life; for I went on with my plea as if Mr. Solmes had not been there.

My mother coloured, and looked at him, at my sister, and at me. My sister's eyes were opener and bigger than ever I saw them before.

The man understood me. He hemmed, and removed from one chair to another.

Solmes's stupidity, her mother's anger, Arabella's dismay, bear in upon Clarissa and force the frantic pleas that contradict duty. The walk, the glances, the gestures, render the scene vivid and manifest the necessity of Clarissa's disobedience. Immersed firmly in the sordid details of economic motivation and physical repulsiveness, Clarissa must revolt and so spring the trap around her.

Following Clarissa's understanding of the necessity of submission, her character begins to approach perfection. As the burden of narrative shifts first to Lovelace, then to Belford, the reader is redirected from Clarissa's response to her situation to the details of her mortification and liberation. Increasingly, the particulars of the compromised world emphasize the disparity between Clarissa's physical surroundings and her spiritual purity. The public humiliation of Clarissa's imprisonment cannot taint the private recesses of her soul. Belford surveys her barred bedroom and then turns to the kneeling lady:

She was kneeling in a corner of the room, near the dismal window, against the table, on an old bolster (as it seemed to be) of the cane couch, half-covered with her handkerchief; her back to the door; which was only shut to [not need of fastenings!]; her arms crossed upon the table, the forefinger of her right hand in her Bible. She had perhaps been reading in it, and could read no longer. Paper, pens, ink, lay by her book on the table. . . . When I surveyed the room around, and the kneeling lady, sunk with majesty too in her white flowing robes (for she had not on a hoop) spreading the dark, though not dirty, floor, and illuminating that horrid corner; her linen beyond imagination white, considering that she had not been undressed ever since she had been here; I thought my concern would have chocked me. Something rose in my throat, I know not what, which made me, for a moment, guggle, as it were, for speech: which, at last, forcing its way, Con—con—confound you both, said I to the man and woman, is this an apartment for such a lady? And could the cursed devils of her own sex, who visited this suffering angel, see her, and leave her, in so damned a nook?

Belford's final words are significant, for Clarissa's environment is damned, partly for its degradation of grace and partly through its fallen nature. But

Clarissa is no longer infected by her compromised surroundings, for she knows that *"this world is designed but as a transitory state of probation; and that she is travelling to another and better."* Details now point to the responses of those who only dimly comprehend her glorification, and illuminate their affinity with the corruption she leaves in eclipse. The discontinuity between the quotidian and the absolute permits private triumph despite public disgrace; now liberated from the cloying details of the mundane world, Clarissa prepares her spiritual dowry even behind physical bars.

When Clarissa takes up the narrative once more, writing to Anna Howe and Mrs. Norton from her deathbed, the details which fill her letters are not primarily of external reality but of the minute development of her spiritual progress. She is increasingly detached from and impervious to the particulars of her environment, and those details which do concern her— the preparation of her coffin, the distribution of her testimonials and gifts— achieve the status of sanctified emanations of a soul. As Clarissa approaches perfection—and death—the details by which she is circumstanced assume the quality of symbols, so that her final gestures seem to proceed from Heaven rather than earth.

> She waved her hand to us both, and bowed her head six several times, as we have since recollected, as if distinguishing every person present; not forgetting the nurse and the maid-servant; the latter having approached the bed, weeping, as if crowding in for the divine lady's last blessing; and she spoke faltering and inwardly: Bless—bless—bless—you all—and now—and now [holding up her almost lifeless hands for the last time]—come—O come—blessed Lord—JESUS!

Clarissa's apotheosis purifies even the language of corrupt sexuality, as ecstasy and consummation achieve their unfallen denotations in Clarissa's climactic union with Christ. After her death the terms in which Clarissa is described and the details with which she is associated reflect this transfiguration of the quotidian through association with the absolute. Anna Howe's description of Clarissa's offer of cream to her sister resounds with overtones of ritual: "And now, methinks, I see my angel-friend . . . courting her acceptance of the milk-white curd from hands more pure than that." And to Lovelace, even Clarissa's heart assumes absolute characteristics; he would cut it out and preserve it in spirits so as to possess the love he was never able to earn.

That the absolute is incompatible with the fallen world is a given of which Clarissa, even before the perfection of her heart, is aware. "Let me repeat that I am quite sick of life; and of an earth in which *innocent* and *benevolent* spirits are sure to be considered as *aliens,* and to be made sufferers by the *genuine sons* and *daughters* of *that earth.*" The absolute can rise out of the quotidian but cannot coexist with it. Thus Richardson's realism is of particular incidents rather than of completed action. The pattern of Clarissa's perfection is anagogical, but is occasioned and rendered accessible as a model for imitation by its original immersion in the details of the mundane world. The final discrepancy between the absolute characterization of Clarissa and the fallen world she transcends underscores the need for the providential promise she embodies.

The discontinuity between Clarissa's spiritual perfection and the blighted world which culminates in Clarissa's apotheosis is, in its seminal stage, the conflict which initiates the catastrophe of the temporal plot. To marry the odious Mr. Solmes, either to gratify her siblings' greed or her parents' compromised concept of duty, would be to violate the dictates of her conscience. It is because this private obligation to God can never be reconciled with society's relative values that Clarissa must leave her father's estate and, ultimately, the larger prison of a community of Lovelaces of which Mrs. Sinclair's brothel is symptomatic. That Clarissa can consult, by turning inward, an intuitive faculty of judgment which is directly related to God, is consistent with the doctrines of such seventeenth-century divines as John Tillotson. By the late seventeenth century *conscience* was used interchangeably with *heart* and signified not the innate, infallible voice of natural reason, but an affective principle, "a function of the sensibility." Thus an important step in the progress toward salvation could be expressed as the cultivation of the heart, a process which begins in self-scrutiny. Clarissa's spiritual development originates with just such an interior survey: "my calamities have humbled me enough, to make me turn my gaudy eye inward; to make me look into myself! And what have I discovered there? Why, my dear friend, more *secret* pride and vanity than I could have thought had lain in my unexamined heart." As the minute examination of the details of Clarissa's responses and decisions indicate, the perfection of Clarissa's understanding of her heart constitutes the significant action of the novel. From this internal development emanate all external actions: Clarissa's attempt to reform Lovelace, her struggles to escape persecution, her eventual submission to and preparation for her Heavenly Father. The rectification of Clarissa's pride originates in a cleansing of the inner eye and culminates in a consolidation of the implied relationship between her heart and her God.

It is a paradox of the faith that the action which Clarissa's perfected heart dictates is complete passivity, patient acquiescence to the mysterious workings of the hand of God. In the providential labyrinth of Richardson's fiction, suffering is the trial of true humility, Job the model of the Christian hero. Job's proud and contumacious spirit must be rectified through a trial of depredation similar to Clarissa's persecution. Thus it is no surprise that Job is, as Lovelace notes, Clarissa's "favourite": she studies that book while in prison, derives the inscription for her coffin from its pages, and chooses Job's speech on vanity as the subject of her funeral oration. It is not only Job's ritual of suffering that qualifies him as a suitable model of Christian heroism, but, ultimately, his complete submission to the will of God. For, in a universe discontinuous with but set in motion and governed by God, any action or exertion of will constitutes a defiance of providence. True piety can thus be expressed only through perfect passivity, for only when passive can one acquiesce to and serve as an adequate vehicle for the enactment of God's will. Paradoxically, action, too, becomes inadvertent passivity, as God's will subsumes all human action. In Richardson's fictional model of the providential scheme, blasphemy takes the form of manipulation and scheming; Clarissa's initial pride manifests itself in pernicious stratagems of reformation and escape,and Lovelace proves himself a "perverse providential surrogate" who must fall victim to his own elaborate structures of deceit.

Clarissa's first intuition of the nature of her pride involves a partial understanding of its gravity: "O my dear! what is worldly wisdom but the height of folly? I, the meanest, at least the youngest, of my father's family, to thrust myself in the gap between such uncontrollable spirits!—to the interception perhaps of the designs of Providence, which may intend to make these hostile spirits their own punishers. If so, what presumption!" From her initial artifices of conducting a private correspondence with Lovelace and hiding letters for Anna Howe in the gatehouse wall grows a malignancy of deceit. She hides pens and papers from her maid, plans elaborate stratagems of escape, and plots to meet Lovelace in the ivy house. Following her terrorized flight with Lovelace, she suddenly realizes the ineluctability of her initial exercise of will: "one devious step at setting out!—that must be it—which pursued, has led me so far out of my path, that I am in a wilderness of doubt and error; and never, never, shall find my way out of it: for, although but one pace awry at first, it has led me hundreds and hundreds of miles out of my path." It is only after the mortification of the rape and Clarissa's final, unplanned escape from Mrs. Sinclair's house that Clarissa can fully acknowledge the wisdom of Judith Norton's advice to submit patiently to God and not despair: "for is it not GOD who governs the world, and permits some things, and directs others, as He pleases? And will He not reward *temporary sufferings*, innocently incurred, and piously supported, with *eternal felicity?*" Clarissa's final pride, perfected through suffering and an understanding of her heart, manifests itself in complete passivity and submission:

> I will do everything I can do to convince all my friends, who hereafter may think it worth their while to inquire after my last behaviour, that I possessed my soul with tolerable patience . . . for thus, in humble imitation of the sublimest Exemplar, I often say: Lord, it is Thy will; and it shall be mine. Thou art just in all Thy dealings with the children of men; and I know Thou wilt not afflict me beyond what I can bear: and, if I *can* bear it, I *ought* to bear it; and (Thy grace assisting me) I *will* bear it.

The counterpoint to Clarissa's divine progress is provided throughout the novel by the actions of Lovelace, the self-proclaimed libertine who undermines his own desperate search for the providential promise of Clarissa by the very art with which he pursues her. Lovelace is the fallen artificer, variously referring to himself as a puppet master, a conjurer, a general, a dramatist. His heroes are pagan rather than Christian, and the characteristic quality of his personality is the capricious energy that erupts in countless strategies of craft and guile. His multifarious plots are the products of a confused and restless imagination; the intricate machinations spin off from the clash of his three warring passions: love, revenge, and pride. As Clarissa realizes, Lovelace has no active conscience; his only "heart" is "a plotting villain of a heart" that courts damnation by toying with providence. In a triumphant letter to Belford, Lovelace applauds the device of his forged letter to Miss Howe: "If thou art capable of taking in all my *providences*, in this letter, thou wilt admire my sagacity and contrivance almost as much as I do myself."

But all of Lovelace's "sagacity and contrivance" can only turn in upon itself, for, in the providential pattern of Richardson's world, any exertion of will is necessarily frustrated by God's larger design. As Clarissa predicts, Lovelace becomes his own punisher. The puppets he set in motion at Mrs. Sinclair's house suddenly snap their strings and initiate Clarissa's arrest, thus compounding Lovelace's guilt and grief. And the emptiness of his "conquest" of Clarissa drives him into a paroxysm of frustration and despair. "I am a machine at last," he moans, "and no free agent." "What a devil are all my plots come to! What do they end in, but one grand plot upon myself, and a title to eternal infamy and disgrace!"

If the absolute and quotidian realms are conceptualized as mutually exclusive, then participation of any kind in the temporal world is necessarily contaminating. It is this assumption that governs the choice of Job as a model for heroism and the frustration of Lovelace's energy. Richardson can only fictionalize the pattern of absolute perfection as alien to this world but as growing out of its fallen state. Any action, because it contributes either directly or indirectly to the providential design, must initiate the progress of Clarissa's salvation. She transcends the world, proves God's promise, and demonstrates, through her spiritual development, the poverty of the particularized community she leaves behind.

It is Fielding's conception of the coexistence of the absolue and mundane worlds that determines the characteristically metaphorical mode of his fiction. In *Tom Jones* social situations and behavior do not simply constitute components of the temporal plot but also provide vehicles for the controlling providential metaphor. The scene of Tom's imprisonment, for instance, does not derive its power from the wealth of physical detail that distinguishes the equivalent passage in *Clarissa*, for, beyond Mrs. Waters's observation that Tom's face is "more miserable than any dungeon in the universe," we are provided no particulars at all. Tom's incarceration is only incidentally physical; in its most important sense it is a metaphorical expression of his spiritual condition. Having feigned a marriage proposal to Lady Bellaston, having lost Sophia through his imprudence, and having stabbed a man in confused self-defense, Tom is trapped by the consequences of his indiscretion (book 18, chap. 1). The rendition of this spiritual dungeon in terms of its physical counterpart points to Fielding's assumption of the ideal continuity between the abstract and the concrete, between spiritual and physical realms.

Part of the difficulty of discussing this fundamental dimension of Fielding's art resides in an imprecise and colloquial use of our critical vocabulary. Key episodes and encounters in *Tom Jones* have been variously described as paradigms, symbols, allegories, and emblems, but each of these terms, while suggesting the crucial correspondences of the plot with spiritual, absolute reality, seems to minimize the significance of the temporal action of the novel. The story of *Tom Jones*, unlike that of such a conventional allegory as *The Faerie Queene*, is "primary and autonomous"; Tom is not only a sort of Everyman but also the attractive, generous, occasionally indiscreet young man that Sophia loves; his exile from and return to Paradise Hall is not only a figure for his spiritual progress but also represents a plausible pattern of human experience. Because the word *metaphor* suggests a correspondence in which the *signifiant* is as meaningful as the *signifié*, that term protects the significance of the temporal action of the novel. *Metaphor* also insists upon a necessary resemblance between vehicle and tenor, thus stressing the specificity of the relationship between temporal actions and their absolute counterparts that a term like *symbol*, with its imprecise denotation, cannot suggest.

The "iconomatic impulse" [as Martin C. Battestin terms it] which directs Fielding's metaphorical mode suggests a vision of human nature as static and definable. As Robert Alter notes, there is, in Fielding's novels, a "metaphysical certainty about identity which implies a novelistic certainty about character, so that character in his fiction is less fluctuating, finally less dynamic, than it is in the work of most other major novelists." This conception of static character is revealed in part through the procedure by which characters are introduced. Whatever temporary blindnesses Squire Allworthy's good nature might occasion, he is essentially possessed of and distinguished by those qualities with which he is initially identified: "an agreeable person, a sound constitution, a sane understanding, and a benevolent heart" (book 1, chap. 2). Thus the movement of Fielding's fiction is not toward delineating the complexities of character, but toward the ultimate clarification of those essential qualities by which each character is defined. In the introductory chapter to book 8, Fielding discusses the importance of "conservation of character," the maintenance of consistency of action and character. Once defined and set in motion, each character must fulfill the logic of his or her static personality; progress is defined not by development but by clarification.

What keeps this kind of characterization from resulting in a perfectly predictable plot are the encrustations of "affectation" which shroud individual actions with a cloak of momentarily deluding appearances. Blifil's liberation of Sophia's bird could originate in generous motives; the philosopher Square's apparent moral righteousness seems to emanate from his professed Platonism. But the development of plot in *Tom Jones* relentlessly exposes the hypocrisy of such pretense and moves toward the essence rather than appearance of character through action. The penetrating vision which permits the author to identify the "true Ridiculous" through the discovery of affectation is for Fielding the characteristic impulse of art, designated both as "genius" and "invention." In the introductory chapter to book 9 he characterizes "genius" as "that power, or rather those powers of the mind, which are capable of penetrating into all things within our reach and knowledge, and of distinguishing their essential differences"— and "invention" as "discovery, or finding out . . . a quick and sagacious penetration into the true essence of all the objects of our contemplation." The celebrated scene in Molly Seargrim's bedroom revealing the philosopher Square in the nakedness of his true desires typifies the thrust of Fielding's art. Through a process of exposure and clarification he consistently illuminates the single impulse that motivates and defines character.

Fielding's elaborate machinery of plot yields a variety of incidents and encounters, the function of which is to provide a number of partial insights into the contortions of affectation. The depths of Blifil's selfishness are plumbed through repeated depictions of his contrivances. His mercenary lust for Sophia, his continued manipulation of truth and the lawyer Dowling clarify the essential malignity of his heart. The intricacy of deceit which complicates the action of the novel emerges from Blifil's self-serving imagination but results in a relentless pursuit of the villainy which perpetrates Tom's persecution.

With respect to Fielding's "mixed characters"—those figures whose essential good qualities are tainted by temporary weaknesses or flaws— the range of incidents of Fielding's plot also provides a proving ground— in these cases, for the deleterious effects of moral frailty. The shortsightedness of Allworthy, the blustering stubbornness of Western, and the impetuous exuberance of Tom are temporary deterrents to the expression of their distinguishing good natures. To varying degrees each character stands in need of prudence, "that perspicacity of moral *vision* which alone permits us to perceive the truth behind appearances and to proceed from the known to the obscure." The complication of plot depends in part upon the snowballing of the consequences of these imprudences: Allworthy's misinterpretation of Tom's exultation drives Tom into exile; Western's refusal to attend to Sophia's heart frightens her into flight; and Tom's repeated sexual indulgences alienate Sophia and embroil him with Lady Bellaston. By the nadir of Tom's imprisonment the consequences of imprudence are clear. Each of the various incidents manifests Tom's essential spiritual condition, clarifying his need for purification, the realization of the providential promise.

Thus despite the range of episodes in *Tom Jones*, external action does not contribute to internal development. In the case of each character the final purification is the result of narrative fiat. With the same dramatic suddenness that characterized Square's exposure, a single letter dispels Allworthy's blindness and explodes Blifil's elaborate deceit. Western acknowledges his daughter's good sense, and Tom embraces in Sophia all the wisdom he has lacked. " 'The delicacy of your sex cannot conceive the grossness of ours, nor how little one sort of amour has to do with the heart.'—'I will never marry a man,' replied Sophia, very gravely, 'who shall not learn refinement enough to be incapable as I am myself of making such a distinction.'—'I will learn it,' said Jones. 'I have learnt it already. The first moment of hope that my Sophia might be my wife taught it me at once' " (book 18, chap. 12). This instantaneous purification of character obliterates the complexity of affectation that permitted the complication of the plot and solidifies character into concept. Tom's marriage to Sophia is the metaphorical expression of the union of energy and wisdom. Their implied issue is the promise of generous, prudential social behavior.

Because the incidents of the providential plot of *Tom Jones* bear an additive as well as causal relationship to each other, the absolutism of action that determined Clariss'a development is meaningless in the world of Fielding's novel. Individual actions cannot define character; consequently, even Tom's multiple indiscretions do not indicate or occasion material moral blemishes. In book 7 Fielding defines the relativity of action. "A single bad act no more constitutes a villain in life than a single bad part on the stage. The passions, like the managers of a playhouse, often force men upon parts without consulting their judgment,and sometimes without any regard to their talents. Thus the man, as well as the player, may condemn what he himself acts; nay, it is common to see vice sit as awkwardly on some men, as the character of Iago would on the honest face of Mr. William Mills" (book 7, chap. 1). The metaphorical expression of the course of salvation in the relative terms of social behavior militates against absolute judgment. The final narrative purification subsumes individual indiscretions and fulfills our initial impression of Tom's good nature.

The abiding sympathy which predisposes us to pardon Tom's temporary lapses of judgment is aroused and sustained by the repeated interpolations of the narrator. Early in the novel, in the depiction of Tom's potentially compromising protection of Black George, the narrator informs us that Tom is possessed of that principle "whose use is not so properly to distinguish right from wrong, as to prompt and incite . . . to the former, and to restrain and withhold . . . from the latter" (book 4, chap. 6). Tom is, in other words, distinguished by innate good nature and is constantly attentive to the decisions of the "Lord High Chancellor" of his mind. As suggested by this image, conscience is for Fielding, as for Richardson, an innate faculty of judgment and guidance. But unlike Richardson, Fielding is not concerned with the gradual sharpening of Tom's inner vision. Clarissa's original pride blinds her to the evidence of God in her own heart, but Tom, as the narrator here suggests, never loses sight of that intuitive faculty which unfailingly "presides, governs, directs, judges, acquits, and condemns according to merit and justice." It is this feeling heart that guarantees that even Tom's apparent culpability in the relationship with Lady Bellaston is merely a momentary and rectifiable indiscretion. The narrator sustains our sympathy for Tom throughout the novel by means of similar didactic asides, repeatedly interrupting the action to comment upon the generosity of Tom's motives, the overriding benevolence of his heart. These narrative interpolations serve an additional function, for, as a true providential surrogate, the narrator guarantees the comic structure of the whole. Despite his protestations against the use of supernatural machinery, the narrator's self-conscious and absolute control pervades and directs the flow of action of the novel. "This work," he reminds critics in the introduction to book 10 "may, indeed, be considered as a great creation of our own."

Because actions metaphorically express spiritual states in *Tom Jones*, by controlling the flow of action the narrator also controls the work's metaphorical structure. His insistence upon Tom's essential goodness delineates the tenor of the novel's informing metaphor, guaranteeing the ultimate validation of the providential pattern despite the relative terms its expression assumes. The comic structure, not only of the overall epic movement, but of each particular incident, is insured. Once he establishes the pattern of alternating catastrophe and recovery, the potential calamities that threaten to overturn the comic structure—Allworthy's misunderstanding, Tom's incarceration, the charge of incest—no longer jeopardize our expectations. In a world presided over by a deity distinguished by a "good heart . . . capable of feeling," felicitous resolution is simply a matter of the unfolding of the design.

Similarly, by emphasizing the truly "mixed" nature of Tom's spiritual condition through the juxtaposition of imprudent actions (metaphors for Tom's impure state), and exercises of charity (metaphors for his potential regenerated state), the narrator demonstrates both the continuing need for spiritual purification and its implied realization. In this movement from metaphors of fallen action to those of unfallen action is the outline of the providential pattern which informs the whole. The narrator's ultimate fiat of purification simply fulfills the promised design.

The repeated metaphorical affirmations of that design directly affect our responses to the emotional states of the characters. Whereas in *Clarissa* our sympathies are directly engaged, as tragic overtones arise from detailed descriptions of the heroine's anguish, in *Tom Jones* the narrator's commentary replaces particularized description, militating against engagement and immediately subsuming the tragic in the comic context. In the scene in *Tom Jones* equivalent to the imprisonment of Clarissa, for instance, the narrator does not detail Tom's agony, thus avoiding any tragic implications. "Of the present situation of Mr. Jones's mind, and of the pangs with which he was now tormented, we cannot give the reader a better idea than by saying, his misery was such that even Thwackum would almost have pitied him. But, bad as it is, we shall at present leave him in it, as his good genius (if he really had any) seems to have done. And here we put an end to the sixteenth book of our history" (book 16, chap. 10). The same power that permits the narrator to curtail the episode enables him to generate and fulfill our expectations in the realization of the promise he momentarily threatens to withhold.

Fielding's choice of quotidian terms for the metaphorical representation of the providential pattern suggests his overriding interest in the social expression of spiritual behavior. In the introduction to book 15, he distinguishes between the "cardinal virtues which, like good housewives, stay at home, and mind only the business of their own family" and "a certain relative quality which is always busying itself with-out-doors, and seems as much interested in pursuing the good of others as its own." It is clearly this active good nature with which Fielding is concerned. As the tightfisted Parson Trulliber in *Joseph Andrews* proves, knowledge of virtue is meaningless in this world unless it overflows into action. Fielding's definition of good nature stresses the necessarily social dimension of that essential quality: "Good-Nature is that benevolent and amiable Temper of Mind which disposes us to feel the Misfortunes, and enjoy the Happiness of others; and consequently pushes us on to promote the latter, and prevent the former." Consistent with the emphasis of the latitudinarian divines on good works rather than faith as the determinant of salvation, Tom's charity to Black George, the Old Man of the Hill, Mrs. Waters, and Mrs. Miller's daughter represents metaphorically the active role which good nature must take in the quest for salvation.

Because the absolute and quotidian worlds can coexist through metaphor, action is fulfillment rather than defiance of the providential plan. Thus the model for Tom's heroism (as, more obviously, for that of Parson Adams in Fielding's first novel) is not Job but Abraham. Representing human faith expressed in works rather than passivity, Abraham, in his role as pilgrim in search of a homeland, perfectly prefigures Tom's exile from and return to Paradise Hall.

The conception of the coexistence of absolute and temporal worlds that informs *Tom Jones* also dictates the consolidation of spiritual and ethical obligations. Thus the fulfillment of social duty proceeds from and satisfies the heart. The profound conflict which arises in *Clarissa* between public and private obligation is replaced, in *Tom Jones*, by a concept of reciprocity. Fielding's doctrine of good works emphasizes "the glorious Lust of doing Good," the self-serving but not selfish aspect of charity. When Sophia's "scrupulous obedience" to her father is questioned, she responds with this explanation: " 'You mistake me, madam, if you think I value myself upon this account; for besides that I am barely discharging my duty, I am likewise pleasing myself. I can truly say I have no delight equal to that of contributing to my father's happiness' " (book 6, chap. 10). Similarly, Tom considers his intercessions in behalf of the Old Man of the Hill and Mrs. Waters as mere discharges of "the common duties of humanity" (book 8, chap. 10; book 9, chap. 2). Because the absolute is represented in terms of such action, these expressions of Tom's generous heart are ultimately rewarded by Sophia, Wisdom herself.

There are questions in literature that continue to perplex. For me, as for many of Richardson's contemporaries, one such puzzle has been the necessity of Clarissa's death. Tom Jones can realize his reward in this world, but Clarissa must leave her father's house in order to reach its divine counterpart. This exploration of assumption and design has had that dichotomy constantly in sight. I think the recognition of Richardson's rigorously realistic conception of the temporal world begins to offer some answers. Richardson conceives of the fallen world in its realistic particulars, and the absolute nature of Clarissa's consolation cannot be represented in the details of compromise. Fielding's conception of the metaphorical relationship between this world and the next explains his much brighter landscape. In the artistic representation of the world as a figure of spiritual reality, temporal effort both earns and mirrors the providential promise. Prudence is a rational faculty; Clarissa's conscience is God's oracle. The one facilitates practical expression of a generous heart; the other precludes compromise in a less than perfect world.

Comic Resolution in Fielding's
Joseph Andrews

Mark Spilka

Though the night adventures at Booby Hall are among the most memorable scenes in *Joseph Andrews*, many scholars tend to ignore them or to minimize their importance. Generally speaking, they pluck the adventures out of context and file them away—out of sight, out of mind—among even more colorful bedroom antics within the picaresque tradition. Thus, J. B. Priestley writes:

> Such chapters of accidents are very familiar to students of the *picaresque,* and all that need be said of this one is that there is some slight relation to character in it . . . but that it is not enough to make the episode anything more than a piece of comic business of a very familiar type. Smollett could bustle through such rough-and-tumble business just as well, if not better.

Priestley is right as far as he goes, but he forgets that *Joseph Andrews* is more novel than picaresque tale and that the novel requires special handling. In the picaresque tale there is little or no dramatic connection between one episode and the next, and the critic can lift things out of context to his heart's content. But with the more fully developed novel form he must show how an episode—lifted *from* a tradition—has been fitted *into* the scheme of a given book. Certainly this is the proper approach to the escapades at Booby Hall, the last major comic scenes in *Joseph Andrews*—scenes which involve all the major characters in the book and both aspects of the central theme, the lust-chastity theme.

Yet with all this in mind it may still be argued that the Booby Hall affair is a simple comic interlude, or diversion, which Fielding inserted at

From *College English* 15, no. 1 (October 1953). © 1953 by the National Council of Teachers of English.

the most crucial point in the novel to increase suspense and at the same time to vary the fare. On the surface there is some truth to this assertion: the night adventures are sandwiched between the all-important chapters in which the incest problem is first introduced then happily solved. But the argument breaks down before a simple comparison: in the famous knocking-at-the gate scene in *Macbeth,* the commonplace is used (according to De Quincey) to offset and heighten the essential strangeness and horror of murder; if the "diversion" argument holds true, the same function should be performed by the bedroom scenes in *Joseph Andrews;* but as any honest reader will admit, these scenes perform precisely the opposite function— that is, they neither increase nor heighten the dramatic intensity of the incest plot; rather, they lessen its seriousness and achieve a special importance of their own. In the next chapter, for example, the company are "all very merry at breakfast, and Joseph and Fanny rather more cheerful than the preceding night"; it becomes obvious that some sort of emotional purgation has occurred and that the resolution of the main plot will be anticlimactic.

All this seems normal enough for a comedy based on character rather than on situation. As Aurelien Digeon points out, "The ending is necessarily the weak point in works of this kind. It is almost always engineered from without; for passions never stop working nor come to an 'end.' " Unfortunately, Digeon fails to add here that if passions never stop working, they are sometimes resolved, and that it is the business of a good comic writer to resolve them. In the night adventures at Booby Hall, Fielding has done just that; with the aid of condensed, violent action, he has stood his book on its head, shaken out all the themes and passions, and resolved them through warmhearted laughter. If this interpretation seems far-fetched, its essential soundness may become evident as we pay more attention to the lust-chastity theme, to Fielding's theory of humor, to the role of nakedness in the novel, and, finally, to two of the most comic figures in the book, Parson Adams and Mrs. Slipslop. As for the other relevant characters—Joseph Andrews, Fanny Goodwill, Lady Booby, and Beau Didapper—we need only note here that the first two embody all the natural health, goodness, and beauty which Fielding admired, while the last two embody much of the vice and artificiality he deplored.

II

In order to parody Richardson's *Pamela,* Fielding built *Joseph Andrews* around a central moral problem: the preservation of (and the assault upon) chastity. On the one hand, Joseph Andrews must protect his virtue from such lustful creatures as Lady Booby, Mrs. Slipslop, and Betty the chambermaid; on the other, Fanny Goodwill must withstand the attacks of a beau, a squire, a rogue, and a servant. But as most writers have observed, the scope of the novel is much broader than this. Fielding saw affectation in two of its forms, vanity and hypocrisy, as the "only source of the true Ridiculous," and he hoped to expose these qualities wherever he found them. Accordingly, he also designed his novel along more general lines: three virtuous, good-natured persons—Joseph, Fanny, and Adams—must be thrust through every level of society as exemplars or as touchstones and instruments for exposing vanity and hypocrisy, and, just as important, goodness and kindness, in whomever they meet. Adams will be the foremost touchstone, since his religious position and his personal traits—innocence, simplicity, bravery, compassion, haste, pedantry, forgetfulness—will always pitch him into a good deal of trouble; yet, once in trouble, his virtues will make him stand out in complete contrast to those who take advantage of him. Finally, in his perfect innocence he will always be the main instrument for exposing his own mild affectations.

But, as these remarks indicate, Adams's position is somewhat ambiguous with regard to Fielding's formula for the ridiculous in humor. Like his predecessor, Don Quixote, he cuts a bizarre figure outwardly, but, at the same time, his inner dignity remains unassailable: as Joseph Andrews tells us, true virtue can never be ridiculed, and we know that Adams, however outlandish, is truly virtuous—so that he stands half within Fielding's theory of humor and half without. (In book 3, chapter 6, Joseph says, "I defy the wisest man in the world to turn a good action into ridicule. . . . He, who should endeavour it, would be laughed at himself, instead of making others laugh.") But this theory is, after all, static and reductive rather than organic. Through shrewd analysis Fielding has called attention to the affectations, the *particular* qualities which make men appear in a ridiculous light. But through his admiration for Cervantes he has unconsciously seized on the principle of the *comic figure*—the whole man who is at once lovable and ridiculous, whose entire character is involved in each of his humorous actions, and whose character must be established through time and incident, in the reader's mind, before he becomes "wholly" laughable. To put it in different terms, when someone we know and like is involved in a ridiculous action, then the humor of the situation broadens and quickens to include our identification with and sympathy for that person. A sudden or prolonged juxtaposition of his inner dignity with his outer "awkwardness" produces a state of mixed emotions in us—love, sympathy, and identification, as well as condescension—and this state is released or resolved, in turn, through laughter. The point can be made clearer perhaps through a modern analogy: the amorphous Keystone Cops amuse us (at least they used to) in accord with Fielding's theory of the ridiculous—that is to say, they lose their false outer dignity in falls and madcap fights; yet when Charlie Chaplin puts up a magnificent bluff in the boxing ring (as in *City Lights*), our laughter becomes much warmer and far more sympathetic in quality—Chaplin's bluff may be ridiculous, but the man who bluffs is brave, and we have learned something of this through time, situation, and the development of character; we are prepared, that is, for his simultaneous display of inner dignity and outer vanity in the boxing ring, and our laughter is accordingly that much richer. One Keystone Cop is much like the next but Chaplin has become a unique and appealing figure in our eyes—and in a similar manner so has Parson Adams. Our respect, love, and admiration for Adams continue to grow through the length of *Joseph Andrews*. And only when his character has been firmly established in our minds (and in the same vein, only when the lust-chastity theme has been worked for all it is worth) can the night scenes at Booby Hall occur. Place these scenes earlier in the book and they will strike us as meaningless horseplay; but at the end of the book we are prepared for them—Parson Adams is now familiar to us as a well-developed comic figure, and his nakedness strikes us with symbolic force.

As a matter of fact the spectacle of nakedness is significantly common (though not always symbolic) in *Joseph Andrews*. Fanny, Joseph, Adams, Lady Booby, Mrs. Slipslop, Beau Didapper, Betty the chambermaid, Mr. Tow-wouse—all appear at one time or another and for various reasons, in a state of partial or complete undress. In the early chapters, for example, Joseph is beaten and stripped by robbers and left on the road to die; when a carriage passes, Fielding "tests" each of the passengers by his willingness to accept Joseph *as he is*, for what he is—a defenseless human being. And late in the book, when Adams appears in a nightshirt (the usual eighteenth-century equivalent for nakedness), Fielding tests, in effect, *our* willingness as good-natured readers, to take Adams for what he is. It should not surprise us, therefore, that a definite symbolic equation between nakedness, on the one hand, and innocence and worth, on the other, occurs in other portions of Fielding's work: Squire Allworthy also appears in his nightshirt, for example, in the opening pages of *Tom Jones*; and in *The Champion* for January 24, 1740, Fielding even cites Plato to the effect that men would love virtue if they could see her naked. This platitude is put to good use in *Joseph Andrews*, though the problem there is too "expose" or "lay bare" both virtue and affectation, often in the same man.

With regard to affectation, Fielding's theory of the ridiculous fits in well with our "nakedness" theme. Affectations are "put on," and it is the humorist's job (or more properly the satirist's) to "strip them off." This much Fielding knew by rote from his earliest published work, a poem against masquerades, to his attack on masquerades in his last novel, *Amelia*: take off the mask, remove the outer pretense, and expose the "bare facts" which lie beneath—vanity, hypocrisy, smugness. But his chief accomplishment, as well as his chief delight, was to distinguish between a man's defects and his essential goodness; and we think in this respect of Adams, Tom Jones, Captain Booth, and dozens of the minor creations. If a man is good-natured "at bottom," then the problem for the novelist is how to get to the bottom. Fielding usually arrives there by playing off the man's faults against his virtues, as when Adams first cautions Joseph against immoderate grief, then grieves immoderately, like any compassionate man, at the news of his son's supposed drowning. But a more pertinent example occurs in one of the inn scenes in *Joseph Andrews*, when Fanny faints and Adams, in his haste to rescue her, tosses his precious copy of Aeschylus into the fire. Here Adams has literally stripped off an affectation while revealing his natural goodness—the book is a symbol, that is, of his pedantry, of his excessive reliance upon literature as a guide to life, and this is what is tossed aside during the emergency. Later on, when the book is fished out of the fire, it has been reduced to its simple sheepskin covering—which is Fielding's way of reminding us that the contents of the book are superficial, at least in the face of harsh experience. Thus the whole incident underscores the fact that Adams's faults, like his torn, disordered clothes, are only the outward, superficial aspects of his character and that the essential Adams, a brave, good man, lies somewhere underneath; his heart—not his Aeschylus, not his harmless vanity—is his true guide in all things of consequence.

Mrs. Slipslop is another matter. She is usually praised by critics as the well-rounded comic foil to Lady Booby. But she is something more than this, since her lust for Joseph, and for all manner of men, is more natural and appealing than Lady Booby's hot-and-cold passion. To begin with, Mrs. Slipslop is an unbelievably ugly maidservant who, after an early slip, has remained virtuous for many years. Now, at forty-five, she has resolved to pay off "the debt of pleasure" which she feels she owes to herself. Though Fielding heavily ridicules her vanity and hypocrisy throughout the book, he also brings out the pathetic strain in her makeup, and at times he even reveals an author's fondness for a favorite creation. Mrs. Slipslop may rail at Joseph, for example, but unlike Lady Booby she will never turn him out into the street; in fact, she save or aids him on several important occasions; but, more than all this, there is something almost touching, as well as ridiculous, about her faulty speech, her grotesque body, and her foolish dream of becoming "Mrs. Andrews, with a hundred a-year." All in all, she is a comic figure in her own right, as well as a comic foil, and if Fielding deals her a sound drubbing in the night scenes at Booby Hall, he also "deals" her a last warm laugh.

III

Fielding beds down his entire cast at Booby Hall in preparation for the night adventures. Then, when the household is asleep, he sends Beau Didapper off to ravish Fanny through trickery, and the round of fun begins. By mistake, Didapper enters Mrs. Slipslop's pitch-dark room and, posing as Joseph, tells her that the incest report was false, and that he can delay the enjoyment of her charms no longer; then he climbs into bed with her. She receives him willingly enough—her dream come true—but the two of them soon discover their mutual error. Ever-prudent, Mrs. Slipslop now sees her chance to win back her reputation for chastity, which she had damaged through recent conduct with Lawyer Scout; so she hugs Didapper even more firmly, calls out for help, and Parson Adams comes running to her rescue from the next chamber. But in his haste Adams has forgot to put on any clothes, and this action is far more characteristic of him than any we have yet seen in the novel. For Adams has now become his own true symbol: he stands there as God made him, all courage and kindness, with his affectations, his clothes, left in a heap behind him. He is now the naked truth, quite literally and lovably, and he is never more himself than at this moment, not even while throwing his Aeschylus into the fire to save Fanny. He is brave, true virtue on the march now, stripped clean of all encumbrance and far beyond the reach of ridicule—for true virtue, as we have already see, can never be ridiculed. Of course, Adams is laughable because he is naked and imprudent and we are not; but mainly he arouses those feelings to which we have been conditioned, with regard to him, from the beginning of the novel. For as Fielding and Plato have told us, men will love virtue if they see her—or in this case him—naked. We see him naked now, and we laugh, to a great extent, out of love. But let us return for a moment to the goings-on in Mrs. Slipslop's bedroom.

Obeying, of all things, the dictates of common sense, Adams now passes over the small, whimpering body—obviously the woman—and proceeds to grapple with the large bearded one—obviously the man. Here Fielding ridicules, in Slipslop and Didapper, that vanity by which one poses as a seducible woman and the other as a virile man. For the small body (Beau Didapper) escapes, and Slipslop receives an almost fatal beating. But Lady Booby, attracted by all the noise, enters the room in the nick of time with lighted candle in hand. At which point Adams discovers both his error and his nakedness and leaps under the covers with Mrs. Slipslop. We have then, in one corner of the bed, Vice posing as Virtue, which is hypocrisy; and in the other corner, Virtue hiding its "lovable" nakedness and apparently acting as Vice—which is false, foolish modesty at the very least. And we also have, as Lady Justice with the Lighted Candle, Lady Booby, the far from blinded villainess of the novel.

Shall we stop a moment to straighten things out? We have already seen that vanity has been exposed to ridicule—a normal enough procedure. But now we can see that virtue itself has been exposed to some sort of laughter; moreover, it has been exposed in a worthless cause—until Adams arrived and began pummeling Mrs. Slipslop, no one was in any real danger. This reminds us at once of Don Quixote, and the comparison enables us to see that virtue has been confounded rather than ridiculed and that we laugh once more, in the main, out of sympathy for a brave man in an awkward fix. (This is also Adams's first "real" windmill and therefore the most quixotic moment in the book. Until now Adams's rescues have been much to the point and more or less successful, since Fielding always attempted to show that virtue can be a successful way of life—hence Adams's vigor, his robust strength, is eventual muddling through. As a knight-errant, he is generally far more effective than the gallant Quixote).

There is more to it than this, however. We have been neglecting Mrs. Slipslop, who at long last has had not one but two men in her bed (simultaneously!), but who has been forced by circumstance to reject them both. The sex-starved maiden, with her mountainous breasts and her spur-of-the-moment virtue, has been soundly trounced. In a very real sense this is Waterloo for the prudent gentlewoman, and for the lust half of the lust-chastity theme as well. All, all is resolved through a burst of laughter, though again through laughter of a special kind. In a parody on *Pamela*, one of two lusting ladies (both foils for Richardson's clumsy Mrs. B) was bound to receive a severe comeuppance. Fielding, the sure comic artist, chose the more comic figure; but the very condition which makes Slipslop appear so ridiculous in our eyes—the extreme distance between her desires and her qualifications—also makes her appeal to the warm side of our (and Fielding's) sense of humor. She is a far less harsh figure than Lady Booby and therefore the more proper bed companion for the equally harmless, "sexless," but virtuous Parson Adams.

Nevertheless, we must return to Lady Booby, at the scene of the alleged rape, for the key to all these resolutions and reversals. After berating Adams as a wicked cleric, the stern hostess spies Didapper's telltale cufflinks on the floor. Then, when she hears Adams's story, when she takes in "the figures of Slipslop and her gallant, whose heads only were visible at the opposite corners of the bed," she is unable to "refrain from laughter." For once, then, Lady Booby appears in a good light: until now she has behaved in a completely selfish manner, but the kind of laughter which we cannot withhold *in spite of ourselves*, stems more from the heart than the ego. Even the opinionated Mrs. Slipslop now checks her tongue, and it becomes apparent that evil itself has been dissolved by some strange power. We can say, of course, that Lady Booby laughs at a maid and a parson who are far too old and ridiculous for zealous modesty; but, more to the point, she laughs at Adams's lovable innocence, and perhaps she laughs at herself as well, at her own defeat; for, as we have observed, Mrs. Slipslop is in part her comic foil, and Parson Adams now lies in the place where Joseph Andrews might have lain, if her own hopes had been fulfilled.

At any rate, a general absolution has obviously just occurred: through elaborate contrivance (the creation of Beau Didapper as catalytic agent, the convenient rainstorm, the crisis in the main plot, Slipslop's affair with Lawyer Scout, and so on) Fielding has brought Adams before us in all his nakedness. The good parson has never seemed so ridiculous, nor has he ever been burdened so heavily with the guilt which rightfully belongs to those around him—to Slipslop, to Didapper, to Lady Booby, and even to you and me, as we stand behind the bold hostess in judgment of the scene and see our own sins revealed by flickering candlelight—yet Adams emerges untarnished from under this double burden of guilt and ridicule, and, like the true comic hero, he absolves us all with his naïve triumph over circumstance: for good and bad men alike have a common stake in that perfect, naked innocence which can force a Lady Booby, or even a

Peter Pounce to grin or laugh from some buried store of benevolence. (In book 3, chapter 12, the normally severe Peter Pounce is also forced to grin at the sight of Adams's bedraggled figure. In the same manner, a misanthrope might grin at a mud-spattered child: the outer ridiculousness is reinforced by inward innocence in both Adams and the child, and the responsive grin or laugh is basically sympathetic.) All this is nicely underscored, I think, when the lady retires once more and the scene at hand, which opens with naked Adams running characteristically to the rescue, now closes with naked Slipslop sliding lustfully, pathetically, characteristically, and as Fielding puts it, "with much courtesy," across the bed toward Parson Adams, who takes the hint and quickly leaves the room. One can't help thinking that at long last, among all those thorns, Fielding has placed a rose for Mrs. Slipslop—for the last warm laugh is hers, in a madcap world where virtue is masked as vice, and vice as virtue, while, in the unmasking, warmheartedness prevails over all morality.

In the next half of the chapter things begin to settle down. Adams, in his haste, inadvertently takes the wrong turn; he climbs quietly into what he thinks is his own bed and prepares for sleep. But in reality the poor man has moved directly from the bed of the ugliest, most indiscriminately lustful woman in the book to that of the loveliest and most chaste. On the other side of him lies Fanny "Goodwill" Andrews (not yet Joseph's wife but his supposed sister) in profound, peaceful, naked slumber; and Fielding promptly reminds us that Adams has done what every red-blooded man in the novel has been trying to do, unsuccessfully, since book 2, chapter 9: he has climbed into bed with Fanny:

> As the cat or lap-dog of some lovely nymph, for whom ten thousand lovers languish, lies quietly by the side of the charming maid, and, ignorant of the scene of delight on which they repose, meditates the future capture of a mouse, or surprisal of a plate of bread and butter, so Adams lay by the side of Fanny [writes Fielding], ignorant of the paradise to which he was so near.

The book has now come full circle, for not only Fanny's incomparable charms but her priceless chastity as well are treated with the utmost indifference by the one man who has succeeded, so far, in sharing her bed; nor is she in any real danger, for his man, this cat or lap dog, neither knows nor cares, nor would care if he knew, about the "paradise" beside him; he simply wants to go to sleep. We can safely say, then, that the lust-chastity theme has been fully and ironically resolved or, if you will, stood on both its ears.

But it is daybreak now, and Joseph Andrews has come for an innocent rendezvous with Fanny. When he raps at the door, the good-natured, hospitable parson calls out, "Come in, whoever you are." Consternation follows, and for the first time in the novel the three paragons of virtue, the three touchstones, are at complete odds with one another. Adams is again burdened with undeserved guilt and can only blame the affair on witchcraft; but, once he recounts his story, Joseph explains to him that the must have taken the wrong turn on leaving Slipslop's room. Then Fielding makes a significant emendation: he has already told his readers that the naked Adams is wearing a nightcap; now he reminds them that he is also wearing the traditional knee-length nightshirt—all this in deference, perhaps, to Fanny's modesty but nevertheless a sign that things are back to normal once more and that the naked truth no longer roams through the halls of night. Fanny and Joseph forgive the parson with the indulgence one shows to an innocent child, and again the scene ends on a benevolent note.

What are we to make of night adventures which serve as a kind of parody on the whole novel; which apparently involve no real problems but in which lust and self-love appear, momentarily, in an almost friendly light; in which chastity is ignored, brave virtue confounded, and a whole comic method thrown thereby into reverse? One solution seems obvious: by sending his beloved parson from bed to bed, Fielding has put a kind of comic blessing upon the novel; he has resolved the major themes and passions through benevolent humor. Or to push on to a more inclusive theory, the comic resolution in *Joseph Andrews* depends for its warmth upon the flow of sympathy which Fielding creates between his readers and his comic figures; for its bite, upon his ridicule and deflation of those figures; and for its meaning, upon the long-range development of character and theme, as well as the local situation at Booby Hall. Apparently Fielding, like Parson Adams, did not always practice the simple theories he preached. But as Adams insists at the close of the night adventures, there is such a thing as witchcraft, and perhaps this is what Fielding practiced upon Adams and upon his readers, and with a good deal of awareness of what he was doing.

Fielding as Novelist: *Tom Jones*

Ian Watt

Literature yields few more interesting causes célèbres than the debate over
the respective merits of the novels of Fielding and Richardson, a debate
which continues today even though during the last century or so the sup-
porters of Fielding have been in almost complete command of the field.
The main reason for the vitality of the controversy is the exceptional range
and variety of the issues—the opposition is not only between two kinds
of novel, but between two kinds of physical and psychological constitution
and between two social, moral and philosophical outlooks on life. Not only
so: the dispute has the advantage of a spokesman whose strong and paradoxical support for Richardson acts as a perennial provocation to the sup-
porters of Fielding, who are dismayed to find Dr. Johnson, the authoritative
voice of neoclassicism, pronouncing anathema on the last full embodiment
of the Augustan spirit in life and literature.

One way of resolving this last difficulty has been to suggest that Dr.
Johnson's attitude should not be taken too seriously because it was dictated
by friendship and personal obligation—Richardson had once saved him
from being arrested for debt. Johnson's critical judgment, however, was
not usually at the mercy of such considerations, and the supposition in
any case runs counter to the fact that his enthusiastic endorsement of
Richardson's novels was accompanied by a merciless awareness of the
shortcomings of the man—witness his lethal jibe that Richardson "could
not be content to sail quietly down the stream of reputation without longing
to taste the froth from every stroke of the oar."

We should, then, consider Johnson's preference seriously, particularly
in view of the consistency with which he recurred to his main charge. "All

From *The Rise of the Novel: Studies in Defoe, Richardson and Fielding.* © 1957 by Ian Watt.
University of California Press, 1962.

the difference between the characters of Fielding and those of Richardson," he maintained, according to Boswell, was that between "characters of manners" and "characters of nature." "Characters of manners," of course, Johnson ranked much lower on the grounds that although "very entertaining . . . they are to be understood by a more superficial observer than characters of nature, where a man must dive into the recesses of the human heart." This distinction between Richardson and Fielding was more memorably expressed when Johnson said that "there was as great a difference between them as between a man who knew how a watch was made, and a man who could tell the hour by looking on the dial plate"; and the same idea is present in the even more plainly invidious statement reported by Mrs. Thrale that "Richardson had picked the kernel of life . . . while Fielding was contented with the husk."

The basic distinction does not involve any direct divergence from critical orthodoxy, but it perhaps does so implicitly, since the basis of Richardson's "diving into the recesses of the human heart" was his detailed description of individual states of mind, a description which requires a minute particularly in the presentation of character, and which is therefore contrary to the usual neoclassical bias towards the general and the universal. There is no doubt that Johnson's theoretical presuppositions were strongly in this direction, as he often proclaimed the doctrine that the poet "must not dwell on the minuter distinctions by which one species differs from another." Yet his operative premises for fiction were apparently quite different, since he reproached Fielding for his reluctance to dwell on these very distinctions, telling Mrs. Thrale, for example, that "Fielding could describe a horse or an ass, but he never reached to a mule."

It would seem, then, that Johnson's vigorously independent literary sensibility tended to confirm at least one of the elements of the opposition described [elsewhere] between neoclassical theory and the novel's formal realism. As for the discrepancy between Johnson's literary theory and his practical judgment, it need occasion little surprise: any body of doctrine is ambiguous in some of its applications, and especially when it is applied in areas for which it was not originally designed. In any case, Johnson's neoclassicism was not a simple thing (neither, for that matter, was neoclassicism); and his divergence from his usual principles in the present instance must surely be regarded as yet another example of how the radical honesty of his literary insight raised fundamental issues so forcibly that later criticism cannot but use his formulations as points of departure; any comparison between the two first masters of the novel form certainly must begin from the basis which he provided.

I

Tom Jones and *Clarissa* have sufficient similiarity of theme to provide several closely parallel scenes which afford a concrete illustration of the differences between the methods of Fielding and Richardson as novelists. Both, for example, show us scenes where the heroine is forced to receive the addresses of the hated suitor their parents have chosen for them, and both also portray the later conflict between father and daughter which their refusal to marry this suitor provokes.

Here, first, is how Fielding describes the interview between Sophia Western and the odious Blifil:

> Mr. Blifil soon arrived; and Mr. Western soon after withdrawing, left the young couple together.
>
> Here a long silence of near a quarter of an hour ensued; for the gentleman, who was to begin the conversation, had all that unbecoming modesty which consists in bashfulness. He often attempted to speak, and as often suppressed his words just at the very point of utterance. At last, out they broke in a torrent of far-fetched and high-strained compliments, which were answered on her side by downcast looks, half bows, and civil monosyllables.—Blifil, from his inexperience in the ways of women, and from his conceit of himself, took this behaviour for a modest assent to his courtship; and when, to shorten a scene which she could no longer support, Sophia rose up and left the room, he imputed that, too, merely to bashfulness, and comforted himself that he should soon have enough of her company.
>
> He was indeed perfectly well satisfied with his prospect of success; for as to that entire and absolute possession of the heart of his mistress, which romantic lovers require, the very idea of it never entered his head. Her fortune and her person were the sole objects of his wishes, of which he made no doubt soon to obtain the absolute property; as Mr. Western's mind was so earnestly bent on the match; and as he well knew the strict obedience which Sophia was always ready to pay to her father's will, and the greater still which her father would exact, if there was occasion.
>
> (book 6, chap. 7)

Structurally, the scene is based on that typical device of comedy, total ignorance by one character of the intentions of the other as a result of a misunderstanding between third parties—Squire Western has been misled by the ineffable Mistress Western into thinking that Sophia loves Blifil, not Tom Jones. It is perhaps because this misunderstanding must be kept up that there is no actual conversation and little feeling of personal contact between the characters concerned. Instead, Fielding, acting as omniscient author, lets us into Blifil's mind, and the meanness of the considerations by which it is governed: at the same time the consistent irony of Fielding's tone suggests to us the probable limits of Blifil's role: we need not fear that he will ever get possession of Sophia's fortune or of her person, for, although he is cast as a villain, it is patently as the villain in comedy.

Blifil's misunderstanding of Sophia's silence leads on to the next comic complication, since it causes him to give Squire Western the impression that his suit has prospered. Western at once goes to rejoice with his daughter, who of course is unaware of how he has been deceived:

Sophia, perceiving her father in this fit of affection, which she did not absolutely know the reason of (for fits of fondness were not unusual in him, though this was rather more violent than ordinary), thought she should never have a better second opportunity of disclosing herself than at present, as far at least as regarded Mr. Blifil; and she too well foresaw the necessity which she should soon be under of coming to a full explanation. After having thanked the squire, therefore, for all his professions of kindness, she added with a look full of inexpressible softness, "And is it possible that my papa can be so good as to place all his joy in his Sophy's happiness?" which Western having confirmed by a great oath and a kiss, she then laid hold of his hand, and falling on her knees, after many warm and passionate declarations of affection and duty, she begged him "not to make her the most miserable creature on earth, by forcing her to marry a man she detested. This I entreat of you, dear sir," she said, "for your sake, as well as my own, since you are so very kind to tell me your happiness depends on mine."—'How! What!" says Western, staring wildly. "O, sir," continued she, "not only your poor Sophy's happiness, her very life, her being, depends upon your granting her request. I cannot live with Mr. Blifil. To force me into this marriage would be killing me."—"You can't live with Mr. Blifil!" says Mr. Western—"No, upon my soul, I can't," answered Sophia.—"Then die and be d—ned," cries he, spurning her from him . . . "I am resolved upon the match, and unless you consent to it, I will not give you a groat, not a single farthing; no, though I saw you expiring in the street, I would not relieve you with a morsel of bread. This is my fixed resolution, and so I leave you to consider on it." He then broke from her with such violence, that her face dashed against the floor; and he burst directly out of the room, leaving poor Sophia prostrate on the ground.

Fielding's primary aim is certainly not to reveal character through speech and action. We cannot be meant to deduce, for instance, that Sophia knows her father so poorly as to entertain any hopes of being able to hold him down to one position by force of logic; what Fielding tells us about Sophia's decision to break the matter to her father is obviously mainly aimed at heightening the comic reversal that is to follow. Similarly we cannot consider Western's threat—"No, though I saw you expiring in the street, I would not relieve you with a morsel of bread"—as characteristic of the man either in diction or sentiment—it is a hackneyed trope that belongs to any such situation in melodrama, not to a particular Squire who habitually speaks the most uncouth Somersetshire jargon, and whose childish intemperateness is not elsewhere shown capable of such an imaginative flight. To say that Sophia's and Western's speeches are grossly out of character would be an exaggeration; but they are undoubtedly directed entirely towards exploiting the comic *volte-face* and not towards making us witnesses of an actual interview between a father and daughter in real life.

It is probably an essential condition for the realisation of Fielding's comic aim that the scene should not be rendered in all its physical and psychological detail; Fielding must temper our alarm for Sophia's fate by assuring us that we are witnessing, not real anguish, but that conventional kind of comic perplexity which serves to heighten our eventual pleasure at the happy ending, without in the meantime involving any unnecessary expenditure of tears on our part. Fielding's external and somewhat preemptory approach to his characters, in fact, would seem to be a necessary condition of the success of his main comic purpose: attention to the immediate counterpoint of misunderstanding and contradiction must not be dissipated by focussing interest on Sophia's feelings or on any other tangential issue.

A total contrast of purpose and method is offered by the way Richardson presents Clarissa's interview with Solmes, after her maid Hannah has warned her secretly that he is the husband that has been decided on for her. It is thus described in a letter to Anna Howe:

> I went down this morning when breakfast was ready with a very uneasy heart . . . wishing for an opportunity to appeal to my mother, in hopes to engage her interest in my behalf, and purposing to try to find one when she retired to her own apartment after breakfast; but, unluckily, there was the odious Solmes sitting asquat between my mother and sister, with *so much* assurance in his looks! But you know, my dear, that those we love not cannot do anything to please us.
>
> Had the wretch kept his seat, it might have been well enough: but the bent and broad-shouldered creature must needs rise and stalk towards a chair; which was just by that which was set for me.
>
> I removed it to a distance, as if to make way to my own: And down I sat, abruptly I believe; what I had heard all in my head.
>
> But this was not enough to daunt him. The man is a very confident, he is a very bold, staring man! Indeed, my dear, the man is very confident!
>
> He took the removed chair and drew it so near mine, squatting in it with his ugly weight, that he pressed upon my hoop. I was so offended (all I had heard, as I said, in my head) that I removed to another chair. I own I had too little command of myself. It gave

my brother and sister too much advantage. I dare say they took it. But I did it involuntarily, I think. I could not help it. I knew not what I did.

I saw that my father was excessively displeased. When angry, no man's countenance ever shows it so much as my father's. Clarissa Harlowe! said he with a big voice—and there he stopped. Sir! said I, trembling and curtsying (for I had not then sat down again): and put my chair nearer the wretch, and sat down—my face, as I could feel, all in a glow.

Make tea, child, said my kind mamma: sit by me, love, and make tea.

I removed with pleasure to the seat the man had quitted; and being thus indulgently put into employment, soon recovered myself; and in the course of the breakfasting officiously asked two or three questions of Mr. Solmes, which I would not have done, but to make up with my father. *Proud spirits may be brought to!* whisperingly spoke my sister to me over her shoulder, with an air of triumph and scorn: but I did not mind her.

My mother was all kindness and condescension. I asked her once if she were pleased with the tea . . .

Small incidents these, my dear, to trouble you with; only as they lead to greater, as you shall hear.

Before the usual breakfast-time was over my father withdrew with my mother, telling her he wanted to speak to her. Then my sister and next my aunt (who was with us) dropped away.

My brother gave himself some airs of insult, which I understood well enough; but which Mr. Solmes could make nothing of: and at last he arose from *his* seat. Sister, says he, I have a curiosity to show you. I will fetch it. And away he went; shutting the door close after him.

I saw what all this was for. I arose; the man hemming up for a speech, rising and beginning to set his splay feet (indeed, my dear, the man in all his ways is hateful to me!) in an approaching posture. I will save my brother the trouble of bringing to me his curiosity, said I. I curtsied—your servant, sir. The man cried, madam, madam, twice, and looked like a fool. But away I went—to find my brother to save my word. But my brother, indifferent as the weather was, was gone to walk in the garden with my sister. A plain case that he had left his *curiosity* with me, and designed to show me no other.

The passage is characteristic of Richardson's very different kind of realism. Clarissa is describing what happened "this morning," and is "as minute as" she knows Anna wishes her to be; only so can Richardson convey the physical reality of the scene—the party at breakfast, the jockeying for position over trifles, and all the ordinarily trivial domestic details which bear the main burden of the drama. The letter form gives Richardson access to thoughts and emotions of a kind that cannot issue in speech, and are hardly capable of rational analysis—the flux and reflux of Clarissa's lacerated sensibility as she struggles against parental tyranny on the battlefield of petty circumstance: as a result we have quite a different kind of participation from that which Fielding produces: not a lively but objective sense of the total comic pattern, but a complete identification with the consciousness of Clarissa while her nerves still quiver from the recollection of the scene, and her imagination recoils from the thought of her own strained alternation between involuntary revolt and paralysed compliance.

Because Richardson's narrative sequence is based on an exploration in depth of the protagonist's reaction to experience, it encompasses many minor shades of emotion and character that are not found in the passages from *Tom Jones*. Fielding does not attempt to do more than to make us understand the rational grounds on which Sophia acts as she does—there is nothing which would not fit almost any sensible young girl's behaviour in the circumstances: whereas Richardson's epistolary technique, and the intimacy of Clarissa with Anna, encourages him to go far beyond this, and communicate a host of things which deepen and particularise our picture of Clarissa's total moral being. Her shuddering ejaculation—"Indeed, my dear, the man is very confident," her scornful comment on her sister's intervention—"I did not mind her," and her admission of involvement in petty family rivalries—she regrets moving away from Solmes because "It gave my brother and sister too much advantage"—all these details of characterisation must surely be overlooked by those who describe Richardson as a creator of "ideal" characters: there is, of course, great will and tenacity in Clarissa, but it is very definitely that of an inexperienced young woman, who has her fair share of sisterly vindictiveness and pert self-assertion, and who, far from being an idealised figure of virgin sainthood, is capable of the catty and sardonic emphasis on Mr. Solmes as a "curiosity." Nor is she by any means a disembodied being; we have no indications of any physical reaction on Sophia's part toward Blifil, but we are given Clarissa's very intense one to Solmes—an instinctive sexual revulsion from "his ugly weight."

The same setting of personal relationship in a minutely described physical, psychological and even physiological continuum is shown in the brief scene which is the counterpart of the second passage quoted from *Tom Jones*. After two private interviews with her mother, Clarissa has been faced with a family ultimatum, and her mother is with her to receive an answer:

Just then, up came my father, with a sternness in his looks that made me tremble. He took two or three turns about my chamber, though pained by his gout. And then said to my mother, who was silent, as soon as she saw him:

My dear, you are long absent. Dinner is near ready. What you had to say lay in a very little compass. Surely, you have nothing to do but to declare *your* will, and *my* will—but perhaps you may be talking of the preparations. Let us soon have you down—your daughter in your hand, if worthy of the name.

And down he went, casting his eye upon me with a look so stern that I was unable to say one word to him, or even for a few minutes to my mother.

Richardson and Fielding portray the cruelty of the two fathers very differently; that of Squire Western has an involuntary and exaggerated quality, whereas Mr. Harlowe's is that of ordinary life; the latter's callous resolve seems all the more convincing because it is only manifested in his refusal to speak to Clarissa—our own emotional involvement in the inner world of Clarissa makes it possible for a father's silent look to have a resonance that is quite lacking in the physical and rhetorical hyperbole by which Fielding demonstrates the fury of Squire Western.

II

On further analysis, then, it appears that Johnson's comparison between Richardson and Fielding does not directly raise the question of which was the better psychologist, but depends rather on their quite opposite literary intentions: those of Fielding alotted characterisation a much less important place in his total literary structure, and precluded him even from attempting the effects which were suited to Richardson's very different aim. The full implications of the divergence can perhaps be most clearly and inclusively demonstrated in Fielding's handling of the plot in *Tom Jones*, for it reflects the whole of his social, moral and literary outlook.

Fielding's conduct of the action, despite a few excrescences such as the interpolated story of the Man of the Hill, and some signs of haste and confusion in the concluding books, exhibits a remarkably fine control over a very complicated structure, and abundantly justifies Coleridge's famous eulogy: "What a master of composition Fielding was! Upon my word, I think the *Oedipus Tyrannus*, the *Alchemist*, and *Tom Jones*, the three most perfect plots ever planned."

Perfect for what? we must ask. Not, certainly, for the exploration of character and of personal relations, since in all three plots the emphasis falls on the author's skillfully contrived revelation of an external and deterministic scheme: in *Oedipus* the hero's character is of minor importance compared with the consequences of his past actions, which were themselves the result of a prophecy made long before his birth; in the *Alchemist* the portrayal of Face and Subtle does not go far beyond the need for suitable instruments to carry out Johnson's complex series of chicaneries; while the plot of *Tom Jones* offers a combination of these features. As in Sophocles, the crucial secret, that of the hero's actual birth, is very elaborately prepared for and hinted at throughout the action, and its eventual disclosure brings about the final reordering of all the main issues of the story: while, as in Johnson, this final reordering is achieved through the unmasking of a complicated pattern of villainy and deception.

The three plots are alike in another respect: their basic direction is towards a return to the norm, and they therefore have a fundamentally static quality. In this they no doubt reflect the conservatism of their authors, a conservatism which in Fielding's case is probably connected with the fact that he belonged, not to the trading class like Defoe and Richardson, but to the gentry. The plots of the novels of Defoe and Richardson, as we have seen [elsewhere], mirrored certain dynamic tendencies in the outlook of their class: in *Moll Flanders,* for example, money has a certain autonomous force which determines the action at every turn. In *Tom Jones,* on the other hand, as in the *Alchemist,* money is something that the good characters either have or are given or momentarily lose: only bad characters devote any effort either to getting it or keeping it. Money, in fact, is a useful plot device but it has no controlling significance.

Birth, on the other hand, has a very different status in *Tom Jones:* as a determining factor in the plot it is almost the equivalent of money in Defoe or virtue in Richardson. In this emphasis, of course, Fielding reflects the general tenor of the social thought of his day: the basis of society is and should be a system of classes each with their own capacities and responsibilities. The vigour of Fielding's satire on the upper classes, for example, should not be interpreted as the expression of any egalitarian tendency: it is really a tribute to the firmness of his belief in the class premise. It is true that in *Amelia* he goes so far as to say that "of all kinds of pride, there is non so unChristian as that of station." But that, of course, is only a matter of noblesse oblige; and in *Tom Jones* Fielding also wrote that "liberality of spirits" was a quality which he had "scarce ever seen in men of low birth and education" (book 9, chap. 1).

This class fixity is an essential part of *Tom Jones.* Tom may think it unfortunate that, as a foundling of presumed low ancestry, he cannot marry Sophia; but he does not question the propriety of the assumption on which their separation is decreed. The ultimate task of Fielding's plot therefore is to unite the lovers without subverting the basis of the social order; and this can only be done by revealing that Mr. Jones, though illegitimate, is genteel. This, however, is not wholly a surprise to the perceptive reader, for whom Tom's eminent "liberality of spirit" has already suggested his superior pedigree; the recent Soviet critic, therefore, who sees the story as the triumph of a proletarian hero is neglecting, not only the facts of his birth, but its continuing implications for his character.

Fielding's conservatism accounts for another and much more general difference between the plots of *Tom Jones* and *Clarissa:* for whereas Richardson depicts the crucifixion of the individual by society, Fielding portrays the successful adaption of the individual to society, and this entails a very different relation between plot and character.

In *Clarissa* the individual must be given priority in the total structure: Richardson merely brings together certain individuals, and their proximity is all that is necessary to set off an extended chain reaction which then proceeds under its own impetus and modifies all the characters and their mutual relationships. In *Tom Jones*, on the other hand, society and the larger order which it represents must have priority, and the plot's function, therefore, is to perform a physical rather than a chemical change: it acts as a kind of magnet that pulls every individual particle out of the random order brought about by temporal accident and human imperfection and puts them all back into their proper position. The constitution of the particles themselves—the characters—is not modified in the process, but the plot serves to reveal something much more important—the fact that all human particles are subject to an ultimate invisible force which exists in the universe whether they are there to show it or not.

Such a plot reflects the general literary strategy of neoclassicism; just as the creation of a field of force makes visible the universal laws of magnetism, so the supreme task of the writer was to make visible in the human scene the operations of universal order—to unveil the handiwork of Pope's "Unerring Nature, still divinely bright, / One clear, unchanged and universal light."

This much wider perspective on character obviously reduces the importance which will be attached to the nature and actions of any particular individual entity—they are mainly interesting as manifestations of the great pattern of Nature. This informs Fielding's treatment of every aspect of characterisation—not only the extent to which his dramatis personae are individualised, but the degree of attention paid to their subjective lives, to their moral development, and to their personal relationships.

Fielding's primary objectives in the portrayal of character are clear but limited: to assign them to their proper category by giving as few diagnostic features as are necessary for the task. Such was his conception of "invention" or "creation": "a quick and sagacious penetration into the true essence of all the objects of our contemplation" (book 9, chap. 1). This meant in practice that once the individual had been appropriately labelled the author's only remaining duty was to see that he continued to speak and act consistently. As Aristotle put it in the *Poetics*, "character" is "that which reveals the moral purpose," and consequently "speeches . . . which do not make this manifest . . . are not expressive of character." Parson Supple must never cease to be supple.

So it is that Fielding does not make any attempt to individualise his characters. Allworthy is sufficiently categorised by his name, while that of Tom Jones, compounded as it is out of two of the commonest names in the language, tells us that we must regard him as the representative of manhood in general, in accordance with his creator's purpose to show "not men, but manners; not an individual, but a species."

The scope of the word "manners" has dwindled so drastically in the last few centuries—no doubt as a result of the way individualism has reduced the areas in which identity of thought and action is generally expected—that the phrase "characters of manners" no longer means very much. It can perhaps be best explained in terms of the contrast with Richardson's "characters of nature." Richardson's literary objective, as B. W. Downs has pointed out, is not so much character—the stable elements in the individual's mental and moral constitution—as personality: he does not analyse Clarissa, but presents a complete and detailed behavioural report on her whole being: she is defined by the fullness of our participation in her life. Fielding's purpose, on the other hand, is analytic: he is not interested in the exact configuration of motives in any particular person's mind at any particular time but only in those features of the individual which are necessary to assign him to his moral and social species. He therefore studies each character in the light of his general knowledge of human behaviour, of "manners," and anything purely individual is of no taxonomic value. Nor is there any need to look inside: if, as Johnson said, Fielding gives us the husk, it is because the surface alone is usually quite sufficient to identify the specimen—the expert does not need to assay the kernel.

There are many other reasons for Fielding's predominantly external approach to character, reasons of a social and philosophical as well as of a literary order. To begin with, the opposite approach involved a breach of decorum: as Fielding's cousin Lady Mary Wortley Montagu pointed out, it was very bad manners for Richardson's heroines to "declare all they think," since "fig leaves are as necessary for our minds as our bodies." It was also consistent with the classical tradition as a whole, as we have seen, to avoid the intimate and confessional approach to personality; and in any case the philosophical problems of self-consciousness had only begun to receive attention some six centuries after Aristotle in the works of Plotinus. Lastly, as was evident in the treatment of Blifil and Sophia, Fielding's comic purpose itself required an external approach, and for a compelling reason. If we identify ourselves with the characters we shall not be in any mood to appreciate the humour of the larger comedy in which they are risible participants: life, we have been told, is a comedy only to the man who thinks, and the comic author must not make us feel every stroke of the lash as his characters squirm under his corrective rod.

At all events, Fielding avowedly and even ostentatiously refused to go too deep into the minds of his characters, on the general grounds that "it is our province to relate facts, and we shall leave causes to persons of much higher genius" (book 2, chap. 4). We have noted how little was said about the feelings, as opposed to the rational determinations, of Blifil and Sophia. This was quite conscious on Fielding's part: he had already remarked ironically of Blifil that "it would be an ill office in us to pay a visit to the inmost recesses of his mind, as some scandalous people search into the most secret affairs of their friends, and often pry into their closets and cupboards, only to discover their poverty and meanness to the world"; similarly when Fielding came to present Sophia's feelings when she first learned of Tom's love, he excused himself in the words: "as to the present situation of her mind I shall adhere to the rule of Horace, by not attempting to describe it, from despair of success" (book 4, chaps. 3 and 14).

Fielding's avoidance of the subjective dimension, then, is quite intentional: but that does not, of course, mean that it has no drawbacks, for it undoubtedly has, and they become very apparent whenever important emotional climaxes are reached. Coleridge, for all his love of Fielding, pointed out that in the soliloquies between Sophia and Tom Jones before their final reconciliation, nothing could be "more forced and unnatural: the language is without vivacity or spirit, the whole matter is incongruous, and totally devoid of psychological truth." In fact, Fielding merely gave us a stock comic scene: elevated sentiments of penitent ardour on the hero's part were countered by wronged womanhood's equally elevated scorn of her faithless suitor. Soon after, of course, Sophia accepts Tom, and we are surprised by her very sudden and unexplained reversal: the dénouement has been given a certain comic life, but at the expense of the reality of emotions involved.

This emotional artificiality is very general in *Tom Jones*. When the hero, for instance, is expelled from Allworthy's house we are told that "he presently fell into the most violent agonies, tearing his hair from his head, and using most other actions which generally accompany fits of madness, rage and despair"; and later that he read Sophia's parting letter "a hundred times over, and kissed it a hundred times as often" (book 6, chap. 12). Fielding's use of these hackneyed hyperboles to vouch for the intensity of the emotions of his characters underlines the price that he pays for his comic approach: it denies him a convincing and continuous access to the inner life of his characters, so that whenever he has to exhibit their emotional life, he can only do it externally by making them have exaggerated physical reactions.

The fact that Fielding's characters do not have a convincing inner life means that their possibilities of psychological development are very limited. Tom Jones's character, for example, exhibits some development, but it is of a very general kind. Tom's early imprudences, his youthful lack of worldly wisdom, and his healthy animality, for example, lead to his disgrace, his expulsion from the Allworthy household, his subsequent difficulties on the road and in London, and his apparently irrecoverably loss of Sophia's love. At the same time his good qualities, his courage, honour and benevolence, all of which have been glimpsed at the beginning, eventually combine to extricate him from the nadir of his misfortunes, and restore him to the love and respect of those who surround him. But although different qualities come to the fore at different times they have all been present from the beginning, and we have not been taken close enough to Tom's mind to be able to do anything but take on trust Fielding's implication, which is that his hero will be able to control his weaknesses by the wisdom he has learned of experience.

In taking this essentially static view of human nature Fielding was following the time-hallowed Aristotelian view, which was actually held with much greater rigidity by most of the philosophers and literary critics of his time. It is, of course, an a-historical view of character, as Fielding showed in *Joseph Andrews,* when he asserted that his characters were "taken from the life," but added that the particular lawyer in questions was "not only alive, but hath been so this four thousand years." It follows logically that if human nature is essentially stable, there is no need to detail the processes whereby any one example of it has reached its full development; such processes are but temporary and superficial modifications of a moral constitution which is unalterably fixed from birth. Such, for example, is the premise of the way that although Tom and Blifil share the same mother and are brought up in the same household by the same tutors, their respective courses are unalterably set in different directions from the very beginning.

Once again the contrast with Richardson is complete. Much of our sense of Clarissa's psychological development arises from the way that her experience brings a continual deepening of her understanding of her own past: as a result character and plot are indivisible. Tom Jones, on the other hand, is not in touch with his own past at all: we feel a certain unreality in his actions because they always seem to be spontaneous reactions to stimuli that the plot has been manipulated to provide; we have no sense that they are manifestations of a developing moral life. We cannot but feel surprise, for instance, when, immediately after accepting fifty pounds from Lady Bellaston, Tom gives his famous lecture to Nightingale on sexual ethics. It is not that the two actions are inherently contradictory—Tom's ethics have throughout been based on the much greater heinousness of harming others than of failing to live up to one's moral code oneself; but if we had been given some indication that Tom was aware of the apparent contradictions between his speech and his own past practice he might have sounded less priggish and more convincing. Actually, of course, separate parts of Tom's nature can hold very little converse with each other, because there is only one agency for such converse—the individual consciousness through which the whole repertoire of past actions operates—and Fielding does not take us into this consciousness because he believes that individual character is a specific combination of stable and separate predispositions to action, rather than the product of its own past.

For the same reasons personal relationships are also relatively unimportant in *Tom Jones.* If there is a controlling force independent of the individual actors and their positions with respect to each other, and if their own characters are innate and unchanging, there is no reason why Fielding should give close attention to their mutual feelings, since they cannot play a decisive role. Here, again, the scene between Sophia and Blifil was typical in that it reflected the extent to which the structure of *Tom Jones* as a whole depends on the lack of any effective communication between the characters: just as Blifil must misunderstand Sophia, so Allworthy must fail to see Blifil in his true light, and Tom must be unable either to understand Blifil's true nature or to explain himself properly either to Allworthy or Sophia until the closing scenes. For, since Fielding's view of human life and his general literary purpose did not permit him to subordinate his plot to the deepening exploration of personal relationships, he needed a structure based on an elaborate counterpoint of deception and surprise, and this would be impossible if the characters could share each other's minds and take their fates into their own hands.

There is, then, an absolute connection in *Tom Jones* between the treatment of plot and of character. Plot has priority, and it is therefore plot which must contain the elements of complication and development. Fielding achieves this by superimposing on a central action that is, in essentials as simple as that in *Clarissa*, a very complex series of relatively autonomous subplots and episodes which are in the nature of dramatic variations of the main theme. These relatively independent narrative units are combined in a concatenation whose elaboration and symmetry is suggested in the most obvious outward aspect of the book's formal order: unlike the novels of Defoe and Richardson, *Tom Jones* is carefully divided into compositional units of different sizes—some two hundred chapters which are themselves grouped into eighteen books disposed into three groups of six, dealing respectively with the early lives, the journeys to London, and the activities on arrival, of the main characters.

This extreme diversification of the narrative texture reinforces, of course, Fielding's tendency not to dwell for long on any one scene or character. In the passages quoted, for example, there was none of the intensive treatment which Richardson gave to Clarissa's interview with Solmes; most of Fielding's time was spent on making clear the initial misunderstanding, and the scale of the scene allowed no more in the way of characterisation than a designing hypocrite, a trapped maiden and a heavy father. But even if there had been any full absorption in the feelings of Sophia, for example, it would soon have been terminated by the management of the ensuing scenes: for, just as we left Sophia immediately after Squire Western had stormed out of the room, and were thus spared any prolonged awareness of her sufferings, so in the next chapter our attention was soon switched away from her parting interview with Tom Jones by Fielding's announcement that "the scene, which I believe some of my readers will think had lasted enough, was interrupted by one of so different a nature, that we shall reserve the relation of it for a different chapter" (book 6, chap. 8).

This is typical of the narrative mode of *Tom Jones:* the author's commentary makes no secret of the fact that his aim is not to immerse us wholly in his fictional world, but rather to show the ingenuity of his own inventive resources by contriving an amusing counterpoint of scenes and characters; quick changes are the essence of Fielding's comic manner, and a new chapter will always bring a new situation for the characters, or present different characters in a similar scene for ironical contrast. In addition, by a great variety of devices, of which the chapter headings are usually significant pointers, our attention is continually drawn to the fact that the ultimate cohesive force of the book resides not in the characters and their relationships, but in an intellectual and literary structure which has a considerable degree of autonomy.

The effects of this procedure and its relationship to Fielding's treatment of character can be summarised in relation to a brief scene which occurs after Tom has heard that Allworthy is to recover from his illness. He takes a walk "in a most delicious grove," and contemplates the cruelty of fortune which separates him from his beloved Sophia:

> Was I but possessed of thee, one only suit of rags thy whole estate, is there a man on earth whom I would envy! How contemptible would the brightest Circassian beauty, dressed in all the jewels of the Indies, appear to my eyes! But why do I mention another woman? Could I think my eyes capable of looking at any other with tenderness, these hands should tear them from my head. No, my Sophia, if cruel fortune separates us for ever, my soul shall dote on thee alone. The chastest constancy will I ever preserve to thy image. . . .
>
> At these words he started up and beheld—not his Sophia—no, nor a Circassian maid richly and elegantly attired for the grand Signior's seraglio,
>
> (book 5, chap. 10)

but Molly Seagrim, with whom, "after a parley" which Fielding omits, Tom retires to "the thickest part of the grove."

The least convincing aspect of the episode is the diction: the speech habits manifested here obviously bear little relation to those we expect of Tom Jones. But, of course, they are a stylistic necessity for Fielding's immediate purpose—the comic deflation of the heroic and romantic pretences of the human word by the unheroic and unromantic eloquence of the human deed. Tom Jones is no more than a vehicle for the expression of Fielding's scepticism about lovers' vows; and he must be made to speak in terms that parody the high-flown rhetoric of the pastoral romance to give point to the succeeding wayside encounter which belongs to the very different world of the *pastourelle*. Nor can Fielding pause to detail the psychological processes whereby Tom is metamorphosed from Sophia's romantic lover to Moll's prompt gallant: to illustrate the commonplace that "actions speak louder than words," the actions must be very silent and they must follow very hard upon very loud words.

The relation of this episode to the larger structure of the novel is typical.

One of Fielding's general organising themes is the proper place of sex in human life; this encounter neatly illustrates the conflicting tendencies of headstrong youth, and shows that Tom has not yet reached the continence of moral adulthood. The scene, therefore, plays its part in the general moral and intellectual scheme; and it is also significantly connected with the workings of the plot, since Tom's lapse eventually becomes a factor in his dismissal by Allworthy, and therefore leads to the ordeals which eventually make him a worthier mate for Sophia.

At the same time Fielding's treatment of the scene is also typical in avoiding any detailed presentation of Tom's feelings either at the time or later—to take his hero's faithlessness too seriously would jeopardise Fielding's primarily comic intention in the episode, and he therefore manipulates it in such a way as to discourage us from giving it a significance which it might have in ordinary life. Comedy, and especially comedy on an elaborate scale, often involves this kind of limited liability to psychological interpretation: it applies to Blifil's malice and to Sophia's sufferings in the scenes quoted earlier, and Allworthy's sudden illness and recovery, which have led to Tom's lapse, must be placed in the same perspective. We must not dwell on the apparent fact that Allworthy is incapable of distinguishing between a cold and a mortal illness, since we are not intended to draw the implications for his character that he is either an outrageous hypochondriac or lamentably unskilled in choosing physicians: Allworthy's illness is only a diplomatic chill, and we must not infer anything from it except a shift in Fielding's narrative policy.

Tom Jones, then, would seem to exemplify a principle of considerable significance for the novel form in general: namely, that the importance of the plot is in inverse proportion to that of character. This principle has an interesting corollary: the organisation of the narrative into an extended and complex formal structure will tend to turn the protagonists into its passive agents, but it will offer compensatingly greater opportunities for the introduction of a variety of minor characters, whose treatment will not be hampered in the same way by the roles which they are allotted by the complications of the narrative design.

The principle and its corollary would seem to lie behind Coleridge's contrast of the "forced and unnatural quality" of the scenes between the protagonists in *Tom Jones* and Fielding's treatment of the "characters of postilions, landlords, landladies, waiters" where "nothing can be more true, more happy or more humorous." These minor characters figure only in scenes which require exactly the amount of psychological individuality which they are possessed of; relieved of any responsibility for carrying out the major narrative design Mrs. Honour can get herself dismissed from the Western household by methods which are at once triumphantly comic, sociologically perceptive and eminently characteristic; nor is there any question of the violence to character and probability which colours the ways whereby Tom Jones, for example, or Sophia leave home.

Such is the pattern of most comic novels with elaborate plots, from

Fielding and Smollett to Dickens: the creative emphasis is on characters who are minor at least in the sense that they are not deeply involved in the working out of the plot; whereas the Tom Jones's, the Roderick Randoms and the David Copperfields are less convincing as characters because their personalities bear little direct relation to the part they must play, and some of the actions in which the plot involves them suggests a weakness or folly which is probably in variance with the actual intentions of their author towards them.

On the other hand, the type of novel which is perhaps most typical of the genre, and which achieves effects which have not been duplicated in any other literary form, has used a very different kind of plot. From Sterne and Jane Austen to Proust and Joyce the Aristotelian priority of plot over character has been wholly reversed, and a new type of formal structure has been evolved in which the plot attempts only to embody the ordinary processes of life and in so doing becomes wholly dependent on the characters and the development of their relationships. It is Defoe and above all Richardson who provide this tradition with its archetypes, just as it is Fielding who provides that for the opposite tradition.

III

Johnson's most famous criticism of Fielding's novels is concerned with their basic technique, but from his own point of view it was probably their moral shortcomings which were the decisive factor. It is certainly this with which he was concerned in his only published reference to Fielding, although even here it is only by implication. In the *Rambler* (1750) Johnson attacked the effects of "familiar" histories whose wicked heroes were made so attractive that "we lose abhorrence of their faults," apparently with *Roderick Random* (1748) and *Tom Jones* (1749) chiefly in mind. He certainly later told Hannah More that he "scarcely knew a more corrupt work" than *Tom Jones*, and, on the other hand, praised *Clarissa* on the significant grounds that "It was in the power of Richardson alone to teach us at once esteem and detestation; to make virtuous resentment overpower all the benevolence which wit, elegance, and courage naturally excite, and to lose at last the hero in the villain."

We find it difficult today to share much of Johnson's abhorrence of the morality of *Tom Jones* and are, indeed, more likely to be unjust to Richardson, and to assume without question that his concern, and that of his heroines, for feminine chastity, can only be explained by prurience on his part or hypocrisy on theirs. But this may not be so, and, conversely, we must in fairness recognise that there are many moral offences in *Tom Jones* which receive a much more tolerant treatment than any Puritan moralist would have accorded them. Defoe and Richardson, for example, are unsparing in their denunciation of drunkenness; but when Tom Jones gets drunk in his joy at Allworthy's recovery, Fielding shows no reprobation: it is admittedly an imprudence which later contributes to the hero's expulsion, but Fielding's only direct comment is a humorous editorial development of the in vino veritas commonplace.

It is the sexual issue, however, which is crucial, both in the moral scheme of *Tom Jones*, and in the objections of its critics. Fielding certainly does not endorse his hero's incontinence, and Tom himself admits that he has been "faulty" in this respect; but the general tendency throughout the novel is surely to qualify the condemnation and make unchastity appear a venial sin—even the good Mrs. Miller, for example, seems to think she has put a fairly good face on matters by pleading to Sophia that Tom has "never been guilty of a single instance of infidelity to her since . . . seeing her in town" (book 18, chap. 10).

Fielding's plot obviously does not punish the sexual transgressions either of Tom Jones or of the many other characters who are guilty in this respect so severely as Richardson, for example, would have wished. Even in *Amelia*, where Booth's adultery is both more serious in itself than anything that can be charged against Tom Jones, and is treated much more severely by Fielding, the plot eventually rescues Booth from the consequences of his acts. There is therefore considerable justification for Ford Madox Ford's denunciation of "fellows like Fielding, and to some extent Thackeray, who pretend that if you are a gay drunkard, lecher, squanderer of your goods and fumbler in placket holes you will eventually find a benevolent uncle, concealed father or benefactor who will shower on you bags of ten thousands of guineas, estates, and the hands of adorable mistresses—these fellows are dangers to the body politic and horribly bad constructors of plots."

Ford, of course, chooses to disregard both Fielding's positive moral intentions and the tendency of comic plots in general to achieve a happy ending at the cost of certain lenity in the administration of justice. For—although Fielding was long regarded as something of a debauchee himself and did not indeed have full justice done to his literary greatness until scholarship had cleared him of the charges made by contemporary gossip and repeated by his first biographer, Murphy—Fielding was in fact as much of a moralist as Richardson, although of a different kind. He believed that virtue, far from being the result of the suppression of instinct at the behest of public opinion, was itself a natural tendency to goodness or benevolence. In Tom Jones he tried to show a hero possessed of a virtuous heart, but also of the lustiness and lack of deliberation to which natural goodness was particularly prone, and which easily led to error and even to vice. To realise his moral aim, therefore, Fielding had to show how the good heart was threatened by many dangers in its hazardous course to maturity and knowledge of the world; yet, at the same time and without exculpating his hero, he had also to show that although Tom's moral transgressions were a likely and perhaps even a necessary stage in the process of moral growth, they did not betoken a vicious disposition; even Tom Jones's carefree animality has a generous quality that is lacking in Clarissa's self-centred and frigid virtue. The happy conclusion of the story, therefore, is very far from representing the kind of moral and literary confusion which Ford alleges, and is actually the culmination of Fielding's moral and literary logic.

The contrast between Fielding and Richardson as moralists is heightened by the effects of their very different narrative points of view. Richardson focusses attention on the individual, and whatever virtue or vice he is dealing with will loom very large, and have all its implications reflected in the action: Fielding, on the other hand, deals with too many characters and too complicated a plot to give the single individual virtue or vice quite this importance.

Besides this tendency of the plot, it is also part of Fielding's intention as a moralist to put every phenomenon into its larger perspective. Sexual virtue and sexual vice, for example, are placed in a broad moral perspective, and the results do not always produce the kind of emphasis that the sexual reformer would wish. Fielding knows, for example, and wishes to show, that some marriage designs may be more vicious than the most abandoned profligacy: witness Blifil whose "designs were strictly honourable as the phrase is, that is to rob a lady of her fortune by marriage" (book 11, chap. 4). He knows, too, that moral indignation against promiscuity is not necessarily the result of a real love of virtue: witness the passage in which we are told that "to exclude all vulgar concubinage, and to drive all whores in rags from within the walls is within the power of everyone. This my landlady very strictly adhered to, and this her virtuous guests, who did not travel in rags, would very reasonably have expected from her" (book 11, chap. 3). Here Fielding's Swiftian suavity reminds us of the cruelty and injustice with which complacent virtue is too often associated; but a narrow-minded moralist might see behind the irony a shocking failure to condemn "whores in rags," and even, perhaps, an implicit sympathy for them.

Fielding, then, attempts to broaden our moral sense rather than to intensify its punitive operations against licentiousness. But, at the same time, his function as the voice of traditional social morality means that his attitude to sexual ethics is inevitably normative; it certainly does not, as Boswell said, "encourage a strained and rarely possible virtue," but rather reflects, as Leslie Stephen put it, "the code by which men of sense generally govern their conduct, as distinguished from that by which they affect to be governed in language." Aristotle's Golden Mean is often, perhaps, capable of a certain subversion of rigid ethical principles: and it is perhaps as a good Aristotelian that Fielding comes very close to suggesting that too much chastity in Blifil is as bad as Tom's too little.

There is a further reason why Johnson, who was, after all, an ethical rigorist in his own way, should have found *Tom Jones* a corrupt work. Comedy—if only to maintain an atmosphere of good-humour between audience and participants—often involves a certain complicity in acts and sentiments which we might not treat so tolerantly in ordinary life. Perhaps the most insistent note in *Tom Jones* is Fielding's worldly-wise good humour, and it often persuades us to regard sexual irregularities as ludicrous rather than wicked.

Mrs. Fitzpatrick, for instance, is dismissed with the words: "she lives in reputation at the polite end of town, and is so good an economist that she spends three times the income of her fortune without running into debt" (book 18, chap. 13). Mrs. Fitzpatrick must remain true to character, and yet be included in the happy ending; nor can Fielding upset the conviviality of his final meeting with his readers to express his abhorrence at the lamentable source of income which we must surmise for his character.

On other occasions, of course, Fielding's humour on that perennial comic resource, sex, is much more overt: in *Jonathan Wild*, for example, when the captain of the ship asks the hero "if he had no more Christianity in him than to ravish a woman in a storm?" or in *Tom Jones* when Mrs. Honour gives her celebrated retort to Sophia's "Would you not, Honour, fire a pistol at any one who should attack your virtue?"—"To be sure, ma'am, . . . one's virtue is a dear thing, especially to us poor servants; for it is our livelihood, as a body may say: yet I mortally hate firearms" (book 7, chap. 7). There is, of course, the same broadening tendency in Fielding's humour here as in his treatment of moral issues in general: we must not forget that even the most virtuous indignation is capable of elementary logical fallacies, or that humankind's allegiance to virtue is capable of cautious afterthoughts. But the tacit assumption of much of Fielding's humour is surely one which suggests that "broad-mindedness" in its modern sense, which typically tends to have a sexual reference, is part of the expansion of sympathy to which his novels as a whole invite us: a relish for wholesome bawdy, in fact, is a necessary part of the moral education of a sex-bedevilled humanity: such, at least, was the classical role of comedy, and Fielding was perhaps the last great writer who continued that tradition.

IV

As far as most modern readers are concerned it is not Fielding's moral but his literary point of view which is open to objection. For his conception of his role is that of a guide who, not content with taking us "behind the scenes of this great theatre of nature," feels that he must explain everything which is to be found there; and such authorial intrusion, of course, tends to diminish the authenticity of his narrative.

Fielding's personal intrusion into *Tom Jones* begins with his dedication to the Honourable George Lyttleton, a dedication, it must be admitted, which goes far to justify Johnson's definition of this form of writing—"a servile address to a patron." There are numerous further references in the body of his work to others among Fielding's patrons, notably Ralph Allen and Lord Chancellor Hardwicke, not to mention other acquaintances whom Fielding wished to compliment, including one of his surgeons, Mr. John Ranby, and various innkeepers.

The effect of these references is certainly to break the spell of the imaginary world represented in the novel: but the main interference with the autonomy of this world comes from Fielding's introductory chapters, containing literary and moral essays, and even more from his frequent discussions and asides to the reader within the narrative itself. There is no doubt that Fielding's practice here leads him in completely the opposite direction from Richardson, and converts the novel into a social and indeed into a sociable literary form. Fielding brings us into a charmed circle composed, not only of the fictional characters, but also of Fielding's friends and of his favourites among the poets and moralists of the past. He is, indeed, almost as attentive to his audience as to his characters, and his narrative, far from being an intimate drama which we peep at through a keyhole, is a series of reminiscences told by a genial raconteur in some wayside inn—the favoured and public locus of his tale.

This approach to the novel is quite consistent with Fielding's major intention—it promotes a distancing effect which prevents us from being so fully immersed in the lives of the characters that we lose our alertness to the larger implications of their actions—implications which Fielding brings out in his capacity of omniscient chorus. On the other hand, Fielding's interventions obviously interfere with any sense of narrative illusion, and break with almost every narrative precedent, beginning with that set by Homer, whom Aristotle praised for saying "very little *in propria persona*," and for maintaining elsewhere the attitude either of a dispassionate narrator, or of an impersonator of one of the characters.

Few readers would like to be without the prefatory chapters, or Fielding's diverting asides, but they undoubtedly derogate from the reality of the narrative: as Richardson's friend, Thomas Edwards, wrote "we see every moment" that it is Fielding who "does *personam gerere*," whereas Richardson is "the thing itself." So, although Fielding's garrulity about his characters and his conduct of the action initiated a popular practice in the English novel, it is not surprising that it has been condemned by most modern critics, and on these grounds. Ford Madox Ford, for instance, complained that the "trouble with the English nuvvelist from Fielding to Meredith, is that not one of them cares whether you believe in their characters or not"; and Henry James was shocked by the way Trollope, and other "accomplished novelists," concede "in a digression, a parenthesis or an aside" that their fiction is "only make-believe." James went on to lay down the central principle of the novelist's attitude to his creation, which is very similar to that described above as inherent in formal realism: Trollope, and any novelist who shares his attitude, James says,

> admits that the events he narrates have not really happened, and that he can give the narrative any turn the reader may like best. Such a betrayal of a sacred office seems to me, I confess, a terrible crime; it is what I mean by the attitude of apology, and it shocks

me every whit as much in Trollope as it would have shocked me in Gibbon or Macaulay. It implies that the novelist is less occupied in looking for the truth (the truth of course I mean, that he assumes, the premises that we must grant him, whatever they may be) than the historian, and in so doing it deprives him at a stroke of all his standing room.

("The Art of Fiction")

There is not, of course, any doubt as to Fielding's intention of "looking for the truth"—he tells us indeed in *Tom Jones* that "we determined to guide our pen throughout by the directions of truth." But he perhaps underestimated the connection between truth and the maintenance of the reader's "historical faith." This, at least, is the suggestion of a passage towards the end of *Tom Jones* when he proclaims that he will let his hero be hanged rather than extricate him from his troubles by unnatural means "for we had rather relate that he was hanged at Tyburn (which may very probably be the case) than forfeit our integrity, or shock the faith of our reader" (book 17, chap. 1).

This ironical attitude towards the reality of his creation was probably responsible in part for the main critical doubt which *Tom Jones* suggests. It is, in the main, a very true book, but it is by no means so clear that its truth has, to quote R. S. Crane, been "rendered" in terms of the novel. We do not get the impressive sense of Fielding's own moral qualities from his characters or their actions that we do from the heroic struggles for human betterment which he conducted as a magistrate under the most adverse personal circumstances, or even from the *Journal of a Voyage to Lisbon*; and if we analyse our impression from the novels alone it surely is evident that our residual impression of dignity and generosity comes mainly from the passages where Fielding is speaking in his own person. And this, surely, is the result of a technique which was deficient at least in the sense that it was unable to convey this larger moral significance through character and action alone, and could only supply it by means of a somewhat intrusive patterning of the plot and by direct editorial commentary. As Henry James put it: Tom Jones "has so much 'life' that it amounts, for the effect of comedy and application of satire, almost to his having a mind"; almost, but not quite, and so it was necessary that "his author—*he* handsomely possessed of a mind—[should have] such an amplitude of reflection for him and round him that we see him through the mellow air of Fielding's fine old moralism."

All this, of course, is not to say Fielding does not succeed: *Tom Jones* is surely entitled to the praise of an anonymous early admirer who called it "on the whole . . . the most lively book ever published." But it is a very personal and unrepeatable kind of success: Fielding's technique was too eclectic to become a permanent element in the tradition of the novel—*Tom Jones* is only part novel, and there is much else—picaresque tale, comic drama, occasional essay.

On the other hand, Fielding's departure from the canons of formal realism indicated very clearly the nature of the supreme problem which the new genre had to face. The tedious asserveration of literal authenticity in Defoe and to some extent in Richardson, tended to obscure the fact that, if the novel was to achieve equality of status with other genres it had to be brought into contact with the whole tradition of civilised values, and supplement its realism of presentation with a realism of assessment. To the excellent Mrs. Barbauld's query as to the grounds on which he considered Richardson to be a lesser writer than Shakespeare, Coleridge answered that "Richardson is *only* interesting." This is no doubt unfair as a total judgement on the author of *Clarissa*, but it indicates the likely limits of a realism of presentation: we shall be wholly immersed in the reality of the characters and their actions, but whether we shall be any wiser as a result is open to question.

Fielding brought to the genre something that is ultimately even more important than narrative technique—a responsible wisdom about human affairs which plays upon the deeds and the characters of his novels. His wisdom is not, perhaps, of the highest order; it is, like that of his beloved Lucian, a little inclined to be easy-going and on occasion opportunist. Nevertheless, at the end of *Tom Jones* we feel we have been exposed, not merely to an interesting narrative about imaginary persons, but to a stimulating wealth of suggestion and challenge on almost every topic of human interest. Not only so: the stimulation has come from a mind with a true grasp of human reality, never deceived or deceiving about himself, his characters or the human lot in general. In his effort to infuse the new genre with something of the Shakespearean virtues Fielding departed too far from formal realism to initiate a viable tradition, but his work serves as a perpetual reminder that if the new genre was to challenge older literary forms it had to find a way of conveying not only a convincing impression but a wise assessment of life, an assessment that could only come from taking a much wider view than Defoe or Richardson of the affairs of mankind.

So, although we must agree with the tenor of Johnson's watch simile, we must also add that it is unfair and misleading. Richardson, no doubt, takes us deeper into the inner workings of the human machine; but Fielding is surely entitled to retort that there are many other machines in nature besides the individual consciousness, and perhaps to express his surprised chagrin that Johnson should apparently have overlooked the fact that he was engaged in the exploration of a vaster and equally intricate mechanism, that of human society as a whole, a literary subject which was, incidentally, much more consonant than Richardson's with the classical outlook which he and Johnson shared.

In Praise of *Rasselas:*
Four Notes (Converging)

W. K. Wimsatt

I. AFTERTHOUGHTS IN *RASSELAS*

Johnson most likely began to write *Rasselas* not long after Saturday, January 13, 1759, when he seems first to have heard of his mother's serious illness. A week later, on Saturday, January 20, he wrote to the publisher William Strahan that he would deliver the book to him on Monday night, and that the title would be "The Choice of Life / or / The History of . . . Prince of Abisinnia." The several learned editors of *Rasselas* have, accordingly, not been inclined to take literally Johnson's later statement to Reynolds, as reported by Boswell, that he not only wrote *Rasselas* "in the evenings of one week," but "sent it to the press in portions as it was written." In portions, as it was corrected during days subsequent to Monday, January 22, perhaps. It is not difficult to imagine revisions and afterthoughts even during the original week of rapid composition. One of the most obvious internal suggestions of such afterthought, or at least of a certain absent-mindedness during the course of writing, appears in the development of the character of the lady Pekuah. We hear of her first, momentarily, in the escape from the happy valley (chap. 15). "The princess was followed only by a single favourite, who did not know whither she was going . . . The princess and her maid turned their eyes toward every part, and, seeing nothing to bound their prospect, considered themselves as in danger of being lost in a dreary vacuity. They stopped and trembled." A second very brief allusion occurs in the next chapter (16), as they arrive at Cairo. "The princess . . . for some days, continued in her chamber, where she was served by her favourite as in the palace of the valley." Thereafter, for

From *Imagined Worlds: Essays on Some English Novels and Novelists in Honour of John Butt,* edited by Maynard Mack and Ian Gregor. © 1968 by Methuen & Co., Ltd.

fourteen chapters (17–30), or during the whole first period at Cairo, including the trip to the cataract of the Nile to visit the hermit, we miss this personage altogether, until in chapter 31, at the great Pyramid, she reappears abruptly: "the favourite of the princess, looking into the cavity, stepped back and trembled. 'Pekuah, said the princess, of what art thou afraid?' " In the first edition, this was the first introduction of the lady's name. For the second edition, Johnson went back and inserted this name after the word "favourite" in the sentence quoted above from chapter 16. We remember that Pekuah, through her terror of the gloomy inside of the pyramid, remains outside and in chapter 33 is kidnapped by a band of Arab horsemen and becomes the central object of attention during six succeeding chapters (to 39). She reappears thereafter, to the end of the story, in every family conversation (chaps. 44, 45, 47, 49); and in chapter 46, her interest in the stars, acquired while she was a prisoner of the Arab chief, is exploited when the ladies invade and civilize the mad astronomer. Once he had conferred a few colours upon this lady, Johnson found her a convenient enough addition to his dramatis personae. It is possible that, having in chapters 15 and 16, provided for presence, he then forgot her, or even deliberately left her out of sight, for seventeen chapters. But it seems at least possible—to me it seems more likely—that he first conceived of the lady Pekuah as his travellers stood at the entrance of the Pyramid, and he bethought himself of Arab horsemen on the horizon and the opportunity to give his story an impetus towards action which at that juncture it badly needed. In that case, he went back (nothing could be simpler) and inserted the allusions to a "favourite" in chapters 15 and 16, and in the second edition the name Pekuah in chapter 16.

As Geoffrey Tillotson has already observed, Johnson throughout *Rasselas* is preoccupied with the passage of time and pays close attention to the number of days, months, and years which measure out his story. At the age of twenty-six, for example, when he first becomes restless in his confinement, Rasselas lets twenty months slip away in daydreaming, then awakes and estimates with chagrin that, since the active life of man, between infancy and senility, amounts to no more than forty years, he has just allowed a twenty-fourth part of his life to run to waste $(12 \times 40 = 480 \div 20 = 24)$. In contrast to such numerical nicety, the following curious sequence occurs in chapters 19, 20, and 21. Rasselas and his friends hear of a hermit, famous for sanctity, who lives near the "lowest cataract of the Nile." They set out to visit him but stop during the "heat" of the [first] day at the tents of some shepherds, whose barbarous conversation proves disgusting to the princess (chap. 19). Presumably they do not linger for the afternoon or spend the night with these shepherds. But: "On the *next day* [the italics are mine] they continued their journey," says the first sentence of chapter 20. Again they stop during the "heat" of the day, but this time at the "stately palace" of a very prosperous gentleman. He entreats them to stay. They do. And the "next day" he entreats them again. They "continued," in fact, "a few days longer, and then went forward to find the hermit." The next chapter (21) begins: "They came on the third day, by the direction of the peasants, to the hermit's cell." By the direction of the peasants? Some might argue that this means simply "*the* peasants" of that region. But this kind of slipshod phrasing is not like Johnson. It appears to me all but certain that "peasants" is one of Johnson's occasional quiet or pronominal "elegant variations." He means the "shepherds" with whom they stopped at midday during chapter 19. After that, and "on the third day" after setting out, they came to the hermit's cell. It seems to me very likely that the episode of the prosperous country gentleman is something which occurred to Johnson at some time after he had written the sequence about the shepherds and the hermit (chaps. 19, 21), and that, wishing to get it in, he wrote it in where he could, but without noticing a slight derangement of the details of the itinerary. The stop with the shepherds is a brief episode which does not sidetrack the journey to the hermit. Chapter 20, on the downfall of a prosperous country gentleman, is an extended intrusion into that journey. *Rasselas* is in a sense a travel story, but it is not on the whole a picaresque story.

The third example of narrative absent-mindedness which I wish to notice does, however, give us another exception to that rule. Chapter 40 (immediately after the narrative of Pekuah's captivity with the Arab) begins: "They returned to Cairo . . . none of them went much abroad. The prince . . . one day declared to Imlac, that he intended to devote himself to science, and pass the rest of his days in literary solitude. 'Before you make your final choice, answered Imlac, you ought to examine its hazards . . . I have just left the observatory of one of the most learned astronomers in the world.' " For the space of five chapters (40, 41, 42, 43, 44) Imlac continues a nonstop lecture upon the mad delusion by which the astronomer believes himself possessed of the power to control the seasons, bringing rain or sunshine to any part of the world as his conscience dictates. We discover that not only Rasselas but Nekayah and Pekuah are present during the whole conversation (chaps. 43, and 44). Then chapter 45 breaks into this sequence as follows: "The evening was now far past, and they rose to return home. As they walked along the bank of the Nile, delighted with the beams of the moon quivering on the water, they saw at a small distance an old man." But this does not really make sense. If we look back through the involvements of Imlac's long discourse on the mad astronomer, to the beginning of chapter 40, we remember that they are already at home and have been during the whole episode. (Looking back yet farther, a long way back, to chapter 25, one might recall that during the first period at Cairo the prince and princess "commonly met in the evening in a private summer-house on the bank of the Nile." But this summer-house either was on the grounds of the main house rented and magnificently furnished in chapter 16, or it was not. If not, if it was away from home, nothing in chapters 40–44 intimates that they have now gone there.) The episode of the mad astronomer has not been concluded. After chapter 45, "They discourse with an old man," the long and dramatically important chapter 46 immediately resumes the story of the astronomer, telling how he is visited by the ladies, Nekayah and Pekuah, and under the softening influence of feminine conversation is gradually cured of his delirious fantasy. Chapter 45, devoted to the old man, a characteristically and passionately Johnsonian projection of the bitterness of old age, is a stark intrusion into the sequence about the astronomer. In its absent-minded opening, it seems to me another of Johnson's afterthoughts, so important that it had to go somewhere. Where else would seem better when the other episodes were already in sequence?

II. "STRUCTURE"

I have been urging genetic inferences and have not meant to imply that the actual inconsistencies which I observe (with the possible exception of Pekuah's long absence from the stage) are in any sense aesthetic deficiencies. They do, however, appear to me as complements of and accents upon a much larger and more clearly observable character of the whole story— what I would describe as its highly episodic, and hence very lumpy or bumpy, structure. One recent critic of *Rasselas*, Professor Kolb, has said that it is arranged in two main parts, one in the happy valley, one after the escape. Another critic, Professor Hilles, has discerned three main parts: 1. In the valley, chapters 1–14; 2. The escape and a period of relatively detached and orderly *observation* at and near Cairo, chapters 15–30; 3. Beginning with the abduction of Pekuah and the grief of Nekayah, a period of greater personal *involvement* and, at the end, of more somber experience, chapter 33–49. In the chapters following the episode of Pekuah's abduction (if I may expand this theme a little), the mad astronomer is not merely observed, but converted from his delirium and received into the family; even the bitter old man comes home with them for a brief conversation. A climax of experience and reflection is reached in the antepenultimate chapters, with the visit to the Catacombs, Imlac's argument for the immortality of the soul, and Nekayah's conclusion: "To me . . . the choice of life is become less important; I hope hereafter to think only on the choice of eternity."

Nevertheless, I believe that the forty-nine chapters of the tale fall even more readily into another and more piecemeal pattern—more readily because with more aesthetic immediacy, more clearly segmented colouring. Thus: 1. Chapters 1–6, the *unrest* of Rasselas in the valley, climaxed by the attempt at flying; 2. Chapters 7–15, the *story* of Imlac (surely too long in proportion to the whole book) and the implausible *escape* by tunnelling through the mountain; 3. Chapters 16–22, the first period at Cairo, *exploratory*, varicoloured, embracing the visit to the hermit; 4. Chapters 23–29, an extended *conversation*, on public and private life, on marriage and celibacy, between Rasselas and Nekayah; 5. Chapters 30–39, *adventures:* the Pyramids, abduction and recovery of Pekuah; 6. Chapters 40–49, return to Cairo and more *somber* experiences: the mad astronomer, the bitter old man, the Catacombs, the end. In each of these six segments, certain subdivisions can of course be seen. The first period in Cairo is notable for the rapid succession of separately sought-out episodes. The relentlessly continued conversation between the prince and his sister (chaps. 23–29) occupies the middle of the whole story as a prolonged central stasis or dead center. The sequence in which Pekuah is the focus of attention (chaps. 31–39) is notable for the relative continuity of the adventure story. The visit to the Pyramids which begins this part, or ends the preceding, seems like a heavy punctuation mark (the accent of antiquity and the tomb), and this indeed is echoed in a second and similar punctuation, the visit to the Catacombs, which signals the end of the whole. The second period at Cairo, though it has fewer incidents than the first, is a sort of counterpart to the first echoing its structure across the interval of the long conversation and the long adventure. Inside one episode in each Cairo period, a shorter and abruptly introduced intercalary episode, as we have seen, stands out like a special bump or knob in the grain of the story. The embittered and malignant old man looks out from his knothole or niche back across the chapters to the fearful and ruined country gentleman. But it is difficult to say just what is accomplished for the whole pattern by features of this sort. It is difficult, on the whole, to speak of the "structure" of *Rasselas* in a sense anything like that in which one speaks of the structure of a play by Shakespeare or of a novel by Fielding or Jane Austen. *Rasselas* has the kind of structure which satisfies, more or less, its modest requirements as a quasi-dramatic narrative—not the causal progression, the beginning, middle, and end of the Aristotelian "whole," but a structure of accumulation, something like that of a series of laboratory reports, or a series of chapters on animals sighted or taken, on a hunt across the veldt with gun or camera. "Eye Nature's walks, shoot Folly as it flies, And catch the Manners living as they rise."

Both Professor Kolb and, with less emphasis, Professor Hilles point out that the story, and especially the section dealing with the first period at Cairo, organizes a series of parallels and oppositions of human states and moral ideas: "prince and princess, male and female," "wise Imlac . . . naïve prince," "normal life . . . the happy valley," "urban life . . . rural," "epicurean . . . stoic," "shepherd, landlord, and hermit," "great and . . . humble," "youth and age, celibacy and matrimony . . . past and present." There is nothing wrong with this kind of analysis. This kind of order, in some degree, may well be one of the requisites for the successful telling of such a tale. On the other hand, some such order is needed too in a moral essay or treatise, and maybe there it is needed even more. (It fits the conversation of the prince and his sister even better than their explorations.) We do not contrive a story for the sake of getting this kind of order, but perhaps the contrary, for the sake of relieving the threat of its rigors.

III. THE STREAKS OF THE TULIP

To put the matter conventionally and moderately, it is a paradox that a man who had Johnson's preference for both the homely and the abstract should undertake an oriental tale at all. Or better, it is a strangely fit incongruity that this tale, which both tries and refuses to be oriental, should contain as one of its most memorable exhibits a discourse on the art of poetry in which occurs the following sequence of assertions: 1. "I could never describe what I had not seen . . . I ranged mountains and deserts for images and resemblances, and pictured upon my mind every tree of the forest and flower of the valley." 2. "The business of a poet . . . is to examine, not the individual, but the species; to remark general properties and large appearances: he does not number the streaks of the tulip." 3. "He must be acquainted likewise with all the modes of life . . . and trace the changes of the human mind as they are modified by various institutions and accidental influences of climate and custom."

The local colour of *Rasselas*, the "oriental imagery" to the "charms" of which Boswell alludes, is not luxuriant. It is even very thin, and we may at moments wish it were thicker. It has a curiously deductive and even conjectual character—like the effort of a man who has read long ago a book of eastern travels for the purpose of translation, perhaps too has dipped into another book or two in the more recent past.

The most conspicuous colour consists simply in the proper names of places, persons, and offices. We are "oriented" at the outset (chap. 1) by the names "Abissinia," "Egypt," and "Amhara." Soon we follow Imlac (chap. 8–12) from "Goiama," near the "fountain of the Nile," by way of "the shore of the red sea," to "Surat," and to "Agra, the capital of Indostan," city of the "great Mogul," and thence to "Persia," "Arabia," "Syria," "Palestine," "many regions of Asia," "Egypt," "Cairo," and "Suez"—the latter names preestablishing for us the route which will be followed by the fugitives from the valley a few chapters hence. Later, the sequence of adventure chapters (30–39) gives us "old Egyptians," the "Pyramids" (over and over), a "troop of Arabs," "Turkish horsemen," the "Bassa" at Cairo, the "borders of Nubia," "the monastery of St. Anthony," "the deserts of Upper-Egypt," the "Arab's fortress" on an "island of the Nile . . . under the tropick."

"How easily shall we then trace the Nile through all his passage," says the aeronautical artist back in chapter 6. This is the first of altogether fifteen allusions by name to that great geographical feature and symbol. The escapees from the happy valley behold "the Nile, yet a narrow current, wandering beneath them." The hermit of chapter 21 lives "near the lowest cataract of the Nile." The "annual overflow" or "inundation" of the Nile is a leitmotif of chapters 41–45, dealing with both the mad weather-maker and the sad old man. ("I rest against a tree, and consider, that in the same shade I once disputed upon the annual overflow of the Nile with a friend who is now silent in the grave.") In chapter 49, the conclusion, a final "inundation of the Nile" confines the prince and his friends to reflection at home (as, long since, in the happy valley, Rasselas and Imlac had been brought together in "domestick amusements" forced upon them by an "inundation" from the lake). "No man," says the wise and aphoristic Nekayah, concluding an earlier chapter of conversation (29), "can, at the same time, fill his cup from the source and from the mouth of the Nile." But Johnson has come close to doing just this.

Another vehicle of exoticism may be identified here and there in a certain courtly, ceremonious, and archaic flourish of words—what Professor Hilles has called "the Grand Style," an aspect of the sublime. This occurs a few times in the author's own voice, as in the opening of the first chapter: "Ye who listen with credulity to the whispers of fancy . . . attend." More often it is from the mouths of the characters—no doubt what the country gentleman of chapter 20 detected as the "eloquence of Imlac . . . and the loft courtesy of the princess." (It is Miltonic—like "Daughter of God and Man, immortal Eve.") As Rasselas saw the animals by moonlight, " 'Ye,' said he, 'are happy . . . nor do I, ye gentle beings, envy your felicity' " (chap. 2). " 'Dear princess,' said Rasselas, 'you fall into the common error of exaggeratory declamation' " (chap. 28). " 'My dear Pekuah,' said the princess . . . 'Remember that you are companion of the princess of Abissinia' " (chap. 31). "Whoever thou art, that . . . imaginest happiness in royal magnificence, and dreamest . . . perpetual gratifications, survey the pyramids, and confess thy folly!" (chap. 32). Here Imlac echoes the rhythm of the narrator in the first sentence of the book. "Illustrious lady," said even the Arab outlaw, "my fortune is better than I had presumed to hope." "Lady," said he, "you are to consider yourself as sovereign" (chaps. 38, 39). Probably the most full-blown instance in the book returns us, characteristically, to geography and to the mighty river. In chapter 25, "The princess and her brother commonly met in the evening in a private summer-house on the bank of the Nile . . . As they were sitting together, the princess cast her eyes upon the river that flowed before her." And:

> "Answer," said she, "great father of waters, thou that rollest thy floods through eighty nations, to the invocations of the daughter of thy native king. Tell me if thou waterest, through all thy course, a single habitation from which thou dost not hear the murmurs of complaint?"

Certain other details of local colour are much less distinctive. At the start (chap. 1) we are treated to "mountains," "rivulets," a "lake," "fish of every species," water falling "from precipice to precipice," "the banks of the brooks . . . diversified with flowers," "beasts of prey," "flocks and herds," "beasts of chase frisking in the lawns." We hear also of a "palace" with "squares or courts," "arches of massy stone," "upper stories," "private galleries," "subterranean passages," "columns," and "unsuspected cavities" closed with "marble." Such terms, so frequent throughout the work, whenever the argument seems to call for some evocation of physical decor, work as local colour mainly or only in conjunction with the proper names of places and persons which we have seen. It seems scarcely extreme to say that these combinations make the kind of local colour a schoolboy might supply. When I was in the eighth grade, we studied geography (which that year was Africa), and we had to write an imaginary journey through Egypt. I can still remember, approximately, one sentence of my composition—because it struck me at the time as so neatly yet richly executed. "Turning a bend in the Nile, we came in sight of the giant Assouan Dam."

Certain other descriptive details are indeed more specially exotic. These, however, are scarce. I attempt the following approximately exhaustive list. In the "torrid zone" of chapter 1, we find the "monkey" and the "elephant." At the start of Imlac's travels in chapter 8, we have "camels" and "bales" of goods. In chapter 9 and again in 12, we have a "caravan," and in chapter 10 the "mosque of Mecca." In chapter 18, at Cairo, a "spacious building," with "open doors," housing a "school of declamation, in which professors read lectures," seems, in spite of its vagueness, much like a part of the ancient Alexandrian world. The shepherds in chapter 19 live in "tents." At the estate of the prosperous country gentleman in chapter 20, "youths and virgins" are "dancing in the grove" near a "stately palace." In 21, the hermit's "cell" is a "cavern" beneath "palm-trees." In 30, as we begin to think of the Pyramids, we hear of "fragments of temples" and "choaked aqueducts." In 32 appear "galleries" and "vaults of marble"; in 33, "dark labyrinths." The travel in the desert (chaps. 31–39) gives us "tents" (nine times), "camels" (three), "ounces of gold" (three), "deserts" and "the desert," a "monastery," a "refectory," and a "prior"; in 38 appear "carpets," "finer carpets," Pekuah's "upper vest" (with "embroidery"), "the lance," "the sword," "palaces," "temples," "granite," "porphyry"; in 39, "the tropick," a "couch," "turrets," two special plums: "crocodiles" and "river-horses," "needlework," "silken flowers," and another plum: the "seraglio." In the final expedition, to the catacombs (47–48), we have a "guard of horsemen," "sepulchral caves," a "labyrinth of subterraneous passages," "embalming" and "embalmed" bodies, "caverns."

A few ingenious manipulations of this slender exotic store, cunning jointures of it with the Johnsonian philosophic and plastic staple, stand out. In chapter 1, just as I become mildly annoyed at "beasts of chase frisking in the lawns" and "the sprightly kid . . . bounding on the rock," I am moderately diverted by "the subtle monkey frolicking in the trees, and the solemn elephant reposing in the shade." (No matter whether ele-

phants would really be found in that mountain fastness.) By a somewhat
different sort of conjunction, it seems to me, Johnson creates a moment of
interesting local colour in chapter 39, as Pekuah looks out on the "winding"
river from her island prison: "The crocodiles and river-horses are common
in this unpeopled region . . . For some time I expected to see mermaids
and tritons, which, as Imlac has told me, the European travellers have
stationed in the Nile." And here let us quote too that moment of pregnant
phrasing from chapter 30: "The most pompous monument of Egyptian
greatness, and one of the most bulky works of manual industry . . . are
the pyramids." And from chapter 38, the Arab's observation to the lady
Pekuah that

> buildings are always best preserved in places little frequented, and
> difficult of access: for, when once a country declines from its prim-
> itive splendour, the more inhabitants are left, the quicker ruin will
> be made. Walls supply stones more easily than quarries, and pal-
> aces and temples will be demolished to make stables of granite,
> and cottages of porphyry.

By a slight extension of the idea of the exotic, perhaps we can bring
in such learned words from the realm of *Mathematical Magick* as Johnson
borrowed from his archaic dictionary source of that title, or from other
"philosophic" sources, and worked into chapter 6, the story of an attempt
at the art of flying: "the tardy conveyance of ships and chariots," "the
swifter migration of wings," "the pendent spectator," "volant animals,"
"the folding continuity of the bat's wings." And with these we come close
to yet a wider category of somewhat notable descriptive phrases—all those,
I should say, which, without including any words in any way exotic or
bizarre, yet by some special energy of compression are likely to strike our
attention or force on us the feeling that the description has "texture." In
chapter 1, the lake is "frequented by every fowl whom nature has taught
to dip the wing in water . . . every blast shook spices from the rocks, and
every month dropped fruits upon the ground. All animals that bite the
grass, or brouse the shrub . . . wandered in this extensive circuit." Such
phrases as these may be looked on as Johnsonian substitutes for local
colour.

A recent observer from the vantage point of Saudi Arabia has ex-
pounded the extreme unrealism of the journey made by the princely party
of fugitives, by ups and downs, through the nearly impassable tropical
forests of the Abyssinian plateau, and then down the steep seven or eight
thousand feet from the eastern escarpment to the narrow coastal plain and
the port where they stayed several months. (This was probably Massawa,
a typical Red Sea port, a "horrible place," lying under relentless sun, in
saturation humidity.) No less dimly realized seem their "quick and prosperous" coastal voyage [of twenty or thirty days] in a primitive sailing
dhow, their slow trip by camel caravan under the desert stars to Cairo, and

finally what must have been the astonished arrival of this party of Coptic Christians amid the teeming contrasts of a vast Islamic city.

Johnson, we know, had long enjoyed some awareness of the Abyssinian locale, for as a young man he had written and published (1735) a translation from a French version of the seventeenth-century Portuguese Jesuit Father Jerome Lobo's *Voyage to Abyssinia*. Of recent years, the scholarship of sources has been urging Johnson's debt to other writers on Abyssinia. Lobo, it is clear, could not have been his only source, for Lobo said the prison of the princes was a rocky and "barren summit." But the paradise on the Abyssinian hill was a commonplace—"where Abassin kings their issue guard, Mount Amara—by some supposed True Paradise, under the Ethiop line." One of the reasons why Johnson was interested in Lobo's *Voyage* was that the Jesuit missionary and diplomat himself was more interested in human character and mores, the hardships and vicissitudes of the human adventure, than in exotic or fantastic colourations. Thus, Lobo reports of the crocodiles (which Pekuah saw from the Arab's island fortress): "Neither I nor any with whom I have convers'd about the *Crocodile*, have ever seen him Weep, and therefore I take the Liberty of ranking all that hath been told us of his Tears, amongst the Fables which are only proper to amuse Children." And Johnson, in a preface to Lobo which Boswell by quoting has made the best-known part of the book:

> THE *Portugese* Traveller, contrary to the general Vein of his Countrymen, has amused his Reader with no Romantick Absurdities or Incredible Fictions . . . HE appears by his modest and unaffected Narration to have described Things as he saw them, to have copied Nature from the Life, and to have consulted his Senses not his Imagination; He meets with no *Basilisks* that destroy with their Eyes, his *Crocodiles* devour their Prey without Tears, and his *Cataracts* fall from the Rock without Deafening the Neighbouring Inhabitants.

Samuel Johnson—both Johnson the man and Johnson the translator of Lobo and the narrator of *Rasselas*—no doubt believes that even the local colours, the geography, the flora, the fauna, the architecture, and the costumes, of exotic places are far less exotic than is commonly reported. Beyond doubt, he believes that human living and human nature in Amhara or in Cairo are far less exotic than is commonly supposed, are indeed essentially the same as in London.

> THE Reader . . . will discover, what will always be discover'd by a diligent and impartial Enquirer, that wherever Human Nature is to be found, there is a mixture of Vice and Virtue, a contest of Passion and Reason.

General human nature is of course Johnson's theme—vice and virtue, passion and reason. Why not then generalized local colour? The deliberate simplification, even complacent ignorance about the actual colours of life in the supposed locale of Johnson's story, is a kind of counterpart and symbol of the general human truth he would be getting at.

IV. A CHORUS OF SAGES

Various critical questions might be asked about *Rasselas*, but surely the main question must always be: What are we to make of the fact that the obvious element of morality is cast in the shape of an oriental tale? Or, what are we to make of the fact that the equally obvious oriental tale is invested with so much morality? The problem, or the task, of a writer who would tell a moral tale is, of course, to get the story and the morality together. He will have to do better than give us a close juxtaposition or rapid alternation of plot and sermon (programme and commercial plug), or a set of essays in a curiously wrought frame, a series of *Ramblers* inserted in a version of the *Arabian Nights*. "We do not read *Rasselas* for the story," says Professor Hilles. "We read it for a view of life that is presented majestically in long sweeping phrases." But he immediately adds: "Diction, rhythms, character and plot are all of a piece." So that he really has a warmer affection for the story (character and plot) than, for instance, Professor Kolb, who, while implying some distress at those critics who "have been content to praise the wisdom and ignore the narrative," at the same time (and on the same page) concludes "that the tale is not the principle which best explains . . . the book . . . the problem of happiness rather than the element of 'story' emerges . . . as the determinant by reference to which questions about the book's structure may be most adequately answered." The structure is "didactic." And this seems to imply somehow that we can call it a "narrative," but not a "tale" or a "story."

In the second section of this essay, I have already given up the "structure" of *Rasselas* so far as that idea pretends to any Aristotelian or organistic and dramatic implications. But then a story does not have to have *much* structure in order to be a story. It is a story if it has any characters and places at all, and if the characters do any talking at all and move about a little, from one place (or one state) to another. The story of *Rasselas* as such, a certain movement of certain persons in certain places—loosely constructed, vaguely characterized, largely undramatic or half-heartedly dramatic as it may be, unfictional fabric of a fiction that it is—has, nevertheless, some kind of imaginative bearing on the moral ideas. This is not an original thesis. "The eastern background," says Professor Kolb, "provides . . . the aura of strange and distant lands where human happiness is commonly thought to be complete and lasting; . . . reminding us of the superficial likenesses and essential differences between *Rasselas* and ordinary oriental tales with their happy-ever-after conclusions." "The judgement of human life," says Professor Leyburn, "would leave a very different impression if it were presented stripped of such aesthetic distance as the regions of the

Nile provide." Oriental decor had been used in Augustan England for stories of adventure and fantasy (*Arabian Nights* and *Persian Tales*). It had well-established didactic uses too—as in *Spectator* and *Rambler* visions and apologues. An oriental spokesman could be used to throw a strange and skeptical perspective on Western mores (Montesquieu's *Persian Letters*, Goldsmith's *Chinese Letters*—just after *Rasselas*). The peculiar twist of Johnson's *Rasselas* is that he uses a sort of nominally or minimally exotic tale for the purpose of displaying the most homely human materials and of asserting a workaday perspective upon them. The philosophy of *Rasselas* (Johnson's resistance to eighteenth-century "optimism") might readily enough become our theme now, but I am pushing, not the philosophy but the literary actualization of it, trying to improve the view that it is important for Johnson's anti-rationalist and conservative purpose that he *should* have a story, of sorts, and a foreign scene.

The Johnsonian substitutes for local colour, we have said, are abstractive, at moments "philosophic," and all but invisible. They may, for that very reason, have a broader spread than we have so far mentioned. It was Johnson himself who observed of Sir Thomas Browne that he "poured a multitude of exotick words," and Johnson's friends Boswell and Arthur Murphy who thought that Browne was a main source for Johnson's own "Anglo-Latian" peculiarities. "How he differed so widely from such elegant models [the Augustans] is a problem not to be solved, unless it be true that he took an early tincture from the writers of the last century, particularly Sir Thomas Browne." Twenty-five years ago I ventured the opinion that Browne "deserves the name 'exotick' which Johnson applies to him," but that this name would sit "curiously on Johnson himself." "Where Browne uses remote terms to make us think of remote things"—Pharaoh, mummy, golden calf, scorpion, and salamander—"Johnson 'familiarizes.' " That much is still true. But, on the other hand, I will now undertake to argue that Johnson's whole way of moral writing, what we may call the *Rambler* style, is a form of moderate exoticism which did not find its ideal setting until he wrote *Rasselas*. During the course of producing his 208 *Ramblers*, Johnson tried out a number of domestic settings of voices for the Rambler mood: the country housewife and her kitchen (no. 51), Mr. Frolick the Londoner in the country (no. 61), Quisquilius the curio-collector (nos. 82–83), Nugaculus the gossip (no. 103), Mrs. Busy (no. 138), Captator the legacy-hunter (nos. 197–98). But in all such instances, the more dramatic he makes the treatment, the more the peculiar Rambleresque pomp of phrasing thins out. This happens even in the exotic setting of the Greenland idyll of Anningait and Ajut (nos. 186–87). Perhaps it happens too with the several oriental tales, including that of the Emperor Seged of Ethiopia (nos. 204–5). Yet with the Emperor Seged, Johnson was verging on the discovery of a curiously heightened affinity between story and philosophic idiom. Perhaps the *Rambler* had been all along a series of oriental apologues without the plot and local colour?—the Rambler himself a kind of Abyssinian sage without the name and the overt ethnic colouration? It was a strange language, that language of the Rambler in his own persona. Who really talked that way? Not Dryden or Addison, or Lord Chesterfield. Not really Johnson himself, except perhaps in the moments of his conversation when he was being the consciously pompous self-parodist or when Mrs. Thrale and Burney had come into the library at Streathem to "make" him "speak" a *Rambler*.

The part of *Rasselas* which we remember best and carry away with us for allusion and quotation—the portable part—is beyond question the aphoristic moralism, the lugubrious orotundity. "We do not read *Rasselas* for the story." "Human life is everywhere a state in which much is to be endured, and little to be enjoyed." Who says this? Imlac, Rasselas, Nekayah, the Stoic philosopher, the hermit, the Arab, the mad astronomer, the old man? Any one of these, at the right moment, might say it. Actually, of course, we remember it is Imlac, near the end of his narrative of his own life (chap. 11)—the same Imlac who later, seated in one of the "most spacious chambers" of the great Pyramid, discourses so eloquently, in a vein of inverse romantic vision: "It seems to have been erected only in compliance with that hunger of imagination which preys incessantly upon life, and must be always appeased by some employment . . . I consider this mighty structure as a monument of the insufficiency of human enjoyments" (chap. 32). The same Imlac, who when the prince looks on a fissure in the rocks as a "good omen" of escape from the valley, replies—almost like a wound-up automaton, a speaking toy-philosopher: "If you are pleased with prognosticks of good, you will be terrified likewise with tokens of evil . . . Whatever facilitates our work is more than an omen, it is a cause of success . . . Many things difficult to design prove easy to performance."

"Marriage has many pains, but celibacy has no pleasures." Who says this? Any one of several characters might say it. Actually the speaker is the maiden princess Nekayah, in the course (chap. 26) of that lengthy and soon quarrelsome conversation with her brother about such profound issues: public and private life, youth and age, celibacy or marriage. The same princess who a few pages later, in the accents of a proto-Screwtape, "reckons" for us "the various forms of connubial infelicity . . . the rude collisions of contrary desire . . . the obstinate contests of disagreeable virtues, where both are supported by consciousness of good intention . . . " (chap. 28). The same princess whom we have already heard, seated in the summer-house by the bank of the Nile, utter her apostrophe to that mighty "father of waters" who rolls his "floods through eighty nations."

The courtly and ceremonious discourse which we have already noticed as a kind of local colour is only the most obvious instance of a lofty and reflective idiom which plausibly pervades nearly the whole of this oriental tale. (The notion of an oriental sage, philosopher, poet, emperor, prince, is an easy one for us to entertain. Who ever heard of an oriental buffoon or ninny?) The *Rambler* idiom, Johnson's own idiom, if we like, an expansion of homely human wisdom into the large perspective of Latinate philosophic diction, is projected across time and space, straight from London and Fleet Street, to cover appropriately, with a veil of the delicately exotic, scenes which we know, by a more than willing suspension of disbelief are enacted at places along the Nile from Amhara to Cairo.

The notion of *Rasselas* as a "comedy" (Johnson's "greatest comic work") has been urged by two recent writers. A third, Professor Hilles again, thinks that they "overstress" the "comic element." Probably they do overstress it. Professor Tracy sees a "comic" (perhaps, rather, a "satirical") reduction of man's fatuousness, shrewd laughter at the prince's chronic failure of common sense, demolition of the poet Imlac's "grandiloquent. . . rapture." Professor Whitley finds "pure comedy of ideas" in the episodes of the first period at Cairo, "comedy of emotion and behaviour," and "deflated oriental romance," in Pekuah's abduction, "dark comedy" in the later chapters about the mad astronomer and the catacombs. Probably we are on safer ground if we are content to say, with Professor Hilles, simply that the attitude prevailing in the story is not, as so often said, "pessimistic," not morose, not cynical, not even satirical; it is rather, gently "ironic" and "realistic." The "smile of the author is a sad smile." Yes—though one may need to insist that it *is* a smile. With Professor Hilles, we must differ from certain critics who have supposed that a "tragic sense of life . . . informs it." It appears to me next to impossible that anyone should be moved either to tears or to shudders at any part of *Rasselas*. "In a short time the second Bassa was deposed. The Sultan [at Constantinople], that had advanced him, was murdered by the Janisaries." But that was, if not a long time ago, yet very far in another country. (The chapter, 18, where the Stoic philosopher mourning the death of his daughter is put in a position of nearly laughable contrast to his declamation of the preceding day is perhaps the only part of the whole book that verges on the uncomfortable.) "In a year the wings were finished and, on a morning appointed, the maker appeared furnished for flight on a little promontory: he waved his pinions a while to gather air, then leaped from his stand, and in an instant dropped into the lake." There we have the characteristic motion of the story as action— the immediate and inevitable plunge, so inevitable and so confidently foreseen as to warrant not the smallest flourish or comment. " 'I . . . resolve to return into the world tomorrow' . . . He dug up a considerable treasure which he had hid among the rocks, and accompanied them to the city, on which, as he approached it, he gazed with rapture" (chap. 21). At many moments the comic smile of the narrator is turned directly on one or another of his characters. " 'But surely, interposed the prince . . . Whenever I shall seek a wife, it shall be my first question, whether she be willing to be led by reason?' " (chap. 29). More often, however, or in general, the smile of this narrator envelops in a less direct way, in a more reticent parodic spirit, the whole of his own Abyssinian tale. He is very close to the endlessly meditative and controversial nature of each of his personae. What does the narrator think of his own "Tale" when he gives his chapters titles such as these: "The prince continues to grieve and muse," "A dissertation on the art of flying," "Imlac's history continued. A dissertation upon poetry," "Disquisition upon greatness," "Rasselas and Nekayah continue their conversation," "The dangerous prevalence of imagination," "The conclusion, in which nothing is concluded"?

In real life, Johnson sometimes indulged in a complacent self-consciousness and amusement at his own inflations. His moments of self-parody are celebrated. In his essays too, *Ramblers* and *Idlers*, a sort of shackled playfulness often parodies the solemn parade. A shadow of grimace accents some restrained contrast between gravity of diction and homeliness or meanness of sentiment. In *Rasselas*, the Johnsonian speaker has translated himself into a realm of sober fantasy where the grim smile, the sad smile, the wan smile, can be more or less constant. Probably it was some feeling like this about the tale that prompted Voltaire to say that its philosophy was *aimable*. Indeed there are profoundly reflective and even solemn moments—and they occur increasingly in the later chapters—at the Pyramids, in the conversation about the astronomer's madness, in the confrontation with the savagely embittered old man, and finally at the Catacombs, in the contemplation of death and immortality. But the last seems to me the only place where it may be impossible to find a smile. Here the initially dominant tone is metaphysical sobriety ("as thought is, such is the power that thinks; a power impassive and indiscerptible"), and this deepens at the end to theological solemnity ("The whole assembly stood a while silent and collected . . . 'To me,' said the princess, 'the choice of life is become less important: I hope hereafter to think only on the choice of eternity' "). But this is an exceptional moment, not the ground tone of the book and not its conclusion. The conclusion, in which nothing is concluded, reverts to the basic plan.

It is not possible to smile sympathetically at nothingness without a degree of participation. Johnson's way of laughter is not the high-comedy way of the wit and his butts, but a quieter way of partly encumbered rehearsal and laboured formulation. Martin Price has deftly alluded to the "gently preposterous oriental setting" of Johnson's tale, "the self-mocking formality of its dialogue, the balance and antithesis of characters as well as dialogue, and the circularity of its total structure." All this is the *imagination* of Johnson's quasi-oriental and ceremonious no-tale—"the wine of absurdity," or absurdity mitigated only in its own rich self-contemplation. In our day, Albert Camus has explained absurdity in Kantian terms as "the division between the mind that desires and the world that disappoints." Johnson's *Rasselas* has much in common with modern versions of the absurd—with a *Godot* or a *Watt*. One main difference, which may disguise the parallel for us, is that the modern versions of the descent take place at a level which is, to start with, subterranean, the very subcellar or zero level of modern man's three-century decline from the pinnacles of theology and metaphysics. Johnson's descendental exercise, with its saving theological clause in the Catacombs, takes place at a level still near the top of the metaphysical structure. It is of course all the richer for this. In the "end-game" played at the modern level, a nearly complete numbness and boredom is roused only as occasional stabs and jolts of obscenity reach a buried nerve. In the more spacious and better lighted areas available to Johnson, there was still eloquence—an eloquence profound and moving as it verges continually on a smiling absurdity.

Fictions of Romantic Irony:
Tristram Shandy

Lilian R. Furst

"—My good friend, quoth I—as sure as I am I—and you are you—
—And who are you? said he.——
Don't puzzle me; said I."

—*Tristram Shandy*, vol. 7, chap. 33

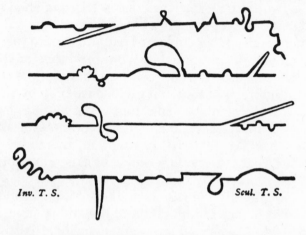

These were the four lines I moved in through my first, second, third, and fourth volumes.—In the fifth volume I have been very good—the precise line I have described in it being this:

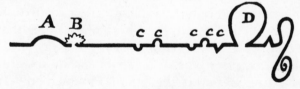

—*Tristram Shandy*, vol. 6, chap. 40

With *Tristram Shandy* doubt and equivocation arise even before the first word of the narrative. Who devised its full title, *The Life and Opinions of Tristram Shandy, Gent.*? Tristram, the fictive author, or Sterne, the actual author? Perhaps it should be attributed to Tristram since he himself refers to "the story of my LIFE and my OPINIONS" (vol. 5, chap. 32). But was it also Tristram who chose the epigraph from Epictetus? There is really no way of knowing. Between the dedication to Pitt, which is unquestionably Sterne's, and Tristram's opening "I wish" stretches a disquieting area of no man's land that invites speculation and induces uncertainty. This neutral space is replicated in those blank pages, dashes, asterisks and the device of aposiopesis for which *Tristram Shandy* is notorious. While stimulating reader participation, these vacuums also provide within and beyond the text room for further hypotheses of the kind that chracterise Tristram's thinking. Such open spaces, temporally as well as narrationally, are the very element of *Tristram Shandy,* and it is these interstices that are the breeding-ground for the ambivalences of irony.

One large and perplexing gap that becomes apparent at the outset and persists to the end is that between the fictive and the actual author. Obviously it is Laurence Sterne who creates Tristram Shandy the writer of his Life and Opinions. Yet though we may smile at the naïveté of the earliest reviewer who praised "the droll Mr Tristram Shandy" as "a writer infinitely more ingenious and entertaining than any other of the present race of novelists," in practice it is far from easy to dissociate the fictive from the real author. Sterne appears without disguise only in the initial dedication to Pitt, in a supplementary dedication to Viscount Spencer that precedes volume 5, and, most interestingly, in five footnotes in which he annotates or corrects what "Mr Shandy" has written, thereby clearly revealing his responsibility as the presenting editor of Tristram's memoirs. Generally, however, he remains concealed behind the persona Tristram Shandy, though his commenting intrusions in those footnotes indicate that the two are not identical. This reduplication of the author in effect thrusts us into a curious double role as readers simultaneously of Tristram Shandy and of Laurence Sterne. Here there would seem to be a likely source for that dual vision that would permit an assured interpretation of ironic alternate meanings. But this is not the case in *Tristram Shandy.* Except in those dedications and footnotes on the outer margins of the narrative, Sterne's perspective is not discernible beside that of his creation, as is that of the narrator in *Don Juan* distinct from his hero, or of J. P. F. Richter, the chronicler of the twins' tale in the *Flegeljahre.* In *Tristram Shandy* the enframing contrivance is an intact, integral part of the fiction, in which only Tristram, not Sterne, addresses us directly. Although we, of course, know of Sterne as the originator of the artifact, we are at most occasionally and dimly aware of his background presence. As we heed to Tristram's voice, we have none of that benevolent, discreet guidance extended to us in *Pride and Prejudice.* We are in fact stranded in the position [Wayne] Booth has so graphically described when "the author has decided to go away and send no letter" (*The Rhetoric of Fiction*). This is, as Booth concedes, a "troubling" narrative situation, and, moreover, one that precludes definitive reconstruction of irony. For while the text emits clues and signals as to Tristram's irony, primarily in his rhetoric, such irony is, like Elizabeth's at Darcy's expense in *Pride and Prejudice,* internal to the fictional realm. Irony of the fiction, on the other hand, emanates in *Tristram Shandy* from that indeterminate expanse between fictive and actual author, and it is from there that we as readers must operate. It is an insecure and uncomfortable spot without any terra firma from which to take our bearings.

With the introductory words of Tristram's tale the nature of the intrinsic equivocation undergoes a change. His "I wish" dispels doubts as to the identity of the writer but heralds others of a different sort. For this "I wish," which will reecho throughout *Tristram Shandy* not only from Tristram's mouth but also from Toby's, Trim's, and Walter's—this "I wish" leads into a world of conjecture, desire, and fantasy. Its tentativeness is in striking contrast to the affirmative assertion: "It is a truth universally acknowledged . . . "that lays the foundation for *Pride and Prejudice*. Whereas that dictum links the narrative to public standards, this "I" removes Sterne's to a private inner space of personal "Opinions." That *Tristram Shandy* is "a history-book, . . . of what passes in a man's own mind" (vol. 2, chap. 2) has often been pointed out. Of utmost importance is the angle from which that history is told; for we experience what passes in Tristram's mind through the record of his own consciousness. If it was, as Lanham maintains, "the application of the older narrative techniques to the new *subject* of realistic narrative, the private life" that shocked Sterne's contemporaries, in retrospect that position is reversed; now it is less the subject than the subjectivity of *Tristram Shandy* that seems its most remarkable feature.

Sterne has not merely made the narrator the theme of his own book; he has made his mind its scene and its organising epicentre. Through his triple role as infant, as adult protagonist, and as writer, Tristram is omnipresent. The doings of Walter, Mrs Shandy, and Toby are related, and implicitly subordinated, to his vision when he constantly refers to them as "my father," "my mother," and "my uncle." The narrative is thus to an extreme degree internalised, for the entire fictional world presented in *Tristram Shandy* is encompassed within a single consciousness. Though Tristram may tell of what passed in Walter's or Toby's mind, in fact he is not entering their minds in the manner of an omniscient narrator; he is reporting *his* perception of what he assumes to be passing in their minds. Whether Tristram's autonomous "I" is ever able to grasp an outer reality is a moot point; it seems rather as if this "I" goes on floating in its self-created amniotic fluid into which it assimilates external phenomena but from which it cannot emerge. Tristram and his narrative remain captive to that enveloping "I," and so do we as readers. We cannot, for example, see and evaluate Walter or Toby directly; our view is solely through the eyes of Tristram, through the mediation and at the remove of his "I." Nor can we judge the degree to which those eyes are distorting, to which he is a reliable or unreliable witness. We have nothing other than his words and his evidence; as he himself acknowledges: "Let us leave, if possible, *myself*:—But 'tis impossible,—I must go along with you to the end of the work" (vol. 6, chap. 20).

This consistent, radical subjectivity of the narrating stance in *Tristram Shandy* has important consequences for the reader's capacity to discern and reconstruct irony. Our reading of the text is conditioned and determined by two inescapable factors: that we are entrapped between overlapping narrators, Sterne and Tristram; and that we are confined within Tristram's mind. The freedom of discrimination essential to the comprehension of an ironic countermeaning is impaired by this distinctive narrative set-up and by the very particular point of view we are made to share. The "I" of the self-advertising narrator represents here not a technique or a device; it is the source of a fundamental problematic, literary and philosophical, for by limiting our horizon, it debars any immediate access to reliable knowledge. Tristram's "I," as it looms over the entire narrative, imprints its unmistakable stamp, casting a shadow which is, despite its jocular aura, quite menacing. For [as Victor Lange writes] "de ausschliessliche Anspruch des Erzählers auf die überlegene Wirklichkeit des eigenen Bewusstseins" ("the narrator's exclusive claim to the superiority of his own consciousness") marks a turning-point, and possibly a crisis, in the art of narration. The axis shifts from communication—overt or covert—with a reader to the introverted exploration of mental states and processes. In practice this means that the narrator is more in colloquy with himself than with any implied reader. And as soon as the narrator's principal commitment is towards his own consciousness, the reader is banished to an outer perimeter of the narrative, where he languishes alone as an uninitiated spectator. Writing becomes an egocentric activity that pays no more than lip-service to the reader, however loud the lip-service may be, as if in compensatory concealment of the lack of true contact. The collusive entente between narrator and reader, which is the precondition for the assured comprehension of irony, tends to wane in proportion to the growing complexity of the narrative strategy.

In *Tristram Shandy* the set-up is further complicated by the tensions inherent in Tristram's own position. He too, like the reader, is the victim of ironic ambiguities, of which he is aware but which he tries to disguise. He faces the difficult task of representing himself as a multilevel persona in his book, balancing the self-detachment of self-presentation with the self-analysis of self-assessment. He is both character and narrator, an actor in the story he is telling and the object of his own contemplation. So he appears at once as an infant controlled by parents and servants and as the controlling animator of the entire scenario. It is a curious result of this twofold continuity that [as John Preston notes] "Tristram is not born of his parents; in a strange way they are born of him," or perhaps it would be more accurate to say that they mutually bear each other. For Tristram functions simultaneously as the experiencing and the telling "I," as the remembered and the remembering figure. One bizarre outcome of this double-take is that he is actually dying while being born. Between the two poles lies his life, the "Life" that he is supposed to be chronicling. Yet here again there is a paradox, for his life is mysteriously and sadly empty, devoid of "adventures" and even of the domesticity of wife and children. The gap that is his life is filled by Toby's martial career and amours. Such life and adventures as Tristram does have—the accidental mashing of his nose and other parts—are socially hardly mentionable. This leads to further ambivalence in so far as the telling of his life implies a social act of communication, specially in the format that Tristram chooses, that of conversational utterance. Appropriating the "double prerogative of narrator and commentator, of observer and material witness, of writer and philosopher" [writes Henri Fluchère], Tristram cloaks his embarrassment in buffoonery. Nevertheless his stance is necessarily a precarious one as he endeavours to convey the unspeakable facts of his life while avoiding offensive explicitness. His mask is that of "the giddy and flexible entertainer, always dynamically involved with his audience and his material, in danger every moment of losing the sympathy of the one and his control over the other" [William Bowman Piper]. His apparently naïve, delirious monologue turns out to be a self-conscious performance. And once the reader begins to realise this, the character of the speaker, one time-honoured touchstone of rhetoric, becomes dubious and shifty. The scene is set for the more intricate enigmas of irony.

The elusiveness of the narrator in *Tristram Shandy* is matched only by his magnetism. "I wish," he muses, "I wish either my father or my mother, or indeed both of them, as they were in duty both equally bound to it, had minded what they were about when they begot me." This is one of the oddest beginnings ever invented. By embarking on his life-story with a consideration of the circumstances of his conception, Tristram immediately thrusts his narrative out of the orbit of normal expectation. His wish induces a disorientation far greater than the "I want a hero" in *Don Juan*, which disrupts the *narrative* process, whereas here it is the most private *human* creative process that is abruptly exposed to public scrutiny. Tristram's wish is the expression of the esoteric non-logic of a mind liberated of all conventional restraints and ready to make inconsequential leaps of the imagination. The gentle hesitancy of its tone emphasises the enormity of its contents. For all its poignant wistfulness it throws the accepted natural order wholly out of joint, not simply through Tristram's voyeuristic prying into his parents' marital bed, but rather through the underlying implicit assumption that the individual can impose his will on the world by the force of his mind. It is no casual usage of a word when Tristram says that his parents should have "minded." This is tantamount to a denial of the validity of outer reality, which is here subjected to the shaping powers of the personal imagination. By subverting the laws of nature, Tristram's wish destroys the familiar ontological schema, which he replaces with a flimsy, idiosyncratic order. It is the individual sensibility, however quirky, that creates the rules of the system in *Tristram Shandy*, and its criteria are the imperatives of an eccentric psychology. The wish of the opening sentence thus postulates the potential for the unlimited reversibility of all the generally recognised bases of human existence. Its deranging iconoclasm is the opposite to the reassuring affirmation of moral axioms and social codes at the beginning of *Pride and Prejudice*. The unexpected is the only standard of expectation in *Tristram Shandy*. Its spaces, its gaps, its subjectivism, its ambiguities, and its profession of the topsy-turvy as its governing principle all point to the fragility of its universe and of its artistic edifice. Everything in *Tristram Shandy* may be other than what it seems.

II

This becomes fully evident in the narrator-reader relationship. At first glance this might appear one of the less controversial aspects of *Tristram Shandy*. The first-person narrator is disposed, indeed anxious, to engage his readers' benign response. He offers him many assurances of his good faith and credibility with such phrases as: "you may take my word," and "Believe me, good folks." At least half of *Tristram Shandy*, according to Ian Watt's reckoning, is taken up with these direct addresses by Tristram to his audience. His rapport with his reader has been characterised as one of "friendship." Certainly he is eager for the reader's attention, and, beyond that, for his active participation in the unfolding of the tale. The rhetoric is designed to impress on the occasionally lazy reader the need for a lively creativity on his part. The technique of insinuation, the famous aposiopesis, is one common goad to provoke cooperation by exciting curiosity, just as the blank page may serve as a concrete invitation: "—call for pen and ink—here's paper ready to your hand.—Sit down, Sir, paint her to your own mind—" (vol. 6, chap. 38). These transparent devices to implicate the fictive reader in the action of Tristram's story have a further function in fostering in the actual reader a consciousness of himself as reader that partners the writer's unremitting awareness of himself as a writer.

However, beside the reader who is internal to the fiction and "who actually becomes a character in the novel," there is another who is external to the fiction. This reduplication of contrived and real reader corresponds to the doubling of fictive and actual author; just as Sterne writes of a writer writing, so we read of readers reading. But though the external reader is superimposed on the internal and at times concurs in his reactions to Tristram's pleas and admonitions, the two by no means coincide. In counterbalance to his involvement in the narrative, the external reader also maintains a detachment from it. Apart from following the action alongside the internal reader, he is in a position, too, to watch Tristram's manipulation of his contrived reader. For the actual reader is distinct from the fictive reader, who is entirely the product of Tristram's invention, in his capacity to distance himself from the action and from the narrator's manoeuvres. He has the independence of judgement that enables him to see what is going on and at the same time to see through it. In other words, he possesses that dual perspective that is the foundation for irony.

This dichotomy between the internal and the external reader is of vital importance for *Tristram Shandy*. Surprisingly it has been largely overlooked. "The text itself . . . ," Preston for instance maintains, "forms the basis for a relationship; it is what reader and narrator share." Certainly it is what the contrived reader and the fictive narrator share because this captive fictive reader's responses are literally dictated by the puppeteer, Tristram. On the other hand, the actual reader, who faces the text from outside the fiction, can evaluate and construct it from his own angle of vision in a manner denied to the contrived reader. So the actual reader, while "sharing" the text with the narrator and being drawn in by some of his tactics, can at the same time take cognizance of its essential slipperiness and the lack of assurance it affords to those who—to borrow its own imagery—use both ears: "whilst I satisfy *that ear* which the reader chuses to *lend* me—I might not dissatisfy the other which he keeps to himself" (vol. 7, chap. 21).

Whether Tristram's contrived reader has two ears is open to question. He repeatedly mishears, misunderstands, misinterprets, jumps to the wrong conclusions, makes mistaken associations. But for this we have only Tristram's word, his constant reprimands and his assiduous corrections of the alleged misreadings. In fact the fictive reader, though strong as a presence, remains shadowy in outline. His image is vexatory: male ("Sir"), female ("Madam"); singular ("your worship"), plural ("your reverences"); "curious and inquisitive" (vol. 1, chap. 5), yet "impatient" (vol. 5, chap. 35); "inattentive" (vol. 1, chap. 20), yet endowed with a good memory (vol. 4, chap. 17); often deemed incapable of understanding (vol. 1, chap. 18; vol. 3, chap. 17), yet capable of imaginative input (vol. 2, chap. 11; vol. 6, chap. 38).

As equivocal as his persona is his relationship to the fictive narrator. On the surface it is one of cordial warmth, in contrast to the contentious tartness in [Diderot's] *Jacques le fataliste*. Tristram shows concern for his reader as he explains his procedures, encourages and reassures him: "don't be terrified, madam, this stair-case conversation is not as long as the last" (vol. 4, chap. 20); he warns him about "a devil" of a chapter (vol. 5, chap. 3), cajoles him to persevere (vol. 5, chap. 41), and even indicates when it is permissible for him to skip or sleep, and when he must pay attention (vol. 5, chap. 7). But despite this apparently close and amiable collaboration, he does not give as much guidance as would seem. He maintains at the outset that he has been "so very particular already" for the sake of those readers "who find themselves ill at ease, unless they are let into the whole secret from first to last" (vol. 1, chap. 4). "Very particular" he may indeed be in the sense of offering massive detail on small matters; "let into the whole secret from first to last": this the reader never is, neither the fictive nor the actual reader. On the contrary, Tristram loves to mystify, to lead on, to drop hints, or asterisks—in short, to leave the reader in a state of uncertainty. He often refuses to answer questions, preferring to retreat into his recital, and he shuns responsibility by sheltering behind characters and events. Consequently he does not develop any intimate, confiding alliance with his audience, let alone establish any steady contract. In a double entendre that reveals the tragicomedy of his position, he confesses that only "with an ass, I can commune for ever" for "I understand thee perfectly" (vol. 7, chap. 32). With human beings his tone is on many occasions begging or apologetic, as he pleads for a tolerant hearing or even for "help" (vol. 9, chap. 20). Gradually it becomes clear to the actual reader with his two ears that Tristram's insistent addresses are a form of public rhetoric, and that his handling of the fictive reader is a facet of his showmanship. A show of genial self-confidence is put on as much for his own benefit as for his reader's. For he tries to hide from himself and from his listener that he cannot fulfil his promises, that he gets nowhere with his tale, that he is quite unable to lead or direct in this journey through the maze of his mind because he himself cannot find the way. Having culled the reader's trust, he cannot live up to the expectations he has fostered. It is even doubtful whether he accomplishes his vaunted goal to write "against the spleen," "to drive the *gall* and other *bitter juices* from the gall bladder, liver and sweet-bread of his majesty's subjects" (vol. 4, chap. 22) by laughter since the contents of his tale with its four deaths, many misadventures, and his own decline, is far from cheering. Tristram's volubility, his animation, and his will to optimism screen out these sombre aspects of his tale. While not deliberately duplicitous, he is both evasive and cunning as a narrator. By cultivating a seemingly intimate relationship with his contrived reader, he is in fact drawing him into an ironic game in which the reader becomes an accomplice to, and a dupe of, deception as well as of self-deception on Tristram's part. Ultimately the narrator's proffered friendship yields only puzzlement and discomfort to a reader who has been inveigled into patience, participation, and perseverance and who is, for all his pains, left in the dark.

The actual reader fares little better, for we too are at the mercy of the fictive narrator's conflicting signals. Though we may perceive the innate shiftiness of the narrative situation, we have no means to overcome it. Instead of enjoying the narrator's confidence, as in *Pride and Prejudice* and *Madame Bovary*, we are relegated here to the position of unacknowledged eavesdroppers. Granted that the problem of evaluation is intrinsic to first-person narratives; as Lowry Nelson has put it, the reader is "on his own and left balancing the evidence as given and evaluated by his first-person fictional collaborator, who happens under the circumstances to be his only source." But, as Nelson goes on to argue in regard to *Moll Flanders*, there can be "a sort of contractual understanding between author and reader that transcends the self-knowledge of Moll." Such a contractual understanding is at best fleeting in *Tristram Shandy*, subject itself to the teasing mobility that pervades the entire work. The restless movement of the eternal present recording the activity of Tristram's consciousness leaves neither time nor space for the reader's deliberations. In the kaleidoscopic verbal and situational commotion no stance is ever sufficiently fixed to provide a reasonably lasting basis for interpretation.

So the actual reader, like his fictive counterpart, is involved in an unceasing process of reassessment and readjustment. This concerns not only the happenings within the tale, but also the personality of the teller. It may well be that "willingly or grudgingly, fully or partially, trust him we must" because we have no choice; yet in fact we can't and we don't trust him. We doubt the reliability of the information he transmits; we wonder how he came to know certain things, and, above all, we speculate whether he is presenting things as they were, or as his imagination perceived them. As Helene Moglen has pointed out, "Tristram's weakness for histrionics, revealed in his liberal use of apostrophe and invocation, places his honesty in a questionable light." His constant need to correct himself and, even more, his inconsistencies evoke an image of confusion that further reduces confidence in his trustworthiness. Our options, however, are scant since any dialogue between actual narrator and reader can occur only through the mediation of the fictive narrator's self-representation.

Occasionally there is a palpable discrepancy that opens up a chink for an alternative view. The most important centres on the matter of power. It is Tristram's reiterated boast that his is the will that controls the protagonists and the reader: " 'tis enough to have thee in my power," he tells his "gentle reader" (vol. 7, chap. 6); most petulantly he asserts his jurisdiction over his mother by abruptly declaring: "In this attitude I am determined to let her stand for five minutes" (vol. 5, chap. 5), and his omnipotence over his whole artifact by giving free rein to his momentary whim: "A sudden impulse comes across me—drop the curtain, *Shandy*—I drop it—Strike a line here across the paper, *Tristram*—I strike it—and hey for a new chapter!" (vol. 4, chap. 10). Here there is firm ground for discriminating irony: beyond the irony that takes place between the fictive narrator and his creation as he plays with his protagonists, his contrived readers and his plot, there is an additional level of irony at Tristram's expense as we realise that the truth is the contrary to what he says. His will does not control and shape his narrative; it seems almost to have a will of its own, to be as susceptible to contingency as Tristram himself is. His physical impotence is the symbol of his lack of power. Through the erratic, inconclusive course of Tristram's narrative, the actual narrator, Sterne, indicates to us the irony of Tristram's claim. Behind Tristram's back, so to speak, a secret collusive intimation passes from the hidden author to the reader, as in *Pride and Prejudice* and *Madame Bovary*.

This is the exception rather than the rule in *Tristram Shandy*. Generally we are hostages to the first-person narrator. Having two ears, we are conscious of the ironic game that is going on, but we do not have sufficient clues to reconstruct any meaning with definity. This is the major reason for the vague malaise which besets readers of *Tristram Shandy*, the uneasy sense, as in Kafka or Beckett, or ineffable implications that are felt but cannot be specified. This method amounts to "warfare with the reader." It is a cross between a guerilla campaign and a sparring match, in which the text seems teasingly to defy us to read it. In the end it is the reader who is made to feel unreliable. For when the author-narrator is a mischievous adversary rather than a sound partner, cooperation between reader and narrator is perforce replaced by the reader's solitary, largely unaided effort. Irony becomes not a matter of reconstructing a covert intended meaning but of confronting a bewildering multiplicity of possible meanings. What began as a pretty innocuous intellectual game turns into a disorienting experience of vertigo. The impact of *Tristram Shandy* has been vividly captured by Virginia Woolf: "our sense of elasticity is increased so much that we scarcely know where we are. We lose our sense of direction. We go backwards instead of forwards." In effect we are circling in search of a categoric meaning where the text is driving us to acknowledge the existence of a plurality of meanings; we are looking for standards of judgement in a work that takes oddity as its norm; we long for closure as we stare into the open spaces. We have no authoritative guide to direct us with discreet promptings. For the highly audible and visible narrating persona has, despite his vociferous presence, a tenuous and problematical relationship with his audience. He is a showman, intent first and foremost on his own performance and on the impression he is making; that is to say, more concerned with himself as narrator than with his narrative. Here we have one of the great paradoxes—and stumbling-blocks—of the art of narration: where the narrator appears closest to the reader, he may be most distant. A surface friendliness may be the ironic mask for a far-reaching alienation. Thus, extensive though Tristram's account is of his Life and Opinions, we remain outsiders, bemused spectators, "in a manner perfect strangers to each other" (vol. 1, chap. 6). Our participation is as illusory and our reading as flawed as that of the fictive reader. What is more, Tristram takes delight in fostering this state of uncertainty: "Sir, I am of so nice and singular a humour, that if I thought you was able to form the least judgement or probable conjecture to yourself, of what was to come, in the next page,— I would tear it out of my book" (vol. 1, chap. 25). But on what grounds should "Sir"—or we—accept at face value even so explicit a statement from the pen of a master-ironist?

III

Such extreme scepticism is supported by the rhetoric of *Tristram Shandy* whose jagged physical surface points to the pitfalls and the brittleness of language as a means of communication. It offers irrefutable evidence for Tristram's contention that it is "the unsteady uses of words" that is "the true cause of the confusion . . . and a fertile source of obscurity" (vol. 2, chap. 2). So the rhetoric, "alienating and seductive," as much a focus of irritation as of fascination, becomes the illustration and the incarnation of the equivocation that is central to *Tristram Shandy*. The language, the syntax, and even the punctuation bring the reader into a direct encounter with the turbulence it both presents and represents. And it is inescapable because this peculiarly fitful use of words, in an irony singularly appropriate to *Tristram Shandy*, is the only element of consistency. The sole constancy of *Tristram Shandy* lies in its very inconstancy.

The one narrating voice is heard by the fictive and the actual reader alike, but what we perceive may differ substantially from the interpretation imputed to "madam." This discrepancy of response is one of the primary spaces for irony in *Tristram Shandy*. Particularly those instances where the fictive reader is chided for misreading or for jumping to wrong conclusions afford an opportunity to alert the actual reader to the correct understanding, though the irony may be a compound one in that the fictive reader's— possibly bawdy—construction may after all be the right one, however strenuously Tristram tries to head it off. Through such complicated manoeuvres the rhetoric becomes an important vehicle for irony in *Tristram Shandy*.

All the traditional stylistic devices of the ironic mode are used freely: hyperbole followed by anticlimax, comic overstatement, blatant nonsequiturs, incongruous combinations and self-evident misstatements. But these tropes, though common in *Tristram Shandy*, are almost incidental, and certainly subsidiary. The major stratagems are at once more gross and more original, the favourite resources being double entendres, puns, innuendoes, suspensions, asterisks, aposiopesis, and sundry typographical capers. All these fulfil the same function: to deprive language of its denotative simplicity and to open it up to other possible meanings. Words themselves are made duplicitous, dubious, "unsteady" by a subversive process of extension. The most famous instance of this technique is with the totally innocent word "nose" which is loaded with sexual overtones by a devious art of suggestion that manages to insinuate exactly what it purports to deny:

> I define a nose, as follows,—intreating only beforehand, and beseeching my readers, both male and female, of what age, complexion, and condition soever, for the love of God and their own souls, to guard against the temptations and suggestions of the devil, and suffer him by no art or wile to put any other ideas into their minds, than what I put into my definition.—For by the word *Nose*, throughout all this long chapter of noses, and in every other part of my work, where the word *Nose* occurs,—I declare, by that word I mean a Nose, and nothing more, or less.
>
> (vol. 3, chap. 31)

By this so-called "definition" "to avoid all confusion," confusion and ambiguity are skilfully nurtured, and this is done again brilliantly with "whiskers" (vol. 5, chap. 1), "Cover-d-way" and "Backside" (vol. 2, chap. 6), and even with such neutral terms as "means," "matters," "things," "it," "affairs," "faculties," whose very vagueness allows them to be laden with insidious implications. The same procedure governs aposiopesis, suspensions, asterisks, dashes, blanks: these are spaces which the reader is invited to fill by the creation of his own meaning. The technqiue is as risky as it is clever; it misfires if the reader cannot discover a meaning; but if the meaning he discovers is scabrous, the responsibility is his.

The rhetoric of *Tristram Shandy* thus enriches the spectrum of ironic communication. "For irony, . . . has passed from the verbal nuance to a still wider range of suggestiveness. It exists now in gesture and mime, as far as the printed page can be adapted to these things" [A. E. Dyson]. On the other hand, this expansion, coupled with the belief in the essential unsteadiness of words, leads also to far greater complexity in the nature of ironies. *Tristram Shandy* has been deemed "annoying and sometimes infuriating because not only are things not what they seem; they are not the opposite of what they seem either" [J. Paul Hunter]. The simpler irony of reversal, such as predominates in *Pride and Prejudice*, is superseded by a progressive deconstruction of meaning. While the traditional ironist "dodges between the innocuous letter of what he says and the subversive spirit of what he means" [Peter Conrad], the romantic ironist darts about in a labyrinth of hypothetical meanings, none of which can be equated with "what he means" because he maintains an awareness of the plurality of meanings and therefore does not settle on any single one as definitive. His perception of the world and, most important, of language as in a state of flux differentiates him decisively from the traditional ironist who believes that words can be used in a steady format to convey a specific meaning. Only the postulate of the stability of language in its denotative as well as in its emotive capacity warrants the assumption—basic to *Pride and Prejudice* and *Madame Bovary*—that the reader will be able to reconstruct the covert intended connotation of a message encoded in irony. Once language, on the contrary, is seen as "unsteady," the comprehension of meaning inevitably becomes uncertain and open-ended. This is one of the major reasons why confident reconstruction is virtually excluded in *Tristram Shandy*. The shiftiness of the linguistic base militates against the hierarchical ordering necessary to the understanding of irony. The rhetoric of *Tristram Shandy* embodies in the sphere of language the same fundamental indeterminacy inherent in the perplexing narrative situation with its dual writers and twofold readers.

The syntax and the tempo of the prose heighten the sense of indefinity through their extreme mobility. The abrupt transitions, the inordinate exploitation of the dash, the rapid shuffling of interrogation and correction, the conversational casualness all contribute to the impression of chaos and incoherence. Whatever is posited in one phrase is restricted, modified or amended in the next; the text of *Tristram Shandy* never rests into fixity literally or figuratively. Even the physical components of the book create a confused motion that militates against the establishment of a steady perspective. The favoured grammatical elements: the optative "I wish," the alternative "or," the reservation "except," the relative clause qualifying what has preceded it—these testify to the precariousness of every statement. As in the style of the *Flegeljahre*, the sheer abundance of *Tristram Shandy* tends to obscure rather than clarify; the minute concentration on the precision of the microcosmic detail serves ironically to highlight the sprawling blurred expanse of the macrocosm. The involuted, apparently aimless flow is objectified in those quirky squiggles (vol. 6, chap. 40) which are at once Tristram's cardiographs of consciousness" [Conrad] and the epitome of the text he is shaping. In *Tristram Shandy* the fractured hyphenated style "demonstrates the impossibility of merely literal meaning; for by means of the very extravagant, foolish syntax attitudes shift and redefine one another" [John Traugott]. Language is being queried through and in its own practices.

The fluidity of meaning and its interconnection with "the unsteady uses of words" is shown in the strange verbal and mental associations that all the main protagonists habitually make. Though the effect is comic, the implications are serious. For each figure has his own personal, frequently idiosyncratic trains of thought on which he drifts away from the accepted understanding of words and ideas. The best example is Toby with his fixation on war-games; to him the "auxiliaries" on which Walter holds forth denote not verbs but troops, while "radical moisture" suggests ditchwater, and "radical heat" brandy (vol. 5, chap. 40). Quite ordinary words too, such as "bridge" and "train," are liable to be misunderstood as a result of mistaken or merely odd associations. Through the repetitive network of misapprehensions the pervasiveness of cross-communication is strongly implied. Every individual, by endowing words with private connotations, comes to speak a language inaccessible to others. The multivalence of words is another symptom of the fragility of a fictional world in which there are no secure points of reference that transcend the subjective vision.

In this sense the problem of the dysfunction of language is crucial to *Tristram Shandy*. Sterne was familiar with Locke's *Essay Concerning Human Understanding*, to which reference is made in *Tristram Shandy*. In book 3 of the *Essay* Locke elaborated his innovative view of words as signs for ideas. While by no means unaware of the potential danger of such a theory, Locke maintains by and large a sanguine optimism. By comparison, Sterne harbours a far deeper scepticism about the prospects of " 'getting something across,' whether it is missiles or people or meanings" [Sigurd Burckhardt]. His witty use of graphic devices—blank pages, a black page, a marbled page—is an attempt to circumvent conventional methods of expression. But these are hardly sufficient grounds for turning Sterne into a crypto-modern writer obsessed with the inadequacy of words and the limitations of language. His reservations about language are counteracted by an exuberant pleasure in words. His fictive narrator is surely one of the most loquacious ever invented, delighting in verbal gymnastics of astonishing agility. If *Tristram Shandy* is about the dysfunction of language, it is also about its hyperactivity. The two, far from being mutually exclusive, are poised in an ironic tension that imparts to *Tristram Shandy* its particular flavour. In its language as in its narrative situation *Tristram Shandy* is a prolonged contradiction of its overt posture: in the same way as the first-person fictive narrator does not maintain any authentic relationship with his contrived or actual reader despite his insistent presence, so none of the manifold conversations—between Tristram and the contrived reader, between Walter and Toby, Walter and his wife, etc.—achieves any true communion. The almost overwhelming mass of words belies—or covers—an unaccountable inner lacuna. Tristram says a great deal about his "Life and Opinions," but in the end, what essential facts are really known about him? and what is the upshot of Toby's affair with Widow Wadham? or of Mrs Shandy's long listening at the chink? Beneath the resonance of the rhetoric there is a space of silence; for the irony of the language is that it reveals, in the very effort at verbal exchange, that there is no exchange because each individual is enclosed within the private confines of his own understanding of words. This fragmentation is the antithesis to the common language shared by the protagonists of *Pride and Prejudice*, whose unproblematic grasp of words and concepts is the basis for their confidence in the truth of knowledge and its attainability. When words are basically "unsteady," they are less usable as the medium for irony because they are in themselves already embodiments of an ironic principle. Language in *Tristram Shandy*, for all its brilliant profusion, is fallible to the point of fallaciousness.

IV

Towards the end of the first volume, Tristram begins to tell Madam of the wound that Toby sustained at Namur, and then suddenly breaks off, thwarting her curiosity by dodging her imputed queries: "The story of that, Madam, is long and interesting—but it would be running my history all upon heaps to give it to you here.—'Tis for an episode hereafter; and every circumstance relating to it in its proper place, shall be faithfully laid before you" (vol. 1, chap. 21). The questions raised here extend well beyond the particular episode of Toby's wound: is there in fact a "proper place" for things in *Tristram Shandy*? and by what or whose criteria is the "proper place" to be determined? Such questions have a direct bearing on any consideration of the organisation of *Tristram Shandy*. For a recognition of its norms must precede exploration of its ironic departure from, or reversal, or subversion of that implicit norm.

However, difficulties immediately arise: by what norm is *Tristram Shandy* to be measured? The generic context that should serve as a yardstick is so blurred that it cannot be invoked as an authoritative standard. Are *The Life and Opinions of Tristram Shandy, Gent.* to be read as a biography, compiled by Laurence Sterne, or as an autobiography being written by Tristram? The peculiar dual texture forces an inclusive and inevitably ambiguous answer. Should the work be regarded as a burlesque? or an improvisation? and what is the place of the digressions in the total disposition? Through the admission of Tristram's "Opinions," the work's scope is so vastly expanded as to warrant the inclusion of everything that passes through his mind, even his so-called "digressions." For "madam," the fictive reader, these matters are settled by Tristram, who is the final arbiter within the fiction; for the actual reader the answers are by no means so simple. Indeed, here once again, he finds himself in an alarming quicksand that denies him a sound footing. Ingenious solutions to this predicament have been put forward, notably by Richard Lanham who sites *Tristram Shandy* in the framework of games of pleasure as an "*ilinx* (games involving loss of balance, the sensation of vertigo—drugs, for example, or a ride on a roller coaster)." The game could also be described as the deployment of a progressive irony that undermines, almost systematically, each and every postulate only to replace it with a further one that will in turn be scuttled in a volatile sequence that captures the evanescence of human existence.

This is the irony that shapes the entire design of *Tristram Shandy*. It consists of overlapping, superimposed components that encroach on each other and displace one another as if in competition for the readers'—and the narrator's—attention. There is no separation into distinct units, as in the incidents of Don Juan's adventures, nor any ordering of the various levels of fiction as in the *Flegeljahre*. What is characteristic of *Tristram Shandy*, on the contrary, is the perpetual state of flux. No single fictional strand ever remains in unchallenged ascendancy; what is the centre of gravity? the story of Tristram's life? or of Toby's *amours*? or of the writing of Tristram's autobiography? The continual breaks, the fluctuations in time and space with the abrupt switch from one focus to another induce a dizzying sense of turbulence. The movement of *Tristram Shandy* has aptly been characterised as "indirect, parabolic, hyperbolic, cycloid" [Burckhardt]. Tristram summarises it more simply but no less puzzlingly: "In a word, my work is digressive, and it is progressive too,—and at the same time" (vol. 1, chap. 22). The paradoxicality of this double, self-contradictory motion is justified by the nature of the story which obliges him "continually to be going backwards and forwards to keep all tight together in the reader's fancy" (vol. 6, chap. 33). The work expands in this seemingly wayward manner because it can progress forwards only by digressing backwards into Tristram's memory. Its structure is governed by an inner irony that determines its architectonics. Digressiveness is in fact an integral and necessary part of this peculiar novel's economy. The earliest to perceive this was Coleridge who noted in jottings for a lecture given February 24, 1818 that "the digressive spirit is not wantonness, but the *very form* of his genius." With his imaginative insight Coleridge places Sterne in the lineage of Cervantes and alongside Jean Paul Richter; he denotes their common features as "humour," "ironical wit," and a "delight to end in nothing, or a direct contradiction." What Coleridge recognised was that an artistic principle governs the apparent capriciousness of *Tristram Shandy*. Its name is not "Muddle," as E. M. Forster averred, but irony in the Schlegelian sense. The configuration of *Tristram Shandy* is that "gebildetes künstliches Chaos" ('shaped artificial chaos') that Schlegel was to extol as the ideal romantic form of narrative.

Such conceptual irony must be distinguished from dramatic irony. Dramatic irony structures plot through the pattern of contrasts and reversals internal to the work. Conceptual irony is intrinsic to the fabric of the work, to its narrative strategies, to its overall organisation as well as to its language. Because it is literally ingrained in the fabric itself as a pervasive determinant, it is not amenable to resolution in the same way as dramatic irony, which is more local, temporary, and limited in its manifestations. And, paradoxically, because of its very centrality, conceptual irony proves more resistant to identification than the ironies closer to the surface and therefore more readily visible, such as the rhetorical or the situational. Extended into a wider format, this distinction amounts ultimately to a differentiation between irony as a device and irony as *Weltanschauung*, between those works, on the one hand, that *use* irony for a specific purpose, such as plot dynamics, or characterisation, or satire, and, on the other hand, those that *are* ironic. *Pride and Prejudice* is the prototype of the one, and *Tristram Shandy* of the other.

One outlet for the conceptual irony of *Tristram Shandy* is in its wholesale sabotage of narrative conventions. Tristram's preface pops up without warning in the middle of the third volume when he has "a moment to spare" with all his heroes off his hands (vol. 3, chap. 20); two chapters are skipped (vol. 9, chaps. 18 and 19) and inserted later; a chapter of ten pages is missing (vol. 4, chap. 14); protagonists are left standing on the stairs or abandoned in the kitchen for pages and hours on end while more urgent business intervenes until they are suddenly recalled and brought back into the story. These flamboyant affronts to narrative syntaxis transmute the straight line of traditional storytelling into those errant squiggles that Tristram draws (vol. 6, chap. 40). By seeming to aim for the straight line, by including a preface, by pretending to aspire to regularity, the incongruity of the text's irregularity is further emphasised. Yet Sterne is more than merely one of the "zany jugglers of narrative convention" [Robert Alter, *Partial Magic*]. The mishaps, interruptions, digressions that beset the narrative are ciphers for the contingencies of existence. The text, too, is subject to accident and susceptible to the unpredictability of life; "if nothing stops us in our way" (vol. 1, chap. 10) is its rueful, poignant, and ironic motto. The innumerable stops, delays, detours and entanglements are an image of the inconsequential, illogical world of *Tristram Shandy*, in which there is no "proper place" for things.

Nor for that matter is there a proper time. The dislocation of plot order has as its corollary a glaring discontinuity in the time sequence. The action swings constantly not only from Tristram's present time of writing to the past of his memory, but well back into the pre-history of the protagonists. The total length of fictional time amounts, according to Mendilow's calculations [in *Time and the Novel*], to three-quarters of a century on the shortest reckoning; other critics arrive at a much longer time-span, dating the events to the years between 1644 and 1766. Whichever is the case, the impression is one of utmost confusion: temporally the narrative has no beginning, middle, or end. In fact it closes four years before Tristram's birth, on whose conception it opened; in the meanwhile, in a series of intersections, interpolations, and superimpositions, it leaps back and forth from the present to various disconnected segments of the past. What makes this technique so disconcerting is not the temporal multidimensionality as such, nor even the jumbling that gives causes after effects, conclusions before happenings; it is rather the absence of any discernible basic linear chronology to which the time-shifts can be related. There is no central point of reference from which the flashbacks and excursions can be arranged and mastered. As a result, the individual incidents appear more like fragmentary spots of time than as parts of a continuum.

Time is thus made relative, shifting, and personal; it is largely removed from the outer objective measure of chronos to the inner subjective realm of duration. Tristram's two journeys to France, many years apart, are telescoped in his mind as if into one: "I have been getting forwards in two different journies together, and with the same dash of the pen—for I have got entirely out of Auxerre in this journey which I am writing now, and I am got half way out of Auxerre in that which I shall write hereafter" (vol. 7, chap. 28). This is one of several instances when the fictive narrator explicitly draws attention to problems of time. In the middle of the fourth volume, for instance, he takes stock of his progress:

I am this month one whole year older than I was this time twelve-month; and having got, as you perceive, almost into the middle of my fourth volume—and no farther than to my first day's life— 'tis demonstrative that I have three hundred and sixty-four days more life to write just now, than when I first set out; so that instead of advancing, as a common writer, in my work with what I have been doing at it—on the contrary, I am just thrown so many volumes back—was every day of my life to be as busy a day as this—And why not?—and the transactions and opinions of it to take up as much description—And for what reason should they be cut short? at this rate I should just live 364 times faster than I should write—It must follow, an' please your worships, that the more I write, the more I shall have to write—and consequently, the more your worships read, the more your worships will have to read.

                                                                    (vol. 4, chap. 13)

The discrepancy between time remembered, time of writing, and time of reading is underlined here. What is more, the time of reading itself, the "hour and a half's tolerable good reading since my Uncle Toby rung the bell" (vol. 2, chap. 8) has a dual connotation since it refers in the first place to Tristram's fictive reader but can apply to the actual reader too. External, mechanical time has therefore been replaced in *Tristram Shandy* by a multifaceted, relativistic, and ironic sense of time that plays the past off against the present, mathematical time against experiential time, reading time against fictional time.

The manipulation of time in *Tristram Shandy* produces a twofold and contradictory effect: a disorientation, almost a feeling of vertigo, arising from the scurrying transition from one temporal segment to another; yet also a haunting apprehension of circularity and indeed of statis. Between Toby's first "I wish . . . you had seen what prodigious armies we had in Flanders" (vol. 2, chap. 18) and his reiteration of the identical phrase (vol. 3, chap. 1) some eight pages intervene and far more than "a minute" (vol. 2, chap. 19) as Tristram inserts what "should have been told a hundred and fifty pages ago" and launches into an account of his father's opinions. The repetition twice of "What prodigious armies you had in Flanders" by Walter (vol. 3, chaps. 2 and 6) together with the triple reprise of "Any man, madam" (vol. 3, chap. 5) suggests that the narrative is, as it were, becalmed; it reechoes the same phrases, retreads the same ground, and in spite of its rhetorical energy it finally gets nowhere. It is by no means coincidental that it ends four years before it began. In the wholly ironic structure of *Tristram Shandy* "proper place" and proper time have become conditional notions.

V

There is still a further dimension of irony in *Tristram Shandy*. It is not only Sterne, the actual author, who is an ironist; the fictive narrator, too, is endowed with a self-questioning ironic intelligence that engages in an incessant scrutiny of the autobiography he is writing. Through the portrayal of an immensely self-conscious writer at work, an internal metafictional irony is woven into *Tristram Shandy*. The arrangement is considerably more complex than in *Don Juan*, where the ironic commentary on the work-in-progress comes from a source external to the fictional myth, from an author who stands beside his artifact and who addresses his scathingly humorous critique to his readers as well as to himself. In *Tristram Shandy*, by contrast, the ironic commentator is a persona within the fiction, and it is he who subverts his own narrative by his perpetual breaks in the fictional illusion. This is the context in which the intruding narrator becomes "a force so disruptive that it transforms the very nature of the work" [Wayne C. Booth]. That transformation occurs through an intensification and a compounding of irony that has the effect of increasing the distance—and the alienation—between the text and the reader. For Tristram's reflections on his writing are primarily a dialogue with himself; at most he extends to his fictive reader the semblance of an apologia or an exhortation. It may be no more than a semblance since he is a showman playing games and cultivating illusions with his tale. As an actual reader takes cognisance of Tristram's dubiousness, he becomes more and more of a sceptical outsider to the narrative process. Not being trusted by Tristram, he in turn grows untrusting. So Sterne's invention of an ironic gamesman as narrator creates a kind of immanent irony that represents a quantum leap in ironic narration.

The immediate impact of Tristram's keen awareness of himself as a writer comes as a threat to the viability of his fiction. He destroys what he creates through his innumerable references to its fragile fictional status. There is hardly a page of *Tristram Shandy* without an overt mention of "my story," "my work," "my book," "this volume," what is to come in "the next chapter," the disturbance caused by "the door harshly opening in the next chapter but one" (vol. 3, chap. 11), what future chapters are being planned (including a chapter on chapters!). The typographical tricks, too, serve as teasing reminders of the printed nature of the entire enterprise. Tristram even portrays himself physically at the time of writing, sitting at his desk "this 12th day of August, 1766, in a purple jerkin and yellow pair of slippers, without either wig or cap on" (vol. 9, chap. 2) or "in the most pensive and melancholy frame of mind, . . . dropping thy pen—spurting thy ink about thy table and thy books" (vol. 3, chap. 28). He envisages himself more as a writer than as an actor in the happenings he is recording. This is hardly surprising since he is either not yet born or an infant at the time he is chronicling, while his present reality is the act of composition. His self-consciousness leads to a continuous anxious assessment of his performance and progress. The hypothetical account of his Life and Opinions is punctuated and punctured by a running critical review of his own methods of narration, the difficulties facing him as a writer and the means whereby he hopes to overcome them.

Yet in endeavouring to bolster the credibility of his text, Tristram is in fact undermining it by drawing attention not merely to the predicaments of composition but also to the essential fictionality of the illusion he is conjuring up. The world of Walter and Mrs Shandy, Toby and Widow Wadham comes across not as a self-sustaining entity enclosed in a well-wrought capsule (as, for instance, the worlds of Elizabeth and Darcy, of Charles and Emma) but as an articulated authorial construct. This does not, of course, imply that the world of Walter and Toby lacks imaginative vitality; that vitality, however, is the outcome of Tristram's creative effort in evoking it. Intervening between that world and the reader—fictive and actual—there is not only a palpable distancing, but also a pronounced refraction through the mediating presence of Tristram, whose vision generates that other removed fictive world within the fiction of *Tristram Shandy*. The recurrent allusions to the business of writing are insistent representations of Tristram's role as author and of the fictionality of his artifact. What is more, the concentration on the techniques of writing, for example on the metaphorical aspects of a phrase, foster in the reader a concomitant consciousness of his involvement in the act of reading. The prominence of this metafictional element, allied with the interruptive mode of narration, results in a fundamental shift of emphasis in *Tristram Shandy*. Its story is not just "in part the story of its telling" [as Preston claims]; the telling of the storytelling becomes so dominant and invasive as to overshadow and virtually oust the story itself. The overt content of *Tristram Shandy*—the lives of Walter, Toby, Le Fever, even Tristram himself—may be likened to branches growing out of the main supporting trunk which is the drama of the birth of this text. Instead of telling the story traditional to the novel, *Tristram Shandy* depicts the processes of shaping the novel. Like Tristram himself in the early volumes, the narrative is in *statu nascendi*. In place of the polished, finished product, the smooth fabric of illusion of *Pride and Prejudice* and *Madame Bovary*, *Tristram Shandy* offers a glimpse of the turmoil in the narrator's workshop. That this workshop is itself fictive, i.e. an invention of Laurence Sterne, is another facet of the multiple play with illusion. The text's prodigious self-reflexiveness is the expression of a progressive irony that takes an impish delight in sapping the foundations of its own edifice.

The same ironic obliquity is characteristic of the act of communication too. Presumably Tristram labours so long and hard at the mechanics of composition in order to convey a meaning or at least to impart some information about his life and opinions. He does no such thing. The facts of his life are of such an embarrassing nature that from the outset he is torn between the urge to disclose and the necessity for discreet reticence. His obsession with the problems of presenting his material becomes a screen and a substitute for his avowed undertaking. In the absence of other commitments, writing comes to be the major adventure of his life. But then the writing that was intended to serve a concrete purpose turns into an end unto itself. His preoccupation with the triumphs and perils of creativity eclipses his original desire to tell his life and opinions. The act of telling in and for itself has primacy over both the living experience on which it is based and also over the tale it is supposed to produce. Absorbed in his own manipulations, the narrator turns his gaze inwards onto himself as a creative being and onto the work he is fashioning. His orientation is towards himself rather than towards the reader, who is extraneous to the central drama that is being enacted between the writer and his text.

What happens to Tristram in this respect is a paradigm for what happens in *Tristram Shandy* as a whole. The story is so disrupted and so reduced in importance as to be subordinate to the circumstances of its evolution. Metafiction here overtakes fiction. It is this that makes *Tristram Shandy* the prototype of ironic reversal in the art of narrative. It tells of itself. In so doing, it destroys itself in the very moment of creation. It denies the reader all the props requisite for confident reading by negating any firm contours, any fixed points of reference, any secure positions or any consistency except its own inconsistency. What it holds out to the reader are the shifting uncertainties of an irony that thwarts and excludes definity.

VI

The contingencies that beset the reader, like the accidents that befall the narrative, parallel the mishaps that dog Tristram's life. In its mobility, its "digressive and progressive," "backwards and forwards" movement, *Tristram Shandy* is itself the tangible incarnation of the unpredictability which rules its fictional world. For this is, as Virginia Woolf recognised, "a world in which anything may happen." It is a world that acknowledges "what nonsense it is, either in fighting, or in writing, or any thing else (whether in rhyme to it, or not) which a man has occasion to do—to act by plan" (vol. 8, chap. 23), that hates "your *ifs*" (vol. 1, chap. 12) but that accepts "*happenings*" as "a matter of contingency, which might happen, or not, just as chance ordered it" (vol. 8, chap. 19) and that submits, however reluctantly, to the "unforeseen stoppages" (vol. 1, chap. 14) which are man's inescapable lot when chance, lucky or unlucky as the case may be, together with time, are "the powers . . . which severally check us in our careers in this world" (vol. 9, chap. 1).

From the point when Mrs Shandy interrupts her husband at the most inpropitious moment with "*a silly question*" (vol. 1, chap. 1) about that other regular domestic ritual of winding up the clock, Tristram's entire life is an illustration of the laws which govern the Shandean universe. He is the "sport of small accidents" (vol. 3, chap. 8) in a series of bizarre reversals. Because of a false alarm the previous year, Tristram's mother had forfeited her legally sanctioned right to confinement in London, so that Tristram is born in the country, where Dr Slop's ineptitude results in the mashing of his nose. Because of his frailty he has to be baptised in haste, and owing to Walter's tardiness and Susannah's distraction he is christened with the one name his father abhors. Because Trim had removed certain vital parts of the sash-windows as building materials for Toby's fortifications and nothing was ever repaired in the ramshackle Shandy home, Tristram suffers the "misadventure" (vol. 5, chap. 18) of a fortuitous circumcision when the window drops at another inopportune moment. And finally because of the slow progress made by his father in compiling the *Tristra-paedia*, his growth outstrips the manual whereby he is to be educated, and "the misfortune was, that I was all that time totally neglected" (vol. 5, chap. 16).

These are ironies of situation when the opposite—or something other—occurs to what might reasonably be expected. They are so common in *Tristram Shandy* as to coalesce into a pattern of perversity in which it becomes natural to anticipate the reverse of what might in the normal course of events be foreseen. For the Shandy family is so prone to "cross-reckonings" (vol. 4, chap. 7) that the coat-of-arms emblazoned on its coach has a *"bend sinister"* (vol. 4, chap. 25) as if to denote "the sinister turn, which every thing relating to our family was apt to take." The "confusion" occasioned by a "jumble of cross accidents" (vol. 7, chap. 37) comes to be the customary (dis)order of this singular household. Surprising turns and wholly contrary outcomes recur with a frequency amounting almost to unfailing regularity. So much so as to contain the tacit but strong implication of a universe turned topsy-turvy because it operates under the aegis of an ontological irony.

Ontological irony has the effect of debarring any systematisation whatsoever. Even to assume the prevalence of reversal is to impose a format on a world whose foremost characteristic is its defiance of rational reckoning. Possibilities go on remaining open in *Tristram Shandy*: with ineradicable optimism and against all odds Toby continues to build his fortifications, Walter to evolve his grandiose schemes, and Tristram to write his book. "Every thing in this world," Walter maintains, "is big with jest,—and has wit in it, and instruction too—if we can but find it out" (vol. 5, chap. 32). That "if" is simultaneously the great hope and the great impediment in *Tristram Shandy*; it supports the protagonists' buoyant faith in potentiality, but only to frustrate ultimate attainment. Tristram's early hesitant phrase: "if nothing stops us in our way" (vol. 1, chap. 10) comes to have an ominous ring, for this is a narrative which not only itself is constantly stopped in its way, but which also takes for its theme the ironic stoppages that halt and hinder human beings on their way through life.

Denied though they are for ever the possession of that positive certainty that resolves ironies in *Pride and Prejudice*, the protagonists of *Tristram Shandy* nonetheless manage to live quite cheerfully by acceding to a state of negative capability. In so far as there is a norm in *Tristram Shandy*, it is equivocation, the suspension of certainty in an open space filled with multiple possibilities:

> Whether *Susannah*, by taking her hand too suddenly from off the corporal's shoulder (by the whisking about of her passions)—broke a little chain of his reflections—
>
> Or whether the corporal began to be suspicious, he had got into the doctor's quarters, and was talking more like the chaplain than himself—
>
> Or whether ....
>
> Or whether—for in all such cases a man of invention and parts may with pleasure fill a couple of pages with suppositions—which

of all these was the cause, let the curious physiologist, or the curious any body determine—

(vol. 5, chap. 10)

Such teasing tactics of prevarication are used again and again in *Tristram Shandy*; often, as in this instance, they have a comic impact through the inflation of small dilemmas into impenetrable predicaments. The comic hyperbole, however, masks a tragic impasse, i.e. that assurance has been dislodged by "suppositions." The erosion of knowledge into doubt is graphically shown in Tristram's account of Toby's disability:

> Now as all the world knows, that no effect in nature can be produced without a cause and as it is as well known, that my uncle *Toby* was neither a weaver—a gardener, or a gladiator—unless as a captain, you will needs have him one—but then he was only a captain of foot—and besides the whole is an equivocation—There is nothing left for us to suppose, but that my uncle *Toby's* leg— but that will avail us little in the present hypothesis, unless it had proceeded from some ailment *in the foot*—whereas his leg was not emaciated from any disorder in his foot—for my uncle *Toby's* leg was not emaciated at all. It was a little stiff and awkward, from a total disuse of it, for the three years he lay confined at my father's house in town; but it was plump and muscular, and in all other respects as good and promising a leg as the other.
>
> I declare, I do not recollect any one opinion or passage of my life, where my understanding was more at a loss to makes ends meet, and torture the chapter I had been writing, to the service of the chapter following it, then in the present case.

(vol. 8, chap. 6)

Beginning with the confident appeal to a publicly accepted sequence of cause and effect—not quite, admittedly, "a truth universally acknowledged"—Tristram slips further into "equivocation," supposition, "hypothesis" and contradiction until he confesses his "understanding . . . at a loss to make ends meet." The failure of logic and reason in the face of an inconsequential world is a corollary of ontological irony.

What is remarkable about *Tristram Shandy* is the good-humoured equanimity with which it acquiesces to a pretty sombre vision of human existence. As Dyson has commented, "the materials for satire exist in plenty, but the will to satire is nowhere to be found." Or only very intermittently and in attenuated form, as for example in the grotesque portrayal of the scholarly disputation in Slawkenbergius's Tale (vol. 4). By and large, the purposefulness and the venom of satire are alien to Sterne; he espouses rather the relativism of irony, aware of ubiquitous incongruities, yet tolerant towards them. An acute sense of the disproportions that typify the jumble of the Shandean living and thinking space is revealed in the strange couplings of disparate particles, outlandish in the discrepancy between their levels. The embryo "HOMUNCULUS" is immediately deemed "as much and as truly our fellow-creature as my Lord Chancellor of England" (vol. 1, chap. 2); Tristram's role as chonicler of "the affairs of the kitchen" is likened to that of Rapin, the illustrious French historian of England (vol. 5, chap. 5); and Trim voices the solemn—and ludicrous—axiom that "there is nothing so awkward, as courting a woman, an' please your honour, whilst she is making sausages" (vol. 9, chap. 7). The unlikely verbal and conceptual combinations of *Tristram Shandy* denote a world so out of joint as to resist rational explanation. Coleridge was surely right when he characterised Sterne as one of those writers "who delight to end in nothing, or a direct contradiction." The unending paradoxicality of a world shaped by an ontological irony was for Sterne not a source of anguish, as it is for most modern writers, but of hilarity, albeit a "sad hilarity." For he remains a child of the eighteenth century even when he foreshadows the concerns of the age of anxiety.

VII

"Did Sterne complete Tristram Shandy?" is the title of a provocative article. The answer given is in the affirmative on the grounds that "from the beginning, Sterne planned the structure of the book as an elaborate and prolonged contradiction of the title-page," that it is literally a cock and bull story consisting "of the substitution of one story-thread for another—Toby's for Tristram's." Clever though this argument is, it addresses a question inappropriate to *Tristram Shandy*. The real issue is whether a narrative that does not merely portray but actually embodies uncertainty can and should be completed; must it not of aesthetic and philosophical necessity remain up in the air? In its concluding exchange:

> L..d! said my mother, what is all this story about?—
> A COCK and a BULL, said *Yorick*—And one of the best of its kind, I ever heard.

(vol. 9, chap. 33)

Tristram Shandy is given a summary, not an ending. It arrives at a provisional halting-place, not a terminal point, when it stops without the finality of closure. The definity implicit in conclusion is alien to the equivocation central to *Tristram Shandy*. Both its perception of the universe as a product of contingency and its associated literary form as process literature prohibit the type of neat resolution that is feasible within either the optimistic assumptions of *Pride and Prejudice* or, alternatively, the pessimistic ones of *Madame Bovary*. In its open-endedness *Tristram Shandy* is more akin to *Don Juan* and to *Jacques le fataliste*. None of these works can repose in a comfortable trust in "truth universally acknowledged"; in place of the security of the finite closure, there is an infinite quest in an unbounded space. "Endless is the Search for Truth!" (vol. 2, chap. 3) could well be the motto (and perhaps the message) of *Tristram Shandy*. Indeed, its scepticism extends even further in its insinuation that truth may ultimately be unattainable:

> 'Tis a pity, cried my father one winter's night, after a three hours painful translation of Slawkenbergius,—'tis a pity, cried my father, putting my mother's thread-paper into the book for a mark, as he spoke—that truth, brother *Toby*, should shut herself up in such impregnable fastnesses, and be so obstinate as not to surrender herself sometimes upon the closest siege.
>
> (vol. 3, chap. 41)

From the concession that truth may be beyond reach to the suspicion that it may be a mirage or an illusion is only a small step. Whether that step is taken in *Tristram Shandy* is debatable; like most of the text's major issues, this remains enveloped in indeterminacy. Clearly, no majestic truth exists here possessing the absolute validity of that posited in *Pride and Prejudice*—truth with a capital "T," so to speak. The truths in *Tristram Shandy* are modest, limited, and frequently questionable. Tristram, for instance, claims certitude in matters generally not amenable to such sureness: "I was begot in the night, betwixt the first *Sunday* and the first *Monday* in the month of *March*, in the year of our Lord one thousand seven hundred and eighteen. I am positive I was" (vol. 1, chap. 4). The proof that he advances by his pseudo-reasoning references to family habits, departures, and returns "brings the thing almost to a certainty," he insists. But his circuitous, digressive ratiocinations, together with the tenuous nature of the evidence he adduces, have the contrary ironic effect of raising serious doubts as to the authenticity of his knowledge. This comical, apparently trifling incident in the opening pages sets the pattern for *Tristram Shandy*. Each protagonist is passionately convinced of the truth of his knowledge; however, the knowledge is purely subjective, the product of an idiosyncratic mind, and based not on verifiable evidence but on intuitive convictions which may be delusions.

The foremost example of this syndrome is Walter Shandy. "I am convinced," he proclaims to Yorick, "that there is a Northwest passage to the intellectual world" (vol. 5, chap. 42). He is just as convinced, on equally gratuitous grounds, that the gateway to enlightenment is through "the use of *Auxiliaries*" whose function is "at once to set the soul a going by herself upon the materials as they are brought her; and by the versability of this great engine, round which they are twisted, to open new tracks of enquiry, and make every idea engender millions." The processes that Walter here extolls are ironically exposed in Toby's misunderstanding of "Auxiliaries" which he associates with troops, not verbs:

> But the auxiliaries, Trim, my brother is talking about,—I conceive to be different things.—
> —"You do?" said my father, rising up.
>
> (vol. 5, chap. 42)

There could hardly be a more telling illustration of the subjectivity of the mental spaces that the characters in *Tristram Shandy* inhabit. Such eccentricity of vision is most strongly emphasised in regard to Walter:

> His road lay so very far on one side, from that wherein most men travelled,—that every object before him presented a face and section of itself to his eye, altogether different from the plan and elevation of it seen by the rest of mankind.—In other words, 'twas a different object,—and in course was differently considered.
>
> (vol. 5, chap. 24)

This holds no less for Toby, or for Tristram himself; they too "saw all things in lights different from the rest of the world" (vol. 6, chap. 26). It is in this context that the epigraph to *Tristram Shandy* must be invoked: "It is not things that disturb men, but their judgements about things." Men's judgement is shown to be grossly fallacious, and consequently understanding either of an extraneous object or between individuals intrinsically fallible. Every attempt at comprehension through logic fails, from Tristram's enquiry into the origins of his misfortunes to Walter's efforts to relate happenings systematically to their causes.

If judgement, intuitive as well as rational, is deceiving, on what can men rely? "For we *trust* we have a good Conscience" is the theme of the interpolated sermon (vol. 2, chap. 17). "Surely," is its postulate, "if there is any thing in this life which a man may depend upon, and to the knowledge of which he is capable of arriving upon the most indisputable evidence, it must be this very thing,—whether he has a good conscience or no." This is promptly translated by Dr Slop into: "I am positive I am right." But "conscience is nothing else but the knowledge which the mind has within herself"; it is "not a law:—No, God and reason made the law, and have placed conscience within you to determine." The sermon in effect proposes a two-tiered ontology: the controlling level is that of God and reason, the source of the law; secondary to them is the personal conscience, intuitive in its workings. Whether conscience is "a matter of *trust*" or whether it can be "a matter of *certainty*" is the pivot of the sermon. The preacher's arguments in favour of certainty are confounded by Dr Slop's simplistic apprehension: "I am positive I am right." Conscience is shown, in ironical contradiction to the thrust of the sermon, to be a matter of trust, in practice a matter of sheer subjectivity. Since God is invisible in *Tristram Shandy*, reason faulty, and the law erroneous, the only recourse is to trust in conscience, and that is, in the last resort, as untrustworthy as judgement.

"No wonder" then, as Walter laments, "the intellectual web is so rent and tatter'd as we see it; and that so many of our best heads are no better than a puzzled skein of silk,—all perplexity,—all confusion within side" (vol. 2, chap. 19). The world of *Tristram Shandy* is "beset on all sides with mysteries and riddles" (vol. 9, chap. 22). As Tristram tells "madam":

we live amongst riddles and mysteries—the most obvious things,
which come in our way, have dark sides, which the quickest sight
cannot penetrate into; and even the clearest and most exalted un-
derstandings amongst us find ourselves puzzled and at a loss in
almost every cranny of nature's works.

(vol. 4, chap. 17)

The protagonists of *Tristram Shandy* are inevitably "puzzled" and "at a loss"
because they can interpret the world only "as we see it," in the light—or
the obscurity—of a subjective perception. The novel admits no criteria, no
norms, no logic and no order external to its enchanted circle, and the radius
of that circle is drawn by the "I" of the fictive narrator. Sterne has devised
the perfect way to represent the solipsistic inner space of subjective
consciousness.

In so doing he also produced the most radical example of literary irony
not only in the eighteenth century but possibly in the entire canon of
Western literature (though this claim might be disputed in regard to Joyce's
Finnegans Wake). In its literary form and in its ontological vision *Tristram
Shandy* demonstrates the impossibility of what it purports to be doing: of
writing a story, of communicating meaning, of capturing definity. As such
it is an ironic self-portrayal whose very failure denotes its success, for it is
the comic incarnation of a tragic paradox.

Yet the irony of *Tristram Shandy*, despite its intensity and its importance, is peculiarly difficult to analyse. Attempts to pin it down seem to
arrive at only partial descriptions. This holds for Dyson's view that the
irony "turns out to be Sterne's way of mirroring the odd complexities of
real life"; for Moglen's contention that: "The overriding irony of the work
derives from the relation of the apparent confusion of form and theme to
the actual structural and conceptual order"; and for [Dietrich] Rolle's thesis
that *Tristram Shandy* shows man at the extreme of his contradictoriness,
and that its irony resides in the attitude of the fictive narrator who relativises
every position he assumes by envisaging its opposite too. All these are
valid assessments, but none of them grasps the core of *Tristram Shandy*'s
highly distinctive irony. It is too dense and too multivalent to be reducible
to a single neat formulation. It cannot be attributed to this or that specific
feature because it so thoroughly pervades the entire text; it seems to be
nowhere special because it is *everywhere*: in the ambiguity of the empty
spaces, in the subjectivity of the time-scales, in the reiterated reminders of
the unsteadiness of words, in the problematical relationships between narrators and readers, in the incessant pointers to the fictionality of the fiction
being created, in the dominance of contingency, and in the insubstantiality
of the private versions of truth. The keystone to *Tristram Shandy* is the
perception of the relativity of all things, just as its ultimate unity lies in its
flexibility.

In effect what Sterne has created—and this is the crux of *Tristram*

Shandy—is an ironic context. A state of perpetual flux, aesthetically as well as philosophically and linguistically, is its controlling factor; so much so that it absorbs into its endless mobility the very bases of judgment. There is no pedestal of security either in the persona of the narrator, or in a sequential time-schema, or in the development of plot, or even in the haven of language or typography from which the reader may take stock so as to exercise his powers of discrimination. When the fixity of perspective is replaced by the multiplicity of perspectivism, no starting-point of sufficient confidence remains for the identification, let alone reconstruction of irony. This is what happens in *Tristram Shandy*; this is the consequence of the wholly ironic context that Sterne has contrived. Where truth and uncertainty have become relative, the notions of "norm" and, therefore, of "opposite" and "reversal" lose their hierarchical significance. Irony then stems not from the contrast to absolute expectations, but from the interaction of elements with each other, and these are in themselves shifting. If, as Lionel Trilling has observed in regard to the concepts of sincerity and authenticity, " 'the whole' is seen as 'confused' rather than as orderly and rational, as, in George Eliot's words, peremptory and absolute, the human relation to it need not be fixed and categorical; it can be mercurial and improvisational."

The outcome is an irony so total and engulfing that it consumes itself, destroying whatever it has just created. However, by withholding the accolade of truth to any one meaning; it leaves all meanings at the level of potentiality. Or there may be no meaning beneath the chaotic surface, no reality behind the appearances. And there is no way of ever knowing for sure. This is the essence of the modern ironic dilemma that *Tristram Shandy* has captured with bewildering brilliance. Its irony may be characterised in the adjectives I have suggested: immanent, intrinsic, conceptual, ontological, progressive; or it may be designated as "romantic."

A Digression on *Tristram Shandy*

Leopold Damrosch, Jr.

For the next century and a half [after *Tom Jones*], the future of the English novel lay in mimetic realism. Jane Austen based her fictions firmly in the contemporary social order, Walter Scott in historical process, and George Eliot in both. Even writers who made overt use of narrative artifice, Thackeray for instance, sought to convey the illusion of a unified and completed world. Social coherence is mirrored by chronological structure: nineteenth-century fiction tends to imitate the biographical course of individual life and to base its realism upon the serial presentation of temporal experience. But it is notable that in many novels the metaphysical dimension of eighteenth-century fiction all but disappears. Grounded upon the immediate experience of social place and personal time, the novel stopped asking the questions about God's plot that had once seemed fundamental.

Eventually the Victorian order broke down and its fictions broke down with it. Among other consequences the literature of the past came in for new consideration, and at the beginning of the twentieth century Laurence Sterne's *Tristram Shandy* unexpectedly emerged, as if from an obscuring mist, as the eighteenth-century work that most anticipates the modern world. As early as 1776, less than a decade after Sterne's last volume appeared, Johnson declared roundly, "Nothing odd will do long. *Tristram Shandy* did not last." But *Tristram Shandy* did last after all, and if Austen and Eliot and Dickens develop certain implications of eighteenth-century fiction, Sterne's peculiar anti-narrative suggests other implications that were for a long time too disturbing to be easily faced. This is not to say that modernism is necessarily good in itself, or (which would be absurd) that *Tristram Shandy* is a greater novel than *Great Expectations* or *Middlemarch*.

From *God's Plot and Man's Stories: Studies in the Fictional Imagination from Milton to Fielding.* © 1985 by the University of Chicago. University of Chicago Press, 1985.

Rather it is to suggest the abyss of undesired possibility that lay just beyond the world view of the 1740s, and to emphasize the urgency with which the fictions of that time strove to hold the future at bay.

Presented as connected series of events, novels of every sort offered themselves as "histories," including *Clarissa, Or, The History of a Young Lady* and *The History of Tom Jones, A Foundling.* Sterne too makes his narrator speak of "the history of myself," but he specifies that it is "a history-book, Sir, (which may possibly recommend it to the world) of what passes in a man's own mind" (vol. 2, chap. 2). Psychology and epistemology were central eighteenth-century concerns; Sterne's interest in Locke and his affinities with Hume have been well documented, and *Tristram Shandy* can fairly be called an exploration of the phenomenology of experience. What we read is a literary artifact which—just as much as Fielding's fictions— selects its details in order to present an imitation of reality. What is offered is an invented image of truth rather than, as Defoe and Richardson pretend, truth itself.

"Writers of my stamp have one principle in common with painters. Where an exact copying makes our pictures less striking, we choose the less evil; deeming it even more pardonable to trespass against truth, than beauty" (vol. 2, chap. 4). For all its jokiness this pronouncement confirms the Aristotelian view that truth is not just the mass of factual detail in which we all live, but the imaginative shaping that detects patterns in the detail, or else imposes patterns upon it. Where Sterne parts from Fielding is in focusing his imitation on connections between mental data instead of on connections between external events, juxtaposing his materials in a spirit of playful *bricolage* rather than causal explanation. The "historiographer," Tristram says,

> will moreover have various
> Accounts to reconcile:
> Anecdotes to pick up:
> Inscriptions to make out:
> Stories to weave in:
> Traditions to sift:
> Personages to call upon:
> Panegyricks to paste up at this door:
> Pasquinades at that.
> (vol. 1, chap. 14)

Like Fielding, Sterne compares his work to a complex machine and boasts of the "good cookery and management" of his materials, but unlike Fielding he glories in connections that can exist nowhere beyond his highly individual imagination, and declares that "Digressions, incontestably, are the sunshine;—they are the life, the soul of reading" (vol. 1, chap. 22). For Fielding as for Aristotle, plot was the soul of a literary work; for Sterne its soul is the imaginative unity in *reading* that is forged by the incorrigibly digressive mind. *Tristram Shandy*, indeed, can be read as a kind of exploded *Tom Jones*.

Insofar as a subtle understanding of the self was a Puritan preoccupation, one might argue that the idiosyncratic shape of *Tristram Shandy* is a direct outcome of Defoe's narratives, attempting "to create a fictional form that grows out of, instead of being imposed upon, what it contains" [Leo Braudy]. But it would be truer to say that *Tristram Shandy* is phenomenological in the sense that traditional philosophy, seeking to understand man's place in the world, had always been so, and that Sterne owes much of his apparent novelty to the tradition of essayists like Montaigne. Anthony Wilden argues that there is a special modernity in the way Montaigne interprets "Know thyself" to mean an endless regress into the self rather than a simple normative ideal, and in Montaigne's conclusion that self-knowledge is mediated through language and relations with other people, rather than achieved by abstract introspection. As Montaigne understands the act of writing, it does not just re-present what he already is, but forms and clarifies his being in an ongoing process.

> In modeling this figure upon myself, I have had to fashion and compose myself so often to bring myself out, that the model itself has to some extent grown firm and taken shape. Painting myself for others, I have painted my inward self with colors clearer than my original ones. I have no more made my book than my book has made me—a book consubstantial with its author, concerned with my own self, an integral part of my life; not concerned with some third-hand, extraneous purpose, like all other books.
> ("Of Giving the Lie," trans. Donald M. Frame)

The Puritan self, though complex and hidden, tended to remain rigidly fixed, and Puritan writing aspired to be transparent (avoiding playfulness at all costs) while seeking earnestly to decipher the messages of the Almighty. *Tristram Shandy*, very differently, insists upon the ceaseless reconstitution of the self in the flux of time, and upon the obligation of writing to shape that experience, not just to report it. There is more than frivolity involved when Tristram remarks, "But this is neither here nor there—— why do I mention it?——Ask my pen,—it governs me,—I govern not it" (vol. 6, chap. 6). Swearingen comments, "There is a perfectly accurate sense in which he may be said not to understand what he says until after he has said it."

Like the other novelists we have been considering, Sterne came late to his literary vocation. His actual profession, which he followed dutifully if not always respectably, was that of a clergyman in the Church of England, and the existential games of *Tristram Shandy* take on a special interest from their grounding in an orthodox view of religious truth.

> Of all the several ways of beginning a book which are now in practice throughout the known world, I am confident my own way of doing it is the best——I'm sure it is the most religious ——for I begin with writing the first sentence——and trusting to Almighty God for the second.
>
> (vol. 8, chap. 2)

This is something very different, however, from Fielding's artist-God whom the human artist emulates. This God connects each separate moment with the others, but we live at the cliff-edge of the latest moment, not knowing what will come next, whereas the harmonious shape of *Tom Jones* encourages a retrospective vision of totality. In earlier novels, including those as different as Richardson's and Fielding's, life is felt to be intelligible even if its causal structure is often mysterious. In Sterne, reality itself is mysterious, and this is felt to be perplexing but also liberating. We now get consciousness rather than story, and what God furnishes is the presiding context for human existence rather than a connected narrative of human actions.

Within *Tristram Shandy* the ingenuous Toby constantly proclaims the goodness of Providence, but this is an act of faith, not a practical demonstration which the narrative enacts. A genuine sermon by Sterne is inserted into the novel and is commented on by a group of characters who nevertheless pay no attention at all to its message (vol. 2, chap. 17). And that *is* its message—that conscience is routinely ignored because we routinely deceive ourselves. Our art forms are no exception: we translate experience into terms that gratify ourselves, whether these are Walter's syllogisms, Toby's innocent war-games, or Tristram's game of writing. It follows that no work of art can hope to be, as *Tom Jones* aspires to be, objective and whole. Like Fielding's God, Sterne's delights in bringing order out of contingency, absorbing chance into Providence; but unlike Fielding's God, he neglects to show us how he does it.

To put it another way, Puritan writers insisted on the interpenetration of this world by the next: Fielding keeps his gaze on this world but claims that comic art can imitate the patterns that are hidden in it by the divine artificer. Sterne, just as much as Fielding, asserts the existence of those patterns, but he implicitly denies that a work of art can reproduce them. In its this-worldly emphasis *Tristram Shandy* is certainly a concord fiction. It brilliantly expresses the ability of the imagination to give meaning to chance occurrences, and to extract pleasure from the most thwarting experiences. And it suggests that although individual persons may act solipsistically, language and consciousness are profoundly social, affirming a stable reality in which even solitary reflection is conditioned by a lifetime of *being with* others. But each of these positions may seem little more than an extenuation: we need not behave solipsistically but we usually do; life can be made bearable by seeing it as play, but the playing cannot neutralize suffering for long. "What a jovial and a merry world would this be, may it please your worships, but for that inextricable labyrinth of debts, cares, woes, want, grief, discontent, melancholy, large jointures, impositions, and lies!" (vol. 6, chap. 14).

In choosing Yorick for his persona Sterne has in mind not only the jester who sets the table on a roar, but also the unclean skull that the gorge rises at. Tristram is a fictional author writing a real book, but Sterne, dying of consumption and telling us so, is a real author writing a fictional book, or at any rate a fictional narrator coughing real blood. [Elsewhere] we noticed Lukács's observation that the early novel broke down into lyric subjectivity, and Lukács speaks also of a mode of irony that is nostalgic and reductive in tone, even when it continues to affirm the existence of providential meaning. "Irony, with intuitive double vision, can see where God is to be found in a world abandoned by God; irony sees the lost, utopian home of the idea that has become an ideal, and yet at the same time it understands that the ideal is subjectively and psychologically conditioned, because that is its only possible form of existence," [*The Theory of the Novel*, trans. Anna Bostock]. For all its comic joy, Sterne's irony is unsettlingly different from the massively stable irony of Fielding's hearty narrator, and both are remote from the certitude of the supreme ironist, Milton's God who laughs his enemies to scorn.

Many readers have sensed something anxious if not unpleasant in Sterne's wit, which is a good deal less joyous than recent critics make it out to be. Some things, but above all the last thing, defy the powers of the imagination to comprehend them. Johnson makes a correspondent in the *Rambler* say that at a friend's deathbed "I felt a sensation never known to me before; a confusion of passions, an awful stillness of sorrow, a gloomy terror without a name." What cannot be named must nevertheless be faced, and Sterne's edgy jokes imply a recognition that conventional literary deaths (Clarissa's for instance) are simply unbelievable, while language balks and makes fun of itself in the face of death.

> Nature instantly ebb'd again——the film returned to its place,
> ——the pulse fluttered——stopp'd——went on——throb'd——
> stopp'd again——moved——stopp'd——shall I go on?——No.
> (vol. 6, chap. 10)

The death that matters most, of course, is one's own, and philosophers and preachers alike have always encouraged the contemplation of it. Augustine says, in remarkably Shandean language, "The whole of our lifetime is nothing but a race towards death, in which no one is allowed the slightest pause or any slackening of the pace." *Tristram Shandy*, in which the race with death is literalized in the seventh volume, ends unfinished (as does *A Sentimental Journey*) because its author has died.

Postponing Tristram's moment of birth is more than a joke about narrative. If you haven't been born then you can't die, and the future is held at bay. By reanimating the dead Yorick, Sterne indulges (like Tom Sawyer and Huck Finn at their funeral) in the fantasy of being posthumous to oneself:

Alas, poor YORICK!

Ten times in a day has Yorick's ghost the consolation to hear his monumental inscription read over with such a variety of plaintive tones, as denote a general pity and esteem for him;——a foot-way crossing the church-yard close by the side of his grave,——not a passenger goes by without stopping to cast a look upon it,—— and sighing as he walks on,
Alas, poor YORICK!

(vol. 1, chap. 12)

But immediately after this feat of self-resurrection come the famous black pages, empty and voiceless, that mark the bourn from which no traveller returns.

Seen in this light, wit is only wit. To be sure, Sterne's wit has successfully created *Tristram Shandy*, but that is only consolation of a sort. When an interviewer asked Woody Allen if he hoped to achieve immortality through his work, he replied magnificently, "I don't want to achieve immortality through my work. I want to achieve it through not dying." And if humor can serve as a means of reconciliation with unpalatable reality, it can also, as Freud urges, serve as an escape from it.

> The grandeur in it clearly lies in the triumph of narcissism, the victorious assertion of the ego's invulnerability. The ego refuses to be distressed by the provocations of reality, to let itself be compelled to suffer. . . . Humor is not resigned; it is rebellious. It signifies not only the triumph of the ego but also of the pleasure principle, which is able here to assert itself against the unkindness of the real circumstances.
>
> ("Humour")

Something like this is surely the deepest explanation for the Puritan distrust of humor.

Tristram Shandy abounds in jokes, whether verbal or practical or both at once. One need not be humorless (though perhaps it helps) to sense something obsessive and unpleasant in much of Sterne's joking, especially about sex. In Fielding sex is a field of activity, in Sterne a field of inactivity, but one which so pervades the imagination that literally nothing is incapable of being sexualized. What is discouraging is the consistency with which this insight is connected with frustration and disappointment.

> Brightest of stars! thou wilt shed thy influence upon some one——
> ——The deuce take her and her influence too——for at that word I lose all patience——much good may it do him!——By all that is hirsute and gashly! I cry, taking off my furr'd cap, and

twisting it round my finger——I would not give sixpence for a dozen such!

——But 'tis an excellent cap too (putting it upon my head, and pressing it close to my ears)—and warm—and soft; especially if you stroke it the right way—but alas! that will never be my luck ——(so here my philosophy is shipwreck'd again)

——No; I shall never have a finger in the pye.

(vol. 8, chap. 9)

Sophia's muff served as an objective correlative for Sophia's deep attraction to Tom, a sexual joke denoting a human reality, as a hostile critic reluctantly admitted:

The little incident of the muff, on which Mrs. Honour, or the author, so profusely wantons, is at the same time a great one against Sophia's delicacy, who could value it more for Mr. Jones's egregious fooling with it; and conveys to young gentlemen and ladies admirable instructions in the art of toying. But whether these instructions contain *nothing inconsistent with the strictest rules of decency,* according to the author's early declaration, must be left to the *chaste eye* of the reader, and need not be further dwelt upon here.

Tristram's cap is an occasion for sexual wordplay that invariably, in the world of the Shandys, substitutes for the thing itself:

All womankind, continued Trim, (commenting upon his story) from the highest to the lowest, an' please your honour, love jokes; the difficulty is to know how they chuse to have them cut; and there is no knowing that, but by trying as we do with our artillery in the field, by raising or letting down their breeches, till we hit the mark.——

——I like the comparison, said my Uncle Toby, better than the thing itself——

(vol. 9, chap. 8)

Language itself becomes a form of involuntary sexual expression, or at least of obscene relief; no wonder then that when Diego scribbles graffiti "he eased his mind against the wall."

Rather than celebrate the comic triumph of Sterne's vision, we would do well to recognize its pathos. He has committed himself fully to the flux of experience which the providential novel, whether Puritan or Augustan, had held at a comfortable distance. In *Tom Jones* the narrator's mastery of chronology reflects an imitation of divine omniscience. In *Tristram Shandy* temporal sequence gives way to the simultaneity of mental impressions, in which psychological order often conflicts with chronological—"A cow broke in (to-morrow morning) to my uncle Toby's fortifications" (vol. 3, chap. 38). Whereas the novels of Richardson and Fielding offer simulacra of perfected memory, in which nothing is forgotten and everything fits together, *Tristram Shandy*—whose sequence of details is impossible to recollect—compels us to immerse ourselves in the strangeness of the ever-unrolling present. But it can only do this because its narrator is reconstructing the data of his own memory, and when he stops, the narrative must stop with him.

The radical and unrelenting arbitrariness of *Tristram Shandy* does amount to a kind of philosophical statement, but it is one whose implications must vary in proportion to one's own beliefs about the arbitrary. A recent critic has well observed,

> Plot and metaphor suggest a triumph of the artist over time. It is not surprising that aestheticians, concerned to replace religion by art, have made so much of these things. *Tristram Shandy* enacts the effort to achieve them and the failure of that effort. The book is all extension and no meaning, all analogy and metonymy and no metaphor or plot.
>
> (Gabriel Josipavici, *Writing and the Body*)

Seen from this angle, *Tristram Shandy* stands in an interesting relation to an allegory like *The Pilgrim's Progress*, which abounds in metaphor, indeed *is* metaphor, but is notably deficient in plot. Sterne can no longer believe, as the earlier novelists did, that the world is pregnant with emblematic meanings which art can reproduce, but his refusal to impose a narrative pattern looks back to Bunyan's world as much as it looks forward to Beckett's. For it would be fair to say that Sterne really does rely on God for the next sentence, and beyond that for the benign control that joins each moment securely with the rest even if human beings are helpless to predict how this will happen. Poring over the hidden connections and implications in his memories, Tristram has much in common with the old Puritan diarists who scrutinized the shifting and mysterious data of their fragmented experience. And for all of Sterne's undoubted interest in *durée*, his book gives an impression finally of existing always in the present moment, even when each present moment is superimposed upon others that lie ahead of it or behind it. In this too *Tristram Shandy* has affinities with the old Puritan narratives, in which urgent attention to the significance of each moment is more important than retrospective display of causal structure. If Defoe struggles to impose pattern upon a mode of experience that resists patterning, then Sterne goes back beyond Defoe.

At the end of the short chapter that began with Trim's analogy of the artillery and their breeches, Sterne abruptly abandons his narrative, wonders about the posthumous fate of his book, and then eloquently concludes,

> I will not argue the matter: Time wastes too fast: every letter I trace tells me with what rapidity Life follows my pen; the days

and hours of it, more precious, my dear Jenny! than the rubies about thy neck, are flying over our heads like light clouds of a windy day, never to return more——every thing presses on—— whilst thou art twisting that lock,——see! it grows grey; and every time I kiss thy hand to bid adieu, and every absence which follows it, are preludes to that eternal separation which we are shortly to make.——

——Heaven have mercy upon us both!

(vol. 9, chap. 8)

That is indeed Sterne's faith, that heaven will have mercy, but his imagination has moved to a vision of impermanence that is more like Shakespeare's than like the stable fictions of his immediate predecessors.

> Sometime we see a cloud that's dragonish,
> A vapor sometime like a bear or lion,
> A towered citadel, a pendant rock,
> A forkèd mountain, or blue promontory
> With trees upon't that nod unto the world
> And mock our eyes with air. Thou hast seen these signs:
> They are black vesper's pageants. . . .
> That which is now a horse, even with a thought
> The rack dislimns, and makes it indistinct
> As water is in water.

(*Antony and Cleopatra* 4.14.2–11)

Meanwhile we have our fictions, which are real enough as feats of imagination, but all too unreal as embodiments of reality. Of course if the religious basis is secure enough, this power may be felt to be exhilarating. "All the world is full of inscape," Hopkins wrote, "and chance left free to act falls into an order as well as purpose: looking out of my window I caught it in the random clods and broken heaps of snow made by the cast of a broom." That is precisely what is at issue in eighteenth-century narrative: the chance and randomness which are perceived as falling into order.

Those signs and footsteps which Michael promised Adam are now very faint indeed, and many readers have seen in *Tristram Shandy* a potential skepticism very similar to Hume's. Flux may conceal divine purpose, or it may not, and in the latter case one might conclude with Sterne's contemporary Diderot that the ever-changing whole is the only unity there is. "Tout change, tout passe, il n'y a que le tout qui reste." But Sterne himself resists the lure of skepticism, and his final position is the one that he poignantly expresses in a sermon: "Wherever thy Providence places me, or whatever the road I take to get to thee——give me some companion in my journey, be it only to remark to, How our shadows lengthen as the sun goes down."

Smollett's Picaresque Games

Philip Stevick

The critical apparatus used to examine picaresque fiction tends to carry us away from a consideration of the picaresque event. The word "episodic," for example, focuses critical attention upon structure; and it is ironically true that when one pays particular attention to episodic structure, one is apt to pay rather little attention to the episodes themselves; or the critic who analyzes the philosophical area indicated by such words as "determinism," "necessity," "choice," "chance," "fortune," "contingency," "luck" may illuminate the world view of picaresque fiction while running the risk of taking for granted the precise structure of those characteristic events upon which that world view is predicated. By using the word "picaresque" at all, we are naming a class of works by pointing to an agent; implicitly we are pointing to the acts the agent does, which we assume to show a remarkable consistency from work to work. We are handicapped by the difficulty of rendering "picaro" into English. If we call him a "rogue," then what he does is indulge in "roguery," a word so effete that it is incredible that it has survived as long as it has in discussions of picaresque fiction. If we speak of the picaresque event as a "trick" or "prank," we both narrow and trivialize it. One word which avoids a number of semantic pitfalls while opening certain fresh ways of looking at the picaresque event is the word "game." The word is neutral of value and allows for any degree of frivolity or intensity, any degree of structural simplicity or complexity, and it allows us to hold together in our minds the ideas both of play and of the urgent relation to matters of survival which most picaresque events contain. It is, in fact, the special condition of picaresque fiction to have invested the game with all of the human tension which it can bear. Lazarillo

From *Tobias Smollett: Bicentennial Essays Presented to Lewis M. Knapp*, edited by G. S. Rousseau and P.-G. Bouce. © 1971 by Oxford University Press.

de Tormes's indigent master, starving, picks his teeth. The picking of his teeth, in its social context, is a game. But there is no mistaking the fact that, as he is playing, he is really starving.

From our point of view in the twentieth century, Smollett appears to link the end of one tradition, the great tradition of classic picaresque, with the beginning of another tradition of related and derivative works, such as, in our century, *Felix Krull* and *Invisible Man*; and the common element of both groups, the one that leads up to Smollett and the one that leads away from him, is the interaction between a hero who is bright, quick, often naïve, and clever, and a society which is both powerful and cloddish, that interaction being a series of what we can loosely call games. Those interactions are at once endlessly various, inventive, surprising *and* limited, constricted, and predictable. Such is the nature of games in or out of books, that they be open to chance or excitement yet constrained by rules and "fields." We do homage to the variety of game in any picaresque work not only by speaking as easily as we do of its inventiveness but also by continuing to read a series of events so basically similar and so potentially monotonous. What we need to do, the variety being apprehensible, is to describe, on the other hand, the continuities of picaresque game, its basic paradigms, for in works so loosely organized it is in the repetitive nature of the game that we perceive the unity of the compositions. Smollett's pivotal position, at the end of the classic picaresque tradition, as translator of Le Sage and assimilator of a wide range of earlier works, and as a precursor of the abrasive absurdities of the neo-picaresque that follows him, guarantees his ability to provide us with patterns of game not only peculiar to himself but suggestive of the nature of the genre.

Midway through *Roderick Random*, an epidemic of fever sweeps Roderick's ship. The climate is wretched, provisions are inadequate, and morale is low. The fever rages "with such violence, that three-fourths of those whom it invaded died in a deplorable manner; the colour of their skin being, by the extreme putrefaction of the juices, changed into that of soot." Roderick soon contracts the fever, suffers deeply yet manages to survive, largely because he has been able to take a berth apart from the ship's hospital, in which the absence of ventilation would virtually have ensured his death. During Roderick's illness he is visited by a friend, not by the ship's surgeon, who has no interest in him, and by the ship's parson, with whom he disputes doctrinal matters with such heat that his fever breaks and he is cured. Not knowing that he is suddenly much better, his friend Morgan returns to his side and, assuming him to be dead, groans, whines, and weeps, while Roderick, feigning death, stifles his own temptation to giggle. Morgan finally closes Roderick's eyes and mouth, "upon which I suddenly snapped at his fingers, and discomposed him so much, that he started back, turned pale as ashes, and stared like the picture of Horror. Although I could not help laughing at his appearance, I was concerned for his situation, and stretched out my hand, telling him I hoped to live and eat some salmagundy of his making in England." Recovered, Roderick uses his recovery as a reproach to Morgan, whose remedies did not cure him, to the ship's doctor, who in his indifference did not attend him, and to his rival, who had wished him dead. Implicitly, his recovery mocks the parson, who, in attempting to ease him into death, had cured him, and the captain, whose mindless neglect of the ship's hospital would have killed Roderick if he had not been able to subvert the captain's discipline.

The gulf that separates Roderick's game from such classic games as chess or such literary games as Holmes's outwitting of Moriarty is enormous. Take the question of choice, for example. Roderick does not self-consciously choose to dispute with the parson or to pretend, with Morgan, that he is dead in the way in which one "makes moves" in chess. There are no alternatives to anything he does, either in his own mind or in ours. There is no particular play of consequences, nor are there any rewards. Tricking Morgan is not, in any sense, winning, and had Morgan seen through his game, Roderick would not have lost. Roderick's game would be of no interest to the fashioners of those chaste mathematical formulae called game theory, which might not surprise us, but there is a basic sense in which Roderick's game would be incompatible also with the classic sociocultural theories of game, namely, those of Huizinga and Caillois, which should surprise us. For to Huizinga and Caillois, game, however central to culture, is defined nonetheless by its discrete separability from the useful and the serious, play being, by definition, gratuitous and nonserious; in Huizinga's word, "fun." In Roderick's game, the snapping at Morgan's fingers is inseparable from the almost dying, the exposure of the fraudulence of the ship's parson, the reality of the fever, the callousness of the captain, and so on. Unlike those moments in experience when we stop being productive and lay out the chess board, Roderick plays at the grimmest business life affords, staying alive in the face of substantial odds, and for him there is no separation between play and seriousness, no dialectic between them, but they are, in fact, identical.

Still, Caillois's categories of game can carry us toward a definition of the precise nature of Roderick's game, a game, or complex of games, representative of large areas of Smollett's fiction and central to Smollett's purposes. Caillois divides game into four types: *agon*, the contest (such as fencing or chess) in which the outcome depends upon superior strength, or tactic, or skill; *alea*, the game (such as dice or roulette) in which the decision is the result of chance; *mimicry*, the free improvisatory expression of the impulse to imitate; and *ilinx*, the pursuit of vertigo (as in skiing or auto racing), a deliberate attempt to confuse momentarily the stability of perception [*Man, Play, and Games*]. We are accustomed, of course, to thinking of agon as the predominant form of picaresque game, in Smollett the perpetual result of humiliation and revenge, provocation and response, challenge and defense; the act of revenge or defense being a contest decided by superior cleverness. In the game I have cited, the agon is diffuse, with several antagonists, no clear conflict, and with a group of minor triumphs rather than a decision. Also elements of the other three games appear: Roderick's recovery depends heavily on chance, Caillois's alea, for example; and the entire action is performed under the disorientation of fever, suggesting Caillois's ilinx, a quality that can remind us of all the rolling eyes, the near swoons, and the drunken reeling about that accompanies so much action in Smollett. Taking for granted the fact, then, that every form in Smollett is apt to be diffuse and every category which one may reasonably apply to Smollett's fiction is apt to be cluttered by the simultaneous presence of a number of other categories, it is still possible to describe Roderick's game. It is as a combination of agon and mimicry that that game, and the typical game elsewhere in Smollett's picaresque fiction, can best be described; mimicry superimpsed upon agon. (By "elsewhere in Smollett's picaresque fiction," I mean in *Roderick Random* and *Peregrine Pickle*. . . . I find neither *Sir Launcelot Greaves* nor *Humphry Clinker* picaresque and have not treated them. *Ferdinand Count Fathom* is a difficult case, for its first two-thirds are as picaresque as the earlier two novels. Yet the nature of its games is quite different from what I take to be the norm in *Roderick Random* and *Peregrine Pickle* and thus I have rather arbitrarily excluded it from consideration.) The agon between Roderick and the captain, the doctor, and the parson is that classic picaresque struggle between the brighter, quicker, more clever picaro and institutional power. We know that Roderick, like every other picaro, will gain temporary victories but no substantial change. The captain will go on being tyrannical, the surgeon indifferent, and the parson full of casuistry. It is the triumph of Roderick to survive, agon by agon, against such institutional stupidity. But it is *not* enough, after all, to survive. In the act of surviving, which is, in itself, a game, Roderick plays at another game only tangentially related to survival. It is as if a chess player, in the act of winning a game of chess, were to occupy himself between moves by mugging, grimacing, and mocking the gestures of his opponent. If we remind ourselves, however, that Roderick's is no chess game but a grim business carried out in a cruel, repressive world in which no victory is more than temporary, the function of Roderick's mimicry becomes clear. Roderick plays his agons to stay alive; he mimics to *be* alive. And in the free invention of his mimicry, he transcends his cloddish antagonists, his limitations of choice, and his brutal world.

II

The shape of the picaresque event is determined to a large extent by its nature as a game. Or rather, in the case of Smollett, the shape of the event is determined by the somewhat discordant nature of its games, especially Smollett's peculiar combination of agon and mimicry. Of all of Caillois's categories, agon is apt to strike one as the most thoroughly circumscribed by rules. Any number of agons, for example, require a disinterested party, an umpire or a referee, for the express purpose of administering rules. Such agons as chess and fencing have vast protocols and elaborate lore accumulated around them. And even such crude agonistic confrontations as Indian wrestling still inevitably carry with them the obligation that they be conducted in some kind of mutually acceptable form. Mimicry, on the other hand, exhibits all of the characteristics shared by other forms of play, as Caillois points out, with one exception: that it is free of rules. It consists of incessant invention. Other pairs of Caillois's categories fit more easily and naturally together than do agon and mimicry, agon and alea, for example: it is easy to think of any number of games containing significant elements both of skill and chance. But agon and mimicry in certain ways pull the participant, and of course the writer as well, in opposite directions. And it is a special triumph of Smollett's art that he is able to reconcile the claims of two such different play impulses, the first tending toward symmetry, regularity, and ultimately, tedium, the other tending toward freedom, spontaneity, and, ultimately, incoherence.

The combination of the two is contained with particular purity in chapter 51 of *Peregrine Pickle*. Pickle and a certain Knight of Malta, having seen a performance of *Le Cid* by Corneille, argue over the comparative merits of the French and English stages.

> Our hero, like a good Englishman, made no scruple of giving the preference to the performers of his own country, who, he alleged, obeyed the genuine impulses of nature, in exhibiting the passions of the human mind; and entered so warmly into the spirit of their several parts, that they often fancied themselves the very heroes they represented; whereas the action of the Parisian players, even in the most interesting characters, was generally such an extravagance in voice and gesture, as is nowhere to be observed but on the stage. To illustrate this assertion, he availed himself of his talent, and mimicked the manner and voice of all the principal performers, male and female, belonging to the French comedy, to the admiration of the chevalier, who, having complimented him upon this surprising modulation, begged leave to dissent in some particulars from the opinion he had avowed.

Presently the argument resumes, although the responses of Pickle tend to be overwhelmed by the learning, the pseudo-learning, and the verbosity of the knight. The mimicry of Pickle does not substantially alter the shape of the event, which follows an agonistic logic of challenge and response; the conventions of the agon are those of the debate, respect for evidence, rhythm between the generalization and the supporting instance, certain features of a public, oratorical rhetoric. But the position of the mimicry allows it to dominate the event; and the values which the mimicry carries alter every value that follows.

Those values can be roughed out with such words as "energy," "spontaneity," "élan"; unlike the learning of the knight, which is made to seem self-congratulatory, pedantic, and quite forced, the mimicry of Pickle is made to seem uncontrived and "natural." M. A. Goldberg has analyzed Smollett's novels by positing a correspondence between their thematic structure and the ideas of the Scottish common-sense philosophers. Certainly the antitheses which Goldberg finds—reason and passion, imagination and judgment, art and nature, social- and self-love, primitivism and progress—are at play in Smollett's works; and there is no doubt that such antitheses are sufficiently stylized and intellectualized that it is defensible to describe the novels' value structures with the aid of "ideas" found outside of the novels, in philosophy. But in Smollett's novels, like anybody else's, there are values and values. What I mean by the values of the mimicry of Pickle as opposed to those of the pompous knight is a good deal more sub-intellectual, or supra-intellectual, than the large thematic patterns which Goldberg finds with the aid of Scottish common sense. In the long run, Pickle may come to be the embodiment, one may feel, of passion, or imagination, or nature. In the short run, it doesn't matter. What does matter is that he is alive.

More than his vitality, Pickle's mimicry has a dimension that draws its power from the attribution to it of supernatural qualities. His mimicry, that is, seems at once perfectly explainable and also magical. Smollett's world is full of people who seem to be what they are not, but Pickle is one person who can transform himself before our eyes into someone else without compromising his integrity of self. And although Smollett does not render the mimicry with any amplitude, it is certainly his intention (note the diction: "male and female," "admiration of the chevalier," "this surprising modulation") to make Pickle's performance seem an extraordinary presentation, virtuoso, unaccountable, unique, and in its way magical.

Such mimicry as Pickle's, moreover, acts as the concrete representation of the picaro's nerviness, his cockiness, his colossal gall. Erving Goffman has chosen to take seriously the idea of "the action" as it is contained in that cant phrase "where the action is." "Action," as he defines it, "is to be found wherever the individual knowingly takes consequential chances perceived as avoidable" [*Interaction Ritual*]. Given characters so imprudent as Roderick Random and Peregrine Pickle, every agon is *un*avoidable. They are bound to suffer humiliation, bound to burn for revenge, bound to be provoked, bound to fight. I have argued that their mimicry is a necessary mode of their continued self-assertion. But in any ordinary causal sense, their mimicry, unlike their agons, is avoidable, perceived as such by the reader and, insofar as we can infer their mental states, perceived as such by the characters. Their mimicry is a kind of chance-taking, always likely to expose them to additional hostility, always likely to fail in its effects, exposing them to still more ridicule. And the consequences of such mimicry may very well be, and often are, triumph and increased confidence, or, on the other hand, embarrassment, futility, a punch in the nose. The mimicry of Smollett's picaros is a splendid instance of Goffman's "action." And to see it as such is to see a linkage between Smollett's picaros and those driven characters of Goffman's essay, the gamblers, the hustlers, the vandals, the criminals, the professional athletes, the skydivers, the mountain climbers, for whom the events of routine experience are not enough and for whom the artificial production of an additional series of events with their own very real peril becomes a personal necessity.

Judged by the agonistic rules that govern the debate between Pickle and the chevalier, the latter wins, easily and decisively. But judged by the complex of values contained in Pickle's mimicry, the chevalier's victory is a hollow one. The mimicry is a small part of the total episode. But its function as a correlative for the high spirits of the hero and as a conveyor of those of his values which we are certainly expected to endorse make the mimicry far more important than its apparent prominence would lead us to believe. Not all mimicry, to be sure, is performed by Smollett's picaros. In chapter 46 of *Roderick Random*, for example, Roderick's new acquaintance Ranter mimicks Roderick's "air, features, and voice." Somewhat later, he makes an elaborate series of mock representations to Roderick's companion Wagtail, who becomes, as the chapter continues, the butt of several others' mimetic ingenuity. Roderick, throughout the chapter, is either victim or spectator, never the chief mime. Yet even though the personages change about, the values attached to certain actions remain substantially the same. People who play at identity are always distinct from people who assume a false identity for self-serving purposes. And the person who plays at identity is likely to be, however morally reprehensible, an interesting person, vital and alive.

Pickle and Pallet at one point in their travels approach Antwerp and the city, being the birthplace of Rubens, reminds Pallet of his idol.

> He swore . . . that he already considered himself a native of Antwerp, being so intimately acquainted with their so justly boasted citizen, from whom, at certain junctures, he could not help believing himself derived, because his own pencil adopted the manner of that great man with surprising facility, and his face wanted nothing but a pair of whiskers and a beard to exhibit the express image of the Fleming's countenance. He told them he was so proud of his resemblance, that, in order to render it more striking, he had, at one time of his life, resolved to keep his face sacred from the razor; and in that purpose had persevered, notwithstanding the continual reprehensions of Mrs. Pallet, who, being then with child, said, his aspect was so hideous, that she dreaded a miscarriage every hour, until she threatened, in plain terms, to dispute the sanity of his intellects, and apply to the chancellor for a committee.

Pallet's mimicry becomes the subject of the chapter. More is made of Pallet's imagined resemblance to Rubens. Ultimately he travels to the tomb of Rubens where he falls onto his knees in apparent adoration, to the considerable dismay of those at the church. Here is an example of mimicry which is patently ludicrous from start to finish. The most obvious reason that Pallet's mimicry is ludicrous is that he is no descendant of Rubens in any sense but is rather an unmitigated fraud, a terrible painter, and the butt of some of Smollett's coarsest humor. But the other reason is that he does not play. His mimicry is not his way of expressing his vitality, as it is with Roderick or Ranter; it is his pathetically serious way of seeking to express his own self-image, an assertion of appearance as if it represented essence. Mimicry which is not play comes close to the pathological.

The mimicry in Smollett's version of picaresque, then, is the chief conveyer of a complicated set of values: energy, vitality, quickness of invention, joy, and, more than all of these, a kind of personal stability, integrity, and authenticity. In a kind of fiction in which every character is more or less flat and every analysis is more or less perfunctory, the way we know who the characters are and the way we know that they have real human substance is through their modes of play. The bare structure, on the other hand, the rhythm and movement of the novel is provided by its successive agons. There are events in Smollett that are more or less pure agon, more or less pure mimicry, or neither, being perhaps melodramatic vignette without anything of the game about them. But ordinarily mimicry and agon interact in a fairly limited number of ways and these can first be set forth by returning to the pattern of Pickle's theatrical mimicry.

Pickle's theatrical mimicry precedes the main substance of the agon, and as the agon continues, Pickle does not return again to his mimicry. The mimicry, occurring at the beginning of the episode, provides Pickle with a means for "winning," at least in the eyes of the reader, for no amount of dialectical skill can really triumph over so splendid a mimetic talent. In the episode cited earlier, Roderick Random mimics, plays dead, at the end of the episode. He had already "won" against the captain, the parson, the disease itself, and his mimicry is a kind of triumphant foolishness, a parting shot not really at Morgan so much as at life itself. A third option allows Smollett to integrate the two, so that a character uses his mimicry as an agonistic tactic, playing back and forth between his strength and skill on one hand and his mocking and posturing on the other. The use of mimicry at the beginning of an agon, as a kind of value base, the use of mimicry at the end of an agon as a self-defining gesture, and the integration of mimicry and agon, Stephen Potter fashion—these are the three basic structures of countless events in Smollett. And limited though these basic paradigms may be, individual instances are capable of demonstrating large dimensions of subtlety and considerable areas of aesthetic choice.

Chapter 45 of *Roderick Random* is rich and diverse enough to demonstrate a number of such choices. After the usual preliminary episodic business of settling into a location, Roderick goes to a playhouse "where I saw a good deal of company, and was vain enough to believe that I was observed with an uncommon degree of attention and applause." Imagining himself to be the center of so much admiration, Roderick rose and sat down, covered and uncovered my head twenty times between the acts; pulled out my watch, clapped it to my ear, wound it up, set it, gave it the hearing again; displayed my snuff-box, affected to take snuff, that I might have an opportunity of showing my brilliant, and wiped my nose with a perfumed hand-kerchief; then dangled my cane, and adjusted my sword-knot, and acted many more fooleries of the same kind, in hopes of obtaining the character of a pretty fellow, in the acquiring of which I found two considerable obstructions in my disposition, namely, a natural reserve, and jealous sensibility.

As a base for the play of values that is to follow, such mimicry is superb, showing, as it does, Roderick's vitality, his passionate wish to define and assert himself together with the gaucherie and the naïveté that makes it all ridiculous and, above all, the honesty toward himself, the insight into his own ridiculousness, the "natural reserve" that makes the passage rather touching to read, and, incidentally, one of the less picaresque events of the novel. As the play proceeds, Roderick is moved by the plight of the heroine and shares her tears, although he notices that no one else is similarly moved. And once again, Smollett has it both ways: Roderick's identification with the tragic situation on the stage is amusing and naïve; yet his susceptibility to the heroine's distress is very much related to his ability to mime—both depend upon an implicit *Einfühlung*, a rich responsiveness to the imagination of what it means to be someone else—and thus Roderick is not only more ridiculous, he is also more admirable, more interesting, more fully human than all of those facile and self-controlled popinjays who surround him in the boxes of the playhouse.

After the play is finished, Roderick encounters an attractive woman and persuades her to accompany him to a tavern. Roderick learns that she is a whore, but as he discovers this, he and the woman exchange tactic and move, precisely that kind of game I have described in which the agonistic structure is integrated with a continuing play of mimicry. The episode of the playhouse whore is followed by several pages of coffee house conversation on that most typical of Smollett's subjects, the merits of the English versus the merits of the French. There is, throughout the conversation, much agonistic maneuvering, much bluster and pretense, much mimicry, although Roderick himself observes more than he participates. Ultimately the chapter works toward its last event, in which Roderick and an acquaintance argue over points of Latin grammar and diction, finally conversing "a full two hours, on a variety of subjects" in Latin. In one sense, the ultimate mimicry consists of an utterly persuasive representation of another person. But in another quite legitimate sense, the ultimate mimicry consists of the sustained conversation (not merely schoolboy disputation) in another language, the language being the product of a culture detached from oneself by several centuries.

It is hard to imagine any system of analytical concepts being brought to bear on that chapter. It is harder still to imagine any critic who judges fiction according to its apparent structural control finding the chapter to be anything but a dismal failure, a sequence of some four main encounters without thematic unity and without even causal necessity. Yet it is a richly expressive chapter and is by no means so disunified as it may seem. For playing across every agon is an intermittent, quite unpredictable, but closely related series of mimicries, containing Roderick at the center and Roderick at the periphery, presenting Roderick, at the end of the chapter, as mimetic virtuoso and Roderick, at the beginning of the chapter, as mimetic fool. To see only the structure of the successive agons is to understand the chapter's events at their crudest level. To see agon and mimicry interrelated, on the other hand, is to understand the events as closely though not sequentially related vehicles for the arrogance and effrontery, the imagination and ingenuity, the energy and vitality, which is the particular source of power in Smollett's version of picaresque.

III

All picaresque novels show face-to-face relations with emphasis upon dissembling, fraud, disguise, and trickery. And to that extent all picaros are skilled mimes. Yet for Defoe's Roxana, to choose a contrast close to Smollett, such dissembling consists of assuming names not her own, wearing clothing that disguises her class or nationality or identity, suppressing her emotions, lying with a straight face. Nothing that she does, however, is comparable to the splendidly exuberant mimicry of Smollett's heroes. Smollett's picaros are not typical of their kind, and the difference lies, as A. A. Parker has pointed out [in *Literature and the Delinquent: The Picaresque Novel in Spain and Europe, 1599–1753*], in the basic goodness of their impulses, a difference that has more than a little to do with their modes of play. "Good" and "bad" are not very relevant categories when applied to the worlds of *Lazarillo de Tormes* or *La Vida del buscón*. In an absolute sense, everybody is bad, the picaro among them. But in Smollett, however fallible or even sometimes cruel his picaros may be, they are generally enraged by evil, compassionate toward the oppressed, honest in the long run if not the short, basically decent. Indeed, Parker maintains that *Roderick Random* is not picaresque at all since it is the world that is wicked in contrast to the hero, who is very far from that "delinquency" which Parker finds common to picaros within the European tradition.

Up to this point I have stressed the expressive value of mimicry in making concrete the vitality of Smollett's picaros. Insofar as they tend to be distinguishable from other picaros by their comparative goodness, it is appropriate to ask whether their mimicry is not merely a function of their vitality but also of their goodness. As a kind of coda to the present discussion, I wish to suggest that it is. Their games, taken together, contain examples of gratuitous malice, insignificant foolishness along with many agons in which their antagonists are unmistakably evil. The point is that even when their games are least ostensibly moral, we never forget that they are basically decent, capable of compassion and remorse. Above all, we never forget the controlling values of Smollett, who hated sham and exploitation with an uncompromising fierceness. Thus I mean to suggest that there is a special resonance in Smollett's picaresque games that is the result of the fact that they exist in relation to the implied limits of certain ethical imperatives.

Neither the historical richness of Huizinga's *Homo Ludens* nor the anthropological richness of Caillois's *Man, Play, and Games* suggests that play has had, and certainly had in the eighteenth century, an ethical dimension. In fact both Huizinga and Caillois, by stressing the gratuitousness of play, implicitly deny its ethical dimension. Caillois further discusses certain tendencies which overtake the play impulse, debasing it, and the idea of measuring play by ethical criteria would certainly be one such. Caillois is perfectly right: if we play because it is "good for us," we *are* debasing the play impulse. And Huizinga is also right: the extraordinary evidences of the play impulse in culture *haven't* anything to do with moral worth. Yet if we shift our perspective somewhat, we are easily enough persuaded that certain kinds of play are vicious and exploitative, hence "bad" or other forms of play are intolerably coarse, dehumanizing, in some other sense, "bad." What kind of games does a good man play? If we didn't think so anyhow, Smollett would demonstrate for us that the question is absurd, that almost any kind of play is possible without compromising one's basic goodness. Yet other fictional settings can as easily demonstrate that play has consequences that cannot finally be separated from the moral world in which it occurs: the manipulative and mendacious games in Samuel Butler's novels, for example, or those games in Evelyn Waugh's that succeed in trivializing the whole of life.

Hugo Rahner has undertaken a study of play, theological in its orientation, which begins by assembling a number of ancient valuations of play: Plato and Plotinus, Tertullian and Origen, Aristotle and Augustine, and above all Aquinas. What emerges from Rahner's study is a synthesis of certain pagan and Christian views of play in history and a remarkable meditation on God at play in the creative act. From the *Nicomachean Ethics* of Aristotle and later from early patristic writings, Rahner revives the ethical concept of "eutrapelia." The "eutrapelos," as Rahner summarizes Aristotle, is the man whose fondness for the playful exists in balance and harmony with his valuation for the serious. "This person," writes Rahner,

> stands between two extremes, the description of which is particularly important as showing how Aristotelian ethics emerged from the cult and politics of the city-state—a description which Aquinas later took over. The one extreme is the "bomolochos," the poor wretch who hung about the altar of sacrifice in the hope of snatch-

ing or begging an odd bit of meat; in a broader sense, one who was ready to make jokes at every turn for the sake of a good meal and himself to be made the butt of cheap gibes. The opposite extreme was the "agroikos," the "boor," whose coarse stiffness was despised by the "asteios," the highly cultured Athenian citizen.

(*Man at Play*, trans. Brian Battershaw and Edward Quinn)

The means by which Rahner shows the transition of this Aristotelian grace and balance into Christian thought is less important for our purposes than the fact that such a transition does exist, that there is a long, impressive continuity in ethical thought, both Christian and non-Christian, which values play while recognizing the ethical perils in its excess.

Even if it could be demonstrated—which it cannot—that Smollett knew and loved the tenth book of the *Nicomachean Ethics*, that would not, I think, establish very much about the values of his fiction. Rahner's treatment does not at all provide the material for a possible "source." What it does provide is the idea that "eutrapelia," in one form or another, is a fairly constant virtue in ethical thought, that it is based so firmly in the cultural patterns of the West that it appears in philosophical writers of widely varying temperaments and world views. To put the matter another way, Rahner's treatment both codifies and confers great dignity upon an idea that is accessible to the common moral sensibilities of great numbers of people who have not read Aristotle and Aquinas. The general accessibility of the idea becomes especially apparent in the eighteenth century since the modes of play in the period are often highly developed and the introspective records of individual people in the period, their letters, journals, and private papers, tend often to be preserved and often to be extraordinarily honest and perceptive. There is scarcely a figure of consequence in literary eighteenth-century England who did not strive daily for "eutrapelia"; we are aware of the importance of the play impulse because it carries over into literature of the first rank more often than in other periods and we are aware of the efforts to keep such play impulses in balance because writers like Boswell tell us how difficult it is. And, as such writers in the eighteenth century make clear, striving for "eutrapelia" comes not merely out of social constraint but out of an implicit conviction of the union of play and ethics.

Of Smollett himself, no reader of the Noyes edition of the letters can fail to have been moved by the last letters in the collection. After the countless personal assaults and defenses, the literary wars, the ills real and imagined of the preceding pages, Smollett prepares to die and describes himself in a letter to Dr. John Hunter which is at once self-deprecatory and dignified, tough and affectionate, stoic and playful.

With respect to myself, I have nothing to say, but that if I can prevail upon my wife to execute my last will, you shall receive my poor carcase in a box, after I am dead, to be placed among your rarities. I am already so dry and emaciated, that I may pass for an Egyptian mummy, without any other preparation than some pitch and painted linen.

The last letter of the collection is only a fragment, undated but evidently written before Smollett's daughter died in 1763.

Many a time I do stop my task and betake me to a game of romps with Betty, while my wife looks on smiling and longing in her heart to join in the sport; then back to the cursed round of duty.

The easiest way to state the most widely held ethical ideal in the eighteenth century is to invoke the phrase that the eighteenth century often invoked itself, "to live well and to die well." The phrase can mean all things to all men, but to Smollett it meant the coexistence of wit and compassion, of "duty," as he puts it himself, and "romps."

Consider, then, the examples of mimicry I have cited as being characteristic of Smollett's picaros. In the first he tricks his best friend, who had thought him dead, but no sooner does he trick him than he is struck with remorse. Although it is proper for Roderick to celebrate his being alive and understandable that he should mock the muddle-headed solicitousness of Morgan, it all becomes, in the act, very close to vicious buffoonery: Roderick soothes the shock of Morgan the moment he has realized the impact of his mimicry. Pickle imitates the actors of the French stage in his disputation with the Knight of Malta not only out of high spirits, not only out of a sense of contest and a knowledge of his own mimetic talent, but out of an implied impulse toward balance in play. Roderick checks his own mimicry at the playhouse precisely out of his own insight that he has been excessive and foolish. As Smollett's picaros always know, although they do not say it, to play badly is to become distorted and grotesque, to join that gallery of living caricatures that forms the human background of the novels.

Pickle's first recorded act, at age nine months, is to contrive an alarming expression of mock pain, apparently for the malicious joy of seeing his elders try to relieve him of some nonexistent pin prick. His last recorded act is to spurn a visiting nobleman who had once behaved contemptuously toward him, by pretending that he is not Mr. Pickle at all. Despite his marriage and good fortune at the end no one would argue that he achieves "eutrapelia." There is scarcely a page of the novel (somewhat less so with *Roderick Random*), in which he is not boorish, coarse, or cruel. Yet it is also true that there is scarcely a page in either *Roderick Random* or *Peregrine Pickle* in which we are not aware of the judgment, either of Smollett or of the picaros themselves, that they are in danger of behaving boorishly, playing to excess. Of Pickle's infant mimicries, for example, we understand that he was treated with gratuitous cruelty in his infancy and that he has been surrounded by grotesques from his very birth; that he should play in a malicious manner is hardly surprising. Yet his games are "a peculiarity of disposition," described with ironic understatement at every point. And no one who reads of the anxiety that Smollett tells us his mock discomfort arouses in his mother is likely to find the infant Pickle's exploitation of her tenderness altogether amusing.

It would be a mistake, I think, to systematize the restraints that act upon the play of Smollett's picaros. Their guilt or embarrassment or remorse is always momentary, always highly specific; they improvise their moral response to experience. Smollett's narrative judgments of them are likely to be problematic, embedded in his rhetoric, every bit as ad hoc as their views of themselves, and just as unsystematic. The texture of Smollett's rhetoric, for example, is filled with man-beast images, which serve, among other things, to remind us of the subhuman possibilities that are always open to his human character, open, certainly, to his exuberantly mimetic picaros who are always in danger (to choose one of Smollett's own favorite beast metaphors) of becoming baboons. And the action of the novels is filled with reminders that the picaros, being skilled mimes, could lie, cheat, steal, and gamble so as to lay waste around them if they wished; but their play most often succeeds against the vain and the arrogant and they never become the vicious and indiscriminate confidence men which they have every native skill to become. In short, Smollett so constructed the characters of the picaros as to keep them in a perpetually unbalanced tension between their lust for game on the one hand and their moral constraint on the other.

Being comic characters set in the repetitive structure of episodic works, Smollett's picaros repeat certain paradigmatic events as the books proceed but they do not change. The unbalanced tension is never resolved. To the end, they are more aggressive than conciliatory. If we were ever persuaded that Roderick Random or Peregrine Pickle had achieved "eutrapelia," we would, I suspect, be disappointed. It is hard to imagine that their perfectly earnest wish for the good life, a life responsive to their own best judgment and their own sensitivity to the distress of others, should ever entirely temper their lust for agon and their delight in mimicry. They do not achieve "eutrapelia" not only because of the structure of the books in which they appear but because "eutrapelia" is a moral ideal difficult to attain. To play strenuously, ingeniously, and joyfully while keeping that play in a morally responsive balance with the whole of one's life, that is the possibility that lies behind Smollett's picaresque events. *Humphry Clinker* is, in a sense, a realization of such an ideal. But in the picaresque novels, "eutrapelia" is as difficult to achieve as Smollett knew it to be in actual experience.

Richardson, Fielding, and Smollett: Private Experience as Public History

Jerry C. Beasley

The broad relevance of the various kinds of pseudohistory and historical biography should be obvious to anyone familiar with the works of Richardson, Fielding, and Smollett. Each of these writers styled himself a historian in a fictional mode, and it is easy enough to see that the popularity of their novels coincided with and perhaps was even reinforced by the currency of spy fictions, secret histories, and feigned memoirs and lives of private people whose experience had imparted to them some kind of real public importance. Such works, we will remember, professed to renounce the extravagances of romance, and they contributed importantly to the climate of interest in narrative accounts of familiar life and contemporary affairs, while they almost invariably proclaimed a moral commitment to the ideals of Christian virtue. Throughout their own novels, Richardson, Fielding, and Smollett exhibit their very serious interest in the historical functions of prose fiction. Our labors, said Fielding of his story of *Tom Jones* (in book 9, chap. 1)—and his words apply equally well to the two other major novelists of the 1740s—"have sufficient Title to the Name of History," for they draw upon the vast materials furnished to the observant eye by life itself, which is interpreted in these fictions by a transforming moral imagination. The exactness with which the authors of *Pamela*, *Joseph Andrews*, and *Roderick Random* reflect the texture of life in their period, the social and moral tensions and the actual feel of day-to-day living, suggests the degree to which they shared some of the impulses of the lesser writers. . . . Their superior gifts and vision enable them to avoid the limitations of mere topicality and voguishness, but Richardson, Fielding, and Smollett were simply the most able and important among a larger community of writers of prose narrative whose varied approaches to the business of representing the realities of public and private life were mutually reinforcing.

The term *history*, as used in the title of *Tom Jones* or *The History of Clarissa Harlowe*, actually suggested a biographical as well as historical method to readers of the day, and the novels of Fielding, and of Richardson and Smollett as well, possess considerable interest as fictionalized history in both important contemporary senses of the term. Like the popular spy fictions and secret histories, they not only register significant truths about familiar life, but sometimes deliberately enter areas of experience hidden from ordinary view. Fielding and Smollett in particular are satiric writers who aim to expose certain ludicrous or odious people and institutions to their readers' scrutiny and derision.

The heroes and heroines of the major novels are all somehow strangers, at least in a moral sense, to the scenes of wickedness and corruption they encounter. Their resemblance to the moralizing spies of Marana and Montesquieu may well have seemed more than just casual to the first readers of their stories. Always innocent in some degree, characters like Pamela Andrews, Abraham Adams, and Roderick Random are outsiders in the real world, where they are confronted by hypocrisy, venality, and cruelty. The role of Richardson's Pamela, as letter-writer and moral agent, is in part that of an observer, a shrewd, articulate, unspoiled country girl whose virtue makes her a kind of alien in genteel society. Her futile efforts to enlist the aid of her captor's neighbors in Lincolnshire reveal the moral shallowness of the country gentry and their upper-class indifference to the rakish carryings-on in their own neighborhoods and their own social circle. In *Clarissa* the picture of life in country houses is narrower than in *Pamela*, but presented in greater depth, and when the novel shifts its scene to London, Richardson bares the inner workings of a circle of libertines and whores as they victimize his beleaguered heroine. The tone of Clarissa's own letters does not differ significantly from that of the epistles written by Mme de Graffigny's Peruvian princess, although they are composed with even greater intensity of personal feeling.

In Fielding's comic "histories" of *Joseph Andrews*, *Tom Jones*, and *Amelia*, it is the narrator who leads the reader behind the façades of contemporary life, but the effect often approximates that of the spy fictions. In the early scenes of *Joseph Andrews*, for example, the author dramatizes the experience of the innocent and therefore alien hero as a means of exposing the vagaries of Lady Booby and her fashionable household. In the same novel he employs Parson Adams as a device for stripping away the mask of an inept, debased clergyman like the swinish Parson Trulliber (book 2, chap. 13), and later draws a vivid picture (in book 4, chap. 5) of the kind of stupidly depraved country justice with whom Fielding the lawyer was well acquainted and who could, if bribed, "commit two Persons to *Bridewell* for a Twig." Trading justices, in fact, as well as other commonly corrupt public servants (lawyers, physicians, prison bailiffs, clergymen), are from this time abundantly examined in Fielding's fiction.

Smollett's "friendless orphan" Roderick Random, as a young Scots-man, is most definitely an outsider in the scenes that come under his view. Smollett's novel generally follows rather closely the model of Le Sage's picaresque romance of *Gil Blas*, but it bears the same relationship to spy fiction as *Gil Blas* does to the same French author's *Le Diable boiteux*, a fantastic adaptation of Montesquieu which Smollett translated in 1750. Rod-erick lacks the detachment of the typical spy, and his own knavery qualifies his reliability as a witness, but his narrative abounds with graphic accounts of country families in strife, of the follies and vices of provincial pharmacists and innkeepers, the twistings of government bureaucracy, the dishonesty of aristocratic ministers, the machinations of gamblers and fortune-hunters. The extended autobiographical episodes describing the ill-fated expedition to Carthagena in 1741 (chaps. 24–37) supply what is probably the most detailed and damning account ever written of the realities of eighteenth-century Navy life. Smollett's journalistic instincts were strong, and his novel reports with great intensity upon the cruelties of the press-gang, the bru-tishness of common sailors, the sickening food and the filth of shipboard life, and the incompetence of officers like the *Thunder's* Captain Oakum and surgeon Mackshane.

The savagely satiric treatment of Captain Oakum, moreover, is a stroke much in the manner of a secret historian as well, for it surely reflects upon some ship's captain, now impossible to identify with any certainty, of the fleet in which Smollett served aboard the *Chichester* during the Carthagena disaster. A number of real people regarded themselves as wounded by the portraits drawn in these episodes, where the author fictionalizes real events for at least the partial purpose of ridiculing public figures. Smollett un-dertook similar treatment of real-life characters in the long prison chapters of his novel (chaps. 61–64) where he avenged himself on Lord Chesterfield, who had once denied him patronage, and on Quinn, Garrick, Lacy, and Rich, the actors and theatrical managers who had refused to produce his unactable tragedy *The Regicide*. He boldly drew their caricatures in the silly figures named Earl Sheerwit, Bellower, Marmozet, Brayer, and Vandal. It was this "set of scoundrels" who had driven the deserving poet Melopoyn to poverty, despair, and jail.

Like Smollett, Fielding more than just occasionally engaged in a gesture recalling the methods of the secret historian. The Beau Didapper of *Joseph Andrews*, to name but one important example, is clearly John, Lord Hervey, Baron Ickworth, the effeminate, diseased, painter courtier whom Fielding loathed for his loyalty to Walpole, and who was known to his enemies by Pope's contemptuous epithet "Lord Fanny." (Fielding, of course, ironically dedicated *Shamela* to Hervey in the person of "Miss Fanny.") Beau Didapper is that "little Person or rather Thing" who, though immensely rich, chose for the "dirty Consideration of a Place of little consequence" to submit his "Conscience," "Honour," and "Country" to the capricious will of a "Great Man" (book 4, chap. 9). In this instance, Fielding's intention is identical with that of Mrs. Manley in *Queen Zarah* or the *New Atalantis*; he aims to embarrass a public person and expose him to ridicule, all for partisan purposes.

Fielding probably read the "*Atalantis Writers*" he sneered at in *Joseph Andrews* (book 3, chap. 1). He certainly despised them, and he would have had no need to turn to them for instruction in the creation of a character like Beau Didapper, or Peter Pounce, or the many other comic figures he drew from real life into the worlds of his fictions for the purpose of ridiculing them. Dryden, Swift, and Pope had all used similar tactics in modes of writing that would have been more likely sources for his inspiration. The point is that the satiric strategies of the secret history were still current in popular fiction, as were the conventions of spy narrative. Richardson, Fielding, and Smollett, as alert members of the reading public, could hardly have been ignorant of these two voguish modes of pseudohistorical writing, or (for that matter) of the degree to which the occasional attractions of their own novels as exposés overlap with the appeal of works like *The Turkish Spy* and *Queen Zarah*. There is no clear evidence to suggest that they borrowed directly from specific conventions of the spy narrative or the *chronique scandaleuse*, but then neither did they, in composing their own works, entirely renounce all association with important attractions of these kinds of popular fiction.

The various forms of historical biogrpahy—the lives of all kinds of public figures and of adventures at sea or on the battlefield—are much more relevant to the novels of Richardson, Fielding, and Smollett than are the spy fictions and secret histories. All three major writers made deliberate attempts to tell stories celebrating the importance of individual men and women, showing how any person, however humble of origin, might rise to a kind of conspicuous moral eminence. Joseph Andrews and Abraham Adams have their counterparts in the Bible, a simple but ingenious allusiveness by which Fielding certifies at once the timeliness and the universal value of their comic experience. The names Tom Jones and Roderick Random in different ways suggest the broad application of the particularized characters they identify and describe—Tom Jones by its very commonness; Roderick Random by its combination of a Christian name drawn from romance and thus hinting at the native nobility of Smollett's hero, with a surname pointing to the dangers of the potentially erratic quality of individual moral life in a vexing, chaotic world. Roderick, like Tom, is projected as a kind of everyman. The epistolary story of Clarissa Harlowe is an intensely autobiographical fiction, and so of course is the first-person tale told by Roderick Random. Yet, as we know from Richardson's emphatic authorial comments, Clarissa herself was conceived as a representative figure whose exemplary functions as Christian heroine, in the author's mind, gives her imagined life high public importance. In the novels of all three major writers, whatever their other attributes or uses of popular narrative conventions, private experience as it touches upon the felt reality of familiar life is deliberately rendered as a special kind of contemporary history—moral history, we may call it, or (in the case of Fielding and Smollett) comic history.

None of this is really news. Every modern reader of *Joseph Andrews*, *Clarissa*, *Roderick Random*, and the other major novels of the 1740s has acknowledged at least the general appropriateness of their claims to a historical function. Their very first readers were surely just as sensitive to the justice of these claims. But the members of the eighteenth-century audience would have read the novels in a context of popular historical biographies, to which they relate in some very interesting ways, and some of these readers—the more sophisticated ones, anyhow—would therefore have enjoyed an enhanced appreciation of their methods and of their authors' performance as contemporary historians in a fictional mode.

There can be no question but that Richardson, Fielding, and Smollett exploited some of the conventions of historical biography, though of course their own complex purposes as artists and as moralists never coincide perfectly with the more limited aims of Simon Berington, or James Annesley, or the author of *Mrs. Christian Davies*, or the other writers of similar narratives. This point may be easily illustrated. The novels of Richardson, Fielding, and Smollett, in pursuit of their didactic purposes, all deliberately employ the motif of the journey, either literal or spiritual, as an extended metaphor for life's entanglements. Furthermore, one might argue that each of the major novels subscribes to an idealism that works itself out in the protagonist's moral progress toward a final reward, usually represented by the happiness to be found in a rural utopia. Clarissa Harlowe's reward comes in heaven, of course, but the principle is the same: like Pamela and the heroes of *Tom Jones*, *Joseph Andrews*, and *Roderick Random*, she ends her journey in a place which, by its very perfections, implies strong criticism of the vexing world through which she has moved. The appeal of this manner of resolution overlaps with the general utopian attractions of a work like Simon Berington's account of the travels of Gaudentio di Lucca, although the kind of ending we find in *Clarissa* had its ultimate origins in pastoral traditions and Christian homiletics, not in utopian voyages, which use a different strategy involving a journey from the real world to a utopia and back again. Clarissa's passage through life to heaven is much more closely related to Christian's journey in *Pilgrim's Progress* than to contemporary travel narratives.

The specifically utopian qualities of the major novels are important, however, and must not be discounted or diminished. Richardson, Fielding, and Smollett were all Christian idealists, though in varying degrees, and surely they were all three aware of the long tradition and continued currency of utopian travel literature, which may have at least indirectly influenced their vision of the meaning of their characters' experience. A more cautious comment, perhaps, is that their Christian understanding of moral life coincided with the idealism expressed in utopian narrative, and that this very real parallel may have been to some degree deliberately emphasized in their novels as an ingredient of their formula for popular success. We may only speculate whether this is so, but the very obviousness of the parallel must have helped to fire the enthusiasm of contemporary readers long since accustomed to the pleasures of utopian tales and to other kinds of stories—the pious novels of Penelope Aubin, for example—that resolved the crises of their beleaguered heroes and heroines' progress toward fulfillment by imposing a Christian utopian vision upon the hard empirical realities of their fictional worlds.

Other kinds of adventure narratives bear much more directly on the practice of the major novelists. In *Jonathan Wild*, Mrs. Heartfree's long story (book 4, chaps. 7–9, 11) of her scarifying experiences with her abductor Wild, of her escape and subsequent adventures on high seas and foreign shores, is Fielding's tongue-in-cheek version of a conventional imaginary voyage. Wild's own adventures after Mrs. Heartfree's departure burlesque the same mode (book 2, chaps. 10–13). Earlier in the book Fielding parodies the Grand Tour (and its literature) by devoting to his "hero's" travels the less than two pages of a "very short chapter" containing "not one adventure worthy the reader's notice" (book 1, chap. 7). In this *Journal of a Voyage to Lisbon* (1755), Fielding would offer a voyage narrative worthy of admiration, as he declared in the preface, because not disfigured either by the introduction of monsters and improbable adventures in unimaginable places, or by the dilation of trivial experience into many dull pages. The voyage narrative, Fielding explained, as a species of historical writing, ought to tell the truth, it ought to be artfully done, and it ought to instruct as well as delight. In *Jonathan Wild* he sought, as did Swift in *Gulliver's Travels*, to expose some of the absurdities of familiar voyage and travel literature. And yet Fielding's purpose, like Swift's, was more complex. By the extravagance and vanities of Mrs. Heartfree's tale, he obviously meant to mix in some foibles that would qualify her otherwise unblemished character, thus bringing it closer to his own theories of characterization. At the same time, he was perfectly serious at another level. Mrs. Heartfree's tale of her trials— of abduction, slavery, leering advances, attempted rape, and so on—illustrates her moral strength and functions as a parable of persecuted virtue triumphant.

Fielding's two great novels of the 1740s, the histories of Joseph Andrews and Tom Jones, present stories of energetic adventurers possessing great personal resilience and powerful moral and emotional interest as ordinary people struggling through life's entanglements. Because the aims of these two works are so very complex, they far surpass anything achieved by the author of the historical biography of Mother Ross or by James Annesley in his autobiographical *Memoirs of an Unfortunate Young Nobleman*. But *Joseph Andrews* and *Tom Jones* do deliberately incorporate some of the same interests as these lesser works. *Tom Jones* does so most conspicuously. The novel is sprinkled with allusions to the Jacobites, and Tom's escapades on the road to London are actually thrown into relief against the turbulent background of the 'Forty-Five. Fielding's lively youth even joins the Hanoverian cause as a soldier ready to die in order to protect the kingdom from the Jacobite invaders. This is all obvious. But the important thing is that for a time at least, the very identity of Tom as familiar hero is partly defined by his direct connection with a great public controversy.

In his last novel, *Amelia*, Fielding exploits still more conspicuously the appeal of the popular historical biographies of military characters in treating the experience of his wayward soldier Billy Booth. Booth is the central figure in a considerable cast of military characters. Though weak and vacillating in his domestic relations, he is a responsible officer who fights valiantly and is wounded at Gibraltar. We see only slightly more of Booth's actual soldiering than we do of Tom Jones's experiences as a military man, but we are led to believe that he was courageous. It is of course impossible to know the degree to which Fielding may have intentionally tried to call to mind the many fashionable tales of soldiering adventurers, but to any reasonably alert reader *Amelia* must have seemed more than just remotely related to works like *Mrs. Davies* and Defoe's *Memoirs of a Cavalier*. Fielding's novel effectually turns the formula of the miliary memoir inside out. The hero's adventures occur mainly in Admiralty offices and the prisons and coffee houses of London, and his enemies are mostly domestic. But the specific effect of the novel's treatment of this gallant soldier is toward defining a higher kind of heroism. Booth, an ordinary man who has benefited from hard experience and finally from the wisdom of Isaac Barrow's sermons, achieves in the teeming world of London what he could not attain in the isolated, remote world of the battlefield, where the dangers were only physical: the status of a Christian hero. In fact, Fielding seems to say in *Amelia* that the real battles, the important moral struggles, are fought in the everyday world, and it is there that they must be won. The circumstances of Booth's seemingly hopeless poverty and his terrible frustrations in trying to get a promotion expose the abuses of privilege in the prevailing military system, and therefore function in the fabric of the novel's social criticism. They link the world of the battlefield with that of daily affairs, which is the novel's main arena, and thus join with Fielding's exposure of a large variety of other social ills—corrupt justices, prison abuses, official favoritism, inadequacies and cruel inequities in the treatment of debtors, the irresponsibilities of an indifferent aristocracy, and so on—in defining the world's resistance to goodness and charity. By surviving his adventures, Booth actually becomes not a warrior hero but, in a very rich sense indeed, a Christian soldier and thus a triumphant figure important to our understanding of Fielding's conception of the deepest meaning of heroism and of his own role as moral historian in a vein of comic fiction.

In *Roderick Random* and *Peregrine Pickle*, with their large casts of fighting sailors, Smollett approaches more nearly than Fielding ever does the actual formula of popular military memoirs. Smollett is a kind of panoramist, and his sailors are less subtly drawn than the soldiers in *Amelia*. Not one of

them possesses the depth of Billy Booth, although Peregrine Pickle's benefactor Commodore Hawser Trunnion, in all his delightfully grotesque
eccentricities, belongs among the most memorable military characters in
eighteenth-century fiction. But Smollett's sailors were drawn from firsthand
observation, and what they lack in subtlety is made up for by the accuracy
and vividness of the portraits. The shipboard scenes of *Roderick Random*,
the battle descriptions, and the accounts of military strategy have the convincing ring of authenticity, and link the Carthagena episodes of the novel
very closely to the memoirs of public careers. In fact, throughout these
pages Smollett almost duplicates the formula of Defoe, allowing for changes
in literary fashion. Roderick himself, by his direct association with such
great events and by virtue of his privileged role as their chronicler, inevitably proclaims the public importance of his own life. In a quite spectacular
way, his performance in giving his account of the Carthagena affair merges
the functions of biographer and historian. Smollett's hero thus demonstrates dramatically how nearly inseparable the two functions could sometimes be in this period. In an extremely explicit manner that neither
Richardson nor Fielding ever quite attempted, Roderick's story also reveals
how very intimately the two dimensions of private and public life were
thought to touch upon one another. Viewed in this light, the Carthegena
chapters of *Roderick Random* appear to be a deliberate as well as complete
paradigm of the most crucial interests cultivated by all the contemporary
kinds of pseudobiographical and pseudohistorical stories. To say the least,
Smollett made capital use of what he knew about these minor but important
works of narrative literature as he readied his own first novel for the press.

The numerous and varied works of pseudohistory and feigned historical biography were, as I have already suggested, deliberate responses
to public tastes. In a kind of circular process familiar enough to anyone
who has studied literary history at all, by catering to those tastes with such
energy and enthusiasm writers inevitably helped to reinforce them, actually
deepening the yearnings of their audience for more of the same. Apparently, contemporary readers could never get enough of stories offering a
fantasy life which exalted private experience, gave it public visibility, and
emphatically affirmed its importance. Certainly that is the lesson of the
popularity earned by the kinds of narrative studied in this chapter, and
the same general appeal, though in different manifestations, characterizes
the more strictly biographical accounts of social outcasts and pious heroes
and heroines. . . . It also, of course, was the chief appeal of the new form
of the novel as it emerged in the 1740s. If authors had not tried to satisfy
popular tastes—an almost unimaginable possibility given the general op-
portunism of the writing and publishing businesses in the period—then
presumably the novel as we know it would have had to await a later birth.
Popular stories in historical and biographical modes were rarely the acknowledged products of the imagination, but by sheer repetition they fa-
miliarized their readers with important conventions and a kind of subject

matter to which novelists like Richardson, Fielding, and Smollett found it easy to turn when composing their own more able and ambitious works.

It is not necessary to argue the degree to which these three major novelists may have copied this or that convention from this or that type of popular history or biography. What they do borrow they adapt or transform, usually quite radically, making it their own. Sometimes their borrowing is very direct, most often it is not so direct, and occasionally (as in the case of the naval chapters of *Roderick Random*) one of their works will combine the attractions of several kinds of narrative in a single episode, a concentrated series of related scenes, and so forth. Nor would it be useful to debate the broader question of whether the ingenious eclecticism of the major novelists was in every instance of its complexity a calculated response to, or borrowing from, some mode of pseudobiography, or pseudohistory, or (for that matter) romance or novelistic narrative. In the present connection at least, it is much more meaningful simply to observe that the biographical histories of Richardson, Fielding, and Smollett were written in a context which included many other lesser works that made something like the same general appeal even while disguising themselves (however transparently) as true stories of real people. The currency of these forgotten tales, we may say, despite their inferior literary quality, very likely helped encourage the chroniclers of the lives and times of Pamela Andrews, Tom Jones, and Roderick Random to write in the manner they all three adopted.

The Vicar of Wakefield:
Goldsmith's Sublime, Oriental Job

James H. Lehmann

The breakdown of typological exegesis in the eighteenth century in England and Germany, which has been documented fully in Hans Frei's *The Eclipse of Biblical Narrative*, was accompanied by two crucial developments in the history of scriptural reading. The first was the *Orientalizing* of the Bible, that is, the reading of it as a product and reflection of an Oriental and therefore of a primitive society. The second involved reading the Scriptures as expressive writing, more specifically as *sublime* poetry. This double transformation is entirely consistent with the dissolution of the old typological framework. For if the Old Testament no longer *means* the New Testament (and that, as Frei argues, is essentially what typology is all about), then it must mean something else. And so its old spiritual referent (the "prefigured" New Testament) is replaced by its geographical and historical referent (the "Orient") and by its emotional and poetic referent (the sublime soul of the ancient Hebrew poet).

These three moments in the history of exegesis—the breakdown in typological reading, the growth of an Orientalizing mode in biblical criticism, and the discovery of the sublime in the Hebrew Scriptures—were all fundamentally *secularizing* moments. Taken as a cultural complex, they constitute a prime example of what Kenneth Burke has called a "secular conversion." Burke's term denotes those attempts by the human mind to neutralize the sacred and terrible by *renaming* them and thus making them more manageable. The Bible, in this sense, was *renamed* "Oriental" and "sublime" as a way of deflecting its theological force. That recourse to the sublime is generally a strategy of avoidance has been noted by Geoffrey Hartman, who claims that the sublime is always a form of sublimation. For

From *ELH* 46, no. 1 (Spring 1979). © 1979 by The Johns Hopkins University Press, Baltimore/London.

our purposes it is sufficient to recall that, as Thomas Weiskel writes in *The Romantic Sublime*, "in the history of literary consciousness the sublime revives as God withdraws from an immediate participation in the experience of men."

It is true that the English critical tradition had long referred to the Hebrew Bible as uniquely sublime, often as a way of excusing its apparent violation of canons of poetic diction. But Robert Lowth, in his Oxford lectures delivered from 1741 to 1750 and published in 1753 as *De Sacra Poesi Hebraeorum*, was the first to combine the claim of biblical sublimity with a detailed treatment of the poetry as Oriental literature. He argued that an understanding of the Bible presupposed an appreciation of the character of the Hebrew "Orientals" to whom it was addressed and by whom it was written. The natural imagery contained in this poetry must be ascribed to the natural surroundings of the ancient Hebrews such as might be reconstructed from modern travelers' reports of Arabia. The sublimity of the Hebrew is related, for Lowth, to the rude origins of the poetry: the didacticism of the poetry, what Lowth calls its "sententiousness," was "more likely to prove efficacious with men in a rude stage of society, for it professed not to dispute but to command, not persuade but to compel." The Oriental quality of the Hebrew mind similarly would make it unable to develop abstract concepts such as that of a future world.

The Oriental quality of the Hebrew mind, its concreteness, its closeness to nature and to the natural context out of which it arose, is closely linked by Lowth to the sublime language of passion that distinguishes Hebrew writing from all others: "The language of Reason is cool, temperate, rather humble than elevated, well arranged and perspicuous, with an evident care and anxiety lest anything should escape which might appear perplexed or obscure. The language of the Passions is totally different: the conceptions burst out in a turbid stream, expressive in a manner of the internal conflict; the more vehement break out in hasty confusion; they catch (without search or study) whatever is impetuous, vivid or energetic. In a word, Reason speaks literally, the Passions poetically." The Rabbis, therefore, must have erred when they declared that prophecy proceeds only from an untroubled mind: "On the contrary, we learn from the testimony of the Prophets themselves that the art of prophesying was often if not always accompanied with a very violent agitation of the mind."

Lowth's use of the sublime as a means of biblical analysis is a *secular* substitute for the earlier spiritual readings of the Old Testament. Significantly, Lowth's lectures generally stay clear of matters Christological, "mystical and visionary." Instead he focuses on the use of parallelism as a rhetorical device in Hebrew verse, and on a theory of parabolic language that permits expression of the sublime through the periodic verse of the Hebrew Bible. He is much less interested in explicating spiritual meanings than in describing the sublime in the Psalms or Isaiah.

Lowth's influence was widespread. M. H. Abrams ascribes particular importance to Lowth: on the mirror/lamp continuum he is something of a proto-lamp. Lowth's notion of the sublime poetic imitation of the poet's soul therefore marks a shift from a more external idea of natural imitation in the Augustan Age (*The Mirror and the Lamp: Romantic Theory and the Critical Tradition*). His work was known and admired by Christopher Smart, whose ecstatic verse utilized Lowthian parallelisms. Hugh Blair's defense of Ossian (1763) rested in large part on the "sublimity" Ossian shared with the Hebrew Bible. Sir William Jones's *Asiatick Researches* (1772) shows an equal debt to the *Lectures on the Sacred Poetry of the Hebrews*. Three years after its first edition, Lowth's *Lectures* were enthusiastically received by Johann David Michaelis, the greatest German Bible scholar of his day. Michaelis's annotations of the *Lectures* (Göttingen, 1758, and Oxford, 1763) led to its wide dissemination in Europe. Finally, Lowth motivated Herder's key work, *Vom Geist de ebräischen Poesie* (1782). Even this cursory history of Lowth's reception would indicate the sentimental and literary possibilities implicit in his new approach to a sublime, Oriental Scriptures: the Sacred Text is sublimely expressive because it is Oriental; it is Oriental because it is so expressive. That these two notions were seen as adequate explanations for Old Testament poetry shows that there was a decided shift away from finding univocal spiritual meanings in the Bible, and instead toward considering the language of the text as a vehicle of poetic expression.

The "sublime" was one secular aspect of Orientalism. Another manifestation of the "secular conversion" I see in biblical Orientalism was the growing prominence of comparative Semitic philology. In a sense what was being undertaken by mid-century Semiticists was nothing less than the demythologizing of Hebrew as the Sacred tongue. As Arabic and Syriac came to be more widely studied, Hebrew lost its privileged position. The claim that Hebrew was not the oldest Semitic language, indeed that it was linguistically poorer than Arabic or Syriac, was made during the 1730s by [Albrecht] Schultens. Not coincidentally, it was Schultens who first proposed the notion of "Semitic languages." The utility of the notion of a comparative Semitics is obvious: if one is going to *rename* (in Burke's sense) the Bible as Oriental literature, then it is important that there be a "related" body to which one may assimilate it.

Crucially, it is the Book of Job that first became the focus for the Orientalizing Bible critics of the eighteenth century. It is this book that was first de-Hebraized by these critics, and so detached from the sacred history of the Jewish and Christian traditions. As long ago as the times of the Talmud, the Rabbis had already sensed something very unbiblical about this book. There never was any consensus regarding its authorship or date of composition. Schultens proposed that the work was not of Jewish origin (a possibility entertained by the rabbis of the Talmud). Some scholars suggested that Job was written in Arabic and then translated into Hebrew.

Dropping Job from the history of the Israelites had obvious theological implications for eighteenth-century students of the Bible. This was remarked over a century ago by the German Hebraist Franz Delitzsch, who noted that

> with the commentary of Albert Schultens . . . a new epoch in the exposition [of Job] begins. He was the first to bring the Semitic languages, and chiefly the Arabic, to bear on the translation and rightly so, for . . . Jerome in his preface to Daniel had before correctly remarked *Iob cum arabica lingua plurimam habet societatem.* Reiske (1779) and Schnurrer (1781) followed later in the footsteps of Schultens but *in proportion as the Israelitish element was considered in connection with the Oriental, the divine distinctiveness of the former was forgotten* [emphasis added].

Lowth, too, saw Job as a non-Jewish work. He believed that although written *in* Hebrew, it was not written *by* a Hebrew, but rather by an Idumean writing somewhere east of Palestine. Although in his novel treatments of Isaiah and the Psalms Lowth at times speaks of spiritual meanings (however halfheartedly), in the case of Job he explicitly and emphatically rejects what he derides as "mystical allegory." The Book of Job has nothing to do, he says, with the religion of the Israelites. Lowth "is not able to trace any vestige of an allegorical meaning throughout the entire poem." For him the central lesson of Job is in no way doctrinal; he scoffs at the numerous allegorical readings and spiritual meanings ascribed to the work. "The truth of the narrative would never . . . have been called into question, but from the immoderate affection of some allegorizing mystics for their own fictions which run to such excess as to prevent them from acceding to anything but what was visionary and typical." Lowth rejects doctrinal readings as utterly irrelevant to "this extraordinary monument of ancient wisdom."

Job is uniquely sublime for Lowth, as it is uniquely Oriental: "The dignity of the style is answerable to that of the subject, its force and energy to the greatness of those passions which it describes, and as this production excels all the other remains of the Hebrew Poetry in economy and arrangement, so it yields to none in sublimity of style." Job is the most sublime of Hebrew works, the most ancient, the most primitive, and the least theological. It is the most clearly Oriental and "has no relation whatever to the affairs of the Israelites."

If Job then is not a doctrinal work for Lowth, it is nevertheless a work containing a profound moral lesson. But that lesson concerns only the sublimity of its poetry as it reflects the sublime passions of its poet-hero, Job. The only doctrine here is the secular doctrine of sublime humility as expressed in the poetry of the work.

Lowth makes this radical point by distinguishing two literary structures in the Book. One, he notes, is the narrative as a whole, embodying the story of Job, his fall from fortune, and his subsequent restoration. The clear message of this Biblical *narrative,* viewed as such, is patience: Job's persistence in his faith leads ultimately to his just reward. Lowth prefers to read the work as poetry, however, rather than as narrative. What Lowth calls the *poem* of Job excludes the prose prologue and epilogue of the book (which contain the fall and restoration) and deals only with its poetry. Viewed this way, as poetry unrelated to narrative action, the point of the book must be something quite different from patience. This Lowth specifies as *humility*. "The true object of the Poem [is] to demonstrate the necessity of humility, of trust in God." Viewed not as narrative but as a Poem, the Book of Job points not to doctrine but to the sublime sentiments of its hero. "The Poem of Job" contains

> no plot or action whatever, not even of the most simple kind . . . it contains merely a representation of those manners, passions and sentiments which might actually be expected in such a situation . . . The poem contains a great variety of sentiment . . . manners and character, remarkable efforts of passion, but no change of fortune, no plot or action.

Since the essence of the poem is the depiction of sublime passions, the characterization of Job's friends is necessarily incomplete: "There appears . . . but little difference in the manners of the three friends; *for in them the Poet has rather studied to display the progress of the passions, than any diversity of character* [emphasis added]. Questions of Divine Providence are not to the point of this most sublime and ancient Oriental poetry: "Neither the nature nor the object of the Poem required a defense of the Divine Providence but merely a reprehension of the overconfidence of Job."

Lowth clearly points the distinction between the *narrative* of Job and the *poem* of Job. His preference for the latter is due not only to the poetic bias of the *Lectures* but also to Lowth's evident impatience with contemporary doctrinal controversies surrounding Job. By emphasizing the poem of Job, Lowth emphasizes the sublime character, whose essential quality is finally sublime humility before God's ineffable power.

II

Lowth on Job is of paramount interest when we consider the possibility of understanding the Vicar as a Job-figure in any "doctrinal" sense. The most sophisticated such view is that of Martin C. Battestin's *The Providence of Wit*. In the chapter entitled "Goldsmith: The Comedy of Job," Battestin confronts a problem that has vexed critics of this novel for some time, namely the abrupt shift of tone and action that occurs midway through the book. Once Charles Primrose leaves his family to retrieve the abducted Olivia, we move from the story of a family to the pilgrimage of an individual, from a controlled comedy of manners with controlled narrator to a rambling tale, often interrupted by other tales, in which sentiment and pathos dominate. One approach to this structural problem has been to treat the first half of the book as novelistic success, while viewing the second half as a sort of failure in its succumbing to the use of romance motifs. Another approach to this problem has been to join the two halves thematically, and Battestin's essay attempts such a solution. He seeks to show that the story of Dr. Primrose in both halves of the novel is the story of the biblical Job. The analogy itself, Battestin admits, is not new. What is new in his treatment is the way he specifies the theological meaning of the Job analogy. In this reading, the hero of the novel follows the path of the biblical Job in the sense that he learns the lesson, which, according to Battestin, was the common reading of Job in the period of *The Vicar*'s composition. This lesson is the doctrine of equal providence, the belief "that, although the dealings of Providence are unequal in this life, the sufferings of good men will be abundantly recompensed in the hereafter." According to Battestin, Primrose learns this Christian "doctrine of futurity" in chapter 28 and shows his new wisdom in chapter 29 by preaching to his fellow prisoners on just this subject. In fact, the title of the latter chapter makes reference to the "equal dealings of Providence."

Primrose's doctrinal revelation marks his attainment of true knowledge. The theological term for Job's new knowledge, Battestin tells us, is "prudence." Whereas one might have knowledge (and Job had knowledge) he might still lack *prudence,* the insight that God's justice persists despite its apparent abrogation in this world. Battestin supports his reading by citing a large number of contemporary theologians who wrote on Job, and by citing too, a particular controversy which raged around Warburton and Bishop Thomas Sherlock during the middle decades of the century. He suggests that Goldsmith sided with the anti-Warburtonians, who maintained that a message of divine reward in resurrection ("equal providence") could be derived from the Book of Job (and hence from a work written before the Christian dispensation).

Battestin's reading is an explicit rejection of recent attempts to read Goldsmith as ironic in his presentation of the hero. Because these readings do not take the theological context into account, he argues, they are anachronistic sophistications imposed on the text by modern critics.

Now Battestin is certainly right in drawing attention to the exegetical tradition in his analysis of *The Vicar of Wakefield*. But it is not at all clear that the Job analogy in the novel is meant to be taken in the spirit he suggests. In fact, Goldsmith plays a good deal with the biblical story; the biblical paradigm is often invoked only to be toyed with. This is so, as my survey of Lowth might have suggested, precisely because the exegetical tradition was itself undergoing a significant change during this period.

As a preliminary but significant example of the ways Goldsmith plays with his biblical model, consider the term "prudence." Battestin wants this term to bear a great weight because it is the technical name of Job's insight; moreover, it is the term which for Battestin ties together the unifying motifs of disguise and blindness (noted [elsewhere] by Curtis Dahl) and the theological understanding of divine providence. The trouble here is that prudence is an ambiguous term in *The Vicar*. Although Battestin refers to prudence only as a term of theological art, its other uses cannot be over-looked in attempting to discern the total meaning of the word in the text. Thus, in the opening chapter, Mr. Wilmot is said to have only prudence left at the age of seventy-two. There is nothing theological about this jesting use of the word. Nor is the term used doctrinally when Primrose tells his family that no prudence could have prevented their misfortune. Actually, prudence would have consisted in Primrose's silence about his Whistonian beliefs on strict clerical monogamy until *after* his family had been joined to the wealthy Wilmots (exactly what the messenger bearing news of the vicar's loss suggests). Prudence may well have theological connotations, but that would only make its use ironic, and irony is finally what Battestin cannot permit.

There are other reversals of the biblical types as well. Job's wife has become the biblical Deborah, the female judge, ruling Israel and ruling, too, her passive nominal leader Barak (Judges 4, 5). And as in Judges, this Deborah is always described in military terms; she is the one who conducts sieges and plans battles. Moses, the son, is something of a lawgiver: he always cites the ancients and argues weakly with Thornhill on matters of doctrine. His sententiousness, in short, is a parody of his biblical namesake and type. And then there are the crucial changes in the order of the biblical narrative, as when Deborah Primrose reprimands her husband for cursing his oppressor whereas Job's wife was the one who begged him to curse God and die. Like Parson Adams of *Joseph Andrews* (the *locus classicus* for Battestin's method), our Vicar often acts at variance with his prototype, deviating subtly but surely from his presumed prefiguration.

There are many such deviations in *The Vicar of Wakefield*, but my purpose is not so much to list them as to indicate where Battestin has gone wrong in his general approach. Battestin's fundamental error arises from his assumption that the *analogical* structure persists in Goldsmith's fiction. Battestin has totally ignored the fact that from the 1740s onward new ways of reading the Bible were gaining ground in England and that such changes in reading would have suggested a number of possible alternatives for the application of a scriptural text to a literary work. He does not consider that the way (a reader of) Pope would have read his Bible might differ from the way (a reader of) Goldsmith would have read the Bible. For example, Pope in his use of Balaam and Job in the *Epistle to Bathurst* (1733) assumes a definite series of theological connotations attached to those figures that can be read as constituting their *meaning;* Earl Wasserman's analysis of the *Epistle* was based on just this premise. But a quarter century later the Bible was being read differently; it was seen not only as the vehicle for theological meanings, but also as a repository of sublime poetry in the Oriental mode. Battestin must be aware of this new Orientalized Bible, yet he pays no attention to it. The results of his exhaustive researches into the theological literature are thus prejudiced by his implicit decision to consider only the homiletic aspects of these writings and to ignore the grammatical and literary-critical work on the Bible that was flourishing at just this time.

Battestin's homiletic bias in this regard forces him also to assume that it was the Warburtonian controversy on "equal providence" that stimulated interest in the Book of Job. Thus, after listing the commentators ranged on each side, he writes, "in the same period appeared several other, more or less neutral, treatises reflecting the widespread interest in the subject which the controversy had generated. These include a variety of studies by Daniel Bellamy, William Worthington, Walter Hodge, Leonard Chappelow, Thomas Heath and Bishop Lowth." The unexamined assumption that these "neutral" studies merely reflect the theological controversy leads Battestin to ignore the new Orientalizing of the Bible undertaken by just these "more or less neutral studies." It also leads him to ignore the fictional possibilities which a newly Orientalized Bible might present to writers such as Goldsmith.

Battestin's evidence of Goldsmith's purportedly sincere interest in the controversy also deserves scrutiny. This consists of a review of Hawkins's contribution to the debate that appeared in the *Critical Review* of August, 1759. Its authorship by Goldsmith is uncertain, but in any case the following hardly reveals real interest in the affair:

> Mr. Hawkins seems to be pretty confident in the advantage of his cause; and this we may venture to say, that he seems to be on the safe side, for he is on the bishop's; and though he loses his cause he may gain a vicarage. As for the controversy, so much has been said on both sides, that we must really acknowledge ourselves sceptic in the debate . . . We can know enough and believe enough without being acquainted with a syllable of the matter: we could wish our divines would therefore rather turn their arms against the common enemy; and while infidelity is at the gate, not waste their time in civil altercation.

This passage is clearly not the strongest basis upon which to found Goldsmith's interest in the Providential controversies surrounding the Book of Job. Rather, in Goldsmith as in other Job studies, the general indifference to the theological issues that Battestin holds most important suggests that he has ignored a crucial development in the mid-century reading of Job. Far from there being a consensus with regard to the specific theology of the work, there was not even unanimity as to whether the book was to be taken as *primarily* theological.

The new Orientalizing Bible readings, as exemplified by Lowth, are important therefore because they force us to reconsider the historical plausibility of a strictly theological reading of Job in *The Vicar of Wakefield*. What we have instead is a *secular* Job. Ronald Paulson has elaborated the distinction between *emblem* and *expression* in the art and literature of the eighteenth century. We might apply this notion by noting that in the Orientalist tradition represented by Bishop Lowth, the emblematic quality of Scripture is confronted with the expressive potentialities of Hebrew poetry. For a new tradition of biblical Orientalism, the emblematic readability of the Bible (the old typological framework in which the Old Testament is emblematic of the New) has been transformed into its sublime expressiveness. Scripture no longer *means* the way it once did. This "secular conversion" is never more manifest than in the Orientalizing of the Book of Job.

III

I would suggest that there is a moral development in *The Vicar* that is closely related to a movement toward the attainment of the sublime. This movement takes our Job-figure from an essentially ironic condition to one that sublimely transcends irony through love and humility. Primrose *becomes* a Job-figure in the course of the novel, not because he acquires specific theological knowledge, but because he moves beyond an artifically self-conscious situation into the condition of genuine passion. He attains the sublime when he is motivated not by concern for appearances and social status, but by the natural and passionate love of his family and his fellow man.

This moral movement in the novel towards humility and the sublime can best be seen in the progress of the work's pictorial imagery. In Goldsmith's time sublime painting, like sublime Hebrew poetry, had to be uniquely expressive not emblematic. As Reynolds put it, painting must strike its viewer in a single blow.

Both halves of our novel contain many scenes with a strongly pictorial quality, but Goldsmith depicts these scenes differently in the two halves. In the "pre-exilic" first portion of the work Primrose's presentation of these pictorial scenes is intensely ironic. This is because his concern in representing his family is to curry favor with his social betters. This concern is morally flawed; in terms of the sublime work of art, Primrose's act of representation is mere parody. Once the vicar sets off on his journey, however, he becomes the object of forces beyond his control. Primrose no longer *creates* scenes; these are discovered or reveal themselves to him. It is just this powerlessness, and the recognition of powerlessness, that allows the narrator to transcend the irony that marks his earlier artifice. The frozen order of the earlier depictions gives way to a series of passionate events. Our hero recognizes moral truth just when these events convey not the ironic fiction-making of their author, but rather his perception of the overpowering significance of human love. As he loses control over his surroundings, he gains his ultimate redemption as a simple and sublime Job (and simplicity is an integral element of the biblical and artistic sublime). Especially in the pictorial culmination of each half of the book—the portrait scene in chapter 16 and the prison scene in chapter 29—we can contrast the irony of artifice with the simplicity of the sublime.

I am suggesting, then, that the identification of Job with the sublime in contemporary biblical discourse allows us to reevaluate the evident break in the style of the novel. While we seem to be moving (unhappily) from a delicate novelistic depiction of life as a social environment, to life as a journey, we are in fact advancing from an artificial and unnatural mode of self-realization to a wiser vision of human existence. I would suggest, too, that a useful general notion for dealing with this transformation of pictorial imagery is that of the *frame*. This notice subsumes, in the first place, the general symbolism of spatial enclosure: frames, enclosures of all sorts, are a fundamental structure in the novel. In addition, we can talk of the *activity* of framing as it pertains to our hero-narrator. In this second sense, framing denotes a selection, delimitation, and depiction of reality by means of the imagery of enclosure. To the extent that scenes in our novel are fictionally enclosed and distanced, successive framings can be seen as the vehicles of Goldsmith's moral statement: if the activity of framing by the hero-narrator consists in the self-conscious wrenching of reality from its human context in order to re-present it (as it does, I believe, in the first half of the novel), then it is a fundamentally ironic activity. When, however, frames disclose a dominant concern for the human and the passionate, then they partake of the sublime. To return to the terminology of contemporary art criticism we might say that the sublime draws us away from the external accentuation of circumstances into the passionate center. Thus the sublime is attained only when the frame encloses that which strikes at a single blow, when the frame yields its own independent significance to the expressive force of its content. In the case of *The Vicar* ironic frames are those created by Primrose as narrator out of concern for external circumstances, social vanity, and acceptance by his social betters. Sublime frames, on the other hand, are those images of enclosure that reveal the passion of true human relationships based on love. Primrose does not create *these* scenes; they effectively create *him* and reshape his character as a sublime Job-figure. As we follow the transformation of frames in *The Vicar of Wakefield*, we follow the progress of a Job-figure transcending irony by assuming the role of sublime character.

The first half of *The Vicar* is replete with examples of framing, but none partakes of the characteristics of the biblical sublime. The women spend their time watching themselves in mirrors. When they move to a new apartment, the narrator describes the new dwelling as if he were showing us a painting ("The eye was agreeably relieved"). We are shown, through the many descriptions of the family's neat little enclosures, the pictorial and fundamentally external quality of their existence. The vicar himself is strongly implicated in this arranging process, and this despite his early assertion that "mere outside is so very trifling a circumstance with me." He speaks of his family as a republic to which he gives laws, but these laws, as he tells us, are entirely ceremonial. This needless form of social creation, which is obviously no more than ornament, is thematically set against a similar scene in a different setting, the prison, in which Primrose does indeed establish a form of useful republic among the prisoners. At the Thornhill estate, however, frames are concerned with external circumstances and, hence, are ultimately ironic.

We have a sense in the novel, also, of the fragility of these self-conscious frames that reflects the precarious social situation of the family. This is emphasized at the beginning of chapter 5 when the pastoral setting in which the Primroses are framed by the narrator is suddenly intruded upon by the hunting squire. The sense of violent intrusion into an enclosed family circle is equally apparent when the Misses Skeggs and Blarney enter in chapter 11. One detects in these scenes the vulnerability of the family circle to the reality that surrounds it, but also the ironic vulnerability of the narrator (the creator of the circle) in his eagerness to appease those powers that surround him. The vicar's language in the course of chapter 11 conveys perfectly the moral ambiguities of concern for the "mere outside"; the concern for the external sets in motion the need to accommodate oneself to the outside. That is what Primrose is doing in this chapter and that is what he does—as hero and as narrator—throughout the first half of the book.

The multiplying ironies in the first half of *The Vicar* should bring us back to the matter of Job. Powerlessness, after all, is the fundamental characteristic of Job in the Bible, and it is Primrose's lack of power that is being pointed out here. Given the general paradigm of Job, there is a pervasive irony underlying the early happy chapters. For Job has already fallen (i.e., lost his wealth) but life goes on. The anguished debate that followed immediately upon the biblical Job's fall has been transformed into the hour and a half set aside daily by the vicar "for innocent mirth between my wife and daughter in philosophical arguments between my son and me," or into the facetious debates between Thornhill and Moses on religious doctrine, or into Olivia's great skill in debating which, according to her proud mother, she has attained from reading the debates of Square and Thwackum, and of Robinson Crusoe and Friday. Clearly, the Job pattern is being parodied precisely to highlight the artificiality of the Primroses' existence.

It is during another framed scene that a simpler, more natural, and more sublime taste is first expressed by the virtuous Burchell. Our narrator describes his discussion of the virtues of the various poetic forms with Moses and the humble Burchell. "Two blackbirds answered each other from opposite hedges . . . every sound seemed but the echo of tranquility." Within this verbally painted enclosure, the disguised lord sings the ballad of Edwin and Angelina. A moment earlier he had attacked the artificiality of the modern classicizing taste in poetry (a taste that had been defended by Moses, who always defends the ancients). The simple and the sublime, of course, were closely identified by contemporary theorists (and especially by apologists for the Bible's style). Burchell's choice of the ballad form and his pronouncements on art introduce an important theme in the novel, and are a key to the new and different structure of its second half.

The artifice of framing and the irony of posturing are most clearly opposed to Goldsmith's ideal of the natural, the simple, and the sublime in chapters 15 and 16. At the end of chapter 15, after the vicar has misconstrued Burchell's letter, he and Deborah confront the disguised Sir William. Primrose cites Pope's line in praise of the honest man. To "the hackney'd maxim of Pope," Burchell responds, "we might as well prefer the tame correct paintings of the Flemish school to the erroneous but sublime animation of the Roman pencil." Burchell rejects the correct in favor of the sublime (this dichotomy had often been applied to the Bible). In a 1760 review of Kedington's *Critical Dissertations upon the Iliad of Homer*, Goldsmith had written:

> The merit of every work is determined not from the number of its faults but of its beauties . . . The great beauties of every work make it inestimable; its defects are only arguments of humanity, not weakness.

For this reason, Goldsmith expresses a preference for the beauties of Italian painting over the more correct French style. Goldsmith on painting and Burchell on Pope should be considered in light of the Advertisement introducing *The Vicar of Wakefield*:

> There are a hundred faults in this thing, and a hundred things might be said to prove them beauties. But it is needless. A book may be amusing with numerous errors, or it may be very dull without a single absurdity.

Opposed to this stands the ridiculous Primrose family portrait, in whose execution the vicar plays no small part. "The family use art which is opposed with still Greater" is the punning title of chapter 16. Literally, it refers to Deborah's schemes to ensnare the young Thornhill, which the narrator knows to be hopeless. But it also echoes the portrait scene in which, to outdo the Flamboroughs, as the vicar approvingly tells us, the family has been artistically represented in a single large frame. The artificiality of this framing is emphasized by the absurdity of the poses: Deborah is Venus surrounded by cupids, and Charles Primrose is depicted handing his sermons on clerical monogamy to his Venus-wife. The painter is asked to fill in "as many sheep as he could for nothing," merely to populate this contrived, unnatural space. The resulting picture, a monstrous caricature of life, won't fit in the house (another, more natural, frame) and we are told that it remained in the kitchen, a monument, it would seem, to the folly and impossibility of the whole enterprise. Coming as it does immediately after the break with Burchell and the latter's discourse on art, and just when Thornhill, junior, successfully invades the family circle (he is to be Alexander the Great at the bottom of the painting), this scene highlights the falsely emblematic activity that betrays and exemplifies the moral flaw of our Job. Just before Olivia is taken, the vicar judges the relative value of the ballad and ode, condemning those odes that "petrify us in a single stanza." The line applies all too well to Primrose's ironic situation as expressed in the grand family portrait.

The transition from scene to sentiment, from emblem to expression, begins with the news of Olivia's abduction. When Primrose learns that his daughter has been taken, a Job scene is played out with a significant reversal. His nature gets the better of him and he immediately curses his oppressor, only to be brought back to his paradigmatic role by his wife and son. (This bears comparison to Parson Adams's reaction to the news of his boy's "drowning" in *Joseph Andrews*.) The passionate outburst by our hero, however, marks a definite progress in Primrose's move toward the sublime, although the description of the family's grief reminds us that the Primroses are still described in *scenic* terms (to use another of Kenneth Burke's useful concepts). Thus we are told:

> In this manner that night the first of our real misfortunes was spent in the bitterness of complaint . . . The next morning we missed our wretched child at breakfast where she used to give life and cheerfulness to us all.

Olivia is perceived as part of a breakfast picture; the scenic and the passionate coexist here. Only gradually will the latter come to dominate.

In the following chapter our narrator-hero recognizes that he may have been deceived as to the identity of the true villain. This is a crucial advance for Primrose, as he begins to recognize the fallibility of his constructions. In his meeting with the company of actors he is shown to appreciate the matter of false imitation as he discourses on the theater. False imitation, too, is the theme of the political harangue that Primrose delivers (tyranny masquerades as liberty, according to the agitated vicar), as well as of the disguise of Arnold's butler. Passion dominates scene when George, the vicar's son, emerges from the company. The pattern of discovery, of emergence from a scene, is repeated in the discovery of Olivia at the inn. Whatever the literary success of Goldsmith's chain of events, we should bear in mind the contrast of the active, ironic creator of scenes, which our narrator is in the book's first half, and the suffering, passionate figure of the book's second half. The inns and rooms, the *frames* of the latter half, are utterly beyond the vicar's control.

The burning of Primrose's house underscores this development. It can be seen as the continuation of the Job motif (in the Bible, Satan is given dominion first over Job's property, then over his family, and finally over Job himself), but it is clearly much more than that. The biblical Job bears no real human relationship to his surroundings, but it is just this relationship that is the subject of Goldsmith's fiction. Crucially, the destruction of the Primrose house is not the beginning of punishment (as it was for Job) so much as the confirmation of a process of salvation that involves a new awareness of the meaning of human and social frames. The burn on the arm, another Job-parallel, is similarly reversed. The sentimental outburst by the vicar following the fire provides an interesting reversal of the biblical *complaint* and a demonstration of a new, passionate perception:

> Observe this bed of straw and unsheltering roof; those mouldering walls and humid floor; my wretched body thus disabled by fire, and my children weeping round me for bread: you have come home, my child, to all this; yet here, even here, you see a man that would not for a thousand worlds exchange situations. Oh, my children, if you could but learn to commune with your hearts, and know what noble company you can make them, you would little regard the elegance and splendour of the worthless.

The culminating revaluation of frames comes in the jail scene. Goldsmith emphasizes the frame aspect of the prison: we see two cells, the general cell, "strongly grated and paved with stone," and the individual cell. It is here, outside of society and away from the false self-dramatization of social framing, that the vicar is most sublime and most passionate. He establishes his society on faith and natural law, not on ceremony. He rejects the idea that property is founded in natural law, and argues that laws should reward as well as punish. The family visiting the vicar, says Primrose, "can make a dungeon seem a palace." Their intrinsic *humanity* now defines them, rather than their self-conscious existence in society.

Finally, after resigning himself to his death and the death of his son, Primrose becomes the center of a culminating transformation of the social frame. At the end of chapter 28 a pathetic scene is presented; Primrose rises to deliver his sermon:

> Thus saying, I made an effort to rise from my straw, but wanted strength, and was able only to recline against the wall. The prisoners assembled themselves according to my directions, for they loved to hear my counsel: my son and his mother supported me on either side; I looked and saw that none were wanting, and then addressed them with the following exhortation.

This is certainly a frame, but it takes us not to the false emblems of the first half of *The Vicar*, but to its biiblical analogue in Exodus 17:12, where Moses' hands are held up by Aaron and Hur. As Meyer Schapiro has shown, this scene has a rich iconographic history: Moses' outstretched arms were taken to figure the sign of the Cross (*Words and Pictures: On the Literal and the Symbolic in the Illustration of a Text*). Thus the artificial self-framing of which our hero was guilty has now reached an opposite extreme. Helped by others, he transcends his scene and delivers his moving sermon. Scene and passion now define one another, and the frame is wholly natural, based entirely on the love of his family and his fellow prisoners. The message of his sermon is therefore doubly appropriate for our transformed (and transfigured) hero:

> No vain efforts of a refined imagination can soothe the wants of nature, can give elastic sweetness to the dank vapours of a dungeon or ease to the throbbings of a broken heart.

Primrose's closing sermon preaches a doctrine of love. Indeed, *The Vicar of Wakefield* is Goldsmith's artistic elaboration of the sublime of love. That Goldsmith considered love and the sublime inseparable can be seen in his review of Burke's *A Philosophical Inquiry into the Origin of our Ideas of the Sublime and Beautiful* in the *Monthly Review* for May 1757. In an otherwise favorable notice, Goldsmith suggested that the author had not sufficiently considered love as an element of the sublime:

> Our Author by assigning terror for the only source of the sublime excludes love, admiration &c. But to make the sublime an idea incompatible with those affections is what the general sense of mankind will be apt to contradict . . . Our astonishment at the sublime as often proceeds from an increased love as from an increased fear.

It is precisely the sublime of love that is attained by the end of the novel.

IV

There is a change, then, that corresponds to the break in the book after chapter 17. That the change relates to Job is undeniable, but that it follows Battestin's theological reconstruction is less likely. Even after the sublime climax in chapter 29, Goldsmith plays with the biblical paradigm:

> The greatest object in the universe, says a certain philosopher, is a good man struggling with adversity, yet there is still a greater which is the good man that comes to relieve it.

This sentiment is as close to romance motifs as it is distant from the point of the Book of Job. And the title of chapter 30, we recall ("Let us be inflexible and fortune will at last change in our favour"), seems to have forgotten the lesson of the earlier chapter.

Goldsmith's use of a biblical type is thus complex in *The Vicar*. Overall, we can say that his free use of the Book of Job, and his emphasis upon a contrast between scene and sentiment, parallels in important ways new biblical-critical notions of the sublimity of the Hebrew poetry and the particular, detheologized sublimity of Job in the works of Lowth and contemporary Semiticists. England's reception of biblical criticism was very halting: Lowth's primary influence on later work in England comes indirectly by way of Michaelis, Herder, and the German Romantics. But that the Bible was sublime and was a species of Oriental literature was widely accepted.

We don't know Goldsmith's precise acquaintance with the work of Lowth, but an Orientalizer like Goldsmith would certain have been receptive to his very popular ideas. Our author's use of Job, then, is to give us a *human* rather than a *divine* message, and that message has much less to do with how we will fare in the next world than it has to do with how we ought to act and to know ourselves in this one.

Money in the Novels
of Fanny Burney

Edward W. Copeland

Three years after Fanny Burney's death in 1843, Macaulay recalled the delight with which he had read her novels: "Her appearance is an important epoch in our literary history," he wrote. "*Evelina* was the first tale written by a woman, and purporting to be a picture of life and manners, that lived or deserved to live." In short, Fanny Burney made writing novels a respectable occupation for women. "She vindicated the right of her sex to an equal share in a fair and noble province of letters." She vindicated the right of her sex, Virginia Woolf might have added, to a share in the *profits* of letters as well. In *A Room of One's Own*, Mrs. Woolf claims that "towards the end of the eighteenth century a change came about which, if I were rewriting history, I should describe more fully and think of greater importance than the Crusades or the War of the Roses. The middle-class woman began to write." And this, Mrs. Woolf reminds us, "was based on the solid fact that women could make money by writing. Money dignifies what is frivolous if unpaid for." "Jane Austen," she concludes, "should have laid a wreath upon the grave of Fanny Burney."

I would like to suggest that the money Mrs. Woolf sees as the motivation for the new female literature of the late eighteenth century was also the subject of that literature—and that from a hitherto unvoiced female point of view. Men of course had written about women and money in novels before Fanny Burney, but the masculine approach was radically different from that of the lady novelist. For the male novelists, the world of money, the getting and the spending, was the stage for aggressive action, a world to be manipulated and managed. Defoe's Moll Flanders—"*Twelve Years a Whore, Five time a Wife (whereof once to her own Brother.) Twelve Times a Thief, Eight Years a transported Felon in Virginia, at last Grew Rich, Liv'd*

From *Studies in the Novel* 8, no. 1 (Spring 1976). © 1976 by North Texas State University.

Honest, and Died a Penitent"—knew her market and exploited it. Richardson's Pamela parlayed her "little mustard seed" of virtue into marriage with a wealthy country squire, a town house *and* a country house, and the approving applause of the neighboring gentry, her author, and herself. The fantasy of Defoe or Richardson by rough analogy might be this: "What would you do if you had a million dollars?" or, "How would you get it?" For the new female novelist there was a significant variation: "What would you do if you *married* a million dollars?" or, more frighteningly, "What if you *don't*?"

The insistent exploration of women's peculiar relationship to money defines the new female fiction. Here is where the heroines of such widely differing novelists as Fanny Burney, Mrs. Radcliffe with her Gothic thrills, and Mary Wollstonecraft, the political radical and feminist, join hands. The topic is approached from every direction: the poor, but nobly virtuous heroine; the wealthy heroine, a prey to fortune hunters; the orphan; the dependent relation; even the unhappily married heroine who in Charlotte Lennox's novel *Euphemia* (1790) confesses that she has "drawn a blank in the great lottery of life." The importance of money in the woman's novel before Jane Austen has eluded the analyzing eye of the critic, I think, because of the large amount of fantasy in this fiction. Pounds sterling are parcelled out at the end of these novels in terms of the wildest, most drunken sort of fantasy fulfillment. But the fantasy money cannot be ignored; it has a reality of its own, first of all, because it is the coin in which an author rewards, dignifies, and, in truth, establishes and confirms the identity of her heroine. Second, the fantasy money exists in a necessary relation to real money, not the real money of the male novelists, but that of the female, domestic budget: the price of theater tickets, the cost of lace, or, in a more serious area of the domestic economy, the price of bread, milk, and eggs. The relationship between these two kinds of money in the woman's novel is at the center of dramatic tension in them all—from romantic castles in the Apennines to the humble vicar's cottage in Surrey. And it is the changing relationship between the fantasy money and the real money that provides a focus for plotting the growth of a new consciousness and self-awareness in women's literature of the last years of the century.

Fanny Burney's novels are particularly revealing since they span so great a period of time, over four decades, from the 1770s to her last novel in 1814: *Evelina*, in 1778, *Cecilia*, 1782; *Camilla*, 1796; and *The Wanderer*, in 1814. Unfortunately, the annoying paradox that has faced every critic of her novels from Croker, Hazlitt, and Macaulay to the present day is that instead of growing more complex, richer, and more resonant as Jane Austen's work did, Fanny Burney's last two novels were written largely in what Macaulay justifiably called "the worst style that has ever been known among men." Even so, as Macaulay recognized, her later style was "not from a decay of power, but from a total perversion of power." "Perversion" is of course unfair, but the criticism does draw attention to the fact that Fanny Burney's later failures were not accidental, but were guided, or misguided, by a shaping principle. I would like to suggest here that the development, or perhaps better, the alteration of her style follows her changing response to the relationships in her novels between real and fantasy money.

What Macaulay does not account for is that the style he calls her "later style," "a sort of broken Johnsonese, a barbarous *patois*, bearing the same relation to the language of Rasselas, which the gibberish of the Negroes of Jamaica bears to the English of the House of Lords," was not exclusive to her later works. Fanny Burney, or Madame d'Arblay as she was in her later years, did use the sharp, comic style of her first novel and her journals in her later work; moreover, her early works and the journals have their share, though less, of high gibberish as well. Variations on that queer, bolloxed style were regularly employed throughout her writing career, from age sixteen to eighty, to dignify the ideal virtues and rewards of her fantasy life. The faults and blemishes of those characters who do not fit this ideal order always attract her low, familiar, comic style; the virtues of the ad- mirable gentry (along with their estates) without fail involve her in reverent, if obscure, circumlocutions.

In *Evelina*, for example, there are two plots: a comic plot of shillings and pence, and a courtship plot of love and pounds sterling. The heroine, Evelina, is the daughter of the sadly misused and beautiful Caroline Evelyn, who, abandoned by her libertine husband, Sir John Belmont, dies in giving birth to Evelina. Evelina is left the ward of the good but aging Mr. Villars, a country clergyman. She is taken on a visit to London by wealthy friends at a young and tender age where unfortunately (and by accident) she meets her maternal grandmother, the vulgar Madame Duval, who before her marriage to Evelina's grandfather was no more than "a waiting girl at a tavern." Madame Duval insists on her rights as the girl's grandmother and, removing the heroine from the protection of her genteel friends, takes her into the company of her vulgar London relations who all talk about money unconscionably. "Pray, if it is not impertinent," the Branghton cousins ask, "what might you give a yard for this lutestring?—Do you make your own caps, Miss?—and many other questions," Evelina writes Mr. Villars, "equally interesting and well-bred." The elder Mr. Branghton is horrified at the price of opera tickets: " 'I thought, at the time,' said Mr. Branghton, 'that three shillings was an exorbitant price for a place in the gallery, but as we'd been asked so much more at the other doors, why I paid it without many words; but then, to be sure, thinks I, it can never be like any other gallery,—we shall see some *crinkum-crankum* or other for our money;—but I find it's as arrant a take-in as ever I met with.' " Madame Duval even touches the sorest of the heroine's nerves by suggesting a marriage with the young Mr. Branghton: " 'Why,' cried she, 'I have had grander views for you, myself, if once I could get you to Paris.' " "I begged her," Evelina says, "not to pursue the subject, as, I assured her, Mr. Branghton was totally disagreeable to me: but she continued her admonitions and reflections with her usual disregard of what I could answer. . . . [S]he concluded, just as she had begun, by saying, that I should not *have him, if I could do better.*"

The romantic plot, of course, discovers quite a different style—and a different kind of money. In her London peregrinations, Evelina falls victim to a fatal prepossession; that is to say, she falls in love with the "sensible and spirited," "open and noble," "gentle, attentive, and infinitely engaging," "animated and expressive" Lord Orville. This condition, one with serious consequences in her later novels, bankrupts her for the marriage market since she can never be happily married to any other man. Fortunately there are no serious impediments to their union; enough time must pass for Lord Orville to see her virtues shining out from the thicket of rude and crude relations that surround her, but as one of the genteel characters says, disguising what she means in appropriately obscure language, "Fortune, alone, has hitherto been sparing of her gifts," which is to say, Evelina is portionless. Lord Orville is, of course, "willing, nay eager" that the union take place even after he has been told her story. But, unwilling to leave the romance at that, Fanny has Evelina recognized by her father ("My God! does Caroline Evelyn still live!") and fall heiress to thirty thousand pounds. Thus, in a separate action, the fantasy money provides the keys to unlimited happiness—and the heroine's identity. In fact, as the first evidence of his paternal affection, Evelina's new-found father sends her a ready one thousand pounds "which he insisted that I should receive entirely for my own use, and expend in equipping myself properly for the new rank in life to which I seem destined." The annoyances and embarrassments of counting pence are left behind as so many comic divertissements on the road to the resolution of the comedy in marriage and a sizable fortune.

Evelina had been written under her father's roof and shows, I think, the marks of that security. Once when her friend, and later her literary adviser, Samuel Crisp pressured her to reconsider her refusal of a well-to-do admirer, Fanny had replied, "My father and Mr. Crisp spoil me for every other male creature"—not the best solution for "an unprotected, unprovided woman," but one that she transposes into her first novel by providing her heroine with a father-husband in Lord Orville, who "when *time had wintered o'er his locks,*" would shine forth "among his fellow creatures, with the same brightness of worth which dignifies my honoured Mr. Villars," and a final fillip of happiness in a wedding trip "to dear Berry Hill, and to the arms of the best of men," Mr. Villars. *Cecilia,* her next novel, was written under considerably different conditions and shows this in its altered tone. Fanny, a celebrity was now out in the world and, though under the protection of Mrs. Thrale and Dr. Johnson, was constantly being reminded by her genteel friends of her financial insecurity. "Now, Miss Burney, if you would write a play," Mrs. Thrale suggested: "Hannah More

. . . got nearly four hundred pounds for her foolish play, and if you did not write a better than hers, I say you deserve to be whipped!" Fanny wrote the play, *The Witlings* (1778–80), which included a heroine who loses her fortune ("Upon my word," one character says, "in my opinion, a Bankruptcy is no pleasant thing!"), an avaricious older woman ("Nothing is so difficult as disposing of a poor Girl of Fashion"), and a high-minded hero ("Her distress shall increase my tenderness, her poverty shall redouble my Respect"). But certain circumstances of the plot and the mockery of the lady wits in the play cut too close to Mrs. Montagu, the Queen of the Blues, and Fanny was persuaded by Mr. Crisp to suppress it.

Cecilia, the novel she wrote to take its place, was, appropriately, about money. The heroine, Cecilia Beverley, an orphan, is heiress to the grand sum of ten thousand pound from her father's estate (which is under her own control) and three thousand pounds per annum from her late uncle, the uncle's money to be received by her upon the condition that when she marry her husband assume *her* name of Beverley. Since she is a minor, her uncle's fortune is left to her in the care of three guardians: the first, Mr. Briggs, a miserly London merchant who is another, grosser version of Evelina's Mr. Branghton; the second, the fashionable Mr. Harrel, the husband of Cecilia's closest girlhood friend and, unfortunately, the heroine discovers, a hopeless gambler; and finally, the aristocratic Mr. Delvile, an unmitigated family snob who will take no hand in managing the money: "why did I degrade myself by accepting this humiliating office?" he laments to his ward. "The head of an ancient and honourable house, is apt to think himself somewhat superior to people but just rising from dust and obscurity." The strategy is obviously different from *Evelina*. In her first novel, Miss Burney had held fairly closely to the simple plan of a Cinderella-type of story; the money could be understood as one more grace added to newly revealed Evelina Belmont. But in *Cecilia* she chose to create an abstract design in the heroine's financial arrangements and explore, through her heroine's difficulties, the problems and anxieties about love and money that she herself was facing—but discretely distanced by the strategy of having the heroine already wealthy. The unhappy fantasy of the novel might be stated: "If you were a woman and had an enormous fortune, how would you go about losing it?" Mrs. Thrale loved the idea: "I'm glad the little book or volume goes on; my notion is that I shall cry myself blind over the conclusion—it runs in my head—'tis so excessively pathetic."

Cecilia is also a novel with two plots that follow roughly the outlines of the division in *Evelina*, a love plot and a plot of hard cash. The novel opens with Cecilia on her way to London to spend the season with her old childhood friend Mrs. Harrel. When she arrives at the Harrels she finds that they are leading a life of shocking dissipation. Mr. Harrel seems "to consider his own house merely as an Hôtel," and Mrs. Harrel is devoted to an acquaintance who are "numerous, expensive and idle." The emotional pressures of the volumes in which she is residing with them are focussed around the Harrels' increasingly serious financial difficulties (brought on by Mr. Harrel's gambling) and Cecilia's progressively more serious involvement in saving them from ruin. Mr. Harrel first borrows from Cecilia as a friend; next he pressures her into loaning him a large amount from her paternal estate (the unencumbered one) in order to save her old friend Mrs. Harrel from the horrors of a complete bankruptcy; and finally he gets almost the last of her ten thousand pounds by threatening suicide if she refuses. Cecilia is tormented by her anxiety for Mrs. Harrel, her guilt for supporting a dissipated establishment, and her increasing fear that she will never see the money again—that her fortune will be lost. This, of course, comes true in a remarkably effective and lurid scene at Vauxhall where Mr. Harrel gets violently drunk before the ladies and then rushes off into the dark walks to shoot himself.

The second plot of *Cecilia*, the love plot, has been faulted, and rightly, for being so loosely attached in the structure to the sections at the Harrels, the only apparent connection being that the heroine falls in love with Mortimer Delvile, the son of one of the other trustees of her estate, the arrogant and name-proud old Mr. Delvile. The relationship between the rough-and-ready financial plot where Cecilia is tricked out of her paternal inheritance and the love plot is, I would like to suggest, closer than has been previously recognized. Cecilia's love is, of course, another fatal prepossession: "she started at her danger the moment she perceived it," Fanny assures us, "and instantly determined to give no weak encouragement to a prepossession which neither time nor intimacy had justified." It was not until a fortnight later "that she was conscious her happiness was no longer in her own power." Much later (two volumes) Mortimer overhears Cecilia in a chat with her dog Fidel to whom she confesses her love. She is horrified: "Delvile, upon whom so long, though secretly, her dearest hopes of happiness had rested, was now become acquainted with his power, and knew himself the master of her destiny. . . . A subjection so undue, and which she could not but consider as disgraceful, both shocked and afflicted her; and the reflection that the man of all men she preferred, was acquainted with her preference, yet hesitated whether to accept or abandon her, mortified and provoked her alternately." This would seem so much girlish posturing were it not for the complicating factor of Cecilia's inheritance. The proposed marriage is anathema to old Mr. Delvile because Mortimer must change his name from Delvile to Beverley; that is to say, if Cecilia gives herself to the man she loves, and takes *his* name, she will have to give up her uncle's three thousand pounds per annum, which sad to say is all she has left after the depredations of the Harrels on her paternal fortune of ten thousand pounds. Unfortunately Mortimer and Cecilia will need the three thousand pounds because the Delviles have no money. Fanny Burney tells us that the barrier to the marriage is the "PRIDE and PREJUDICE" of old Mr. Delvile, but this holds true only by refusing to look at the real barrier: Cecilia's money. The structure that underlies all the inflated style and melodramatic heart-burnings of the love plot, including a burst blood vessel for Mortimer's mother and Cecilia's running mad in the streets of London, is founded in the undecided state of Cecilia's inheritance. Will Cecilia exchange her wealth and independence for a husband? Will or *can* the hero, bound by his father to keep the Delvile name, marry a penniless heroine? Will the Delviles, who need the money, give in and accept the name Beverley? These are the questions that tortured the nerves of her readers old Mrs. Delany and the Duchess of Portland through five volumes: "Cry, to be sure we did," said the Duchess. "Oh, Mrs. Delany, shall you ever forget how we cried?" "I shall never forget," said Mrs. Delany, "your Grace's earnestness when we came to that part where Mrs. Delvile burst a blood-vessel. Down dropped the book, and just with the same energy as if your Grace had heard of some real and important news, you called out, 'I'm glad of it with all my heart.' "

As Fanny Burney approached the economic realities of her own situation, "an unprovided, unprotected woman," the moneys of the love plot and the financial plot at the Harrels seem to grow closer. Together they form a story of helplessness and loss. Cecilia decides to marry Mortimer Delvile, give up her name and give up her fortune. The real money is lost and so is the fantasy money (the projected inheritance from her uncle). As a final loss, so is the marriage: Mortimer deserts her in London when he discovers her, innocent of course, in a compromising interview with a male friend. Cecilia's identity, now resting in the exchange of fortune for love, is totally destroyed, and she runs mad in the streets. Appropriately enough, she is rescued by a pawnbroker. Everything works out of course: hearts are softened by the sight of the poor mad victim; the marriage is recognized by the Delviles; and the reunited couple move into the paternal home—the same happy ending as in *Evelina*, but sadly dimmed.

Fanny Burney cannot get over the loss of the money—nor can Cecilia. Even with the "unremitting fondness of Mortimer" and "all the happiness human life seems capable of receiving. . . . She knew that, at times, the whole family must murmur at her loss of fortune, and at time she murmured herself to be thus portionless, tho' an HEIRESS." Mr. Crisp strongly protested the ending and the loss of fortune; Edmund Burke told her "he wished the conclusion either more happy or more miserable; 'for in the work of the imagination,' said he, 'there is no medium.' " Burke was right. Fanny had tried for realism and fallen between two stools: the work was neither tragedy nor comedy. Instead of the comic norm of a social judgment against absurdity, there is moral judgment against the wicked. Instead of tragedy, or private action within the soul, we have melodrama, public action within the world. Melodrama, I think, is the appropriate word to describe *Cecilia* and the last two novels: "comedy without humor," as Northrop Frye remarks [in *Anatomy of Criticism*]. Melodrama is also a form in which there can be a "cost-accounting" of good and evil, a form, as Frank Rahill notes, that is particularly well-adapted to interpreting the feelings of disenfranchised, disinherited groups [*The World of Melodrama*]. Understanding this, one can hardly blame Fanny for adding a saving grace to Cecilia's loss of fortune: a maiden aunt of young Mortimer's "was so much charmed with her [Cecilia's] character, and so much dazzled by her admiration of the extraordinary sacrifice she had made, that, in a fit of sudden enthusiasm, she altered her will, to leave to her, and to her sole disposal, the fortune which, almost from his infancy, she had destined for her nephew." The secondary title might well have been "Identity Restored."

Unfortunately no young man, rich or poor, presented himself to Fanny Burney, and *Cecilia* brought only two hundred pounds—enough to buy a small annuity, but not sufficient for an independence. It was at this time she was offered a living, "a mess of pottage" according to Macaulay, as "Second Keeper of the Robes" to Queen Charlotte. With deep misgivings she accepted the position: "My dear father is in raptures; that is my comfort." For Fanny herself, the loss of freedom that went with the job was equivalent to marriage, and in this case an unhappy one: "I am *married*, my dearest Susan—I look upon it in that light—I was averse to forming the union, and I endeavoured to escape it; but my friends interfered—they prevailed—and the knot is tied. What then now remains but to make the best wife in my power? I am bound to it in duty, and I will strain every nerve to succeed."

In the journals she kept during this period of service (five years), the "strain" appears in the insistence on the same divisions of style and content that her novels had shown, but with an even more severe separation of roles than in either *Evelina* or *Cecilia*. Just as in the novels, she is unsparing of low, vulgar characters in her accounts of daily life at court, especially the crude and vindictive Mrs. Schwellenberg, her fated companion as the First Keeper of the Robes. Mrs. Schwellenberg's poor English and vulgar ideas are mocked with a sharp eye to the comic and absurd. On the other hand, the King, Queen, and Princesses always rise to the highest level of her novelistic creatures of perfection. The Queen is "the gracious Queen" or "the sweet Queen"; the King, "the good King"; and the Princesses, "the amiable Princesses." The Queen, who actually spoke English no better than Mrs. Schwellenberg, always speaks the most refined English, and if her opinions are paraphrased, Fanny gives them the turn of her own most affected, artificial high style, Fanny's response to the gruelling duties of her service and the daily humiliations of life with Mrs. Schwellenberg was to refuse to see too clearly, to write her life as if it were a novel, to preserve at least one part of it to an ideal order, and to bend truth, if necessary, to meet the urgency of her need.

Although she did not write another novel until after she was finally released from her service to the Queen, the novel to follow, *Camilla*, was outlined at court on small scraps of paper between bouts with Mrs. Schwellenberg and "gracious conferences" with the "sweet Queen." It too was to be a money novel:

A Family brought up in a plain oeconomical, industrious way, all happy, contented, vigorous, & affectionate.

Sudden affluence comes to them—

They are exhilarated

Some exult—some are even—some gallop on to profusion

A Sermon on equanimity

Some grow indolent & insolent

Suddenly all is lost.

Reduced to poverty.

Some humbly sad—some outrageously repining:—some haughtily hardy—some pettishly impatient—one cheerfully submissive

A sermon on disappointments.

What of shifts & cramping before seemed nothing, now appear hardships and sorrow.

The outline seems to offer little more than one of Hannah More's "Repository Tracts," but fleshed out by Madame d'Arblay in the turbulent 1790s, *Camilla* becomes a tale of fearful retreat from the world of real money. In *Evelina*, the love plot with its sentimental language and fantasy money had been reconciled with the low money of the vulgar folk through the conventions of comedy, by laughter and romance that affirmed Fanny's world of the 1770s. In *Cecilia*, Fanny had tried to compromise between the claims of real money and the money of romance by leaving her heroine in a state of tempered happiness. But in *Camilla*, the love plot, which includes one of the "best estates in the country," and the economic plot of real distress are almost completely divorced—in terms of her two styles and in the plot structure itself.

Camilla Tyrold, the daughter of a country clergyman, is warmhearted, virtuous, innocent, and sometimes imprudent in her natural liveliness. Her "imprudence" is the peg upon which the authoress tries to hang both the love plot and the economic plot. The hero, Edgar Mandlebert, for whom, of course, Camilla has a prepossession, and who has all the admirable, elegant, noble, and amiable virtues of the rest of Fanny's ideal people, falls in love with Camilla, cautions her against her imprudence (mainly being seen with a Mrs. Arlbery who is careless of the opinion of others), and finally promises to marry her. But there are occasions after they are engaged in which Camilla, innocently, is trapped in compromising situations. In *Evelina* this kind of flutteration would have been forgiven by the hero, and the heroine's virtue would have continued to shine forth unbesmirched. In *Camilla* there is no forgiveness for a lapse from manners; the firm, but broken-hearted Edgar finds that he must call off the engagement, and he goes to the Continent. In the money plot, Camilla through imprudence—and genuine ignorance of the ways of the world—runs up some fairly minor bills at Bath, where she is visiting with some of her fashionable friends. The debts are not, in fact, incurred by herself, but by an irresponsible intermediary. She finds that she must borrow the sum from a moneylender, Mr. Clykes, to avoid embarrassment. For committing this unforgivable imprudence, she is punished by having her father thrown in jail for her debts. Just as in *Cecilia*, after the heroine's loss of both money and love, there is nothing to do but run mad, which Camilla does, but in this novel more privately. The hero, back from the Continent, luckily stops in the same inn where Camilla is raving (quietly) upstairs, overhears her confessions of love for him and remorse for her financial irresponsibility, forgives her, and offers marriage again. Thus the heroine and her family are enabled to enter the realms of untold wealth and live happily ever after.

Madame d'Arblay, now married and responsible for the support of her estateless husband, the French *emigré* General Alexandre d'Arblay, and a son (born in 1794), had undoubtedly tightened the "cost-accounting" of *Camilla* in response to both personal and public pressures of the nineties. The new and fearful emphasis on the workings of money, I think, comes from her own anxieties as she faced the task of supporting her new family on her small pension from the Queen (one hundred pounds) and by the efforts of her own pen. Joyce Hemlow suggests that the heavy emphasis on manners in the novel may be Madame d'Arblay's desire to prove to the world that she had not completely lost her morals by marrying a Frenchman. Whatever the reason, the manners of *Evelina* have been erected in *Camilla* into a system against which there is no appeal: one false step and all is lost. The economics are even more terrifying: money is an irrational, uncontrollable force. The smallness of Camilla's offense is no hedge against utter destruction. Mr. Clykes, with justice behind him, legally forecloses the loan and imprisons her father. The only salvation for the heroine is in the good offices of her author. The hero and heroine retreat to their country estate, where they spend the rest of their days avoiding the world in the company of her "fond parents and her Enraptured Uncle." Another comedy without humor.

Her last novel, *The Wanderer; or Female Difficulties*, although published in 1814, was set in the 1790s in England. As a novel, the work is a failure, but as a document of one woman's reaction to the social and economic upheaval that had taken place in Europe during the French Revolution it is one of the most intriguing works of the period. Madame d'Arblay raises the conservative standards of manners and her own high style against the savage economic pressures of those years and finds both wanting. The implicit assumption of the early novels, that a woman's identity was to be one and the same with the ideal standards of her society is spelled out clearly in *The Wanderer*—and plaintively.

This last novel begins with the heroine having already suffered all the losses that the other heroines are only threatened with. She has lost all chance for love because she is already married to a brutal French revolutionary (a forced marriage to save the life of her guardian imprisoned in France); she is penniless because she has had to flee France without funds and because, for various complications including some lost papers, she cannot establish her identity as an English heiress; she is nameless because her real name cannot be revealed without endangering the life of her imprisoned guardian. She is in fact the ultimate abstract case for Madame d'Arblay of a woman who must establish her claim to respect and a place in society by the external signs of her virtues. Unfortunately, Madame d'Arblay's vision of the signs, of what constituted female worth, was limited to the manners of another century. The Fair Incognita, the Fair Unknown, The Wanderer, L. S., Ellis, Juliet, and finally Lady Juliet Granville can only establish herself as a woman of rank by fainting at the proper times, by her excellence at playing the harp, by her modulated tones, her regal bearing in distress, her orthography (which the hero cannot praise enough), her landscape drawings—and, of course, by her constant use of the "gibberish" of Fanny's most labored efforts at high style:

> Alas! deprived of all but personal resources, I fixed upon a mode of life [hemming pocket-handkerchiefs] that promised me, at least my mental freedom. I was not then aware how imaginary is the independence, that hangs for support upon the uncertain fruits of daily exertions! . . . but the difficulty of obtaining employment, irregularity of pay, the dread of want,—what is freedom but a name, for those who have not an hour at command from the subjection of fearful penury and distress?

The question is a real one: how to avoid want and penury, but Madame d'Arblay cannot find any way out of the situation for her heroine except by the good fortune of proving her birth and locating her a wealthy suitor. The plots of fantasy and reality are even further apart than in *Camilla*. The real difficulties of a female, at least those of the middle-class woman, are insolvable: "How few, . . . how circumscribed, are the attainments of women! and how much fewer and more circumscribed still, are those which may, in their consequences, be useful as well as ornamental, to the higher, or educated class! those through which, in the reverses of fortune, a FEMALE may reap benefit without debasement! those which, while preserving her from pecuniary distress, will not aggravate the hardships or sorrows of her changed condition, either by immediate humiliation, or by what, eventually, her connexions may consider as disgrace!"

The problem posed is that of every middle-class woman with a fixed or small income attempting to preserve her lady's standing against the encroachments of a troubled economy and rising inflation. Against the rising tides of economic and social chaos, the Fair Unknown erects a rampart of punctilio. "My conduct must be liable to no inference of any sort. Adieu, Sir," she tells the awestruck, admiring hero when he tries to offer her money. The new reading audience of 1814 simply could not understand why this was so important. "The Wanderer raises obstacles, 'lighter than the gossamer that idles in the wanton summer air,' into insurmountable barriers," wrote Hazlitt. "Her conduct never arises directly out of the circumstances in which she is placed, but out of some factitious and misplaced refinement on them. It is a perpetual game of cross purposes." The irony of this is that in the preface to *The Wanderer* Madame d'Arblay makes a special point of claiming to be "past the period of chusing to write or desiring to read, a merely romantic love-tale, or a story of improbable wonders." The expectations for the role of women had undergone a profound revolution in the 1790s, but one that Fanny Burney d'Arblay was only partially aware of, and one to which she was unable to adapt her art. But it was a gallant effort. She did face the fact that times had changed, and she made every effort to face it directly. Mrs. Radcliffe's Gothic novels may actually have found a better response to the chaos of the nineties by moving into the purer realms of fantasy in Italian castles and thinly got-up medievalism. The traps her heroines face are actually the same as those of Madame d'Arblay, but they do not call for the verifying testimony of contemporary society. Jane Austen got over the difficulty by confining society to provincial villages and by rigorously screening out distractions from the outside world—a sound sense of the limitations and strengths of the novel of manners. Where Miss Austen internalized "Female Difficulties" in her heroines, Fanny Burney and the rest of her generation of lady novel writers had turned to the externalizing conventions of melodrama, a notoriously time-bound convention.

For that reason alone, the female writers of the end of the eighteenth century are worth a reconsideration: they define a major shift in woman's consciousness. The middle-class woman had indeed begun to write—about herself. The old covenant with society was broken; the new one yet to be defined, and this, as Jane Austen, the Brontë sisters, and George Eliot found, in terms of the precarious relationship between love and money. But as Fanny Burney looked over the divide from the eighteenth into the nineteenth century, the future seemed bleak: the new woman, she wrote, "was a being who had been cast upon herself; a female Robinson Crusoe, as unaided and unprotected, though in the midst of the world, as that imaginary hero in his unhabited island; and reduced either to sink, through inanition, to nonentity, or to be rescued from famine and death by such resources as she could find, independently in herself" (*The Wanderer*).

Gothic Heroes in the Novels
of Walpole, Lewis, and Radcliffe

Howard Anderson

"The Mysteries of Udolpho . . . is in my opinion one of the most interesting Books that ever have been published. I would advise you to read it by all means, . . . and when you read it, tell me whether you think there is any resemblance between the character given of Montoni in the seventeenth chaper of the second volume, and my own. I confess, that it struck me, and as He is the Villain of the Tale, I did not feel much flattered by the likeness." The intensity of M. G. Lewis's response to Mrs. Radcliffe's novel is well known; still, we can assume he is more playful than serious in urging upon his mother the congruity of his own identity and Montoni's. The passage (written by the man soon to become Monk Lewis, the artist inseparable from his creation) amounts almost to a prescient parody of the readiness to merge all gothic novels into The Gothic Novel, to fuse every gothic hero in The Gothic Hero.

This impulse is the less surprising since many novelists in the last years of the eighteenth century drew at random on the characteristics of Manfred, Montoni, Ambrosio, and Schedoni to formulate their own recipes for the mass production of excitement. The lines of distinction get blurred not only between Montoni and Ambrosio, but between one gothic work and another. But while the male protagonists that Walpole and Radcliffe and Lewis create do of course have qualities in common, including at times an ability to induce excitement, their differences should receive as much attention as their similarities. The differences that seem to me most worth exploring determine the varying ways in which the men in these novels approach being protagonists of education novels: what sort of change, or development, or learning is possible for men in these books? This subject can make

From *The English Hero, 1660–1800*, edited by Robert Folkenflik. © 1982 by Associated University Presses, Inc.

most sense when it includes recognition of the fact that what constitutes "men" is divided, fragmented, split among different characters (usually a young man and mature one) in terms that seem at first mutually exclusive. And finally, what change we see—whether it amounts to permanent growth or mere inconsistency—will depend upon the writer's methods of presenting character.

When Ann Radcliffe looks at men in *The Mysteries of Udolpho*, she sees stability. Emily St. Aubert starts out rather too susceptible to indulgence in "the pride of fine feeling, the romantic error of amiable minds"; her experience at Udolpho and Chateau le Blanc provides for careful articulation of her progress to mental and emotional discipline. No such development is observable in either Valancourt or Montoni. Radcliffe's approach to both men is pictorial. We first encounter Valancourt as a figure in a mountain scene, and though an account of his imminent change and development seems promised, what finally is provided is summary, and in any case the change turns out to have been illusory. Montoni is a part of the rugged terrain and brooding castle from which he emerges. Both men remain essentially a part of a landscape in which only the sensibility of a young woman moves.

The intentions of Walpole and Lewis are quite different. Their men are characterized by neither the unchanging integrity of Emily's lover nor the monolithic malignity of her enemy. Montoni does indeed occasionally allow a moment's weakness to cross his visage, but for Walpole's Manfred and Lewis's Ambrosio (and for Raymond, as well) such inconsistency is a central fact of character. Equally important, these men are presented to us from the inside and are undergoing experience which—whether they learn anything from it or not—is meant to leave them decisively different by the time their stories end.

Such a vision of masculine possibility as embodied in Manfred was insufficient to challenge Ann Radcliffe, but Ambrosio stirred her to respond. When she turned to imagining Vivaldi and Schedoni in *The Italian*, it was with a willingness to incorporate into her pictorial vision an articulation of inner forces that she had earlier preferred (or been able?) only to suggest. To read these four novels in the context of one another is to find them marked by opposing conceptions of the nature and possibilities of men— conceptions that manifest themselves in essentially different modes of characterization.

I

Walpole's *The Castle of Otranto* is often referred to as a blueprint from which later gothic works derive their plans; its subtitle, "A Gothic Story," invites such a conclusion. The hero-villain, Manfred, in particular, along with the castle itself, play roles whose power is felt in many later novels. And no wonder: compared to any of his novelistic predecessors, Manfred is a dangerous hero whom we encounter as mysterious. Or better, as strange. For Manfred's behavior from the first is not so much brooding and inscrutable as it is erratic, irrational, unexpected. The opening of the novel places him in a domestic scene whose interruption by a supernatural surprise leads to responses on Manfred's part that no one—least of all his bewildered family—is prepared for. When his son is crushed by the giant helmet, the servants convey "the disfigured corpse into the hall, without receiving the least direction from Manfred. As little was he attentive to the ladies who remained in the chapel: on the contrary, without mentioning the unhappy princesses his wife and daughter, the first sounds that dropped from Manfred's lips were, Take care of the lady Isabella." Daunted, but determined to be (as usually expected) of service, his wife and daughter keep trying to comfort him, not comprehending that Conrad—formerly the apple of his eye—has been replaced by a new set of concerns.

Not entirely new: Walpole does assert that in fact Manfred's interest all along has been in the dynasty, rather than in its individual components. But the point still holds; Manfred continues to appear not so much passionately determined as frantically active. Having decided to marry Isabella and produce another heir to Otranto (even though it means all the awkwardness of a divorce), he lets her slip out of his hands and out of the castle. Next he is uncertain what to do about Theodore: he is furious at him for helping Isabella escape, but he can't help admiring his courage in admitting it. And for every reference to Manfred's cruelty and his steely courage, there is another to his shame at his conduct, his sliding back to soft feelings for his wife, and to his "heart capable of being touched."

These inconsistencies seem to be signs of Walpole's effort to make Manfred a complex figure, dangerous but not unadmirable. That objective is apparent in a passage early in the novel where he is described as being "not one of those savage tyrants who wanton in cruelty unprovoked. . . . his temper . . . was naturally humane; and his virtues were always ready to operate, when his passion did not obscure his reason." Manfred's characterization does become a little richer through the placement of this passage in a context where his virtues appear to be very close to those of the young Theodore, who is his more consistently noble rival and enemy throughout the story. But while linking Manfred and Theodore does result in ennobling the villain, it also tends to demystify his nature: "the circumstances of fortune had given an asperity to his temper, which was naturally humane."

As the plot thickens, Manfred becomes more erratic: "Ashamed of his inhuman treatment of a princess, who returned every injury with new marks of tenderness and duty, he felt returning love forcing itself into his eyes—but not less ashamed of feeling remorse towards one, against whom he was inwardly meditating a yet more bitter outrage, he curbed the yearnings of his heart, and did not dare to lean even towards pity. The next transition of his soul was to exquisite villainy." He is particularly unimposing when we find him asking for pity from Frederic and his knights. He weeps, and then—inventing a figure of rhetoric somewhere between a whine and a sacrilegious boast—tells them that in him they see "a man of many sorrows." He again edges toward the absurd after the banquet scene when we find him "flushed with wine and love."

Manfred's unsteady behavior does not finally invest him with complexity enough to tease us out of thought, as Walpole seems to have intended. Rather, for all Walpole's attempt at a terrifying exploration of the dark cavern of his hero's mind, what Manfred has of impressiveness abides in what Maurice Lévy call "l'énergie farouche et aveugle" [in *Le Roman "Gothique" Anglais 1764–1820*]. It is his energy that holds our attention and makes it impossible quite to condescend to him—not the turnings of his mind or the richness of what he learns from his experience. *The Castle of Otranto* conforms to what Misao Miyoshi defines [in *The Divided Self: A Perspective on the Literature of the Victorians*] as the gothic dualism: remorse following passion. But though that rhythm provides a link between this book and some very great education novels, what Manfred discovers about himself and what he makes of the discovery does not matter much. The *Castle of Otranto* points the way to a gothic hero fully psychologized and fully transformed by his experience, but it was not a way that Walpole was himself able to take.

II

Ann Radcliffe did not for a long time take that direction, either, though her reasons may have been more fully a matter of choice than were Walpole's. It is not surprising that she stayed in closer touch with the minds of women than of men; she looks out at the heroes and villains of her early novels from inside the consciousness of her heroine. To speak of *The Mysteries of Udolpho* as representative of her early practice, Montoni's terrifying power lies precisely in his impenetrability, and Valancourt's only interestingly ambiguous behavior is presented in a summary report that turns out to be false.

The stress on the "manliness" of their appearance as each is introduced implies what the presentations of the two very different men have in common. Valancourt is exemplary in his manners, habits, and sentiments, he reads the right books, and he has the right feelings about scenery: "a frank and generous nature, full of ardour, highly susceptible of whatever is grand and beautiful, but impetuous, wild, and somewhat romantic. Valancourt had known little of the world. His perceptions were clear, and his feelings just; his indignation of an unworthy, or his admiration of a generous action, were expressed in terms of equal vehemence. St. Aubert smiled at his warmth, but seldom checked it, and often repeated to himself, 'This young man has never been at Paris.' " The stultifying generalizations in the description make us pay attention to St. Aubert's particularizing comment, and indeed it is repeated often enough to build our interest and our hopes concerning what Valancourt will learn about himself (and what we will learn about him) when he finally does get from the provinces to the city.

But Valancourt is not destined to be Julien Sorel. Radcliffe plays with the theme that was to preoccupy the great novelists of the nineteenth century as she allows an acquaintance of Valancourt's to recount to Emily a sordid story of her lover's fall into betrayal and dishonor in Paris. But the account is merely a synopsis (and edited, at that, for the heroine's ears), briefly told, from the point of view of a remote observer. And in the end it turns out not to be true. Insofar as we see inside Valancourt at all, he remains simple—divided only by the most conventional and perfunctorily stated conflicts: he could not come to Udolpho to help Emily because of duty to his regiment. His stay at Paris has presumably taught him that La Vallée is a better place to live, but compared with Emily's painful progress toward that truth, his is unconvincing—or better, unrealized.

Montoni is more fully developed, but we have even less privileged access to his mind. If Valancourt really requires fuller inner treatment to make him an adequate counterpart to Emily (whose imagination, stimulated by Udolpho, will find him at best merely soothing), Montoni maintains himself sufficiently by what appears on his exterior: "A man about forty, of an uncommonly handsome person, with features manly and expressive, but whose countenance exhibited, upon the whole, more of the haughtiness of command, and the quickness of discernment than of any other character." This is how he is first described, and while the passage contains what can be called psychological description, it is characteristic of Radcliffe's representation of her central male figure in stressing the look that implies certain dominant inner qualities. She presents throughout what is essentially a portrait of Montoni. Another early passage defines Emily's response to him as the result of what she discerns in his appearance: "His visage was long, and rather narrow, yet he was called handsome; and it was, perhaps, the spirit and vigour of his soul, sparkling through his features, that triumphed for him. Emily felt admiration, but not the admiration that leads to esteem; for it was mixed with a degree of fear she knew not exactly wherefore."

That fear is rightly understood by most readers to be sexual, but it is important that it is sexual at a remove: nothing we see of Montoni suggests simple lust. His motive, in fact, is defined as greed, and he is sexually predatory toward Emily only to the extent that she is a pawn to be traded for property. This has the effect of making him the more sinister; being the only man at Udolpho (among the socially acceptable) who does not have more immediate designs on the heroine clearly places him out of the common run of humanity. The Byzantine convolutions of his sexuality give him depths that mere greed would not have. Beyond that, greed—or ambition, or any of the associated general terms with which Radcliffe begins to get at Montoni's motivation—is not enough to describe the depths so formidably suggested in the scenes where she captures his restlessness and his arrogance. The restlessness is perhaps best caught in the passage about his gambling that Lewis referred to in his letter to his mother. His vigorous arrogance is here: "Montoni displayed his conscious superiority, by that decisive look and manner, which always accompanied the vigour of his thought, and to which most of his companions submitted, as to a power, that they had no right to question." And these expressive attitudes elicit the response we share with Emily: "O could I know . . . what passes in that mind; could I know the thoughts, that are known there, I should no longer be condemned to this torturing suspense."

There are very few instances in which "what passes in that mind" is described, and even fewer that reveal ambiguous feelings; there is one, however—when Montoni feels pity for Emily and then shame for having felt it. But the depths implied by his peculiar heroic stance are sufficiently frightening—he does not have to be complicated as well. If he is in this monolithic sense a simple character, so also his experience is simple in that so far as we know he never changes, discovers nothing. Montoni's end is conveyed in a description even more disappointingly brief than the story of Valancourt's days in Paris: he is arrested, poisoned—it is all done in a few sentences. If, as Victor Brombert suggests [in *The Hero in Literature*], heroic experience measures freedom and morality, that measurement is registered entirely in its ostensible victim—Emily—who thereby becomes the beneficiary of her suffering. Montoni sees nothing at the end that he did not see at the beginning. Compared to Emily, both he and Valancourt are people to whom nothing ever happens—a form of self-victimization that Henry James takes up without entirely intending to in Gilbert Osmond, and which he treats directly in "The Beast in the Jungle" and "The Jolly Corner." Miyoshi's gothic dualism of passion and remorse is absent from this book. Valancourt sheds some tears when he fears he has acted unworthily, but they turn out to have been unnecessary. For Montoni—who had refused to feel pity, and who disputed about Hannibal while ignoring the sublime Alps—there are no tears.

III

Ambrosio and Raymond in *The Monk* are a pair quite different from the others. They are young—there is no such thing as *established* character in *The Monk*—and the experience of both is distinctly and specifically educational. For the first time we have men who indeed measure freedom and morality, and to a considerable extent, register what they have seen. When we discover at the end that there has been all along a blood relation between the two, the fact serves to suggest that their common problems extend roots into their common past.

Those common problems are sexual in their origins; Lewis's heroes suffer as fully and directly for their sexuality as did Radcliffe's heroines, though of course differently. And what they undergo comes with corresponding directness. The narrative of Ambrosio's story stays very close to his consciousness, tracing its turnings attentively; and Raymond's long account of his love affair is told in the first person. The effects are not pictorial as in Radcliffe, but psychological, and the psychological interest is furthered by unprecedented attention to the formative forces at work in Ambrosio's early life. No earlier novelist, not even Richardson, had traced the causes of his hero's perversity as Lewis does.

In fact, it may come as a surprise to find that in a novel usually considered richly realistic, Richardson had provided only the sketchiest outline of the origins of Lovelace's demonic feelings toward women. And if we are accustomed to thinking of gothic novels as "romances" and of gothic heroes as Northrop Frye's "stylized figures which expand into psychological archetypes" [*Anatomy of Criticism*], we will be even more surprised to find how much Lewis has to say about how Ambrosio came to be the kind of person he is. The destructively adulatory attention that Ambrosio gets from the fellow monks is often touched on early in the book, but it is when he has fallen for the first time into the ready arms of Matilda—and is about to embark on his self-consuming search for ultimate sexual satisfaction—that Lewis provides a detailed account of what the monastery has done to pervert Ambrosio's originally noble nature:

> Had his Youth been passed in the world, He would have shown himself possessed of many brilliant and manly qualities. He was naturally enterprizing, firm, and fearless: He had a Warrior's heart, and He might have shone with splendour at the head of an Army. There was no want of generosity in his nature. . . . His abilities were quick and shining, and his judgment vast, solid, and decisive. With such qualifications, He would have been an ornament to his Country: That He possessed them, He had given proofs in his earliest infancy, and his Parents had beheld his dawning virtues with the fondest delight and admiration. Unfortunately, while yet a child He was deprived of those Parents. . . . The Abbot, a very Monk, used all his endeavours to persuade the Boy, that happiness existed not without the walls of a Convent. He succeeded fully . . . his Instructors carefully repressed those virtues, whose grandeur and disinterestedness were ill-suited to the Cloister. Instead of universal benevolence, He adopted a selfish particularity for his own particular establishment: He was taught to consider compassion for the errors of others as a crime of the blackest dye: The noble frankness of his temper was exchanged for servile humility; and in order to break his natural spirit, the Monks terrified his young mind, by placing before him all the horrors with which Superstition could furnish them: They painted to him the torments of the Damned in colours the most dark, terrible, and fantastic,

and threatened him at the slightest fault with eternal perdi-
tion. . . . While the Monks were busied in rooting out his virtues,
and narrowing his sentiments, they allowed every vice which had
fallen to his share, to arrive at full perfection. He was suffered to
be proud, vain, ambitious, and disdainful: He was jealous of his
Equals, and despised all merit but his own: He was implacable
when offended, and cruel in his revenge.

Lewis may owe something to Godwin in this passage, but neither Walpole
nor Radcliffe had gone into detail about the social forces that could help
account for their villains. Neither goes further than to assume the enormous
influence of social ambition in the lives of men. Lewis particularizes what
society has done to Ambrosio, describing his education as a trap constructed
to separate him from all that was best in his potential; the confining monastery becomes the apt symbol of one side of himself erected to imprison
another aspect of his being.

Most important, Lewis reveals the extent to which Ambrosio has in-
corporated the values inculcated by his education. Alien as monastic standards are to what he was originally, Ambrosio has absorbed them so fully
that they are now a great part of him; he is in fact the head of the monastery,
its chief embodiment. It is precisely because Ambrosio cannot reject the
standards of the monastery that the ensuing explosion in his personality
occurs. In Manfred and Montoni, the individual will chains itself to the
past in the unquestioning service of social prestige and power. Lewis's
contribution is to put the service very much into question, but it is no less
enslaving for that. Ambrosio at thirty suddenly glimpses the ecstatic possibilities of individual fulfillment through sexual experience. But, unable to
imagine foregoing the status and respect attendant on his position in his
world, he cannot even want to break free. His terrible self-destruction is
not caused by revolt against the established order; indeed it may be said
to happen because he does not revolt enough. The sexual insatiability at
the center of his rapid downward spiral in the second half of the book
results from the inadequacy of sexual pleasure to assuage the guilt created
by tension between his lives of license and of order. This is only another
way of describing the tension between his attempts to live in a new world
and an old at once. We are told repeatedly that the Monk's need for the
respect of his community grows in proportion to his failure to deserve it,
and his sense of that failure leads him to the pursuit of stronger, more
intense, and violent anodynes. Artaud's perception that Ambrosio's essential engagement is in an attempt to break the physical and moral boundaries to "le mouvement naturel de l'amour" needs to be adjusted by the
recognition that he does not attempt to break, but rather to circumvent,
the perverse cultural boundaries upon which much of his identity continues
to depend.

There is no suggestion in the novel that Ambrosio's psychic dilemma could be solved by revolt or escape. The tedious, touching story that Elvira tells about her attempt with her husband (Ambrosio's father, though we may not yet know it) to avoid the wrath of his own aristocratic father suggests in fact the impossibility of simply replacing old worlds with new ones. Gonzalvo had married beneath him, against his father's will; when the two escape to Cuba, their love, strong as it is, proves insufficient to supply the place that the old land had occupied in Gonzalvo's life. The poem he wrote to express his unhappiness ("The Exile") is nearly unreadable, but it summarizes Lewis's message on the limitations of trying to find freedom by running away. The novel's long subplot centering on Raymond de las Cisternas reinforces the same theme in rich psychological detail.

Raymond's grand tour through France and Germany parallels Ambrosio's encounter with the social world; each constitutes in its own way the last step in the education of the young man. If the Grand Tour was classically intended to allow investigation of foreign courts, Raymond's is a good deal more a sentimental journey; like Ambrosio's his education as an adult really begins when he encounters a woman. It is important that she is an old woman—too old to interest him, anyway, though not too old to be herself interested. Before his story ends he discovers that he must deal not only with this unappealing lady, but with one who has been around much, much longer. In fact, Raymond's heroic task is precisely Ambrosio's: he must recognize that the most apparently free and individual human impulses have lines of liaison with other people and with the past; he has to reconcile his spontaneous acts with the world of which he is a part. Raymond finally survives this test as Ambrosio does not, but in the process he is driven to the edge of madness and of death.

When Raymond chivalrously saves the Baroness Lindenberg from murderous robbers, the lady falls in love with him, invites him to her castle in Bavaria, and despite the fact that she is married begins a vigorous courtship that he is too naive to comprehend. When he does wake up, he is in love with the baroness's young niece and assumes that a polite explanation of his feelings will suffice to extricate him from the older woman's unwanted embrace. He is wrong, of course: her feelings have been engaged and are by now under neither his control nor her own. She will not agree to let him marry Agnes, and to elude her the two optimistic young people decide to harness local superstition. Agnes will dress in the costume of the Bleeding Nun who is said to have haunted the castle for a hundred years, and when the terrified gate keeper opens to let the "ghost" out, she and Raymond will elope together in his waiting carriage.

The results are predictable: the real ghost joins Raymond in the carriage, gathering him in an embrace even harder to break than the baroness's. What follows is a tale of psychological possession—of his long and laborious effort to rid himself of her haunting presence, to reunite himself with Agnes, and later still to redeem Agnes from the ghastly vault in which she is buried alive. Its interest lies in the suggestiveness of its description of the reasons why autonomous and spontaneous expression of sexual passion is impossible in the world of *The Monk*. The Bleeding Nun, who gets a grip on Raymond when he tries to love where he pleases, turns out herself to have been a woman whose unbridled sexual passions led to murders, and finally to her own. This embodiment of carnal violence—the convent could not hold her long—had been, furthermore, a member of Raymond's own family; the same blood flows in their veins (and hence, not incidentally, in Ambrosio's). It is only by locating her unburied corpse and carrying it to burial in their family vault that Raymond can exorcise her haunting presence. Until he performs that symbolic act of reconciliation between her violent individualism and her family he languishes nervous, sleepless, unmanned.

Having done so, he locates Agnes, and though she has by now taken the veil at her family's insistence, he manages a fatal meeting with her in the convent garden that results in her pregnancy. What the Bleeding Nun has taught about the dangers of attempting sexual freedom is then repeated as another bitter old woman—this time the convent's mother superior—prevents the fulfillment of Raymond's love by consigning Agnes to a living death in a subterranean cell. Raymond's agitation when he cannot find her, followed by another long bout of histerical illness, leads him again near madness and death. At the very least, we can say that the two assertions of his sexuality lead to paralysis from which he is saved only by sheerly fortuitous turns of events. Miyoshi's gothic dualism of passion and remorse reaches its apogee in *The Monk:* both Ambrosio and Raymond exemplify fully this fluctuation of feeling. It is represented in each in such careful and prolonged detail as to constitute the rhythm of the book. Furthermore, the careful attention on the one hand to nuances of feeling, and on the other to the placement of these passions in a context of both environment and heredity, make Lewis's heroes the richest embodiments of a kind of heroism whose origin Maurice Lévy traces to the novels of Sophia Lee—a hero "sensible et malheureux, victime à la fois de ses passions et du Destin."

IV

The rhythm of Radcliffe's *The Italian* is very different: it ends with the wedding of Vivaldi and Ellena, where there is no expression of that regret for what has been lost that pervades the long-delayed weddings in *The Monk*. Furthermore, Schedoni counters Ambrosio's "dread" of death by taking his into his own hands: he poisons himself, and his last expression is a shriek of exultation. Yet to read *The Italian* is to know that *The Monk* was the most interesting book Ann Radcliffe read after she had finished writing *The Mysteries of Udolpho*. In Vivaldi and Schedoni she manages, without at all abandoning the striking visual presentation of her heroes, to combine with it greater psychological range and complexity. These two characters are larger than Radcliffe's other men because she imagines much more their inner experience, she allows that inner experience more contradiction and reversal (if not permanent change), and—particularly in their long mutual confrontation with the Inquisition—she endows the two men with characteristics that link them, hero and villain, in ways that are both admirable and human.

It is a new departure of real importance for Radcliffe to begin her narrative with an exploration of her hero; it is even more important that as the book continues we remain as often with Vivaldi or Schedoni as with Ellena. Vivaldi is described as partaking of the characteristics of his parents, and though he is nobly devoid of their more serious limitations, the ambiguities of his nature are sufficient to provide a real basis for his later problems in achieving that marriage which he considers his "most sacred right": "his pride was as noble and generous as that of the Marchese; but he had somewhat of the fiery passions of the Marchesa, without any of her craft, her duplicity, or vindictive thirst for revenge. Frank in his temper, ingenuous in his sentiments, quickly offended, but easily appeased; irritated by any appearance of disrespect, but melted by a concession, a high sense of honor rendered him no more jealous of offence, than a delicate humanity made him ready for reconciliation, and anxious to spare the feelings of others."

It is exactly Vivaldi's high sense of his own honor that makes him so determined to marry as he chooses, and it is his quickness to take offense that fixes the indomitable Schedoni as his most dangerous opponent in accomplishing that end. In setting himself in opposition to the idea that "you belong to your family, not your family to you," Vivaldi aligns himself with the assertive individuals that Lewis's heroes try to be, far more than with Radcliffe's passive Valancourt. And like Ambrosio and Raymond, he is sometimes inconsistent and self-indulgent. His romantic propensity to find pleasure in fanciful superstition makes him rather like an early Radcliffe heroine, and its effects are double-edged: his curiosity about the supernatural is an element of his sensitivity and openness to experience, but it contributes to his being locked up at Paluzzo while Ellena is being carried away to a mountain convent.

Vivaldi comes to life, then, as something more than a "manly figure" like Valancourt, lending human interest to a sublime mountain landscape. But though in the end he confronts the villain of the piece (as Valancourt never does) and contributes importantly to his destruction, Vivaldi is otherwise no match for Schedoni. The book contains two extended descriptions of the villain's character and his past. The first, while more detailed than anything comparable in *The Mysteries of Udolpho*, carries on brilliantly Radcliffe's visual artistry: the evocation of depths through description of surfaces is epitomized in Schedoni's face, which "bore the traces of many passions." The second passage provides the historical information that culminates in Schedoni's choosing to transform his identity from aristocrat to monk, summed up in his taking a new name. And there are innumerable other passages that provide on the one hand the suggestive hieroglyphs of Schedoni's character (the description of his cell is one sort of example) and on the other analysis of his inner feelings and motives.

But the novel's greatest accomplishment lies in the portrait—visual *and* psychological—of its evil genius, first as he awes the heroine by his mysterious appearance on the barren shores of the Adriatic, and then late at night, when he stalks the confines of her room, struggling to prepare himself to kill her. Caught between rocks and waves, we see Schedoni through Ellena's terrified eyes; she is both terrified and confused—and he appears apparently from nowhere, and then, when she appeals for help to the monk, she is confounded by his aloofness and hostility. It is a stunning nightmare scene that would be sufficient in itself to explain the attraction the gothic novel has had for the surrealists. In it, Schedoni lives fully as an ambiguous nature—the dangerous religious—observed.

The interior scene is quite different. We follow Schedoni to the small upper room where Ellena is asleep (the description is heavy with *Othello*), and we follow his mind as it discovers "an emotion new and surprising" that he tries vainly to suppress so that he can get on with the business at hand. "Had it been possible to shut out consciousness, he would have done so," but his consciousness grinds on, pushing him to discoveries and awarenesses altogether unlike anything Radcliffe had imagined for Montoni. Schedoni's misgivings, his strange forebodings, his unaccustomed paralysis, culminate in the discovery that he has in fact almost killed his own daughter. It does not, I think, finally matter that he is mistaken—she is only his niece—nor that after being so thoroughly shaken he shortly returns to his old ambitions, only now with the aim of ensuring Ellena's marriage to the wonderfully eligible Vivaldi, rather than preventing the match. It is less important that he is very soon again "willing to subject himself to any meanness however vicious, rather than forego the favorite ambition." The fact remains that he has been shaken: Schedoni is a greater novelistic achievement than Montoni because we have been there when something happened to him and have been convinced of it with him. In these scenes on the stormy Adriatic he is at once an austere force of nature and a vulnerable human being.

His appearance before the Inquisition manifests the same combination of superiority and victimization in the face of powers beyond even his own. None of these scenes rises to the dramatic or visual power of those by the shore, but Radcliffe's description of Schedoni being hounded and trapped while at the same time taking command of his own fate (and being certain to bring his betrayer down with him) is not radically anticlimatic. Most important, her attribution of some of the same characteristics to both Schedoni and Vivaldi as they face the relentless Inquisition has the effect of making each seem an instance of the same humanity: where Vivaldi displays "grandeur of mind," Schedoni remains "firm and even tranquil, and his air dignified." And certainly Ann Radcliffe is showing Monk Lewis how a man should die when she allows Schedoni even at the last to conquer "for a moment, corporeal suffering," and speak for himself in firm tones.

Surely it is better, then, not to let the fact that all of these writers divide their masculine worlds among roughly similar casts of characters lead us to ignore what individuates these characters. Walpole, Radcliffe, and Lewis have in common a view of the past as possessing and imprisoning good and bad "heroes" alike. "Are there really *ghosts?*" asks Francis Russell Hart in his valuable essay on gothic characterization, and he replies that the answer of the gothic as a genre is that "*We* are ghosts." The past lives on, paradoxically and terribly, in a whole range of men who try precisely to free themselves from it, to assume individual freedom. Yet, again, each character is related to that haunting past in his own way, and their common effort to transcend it should not prevent attention to Walpole's, Radcliffe's, and Lewis's ways of realizing the terrors that haunted English literature through a revolutionary generation, and which survive into our own.

Feminist Irony and the Priceless Heroine of *Mansfield Park*

Margaret Kirkham

"I do not quite know what to make of Miss Fanny. I do not understand her." So says Henry Crawford. What to make of Miss Fanny is the central moral puzzle Jane Austen presents to her anti-hero. He fails to discover the correct solution. It is also the central puzzle presented to the reader, testing the soundness of his moral attitudes and the quickness of his wits. It may be that the author misjudged what could be expected of her readers, for they have not, by and large, solved the riddle of Miss Price satisfactorily. Even Henry Austen took a bit of time over it. He had the advantage of familiarity with contemporary works to which allusion is made, as well as a knowledge of the author's point of view, and yet he found this puzzle a difficult one. No wonder, then, that later readers, lacking his privileged knowledge, have sometimes blundered.

In this essay, I shall try to show that Jane Austen teases us about Miss Fanny. Irony, far from being suspended in *Mansfield Park*, is turned upon the reader. We are given a heroine who, in some respects, looks like an exemplary conduct-book girl, but this is deceptive. Fanny is not a true conduct-book heroine and, insofar as she resembles this ideal—in her timidity, self-abasement, and excessive sensibility, for example—her author mocks her—and us, if we mistake these qualities for virtue. Jane Austen hated "unmixed" characters in general, and "unmixed" heroines in particular, a point on which she disagreed with the Dr. Johnson of *Rambler 4*. Writing to her niece Fanny Knight (the one with a weakness for Evangelical gentlemen), she discusses the opinions of an aptly named Mr. Wildman, who had not found her novels to his taste:

From *Jane Austen: New Perspectives*. (Women and Literature, n.s., vol. 3), edited by Janet Todd. © 1983 by Holmes & Meier Publishers, Inc.

Do not oblige him to read any more.—Have mercy on him. . . .
He and I should not in the least agree of course in our ideas about
Heroines; pictures of perfection as you know make me sick and
wicked—but there is some very good sense in what he says, and
I particularly respect him for wishing to think well of all young
Ladies; it shows an amiable and delicate Mind—And he deserves
better than to be obliged to read any more of my Works.

If Jane Austen created a conduct-book heroine, it cannot have been
without an ironic intention of some kind. A clue to what it was occurs in
an unsigned article on the "Female Novelists" published in *New Monthly
Review* in 1852: "Then again, in *Mansfield Park,* what a bewitching 'little
body' is Fanny Price." This Victorian writer sees in Fanny, not a paragon
of virtue, but a little enchantress, and it is important to notice that, when
Crawford falls in love, he too sees her in this way. Fanny's apparent saintliness is closely connected with her sexual desirableness, as Crawford shows
in chapter 12 of the second volume, where he tells his sister that he is in
love. His appreciation of "Fanny's graces of manner and goodness of
heart," as well as his recognition of her "being well-principled and religious," is mingled with his dwelling on her "charms," "her beauty of face
and figure," her beautifully heightened color, as she attends to the service
of that stupid woman, her Aunt Bertram, and the neat arrangement of her
hair, with "one little curl falling forward . . . which she now and then
shook back."

Crawford is incapable of understanding that the "religious principles"
he admires in Fanny are formed, as Providence intended rational beings
to form moral principles, out of rational reflection upon experience. His
view of her is deeply sentimental, for he sees her as something like the
ideal woman of Rousseau's *Émile,* innocent, virtuous, tractable, and crying
out for protective love, which her prettiness and gentleness excite in him.
By volume 3, he discovers that she has "some touches of the angel" in her.
Henry Austen must have seen at that point, if he had not seen it before,
that his sister would not allow her heroine to marry Crawford, for Austen's
objection to the comparison of young women to angels is so consistently
maintained that this blunder of Crawford's could not pass unnoticed. Elizabeth Bennet once says, jokingly and critically, that her sister Jane has
angelic characteristics (*Pride and Prejudice*); otherwise, from the *Juvenilia* to
the mature works, only fools or villains make this analogy. It is pointedly
avoided by all the Austen heroes, but used to define the defects of the
more complex anti-heroes, notably Willoughby and Crawford, and to define
Emma's disillusion with Frank Churchill (*Emma*).

The point is of great importance to a right understanding of Fanny
Price and *Mansfield Park,* because it directs us to the criticism of the conduct-
book ethos which is the essential irony of Miss Price's characterization. It
may seem strange to us that physical weakness, or lassitude, should be

thought to enhance a girl's sexual attractiveness, nor do we think religiosity alluring, but it was not always so. The conduct-book ideal of young womanhood was deeply sentimental, and the genre included works in which salaciousness was mixed with moral advice.

Two examples, quoted and proscribed by Mary Wollstonecraft in *A Vindication of the Rights of Woman*, are of especial interest. Wollstonecraft berates James Hervey, whose *Meditations and Contemplations*, written between 1745 and 1746, were "still read" in 1792. Hervey told his readers (mostly female) that:

> Never, perhaps, does a fine woman strike more deeply, than when, composed into pious recollection, and possessed with the noblest considerations, she assumes, without knowing it, superior dignity and new graces; so that the beauties of holiness seem to radiate about her, and the bystanders are almost induced to fancy her already worshipping among the kindred angels.

Mary Wollstonecraft could not stand that sort of thing. "Should," she asks, "a grave preacher interlard his discourses with such folleries? . . . Why are girls to be told that they resemble angels: but to sink them below women." Like Jane Austen, she has no patience either with Dr. Fordyce, whose *Sermons to Young Women* (1766) contain a remarkable passage in which the awfulness of abusing young angels is discussed with salacious relish:

> Behold these smiling innocents, whom I have graced with my fairest gifts, and committed to your protection; behold them with love and respect; treat them with tenderness and honour. They are timid and want to be defended. They are frail; oh do not take advantage of their weakness! Let their fears and blushes endear them. Let their confidence in you never be abused. But is it possible, that any of you can be such barbarians, so supremely wicked, as to abuse it? Can you find in your hearts to despoil the gentle, trusting creatures of their treasure, or do anything to strip them of their native robe of virtue? Curst be the impious hand that would dare to violate the unblemished form of chastity! Thou wretch! thou ruffian! forbear; nor venture to provoke Heaven's fiercest vengeance.

Mary Wollstonecraft says, not unreasonably:

> I know not any comment that can be made seriously on this curious passage, and I could produce many similar ones; and some, so very sentimental, that I have heard rational men used the word indecent when they mentioned them with disgust.

It will be remembered that it was Fordyce's *Sermons* that Mr. Collins chose, after having turned down a novel, to read aloud to the ladies at Longbourn. Perhaps it was at just such a passage that Lydia Bennet, no angel, but "a stout well-grown girl of fifteen," interrupted his "monotonous solemnity" to tell her mother an interesting bit of gossip about the regiment quartered nearby. At all events, Mr. Collins's approbation of Fordyce is a clear indication that Jane Austen disapproved of him.

There is good reason to think, in the light of her novels and letters, that this was a disapproval founded in sympathy with rational, post-Enlightenment feminism. This is not to suggest that Austen was in agreement with Wollstonecraft on anything more than these fundamental ideas: (a) that women, being possessed of the same "powers of mind" as men, have the same moral status and the same moral accountability; (b) that girls should be educated in a manner appropriate to this view of the female sex; (c) that a "respectable" marriage is an "equal" marriage, in which man and woman are "partners," and must therefore rest on "friendship and esteem," and (d) that literary works in which any other view is endorsed are objectionable. Modern feminists may find these very tame, but around 1800 they were the essential convictions of rational feminism. We need not be put off because Austen is "a moralist" after the Johnsonian fashion; so, in many respects, is Wollstonecraft, especially in the *Vindication*, itself a sort of conduct book. The moral argument upon which Wollstonecraft bases her feminist case derives very largely from Bishop Butler's *Analogy of Religion* (1796) and from Richard Price's *Review of the Central Question in Morals* (1758). Butler was a bishop of the established church, whose views accord to a large extent with Johnson's. Price was a Dissenter and, through his influence upon progressive Dissent, associated not only with Wollstonecraft herself but with many of the radicals of his time. His ambience was thus quite different from Butler's, but the essential character of his view of morals was not, as he himself acknowledges.

So far as late-eighteenth-century feminism went, Butler and Price could both be seen as laying down principles upon which a feminist moralist could found her argument. This is crucial to a right understanding of the relationship between the first well-known English feminist theorist, Mary Wollstonecraft, and the first major woman novelist in English. Thinking of them, as we do, as totally different in their religious and political affiliations, life-style, and temperament, we may easily miss what connects them as feminist moralists, whose roots lie in a common tradition of ethical discussion. There is no need to assume that Austen was an undercover Jacobin because she is so close to Wollstonecraft as a feminist moralist.

Austen's implicit demand that men and women be judged, and judge themselves, by the same, somewhat strict, standard in sexual matters, should not be seen as a sign of her commitment to anti-Jacobin fervor. It is no more than the mark of her convinced feminism. Among the radicals, as both Gary Kelly and Marilyn Butler show, feminist feeling went hand in hand with emphasis upon the need for reason and restraint in sexual matters. Butler is impatient with them about it: "In sexual matters, the Jacobins thought and behaved (whatever their opponents claimed) like forerunners of the Evangelicals." Believing in the power of reason to liberate mankind, they renounced the example of "Rousseau, Goethe and Kotzebue . . . when they refused to exploit sexual passion as a powerful natural ally against a moribund society and its repressive conventions." Butler contrasts the English Jacobins unfavorably in this respect with their Continental counterparts, including Madame de Staël.

A feminist point of view is not only compatible with the argumentative style of an eighteenth-century moralist, but may be positively connected with it. Were *Mansfield Park* primarily about political and social questions *other* than feminist ones, the conservative character of the moral argument which it embodies would justify us in supposing it to be fundamentally conservative in outlook, but, if the feminist issues are the central ones, it may be that the orthodox, rather old-fashioned character of the argument indicates feminist radicalism rather than orthodoxy. An example may be useful here. In attacking the education commonly provided for middle-class girls, Mary Wollstonecraft says:

> Though moralists have agreed that the tenor of life seems to prove that *man* is prepared by various circumstances for a future state, they consistently concur in advising *woman* to provide only for the present.

She refers to the belief, best exemplified in Bishop Butler's *Analogy of Religion*, and popularized in many sermons and moralistic works, that the world is so ordered as to teach us moral principle through secular experience. Even without a belief in God, the order of nature, including human nature, of which rational powers are a part, insures that we are rewarded when we act well and punished when we act badly. It was an orthodox belief of established moralists that this was so, but, in applying it to women, Mary Wollstonecraft is able to use it to attack existing practices in education and social custom, which rule out one half of mankind from the benefits of exercise in the moral gymnasium designed to teach moral principles.

In the Austen novels the heroines learn about morals through the application of rational reflection to experience. This is how they are shown to acquire principle. They never learn it from clerical advisers. The process by which they acquire understanding of duty, and of right courses of action, is entirely secular, as [Gilbert] Ryle noted. The way in which they are shown as becoming morally accountable may look a little old-fashioned, if we forget that they are young women, not young men. If we remember it, and see it in relation to contemporary feminist discussion, we may see that Jane Austen is sometimes a radical wolf when she pointedly adopts orthodox moralists' sheep's clothing.

It is time to return to Miss Fanny, and to show further that her characterization is to be illuminated by Mary Wollstonecraft. The implication of this must be that either Austen had read Wollstonecraft or that she was familiar with her works through the filtering through of their arguments and examples to other, less controversial writers. I do not mean to argue the case for direct influence here. During the five years she spent in Bath, with its well-stocked bookshops and circulating libraries, by no means confined to fiction, Austen had access to the works of Mary Wollstonecraft. In the absence of direct biographical information, the case must stand upon the probability implied by closeness of point of view and, in some instances, of allusion and vocabulary.

Vindication is not primarily about the political and constitutional rights of women, but about the ideas referred to above as constituting the essence of post-Enlightenment rational feminism. It is largely an attack upon Rousseau, especially the Rousseau of *Émile,* and upon those sentimental moralists and divines who had followed him in denying women the moral status of rational, adult, moral agents. With them are coupled imaginative writers of both sexes, including Madame de Staël, who, by emphasizing the sensibility of women at the expense of their powers of reason, have "Rendered them Objects of Pity, Bordering on Contempt." Wollstonecraft's animus against Rousseau arises from his having made Sophie—his ideal mate for Émile, the ideal man—a different kind of moral creature. Whereas Émile is to enjoy bodily and mental exercise, Sophie is to be confined to bodily weakness and to obedience. This, Rousseau thought, was in accordance with the nature of the two sexes and with their purposes in life. It was for the man to enjoy the advantages of a free, experiential life; it was for the woman to please him, to arouse his sexual passion, to enjoy his protection, and to obey him. All this was anathema to Wollstonecraft and, to Austen, a fit subject of ridicule.

Take first the question of health and strength, which is of particular importance to the characterization of Miss Fanny. Wollstonecraft objects to Rousseau's belief that genuine weakness and the affected exaggeration of weakness are natural to women and a means by which they gain an ambiguous power over men. She quotes with disgust a passage from *Émile* in which it is asserted of women:

> So far from being ashamed of their weakness, they glory in it; their tender muscles make no resistance; they affect to be incapable of lifting the smallest burdens, and would blush to be thought robust and strong.

Wollstonecraft declares that

> the first care of mothers and fathers who really attend to the education of females should be, if not to strengthen the body, at least not to destroy the constitution by mistaken notions of female excellence; nor should girls ever be allowed to imbibe the pernicious notion that a defect can, by any chemical process of reasoning, become an excellence.

She then attacks such conduct-book authors as have taken their cue from Rousseau and encouraged girls to cultivate either real or affected weakness and low spirits. Among these she reluctantly places Dr. John Gregory, whose *A Father's Letters to His Daughters* (1774)

> actually recommends dissimulation and advises an innocent girl to give the lie to her feelings, and not dance with spirit, when gaiety of heart would make her feel eloquent without making her gestures immodest. In the name of truth and common sense, why should not one woman acknowledge that she has a better constitution than another?

Austen did not admire physical weakness or ill-health or ignorance in young women, but a lot of people, including those who ought to have known better, did. The relevance of this to Miss Price is obvious. Austen created in her a heroine whom the unwary might take for something like the Rousseauist ideal of the perfect woman, but she expects her more discerning readers to see through it, and gives them a good many indications that this is not a proper reading. The most important of these is, of course, the category mistake of the anti-hero, but there is a good deal else. The true hero is never shown as encouraging Fanny in her partly self-imposed fragility and timidity, although he is kind to her when he observes her genuine tendency to tire easily. He gets her a horse, encourages her to ride regularly, and tells her to speak up for herself, even to her uncle. But the major comic emphasis, through which Austen shows that she does not admire hypochondria in women, even beautiful ones, comes through the splendid portrait of pampered indolence in Lady Bertram.

Fanny is quite different from her aunt in that she has, both as a child and as a very vulnerable adolescent, experienced both neglect and hardship. Given Mrs. Price's predilection for sons and her slatternly housekeeping, there is little reason to think that the health (whether of body or mind) of her eldest daughter had ever received much attention. At Mansfield, the somnolence of Aunt Bertram, the sadism of Aunt Norris, and the false regard for wealth and status of Sir Thomas Bertram, his elder son, and his daughters, have all combined to ensure that Fanny's mental and physical health are put in jeopardy. She has not a strong constitution, but she was not as a child devoid of normal impulses to active life. She did not enjoy such freedom as Catherine Morland, rolling down green slopes with her brothers, and it is never positively established that she preferred cricket to dolls or nursing dormice, as Catherine did, but Fanny, in her early years at Portsmouth, was important as "*play-fellow*," as well as "instructress and nurse" to her brothers and sisters. The single instance of remembered childhood activity which Austen mentions concerns dancing. William recalls how he and Fanny used to dance together as children. It is what prompts him to ask Sir Thomas if his sister is a good dancer, Sir Thomas being forced to reply that he does not know. William says, "I should like to be your partner once more. We used to jump about together many a time, did not we? when the hand organ was in the street?" Fanny's excessive fragility of body and lack of self-confidence are the result of inconsiderate, and sometimes humiliating, treatment by her illiberal, selfish aunts, but it has not quite stamped out of her an impulse to life which is to be seen in her continued love of dancing. At her first ball, "she was quite grieved to be losing even a quarter of an hour . . . sitting most unwillingly among the chaperons . . . while all the other young people were dancing." Later, when a ball is given in her honor, the narrator tells us, "She had hardly ever been in a state so nearly approaching high spirits in her life. Her cousins' former gaiety on the day of a ball was no longer surprising to her; she felt it to be indeed very charming." And she actually practices her steps in the drawing room, when she is sure Aunt Norris won't see. She gets tired later at this ball, partly because she is jealous of Miss Crawford, but it is three o'clock in the morning, and she is up earlier than anyone else, apart from William, next day, in order to see him off.

Fanny Price's feebleness is not a mark of Clarissa Harlowe-like saintliness, as Lionel Trilling thought, nor is it to be dismissed, as Marilyn Butler dismisses it, as "quite incidental." It is essential to the play of anti-Rousseauist, feminist irony upon Miss Price and those who seek to interpret her. Once her cousins leave Mansfield, prolonged ill-treatment is seen to have curious effects. The affectation of fragility, which it took an expensive education to achieve, Fanny lacks, but a genuine fragility now makes her seem something like the Rousseauist ideal, and by this Crawford is, as he puts it, "fairly caught." But, if Fanny's physical frailty amounts to more than it seems, the strength of her mind, despite the physical and emotional deprivation she has endured, is truly formidable. Housed within the "bewitching little body," lurking behind the "soft light eyes," is a clear, critical, rationally judging mind, quite unlike the tractable, childlike mind of the true conduct-book heroine. Wollstonecraft says, "The conduct of an accountable being must be regulated by the operation of its own reason; or on what foundation rests the throne of God?" (*Vindication*). Just before Fanny offends her uncle by insisting upon her right to regulate her conduct, by the operation of her own judgment, in a matter of great moment, he is made to say, though without understanding what it implies, "You have an understanding, which will prevent you from receiving things only in part, and judging partially by the event.—You will take in the whole of the past, you will consider times, persons, and probabilities." He is talking about Aunt Norris's past behavior, but he describes exactly what Fanny does in forming her opinion of Crawford.

The moral and comic climax of *Mansfield Park* occurs at the start of volume 3, in the East room, when Fanny confronts her august uncle and defies him. Sir Thomas, once he is able to make out that she intends to refuse Crawford, thunders away at her about ingratitude, selfishness, perversity, and sheer obtuseness as to her own interest. He is forced to wonder if she does not show "that independence of spirit, which prevails so much in modern days, even in young women, and which in young women is offensive and disgusting beyond all common offence." Austen expects us to laugh at him, but she does not spare her heroine either. Returning from her walk in the shrubbery, Fanny finds that a fire has already been lighted, on Sir Thomas's orders, in the bleak East room. She does not say, as a creature wholly regulated by reason might have done, "Well, wrongly though he has judged and acted, he has kind and benevolent aspects." She says—and it is truer to life, as well as to the comic spirit—"in soliloquy," " 'I must be a brute indeed, if I can be really ungrateful. . . . Heaven defend me from being ungrateful.' "

Jane Austen laughs at Fanny when she herself acquiesces, as she often does, in the submissive role in which an unjust domestic "order" has cast her. She exposes, with a more bitter ridicule, the foolishness which has all but stamped out of Fanny her ability to laugh, dance, play, or to act—in any sense. But she does not despair. Reason, and the will of a less insane God than that invoked by such clerics as Fordyce and Mr. Collins or Dr. Grant, will prevail, where men have such sense as Edmund and women such sense as Fanny. "Good sense, like hers, will always act when really called upon," and so it does. Fanny becomes "the daughter that Sir Thomas Bertram wanted," that is, *lacked*, and, together with Edmund, is shown as capable of establishing at the parsonage a more liberal and more securely based domestic order than that of the Great House.

Fanny does not, as some critics, more concerned with mythic elements of plot than sound moral argument, have thought, "inherit" Mansfield Park. She marries the younger son, not the heir (who is pointedly restored to health), and she goes to live at the parsonage, where an enlightened, rational, secular Christianity is likely to be the order of the day. It is, perhaps, unlikely that the next Lady Bertram will waste so many years in a state of semiconsciousness, devoid of mental or physical life, upon a sofa, with a lapdog and a tangled, useless, meaningless bit of needlework, as the former Miss Maria Ward has done. But it is at the parsonage, not the Great House, that there is to occur that "unspeakable gain in private happiness to the liberated half of the species; the difference to them between a life of subjection to the will of others, and a life of rational freedom," of which J. S. Mill was later to write.

In *Mansfield Park*, Austen shows some sympathy with points made in the *Vindication* and anticipates Mill *On the Subjection of Women*. It looks to me as though she may also have profited from a critical reading of Wollstonecraft's two novels. There is no direct evidence that she read them, but Godwin's publication of his *Memoirs of the Author of a Vindication of the Rights of Woman* in 1798 caused a great deal of interest in its subject. The "Advertisement" to *Mary* (1788) tells us that its heroine is "neither a Clarissa, a Lady G. [randison] nor a Sophie." In it, "the mind of a woman who has thinking powers" is to be displayed. Mary, its heroine, had "read Butler's *Analogy*, and some other authors: and these researches made her a Christian from conviction." Austen would not have countenanced the pretentious tone of this, but, in her own ironic way, she shows us that much the same could be said of Fanny. By the time *Maria* was written—it was still unfinished in 1797, when Wollstonecraft died—the author had become a Deist, rather than a Christian, but this does not prevent her from applying Butler's argument about how we learn moral principles in her new work. She says that in most novels "the hero is allowed to be mortal, and to become wise and virtuous as well as happy, by a train of events and circumstances. The heroines, on the contrary, are to be born immaculate."

Both in Wollstonecraft and Austen, the language of law and property as well as the language of capture and captivation are shown as improperly applied to marriage and to decent sexual relationships. *Mansfield Park* opens with the *captivation* by Miss *Ward* of *Hunting*don, of a baronet to whom her uncle, *"the lawyer, himself,* . . . allowed her to be at least three thousand pounds short of any *equitable claim"* (my italics). Wollstonecraft's Maria talks about "the master key of property." Austen, in the Sotherton episode, makes use of the lock and key image in connection with Rushworth and his property. Wollstonecraft's Maria says, "Marriage had bastilled me for life." Maria Bertram, flirting with Crawford while her intended husband has gone off to look for the key to the iron gate, which gives her "a feeling of restraint and hardship," alludes to the starling which Yorick found caged in the Bastille, and which sang incessantly, "I can't get out, I can't get out." She also refers to Sotherton as a prison, "quite a dismal old prison." Wollstonecraft's anti-hero declares "that every woman has her price." Austen borrows, as the name for her heroine, that of Crabbe's in one of *The Parish Register* tales. Crabbe's Fanny Price is a refuser of the captive-captivate game; Austen's is shown as unfit, by her nature, to become a commodity in the marriage market, though capable of paying the price of enduring wrongful abuse and misunderstanding, which secures her "right to choose, like the rest of us."

Jane Austen does not, like Mary Wollstonecraft, present us with an innocent heroine imprisoned in a marriage for which she is not regarded as bearing a responsibility. Austen's Maria chooses her own fate, though neither Sir Thomas nor the moral standards of the society of which he is a pillar are held blameless. Fanny, who avoids an imprisoning marriage, since she enters a partnership based on affection and esteem, does so not because she is "innocent," but because she is what Milton called [in *Areopagitica*] "a true wayfaring Christian." Hers is not "a fugitive and cloistered virtue, unexercised and unbreathed," but one that has been put to "trial . . . by what is contrary."

Once the irony at work in the characterization of Miss Price is recognized, the way is open to consideration of what is shown as truly valuable in the right ordering of domestic society and in the world beyond it. Jane Austen did not believe that individuals had to create their own morality; she believed that moral law was objectively enshrined in the nature of the world itself. To that extent, she supposes that human beings are required to be obedient to moral laws or principles, but she is perfectly clear that the individual human being has the right, and duty, of determining, by the operation of his or her own reason, what these principles are and how they are to be applied in the personal regulation of conduct. By showing that Sir Thomas's niece and his younger son are better to be relied upon in judging correctly, an implicit criticism of "birthright and habit," which debar women and younger sons from influence, even when their superior abilities are known, is made. It is quite in line with Wollstonecraft's attitude to "the Pernicious Effects which Arise from the Unnatural Distinctions Established in Society" (part of the title of chapter 9 of *Vindication*). When Mary Crawford says that Edmund ought to have gone into Parliament, he replies, "I believe I must wait till there is an especial assembly for the representation of younger sons who have little to live on." Sir Thomas is a Member of Parliament, as, presumably, his elder son will also be. It is suggested that Mr. Rushworth will also enter the House when Sir Thomas is able to find him a borough. A rotten borough is not specified but would undoubtedly be appropriate. The case for the recognition of the *equality* of women with men is implicitly allied with the case against such unnatural distinctions and inequalities as are inherent in the law of primogeniture and in the unrepresentative character of Parliament.

Mansfield Park is also pointedly concerned with *fraternity*. What ought to be, and sometimes is—as in the relationship between Fanny and her brother William—the paradigm of equal, affectionate relationships between men and women is always held up as an ideal, having implications beyond the literal meaning of "brother" and "sister." Edmund Bertram treats his inferior little cousin as a sister early in volume 1. He does not fall in love with her until the final chapter, in which this is treated cursorily and ironically. This is not because Jane Austen had suddenly and unselfconsciously become interested in incest; it is because the marriage which provides the necessary happy ending of a comic work carries implications about the right relationships between men and women, both in marriage as a social institution and in society at large. As Mill was to say some fifty or more years later:

> The moral regeneration of mankind will only really commence,
> when the most fundamental of the social relations is placed under
> the rule of equal justice, and when human beings learn to cultivate
> their strongest sympathy with an equal in rights and cultivation.

Austen, in *Mansfield Park*, shows that such an ideal is more readily to be found, in contemporary society, between brothers and sisters than husbands and wives, though she seeks a transference to the marriage relationship of the ideal. With William, Fanny experiences a "felicity" which she has never known before, in an "unchecked, equal, fearless intercourse."

It is, however, with liberty, and the moral basis upon which individual liberty must be founded, that *Mansfield Park* is clearest and boldest. Women, in the Midland counties of England, like servants, were not slaves. Even a *wife*, not beloved, had some protection, "in the laws of the land, and the manners of the age." So Catherine Morland had learnt, under the tutelage of Henry Tilney. "Murder was not tolerated . . . and neither poison nor sleeping potions to be procured like rhubarb, from every druggist" (*Northanger Abbey*). But what of an indulged wife? And a falsely respected one? In the Midland counties of England, murder might not be necessary where a wife could retain all the advantages of outward respect, rank, precedence, and "respectability," while passing her days in a state of partly self-induced semiconsciousness. Lady Bertram had "been a beauty, and a prosperous beauty, all her life; and beauty and wealth were all that excited her respect." She values herself on her possession of these things and, in the corrupt social order of which she is part, is valued for them. Never shown as going outside, or breathing fresh English air, Lady Bertram represents the slavery to which women who accede to such ideas reduce themselves, with the unwitting connivance of those, like Sir Thomas, who see nothing disgraceful in their condition. Not literally a slave and not suffering from the effects of a literal sleeping potion, what is she as a human being? What is she morally, as a rational, accountable one?

It is well known that in America the movement for women's rights was accelerated by the part women played in the movement for the emancipation of the slaves. As they heard, and put, moral arguments against slavery, they made an analogy between the moral status of a slave and of a woman, especially a married woman. This analogy is made in the *Vindication* and implied in *Mansfield Park*. Wollstonecraft says that a "truly benevolent legislator always endeavours to make it the interest of each individual to be virtuous; and thus private virtue becoming the cement of public happiness, an orderly whole is consolidated by the tendency of all the parts towards a common centre." Women, however, are not taught to be virtuous in their domestic life and so are not to be trusted in either private or public life. They learn to be subject to propriety, "blind propriety," rather than to regulate their actions in accordance with moral law as "an heir of immortality" ought. She asks, "Is one half of the human species, like the poor African slaves, to be subjected to prejudices that brutalise them, when principles would be a surer guard of virtue?"

In England, agitation against the slave trade had gone on all through the last quarter of the eighteenth century. The arguments against it were rehearsed widely in the early nineteenth century, leading up to the passing of the Act of Abolition, which became effective in 1808. Jane Austen must have been familiar with them and, in a letter of 1813, speaks of having been in love with Thomas Clarkson's writings. In 1808, Clarkson published *The Abolition of the African Slave Trade*:

> We have lived in consequence of it to see the day when it has been recorded as a principle of our legislation that commerce itself shall have its moral boundaries. We have lived to see the day

when we are likely to be delivered from the contagion of the most barbarous opinions. Those who supported this wicked traffic virtually denied that man was a moral being. They substituted the law of force for the law of reason. But the great Act, now under our consideration, had banished the impious doctrine and restored the rational creature to his moral rights.

It is easy to see here that a woman who rejoiced that the slave trade had been ended might ask whether it had yet been recorded "as a principle of our legislation that commerce itself shall have its moral boundaries"—so far as women were concerned. Was it universally accepted that woman was "a moral being"? Had the rational creature been restored to *her* moral rights?

Clarkson goes over the history of the anti-slavery movement and refers to a particularly famous legal judgment, which established that slavery was illegal in England. This was the Mansfield Judgment, given by the Lord Chief Justice of England in 1772, in a case concerning a black slave, James Somerset, the question being whether, having been brought to England, he could still be held to be "owned" by his master. Arguing that he could not, counsel for the defence, referring to an earlier judgment given in the reign of Queen Elizabeth, said:

> It was resolved that England was too pure an air for slaves to breathe in . . . and I hope my lord the air does not blow worse since—I hope they will never breathe here; for this is my assertion, the moment they put their feet on English ground, that moment they are free.

Lord Mansfield found in favor of Somerset and, by implication, of this view of English air.

In *Mansfield Park* the English patriarch is also the owner of Antiguan plantations and of the slaves who work them. When he returns to England, his niece puts a question to him about the slave trade. We are not told what the question was, nor what answer was given, but, through her title, the making of Sir Thomas a slaveowner abroad, and the unstated question of Miss Fanny, *her* moral status in England is implicitly contrasted, yet also compared, with that of the Antiguan slaves. Since it is often assumed that Jane Austen could not have thought much about anything which did not impinge upon her domestic life and familial relations, or else been said by Dr. Johnson, it may be worth noting that at the house of her brother Edward she met Lord Mansfield's niece on a number of occasions, and that Boswell reported Johnson's view on another slavery case, *Knight* v. *Wedderburn*, as follows: "No man is by nature the property of another. The defendant is therefore by nature free!"

Slaves have masters but cannot truly be said to have a country, since they are neither protected by its laws nor accorded those rights which belong to freeborn citizens. That this was true in England of women is a point made by Wollstonecraft in *Maria*, where the heroine has no redress in "the laws of her country—if women have a country." Austen, not doubting that even such an unpromising feminist as Fanny Price "speaks the tongue that Shakespeare spoke" and, apart, no doubt, from a small difference about Adam and Eve, holds "the faith and morals . . . which Milton held," assumes that enlightened readers will know that she has the same "titles manifold" to British freedom as anyone else. She assures us that the soil at Mansfield is good, especially at the parsonage, and she makes a great point of the wholesomeness of English air, which is frequently associated with health and liberty. At Sotherton, with its prisonlike atmosphere, all the young people share "one impulse, one wish for air and liberty." Fanny's need for fresh English air is stressed again and again, often in ironic contexts. After berating her for not accepting Crawford, Sir Thomas tells her to get some exercise outside, where "the air will do her good," and Henry Crawford says of her, that she "requires constant air and exercise . . . ought never to be long banished from the free air and liberty of the country." Of course, he means the countryside, but does not Austen expect the intelligent, enlightened reader to see a bit further?

Finally, we come to *Lovers' Vows*. It has been thought that, because this play had been attacked in anti-Jacobin circles, Austen's choice of it must be taken as a sign of her reactionary political viewpoint. However, it is quite directly associated with the main feminist themes of this novel. For a start, as its title shows, it is about the sentimental treatment of lovers' promises and is used to point the contrast between the lack of commitment involved in such promises as Baron Wildenhaim made to Agatha before he seduced her, or as Crawford half-makes to Maria, and the binding nature of the marriage contract. *Lovers' Vows* is a work in that tradition of Rousseauist literature which Mary Wollstonecraft objected to as rendering women objects of pity bordering on contempt. Agatha, having endured twenty years of poverty and humiliation because Wildenhaim broke his promise to her, makes a grateful, tearful acceptance of his eventual offer (following their son's intervention) to marry him. The curtain comes down on the following tableau:

> Anhalt leads on Agatha—The Baron runs and clasps her in his arms—supported by him, she sinks on a chair which Amelia places in the middle of the stage —The Baron kneels by her side, holding her hand.
> BARON. Agatha, Agatha, do you know this voice?
> AGATHA. Wildenhaim.
> BARON. Can you forgive me?
> AGATHA. I forgive you (*embracing him*).
> FREDERICK (*as he enters*). I hear the voice of my mother!—Ha! mother! father!

(Frederick throws himself on his knees by the other side of his mother—She clasps him in her arms.—Amelia is placed on the side of her father attentively viewing Agatha—Anhalt stands on the side of Frederick with his hands gratefully raised to Heaven.) The curtain slowly drops.

Anyone who doubts whether Jane Austen laughed at this had better reread *Love and Freindship*, but we have good reason to suppose that she thought the "happy ending" morally objectionable, not because the baron was letting his class down by marrying a village girl, nor the honor of his sex by marrying the girl who had lost her virtue through his agency, but because Agatha should have had more respect for herself, and too much contempt for him to have him at any price.

Mansfield Park remains a puzzling novel, partly, I think, because Jane Austen enjoyed puzzles and thought it both amusing and instructive to solve them. She asks a great deal of her readers—sound moral attitudes, derived from rational reflection upon experience; quick-wittedness and ingenuity in making connections; and a belief in the wholesomeness of laughter. It would be possible to make of *Mansfield Park* something like a piece of feminist propaganda, in which regulated hatred predominates, but it would be false. It is a great comic novel, regulated by the sane laughter of an impish, rational feminist. The pricelessness of Miss Price is its heart—and head.

Chronology

1660   Daniel Foe (later Defoe) born in London to James Foe, tallow chandler, and Alice Foe. He is educated at the Reverend James Fisher's school at Dorking, Surrey, and then at the Reverend Charles Morton's school at Newington Green. (As a Dissenter, he cannot attend Oxford or Cambridge, but receives a comparable education.) Works not very successfully as import-export merchant.

1667   Jonathan Swift born in Dublin to English parents: Jonathan Swift (deceased) and Abigail Swift. He is educated at Kilkenny School and then at Trinity College, Dublin, where he receives a B.A. and works toward an M.A. (studies interrupted by the Glorious Revolution). Is ordained as a priest in the Church of Ireland, and, after living many years in England, eventually becomes Dean of St. Patrick's Cathedral, Dublin.

1685–92   Defoe publishes political tracts.

1689   Samuel Richardson born in Mackworth, Derbyshire, to Samuel Richardson, tradesman, and Elizabeth Richardson. He may have been educated at the Merchant Taylors' School; claims he received "only common School-learning" before being apprenticed to a printer. Later owns his own successful printing business.

1697   Defoe publishes *An Essay upon Projects*.

1701   Defoe publishes *The True-Born Englishman: A Satyr*.

1703   Defoe publishes *The Shortest Way with the Dissenters: or, Proposals For The Establishment of the Church*, for which he is arrested; publishes *Hymn To The Pillory* and an authorized edition of his collected works.

1704   Swift publishes *A Tale of a Tub* and *The Battle of the Books*.

1704–13   Defoe writes and edits *The Review*.

1707	Henry Fielding born at Sharpham Park, Glastonbury, to an army officer. He attends Eton College and studies letters at the University of Leyden and law at the Middle Temple (London), where he is called to the bar. After working in the theater for several years, becomes magistrate for Westminster (London).
1708	Swift publishes *Argument against Abolishing Christianity* and *Letter concerning the Sacramental Test.*
1708–9	Swift publishes *The Bickerstaff Papers.*
1709	Samuel Johnson born in Lichfield, Staffordshire, to a bookseller. He is educated at Lichfield Grammar School and Pembroke College, Oxford, from which he does not take a degree. He works briefly as a schoolmaster, opens his own (unsuccessful) school, and then earns his living by his pen. Swift publishes "Description of a City Shower" and "Description of the Morning" in the newly founded *Tatler.*
1710–13	Swift writes *Journal to Stella.*
1713	Laurence Sterne born in Clonmel, Ireland, to Roger Sterne, an infantryman (and grandson to the Archbishop of York), and Agnes Sterne. He is educated in Yorkshire, then on scholarship at Jesus College, Cambridge, where he receives a B.A. and an M.A. Enters the clergy on graduation and becomes a prebendary of York cathedral.
1715	Defoe publishes *The Family Instructor*, a conduct manual.
1718	Defoe publishes second volume of *The Family Instructor.*
1719	Defoe publishes *The Life and Strange Surprizing Adventures of Robinson Crusoe of York, Mariner* and *The Further Adventures of Robinson Crusoe.*
1720	Defoe publishes *The Life, Adventures, and Pyracies of the Famous Captain Singleton.*
1721	Tobias Smollett born in Cardross, Dumbartonshire, Scotland, to Archibald Smollett, a disinherited laird, and Barbara Smollett. He is educated at Dumbarton Grammar School and attends Glasgow University, where he is apprenticed to a surgeon. Becomes ship's surgeon in the navy and later sets up as a surgeon in London.
1722	Defoe publishes *The Fortunes and Misfortunes of the Famous Moll Flanders, A Journal of the Plague Year,* and *The History and Remarkable Life of the Truly Honourable Col. Jacque.*
1724	Defoe publishes *The Fortunate Mistress: Or . . . Roxana.*
1724–25	Swift publishes the *Drapier's Letters.*
1724–26	Defoe publishes *A Tour Thro' the Whole Island of Great Britain* in three volumes.
1725	Defoe publishes *The Complete English Tradesman* and pirate and criminal "lives."

1726   Swift publishes *Gulliver's Travels.*
        Defoe publishes *The Political History of the Devil.*

1727   Defoe publishes *Conjugal Lewdness (A Treatise Concerning the Use and Abuse of the Marriage Bed), An Essay on the History and Reality of Apparitions, A New Family Instructor,* and a second volume of *The Complete English Tradesman.*

1728   Defoe publishes "Augusta Triumphans: Or, The Way To Make London the most flourishing City in the Universe" and *A Plan of the English Commerce.*
        Fielding's play *Love in Several Masques* produced; he publishes *The Masquerade.*

1729   Swift publishes *A Modest Proposal* and *The Grand Question Debate.*

ca. 1730   Oliver Goldsmith born in Ireland to the Reverend Charles Goldsmith, an Anglo-Irish clergyman. He is educated at schools in Ireland and at Trinity College, Dublin, where he receives a B.A. After studying for the church, considering law, and studying medicine, he works at various medical and literary jobs.

1730–37   Fielding works as playwright.

1731   Defoe dies in London; buried in Bunhill Fields.
        Fielding publishes his play *The Tragedy of Tragedies: Or, The Life and Death of Tom Thumb the Great,* produced the year before.

1734   Richardson publishes *The Apprentice's Vade Mecum.*

1737   The Licensing Act is passed, largely in response to Fielding's play *The Historical Register for 1736;* Fielding can no longer publish or produce plays.

1738   Swift publishes *A Complete Collection of Polite and Ingenious Conversation.*
        Johnson begins writing for the *Gentleman's Magazine* and publishes "London."

1739   Swift publishes *Verses on the Death of Dr Swift.*
        Richardson publishes an adaptation of L'Estrange's *Aesop's Fables.*
        Smollett tries without success to produce a play, *The Regicide.*

1739–41   Fielding edits *The Champion.*

1739–43   Johnson writes miscellaneous journalistic pieces and biographical sketches.

1740   Richardson publishes *Pamela: Or, Virtue Rewarded.*

1741   Fielding publishes *An apology for the life of Mrs Shamela Andrews,* a satire on Richardson's *Pamela.*
        Richardson publishes *Familiar Letters on Important Occasions,* a collection of model letters.

1741–42   Sterne publishes articles in support of Sir Robert Walpole.

1742	Richardson publishes *Pamela in her Exalted Condition*. Fielding publishes *The Adventures of Joseph Andrews and his Friend, Mr Abraham Adams*.
1743	Fielding publishes three volumes of *Miscellanies*, which include *A Journey from this World to the Next* and *The Life and Death of Jonathan Wild the Great*. Sterne publishes "The Unknown World, Verses occasioned by hearing a Pass-Bell" in the *Gentleman's Magazine*.
1744	Johnson publishes *The Life of Mr Richard Savage*.
1745	Swift dies in Dublin following a long, degenerative illness; buried in St. Patrick's Cathedral. Fielding writes pamphlets for the Hanoverian cause: *A Serious Address to the People of Great Britain, The History of the Present Rebellion, A Dialogue between the Devil, the Pope, and the Pretender*. Johnson publishes proposals for an edition of Shakespeare.
1745–46	Fielding edits *The True Patriot*.
1746	Smollett publishes *Advice*, a verse satire, and "The Tears of Scotland."
1747	Fielding edits *The Jacobite's Journal*. Johnson publishes a plan for his dictionary. Smollett publishes *Reproof*, a sequel to *Advice*.
1747–48	Richardson publishes *Clarissa: Or, The History of a Young Lady*.
1748	Smollett publishes *The Adventures of Roderick Random*.
1749	Fielding publishes *The History of Tom Jones, a Foundling*. Johnson publishes *The Vanity of Human Wishes*; David Garrick produces Johnson's *Irene*. Smollett publishes *The Regicide* (still unproduced).
1750–52	Johnson founds and contributes largely to *The Rambler*.
1751	Fielding publishes *Amelia*. Smollett publishes *The Adventures of Peregrine Pickle*.
1752	Frances Burney born at King's Lynn to Dr. Charles Burney, organist, musical historian, and composer, and Esther Burney. She receives no formal schooling, but grows up in London in the midst of her father's Blue Stocking Circle. After several of her books have been successfully published, she becomes Second Keeper of the Robes to Queen Charlotte, until an illness allows her to resign. Marries a poor French emigré, General Alexandre d'Arblay; they live on the proceeds of her writings. Fielding edits *The Covent-Garden Journal*. Smollett publishes an *Essay on the External Use of Water* and is believed to be the author of the attack on Fielding, *A Faithful Narrative . . . of Habbakkuk Hilding*.
1753	Fielding publishes *Proposal for making effective provision for the Poor*. Smollett publishes *The Adventures of Ferdinand Count Fathom*.

1753–54   Richardson publishes *The History of Sir Charles Grandison.*
           Johnson contributes to *The Adventurer.*

1754   Fielding revises *Jonathan Wild.* Fielding dies in Lisbon, Portugal,
           and is buried there.

1755   Johnson publishes *A Dictionary of the English Language.*
           Richardson publishes *A Collection of the Moral and Instructive Sen-
           timents . . . in the Histories of Pamela, Clarissa, and Sir Charles
           Grandison.*
           Fielding's *Journal of a Voyage to Lisbon* published posthumously.
           Smollett publishes a translation of *Don Quixote.*

1756   Smollett cofounds and edits the *Critical Review;* publishes the seven-
           volume anthology, *A Compendium of Authentic and Entertaining Voy-
           ages,* of which he is general editor and one of the authors.
           Johnson publishes further proposals for an edition of Shakespeare.

1756–57   Goldsmith contributes articles to the *Monthly Review.*

1757–58   Smollett publishes the *Complete History of England.*

1758   Smollett publishes a revised edition of *Peregrine Pickle.*
           Goldsmith publishes a translation of Jean Martheile's *Memoires d'un
           Protestant.*

1758–60   Johnson contributes the *Idler* series of essays to the *Universal
           Chronicle.*

1759   Johnson publishes *Rasselas, Prince of Abyssinia.*
           Sterne publishes *A Political Romance* (later retitled *The History of a
           Good Warm Watch Coat*), which is burned by church authorities.
           Publishes the first two volumes of *The Life and Opinions of Tristram
           Shandy.*
           Goldsmith contributes to the *Critical Review;* publishes *An Enquiry
           into the Present State of Polite Learning in Europe;* publishes briefly a
           periodical, *The Bee.*

1759–65   Smollett helps edit *The Modern Part of the Universal History.*

1760   Sterne publishes *The Sermons of Mr Yorick.*
           Smollett publishes *The Life and Adventures of Sir Laucelot Greaves.*

1760–61   Goldsmith writes "Chinese Letters" for the *Public Ledger;* they are
           published in 1762 as *The Citizen of the World: Or, Letters from a Chinese
           Philosopher, Residing in London, to his Friends in the East.*

1760–63   Smollett and Goldsmith found and edit the *British Magazine, or
           Monthly Repository.*

1761   Richardson dies at Parson's Green near London.
           Sterne publishes volumes three through six of *Tristram Shandy.*
           Smollett begins publication of *The Works of . . . Voltaire,* of which
           he is coeditor.

1762   Goldsmith publishes *The Life of Richard Nash, of Bath, Esq.*

1764   Goldsmith publishes *An History of England in a series of letters from a nobleman to his son* and *The Traveller: Or, A Prospect of Society.* Horace Walpole publishes *The Castle of Otranto.*

1765   Johnson publishes his edition of Shakespeare.
Sterne publishes volumes seven and eight of *Tristram Shandy.*
Smollett publishes fifth and final volume of the *Continuation of the Complete History of England.*

1766   Goldsmith publishes *The Vicar of Wakefield* and an anthology of poems for young ladies.
Sterne publishes volumes three and four of *The Sermons of Mr Yorick* (volumes five through seven will be published posthumously by his daughter, Lydia).
Smollett publishes *Travels through France and Italy.*

1767   Sterne publishes volume nine of *Tristram Shandy;* writes the *Journal to Eliza* (published in 1904); publishes *A Sentimental Journey.*
Goldsmith publishes *The Beauties of English Poesie.*

1768   Goldsmith's *The Good Natur'd Man* is produced and published.
Sterne dies in London; after his death, his body is offered by res-urrectionists for anatomy lectures at Cambridge, where it is rec-ognized and reburied.

1768–69 Smollett publishes the eight-volume *Present State of All Nations.*

1769   *Adventures of an Atom* published, attributed to Smollett.
Goldsmith publishes *The Roman History.*

1770   Goldsmith publishes *The Deserted Village.*

1771   Smollett publishes *The Expedition of Humphry Clinker.* Smollett dies at his home near Leghorn, Italy, where he is buried.

1773   Goldsmith's *She Stoops to Conquer* performed at Covent Garden; he publishes the first volume of a *Grecian History.*
Smollett's *Ode to Independence* published posthumously.

1774   Goldsmith dies in London, is buried in Westminster Abbey. *Re-taliation,* the eight-volume *An History of the Earth and Animated Na-ture,* and *Grecian History* all published posthumously in this year.

1775   Jane Austen born in Steventon, Hampshire, to George Austen, a prosperous parish clergyman, and Cassandra Austen. She is ed-ucated by the widow of a Principal of Brasenose College and then attends the Abbey School at Reading; her formal education ends at the age of nine. She spends the rest of her life with her family, chiefly her mother and sister; the three women eventually settle in a house on the estate of Austen's brother.
Johnson publishes *A Journey to the Western Islands of Scotland.*

1776   Smollett's translation of Fenelon's *Adventures of Telemachus* pub-lished posthumously.

1778   Burney publishes *Evelina: Or, The History of a Young Lady's Entrance Into the World.*

1779–81	Johnson publishes *The Lives of the English Poets.*
1782	Burney publishes *Cecilia: Or, Memoirs of an Heiress.*
1784	Johnson dies at his home and is buried in Westminster Abbey.
1786	William Beckford publishes *Vathek, an Arabian Tale.*
1789	Mrs. Ann Radcliffe publishes *The Castles of Athlin and Dunbayne.*
1790	Burney writes *Edwy and Elgiva, Hubert de Vere, The Siege of Pevensey,* and *Elberta,* tragedies. Radcliffe publishes *A Sicilian Romance.*
1791	Radcliffe publishes *The Romance of the Forest.*
1793–95	Austen writes *Lady Susan* and begins *Elinor and Marianne,* which will become *Sense and Sensibility.*
1794	Radcliffe publishes *The Mysteries of Udolpho.*
1796	Burney publishes *Camilla: Or, A Picture of Youth.* Matthew Gregory Lewis publishes *The Monk,* the popularity of which gives him the soubriquet of "Monk" Lewis.
1796–97	Austen tries unsuccessfully to publish *First Impressions,* an early version of *Pride and Prejudice.*
1797	Radcliffe publishes *The Italian.*
1798–1801	Burney writes three comedies, which are not published: *Love and Fashion, The Woman Hater,* and *A Busy Day.*
1803	Austen sells a novel entitled *Susan* (later published, probably in revised form, as *Northanger Abbey*), but it is not published.
1803–5	Austen writes ten chapters of *The Watsons;* she never completes it.
1811	Austen publishes *Sense and Sensibility.*
1813	Austen publishes *Pride and Prejudice.*
1814	Austen publishes *Mansfield Park.* Burney publishes *The Wanderer.*
1815	Austen publishes *Emma;* begins writing *Persuasion.*
1817	Austen begins *Sanditon;* before she completes it, she dies in Winchester; is buried in Winchester Cathedral.
1818	Austen's *Persuasion* and *Northanger Abbey* published posthumously.
1832	Burney publishes *The Memoirs of Dr. Burney.*
1840	Burney dies in London.
1843–46	Burney's *Diary and Letters . . . 1778–1840* published posthumously.
1889	Burney's *Early Diary 1768–1778* published posthumously.

Contributors

HAROLD BLOOM, Sterling Professor of the Humanities at Yale University, is the author of *The Anxiety of Influence, Poetry and Repression,* and many other volumes of literary criticism. His forthcoming study, *Freud: Transference and Authority,* attempts a full-scale reading of all of Freud's major writings. A MacArthur Prize Fellow, he is general editor of five series of literary criticism published by Chelsea House. During 1987–88, he was appointed Charles Eliot Norton Professor of Poetry at Harvard University.

MARTIN PRICE is Sterling Professor of English at Yale University. His books include *Swift's Rhetorical Art: A Study in Structure and Meaning, To the Palace of Wisdom: Studies in Order and Energy from Dryden to Blake,* and a number of edited volumes on literature of the seventeenth, eighteenth, and nineteenth centuries.

PATRICK REILLY is Senior Lecturer in English at the University of Glasgow and the author of *Jonathan Swift: The Brave Desponder.*

RALPH W. RADER teaches in the Department of English at the University of California, Berkeley. His most recent book is *Tennyson's Maud: The Biographical Genesis.*

JOHN J. RICHETTI is Professor of English at Rutgers University. His works include *Defoe's Narratives: Situations and Structures, Philosophical Writing: Locke, Berkeley, Hume,* and *Popular Fiction before Richardson: Narrative Patterns 1700–1739.*

MARY POOVEY, Professor of English at Rutgers University, is the author of *The Proper Lady and the Woman Writer: Ideology as Style in the Works of Mary Wollstonecraft, Mary Shelley, and Jane Austen* and other studies of eighteenth-century fiction.

MARK SPILKA is Professor of English and Comparative Literature at Brown University. He has written extensively on modern fiction—his major books include *The Love Ethic of D. H. Lawrence* and *Dickens and Kafka: A Mutual Interpretation*—as well as on eighteenth-century literature.

IAN WATT is Professor of English at Stanford University. His books include *The Rise of the Novel, Conrad in the Nineteenth Century*, and the forthcoming *Gothic and Comic: Two Variations on the Realistic Tradition*.

W. K. WIMSATT was Professor of English at Yale University. Best known for his works written in collaboration with Monroe Beardsley, *The Verbal Icon* and *Hateful Contraries*, his achievement as a scholar of Johnson and Boswell is formidable.

LILIAN R. FURST is Professor of Comparative Literature at the University of Texas, Dallas. She has written numerous works on Romanticism, such as *Fictions of Romantic Irony* and *Romanticism in Perspective: A Comparative Study of Aspects of the Romantic Movements in England, France, and Germany*.

LEOPOLD DAMROSCH, JR., is Professor of English at the University of Maryland. His most recent book is *God's Plot and Man's Stories: Studies in the Fictional Imagination from Milton to Fielding;* his other publications include *Samuel Johnson and the Tragic Sense* and *Symbol and Truth in Blake's Myth*.

PHILIP STEVICK, Professor of English at Temple University, is the author of *The Chapter in Fiction: Theories of Narrative Division*, as well as works on modern fiction.

JERRY C. BEASLEY is Professor of English at the University of Delaware. His books include *Novels of the 1740s*, and he is coeditor of the plays of Frances Sheridan.

JAMES H. LEHMANN received an M. Phil. in English and a J.D. from Yale University before his early death in 1982.

EDWARD W. COPELAND has written on Fanny Burney, Jane Austen, and Samuel Richardson.

HOWARD ANDERSON is Professor of English at Michigan State University. He has written numerous articles on eighteenth-century literature and edited *Tristram Shandy*.

MARGARET KIRKHAM teaches at Bristol Polytechnic and is the author of *Jane Austen: Feminism and Fiction*.

Bibliography

GENERAL

Armstrong, Nancy. "The Rise of Feminine Authority in the Novel." *Novel* 15 (1982): 127–45.

Backsheider, Paula R., ed. *Probability, Time, and Space in Eighteenth-Century Literature.* New York: AMS, 1979.

Battestin, Martin C. *The Providence of Wit: Aspects of Form in Augustan Literature and the Arts.* Princeton: Princeton University Press, 1974.

Bogel, Fredric V. *Literature and Insubstantiality in Later Eighteenth-Century England.* Princeton: Princeton University Press, 1984.

Braudy, Leo. "The Form of the Sentimental Novel." *Novel* 7 (1973): 5–13.

———. *Narrative Form in History and Fiction: Hume, Fielding, and Gibbon.* Princeton: Princeton University Press, 1970.

Champion, Larry S., ed. *Quick Springs of Sense: Studies in the Eighteenth Century.* Athens: University of Georgia Press, 1974.

Damrosch, Leopold, Jr. *God's Plot and Man's Stories: Studies in the Fictional Imagination from Milton to Fielding.* Chicago: University of Chicago Press, 1985.

Duncan, Jeffrey. "The Rural Ideal in Eighteenth-Century Fiction." *Studies in English Literature 1500–1900* 83 (1968): 517–35.

Ermarth, Elizabeth Deeds. *Realism and Consensus in the English Novel.* Princeton: Princeton University Press, 1983.

Folkenflik, Robert, ed. *The English Hero 1660–1800.* Newark: University of Delaware Press, 1982.

Ford, Ford Madox. *The English Novel from the Earliest Days to the Death of Conrad.* Darby, Pa.: Arden Library, 1979.

Fussell, Paul. *The Rhetorical World of Augustan Humanism: Ethics and Imagery from Swift to Burke.* Oxford: Oxford University Press, 1965.

Hilles, Frederick W., ed. *The Age of Johnson: Essays Presented to Chauncey Brewster Tinker.* New Haven: Yale University Press, 1949.

Hilson, J. C., M. M. B. Jones, and J. R. Watson, eds. *Augustan Worlds: New Essays on Eighteenth-Century Literature.* New York: Barnes & Noble, 1978.

Iser, Wolfgang. *The Implied Reader: Patterns of Communication in Prose from Bunyan to Beckett.* Baltimore: The Johns Hopkins University Press, 1974.

Karl, Frederick R. *The Adversary Literature: The English Novel in the Eighteenth Century: A Study in Genre*. New York: Farrar, Straus & Giroux, 1974.

Kay, Donald, ed. *A Provision of Human Nature: Essays on Fielding and Others in Honor of Miriam Austin Locke*. University: University of Alabama Press, 1977.

Kearn, Jean B. "The Fallen Woman from the Perspective of Five Early Eighteenth-Century Women Novelists." *Studies in Eighteenth-Century Culture* 10 (1981): 457–68.

Leranbaum, Miriam. " 'Mistresses of Orthodoxy': Education in the Lives and Writings of Late Eighteenth-Century English Women Writers." *Proceedings of the American Philosophical Society* 121 (1977): 281–301.

Mack, Maynard, and Ian Gregor, eds. *Imagined Worlds: Essays on Some English Novels and Novelists in Honour of John Butt*. London: Methuen, 1968.

McKee, John B. *Literary Irony and the Literary Audience: Studies in the Victimization of the Reader in Augustan Fiction*. Amsterdam: Rodopi, 1974.

Miller, Nancy K. *The Heroine's Text: Readings in the French and English Novel, 1722–1782*. New York: Columbia University Press, 1980.

Novak, Maximillian. *English Literature in the Age of Disguise*. Berkeley and Los Angeles: University of California Press, 1977.

Paulson, Ronald. *Satire and the Novel in Eighteenth-Century England*. New Haven: Yale University Press, 1967.

Perry, Ruth. *Women, Letters, and the Novel*. New York: AMS, 1980.

Preston, John. *The Created Self: The Reader's Role in Eighteenth-Century Fiction*. London: Heinemann, 1970.

Price, Martin. *To the Palace of Wisdom: Studies in Order and Energy from Dryden to Blake*. Carbondale: Southern Illinois University Press, 1964.

Rawson, C. J. *Order from Confusion Sprung: Studies in Eighteenth-Century Literature from Swift to Cowper*. London: Allen & Unwin, 1985.

Richetti, John J. *Popular Fiction before Richardson*. Oxford: Oxford University Press, 1969.

Rivers, Isabel, ed. *Books and Their Readers in Eighteenth-Century England*. Leicester: Leicester University Press, 1982.

Rogers, Katharine M. "Dreams and Nightmares: Male Characters in the Feminine Novel of the Eighteenth Century." *Women and Literature* 2 (1982): 9–24.

Rothstein, Eric. *Systems of Order and Inquiry in Later Eighteenth-Century Fiction*. Berkeley and Los Angeles: University of California Press, 1975.

Spacks, Patricia Meyer. *Gossip*. New York: Knopf, 1985.

———. *Imagining a Self: Autobiography and Novel in Eighteenth-Century England*. Cambridge: Harvard University Press, 1976.

Spearman, Diana. *The Novel and Society*. London: Routledge & Kegan Paul, 1966.

Van Ghent, Dorothy. *The English Novel: Form and Function*. New York: Holt, Rinehart & Winston, 1953.

Watt, Ian. *The Rise of the Novel: Studies in Defoe, Richardson, and Fielding*. Berkeley and Los Angeles: University of California Press, 1957.

GOTHIC

Auerbach, Nina. *Woman and the Demon: The Life of a Victorian Myth*. Cambridge: Harvard University Press, 1982.

Durant, David. "Ann Radcliffe and the Conservative Gothic." *Studies in English Literature 1500–1900* 22 (1982): 519–30.

Fleenor, Juliann E., ed. *The Female Gothic*. Montreal: Eden, 1983.

Hart, Francis Russell. "The Experience of Character in the English Gothic Novel."

In *Experience in the Novel,* edited by Roy Harvey Pearce. New York: Columbia University Press, 1968.

Hogle, Jerrold E. "The Restless Labyrinth: Cryptonomy in the Gothic Novel." *Arizona Quarterly* 36 (1980): 330–58.

Kahane, Claire. "Gothic Mirrors and Feminine Identity." *The Centennial Review* 24 (1980): 43–64.

Liu, Alan. "Toward a Theory of Common Sense: Beckford's *Vathek* and Johnson's *Rasselas.*" *Texas Studies in Literature and Language* 26 (1984): 183–217.

DANIEL DEFOE

Allen, Walter. *The English Novel: A Short Critical History.* London: Phoenix House, 1954.

Alter, Robert. *Rogue's Progress: Studies in the Picaresque Novel.* Cambridge: Harvard University Press, 1964.

Anderson, Hans H., "The Paradox of Trade and Morality in Defoe." *Modern Philology* 39 (1941): 23–46.

Boardman, Michael M. *Defoe and the Uses of Narrative.* New Brunswick, N. J.: Rutgers University Press, 1983.

Braudy, Leo. "Daniel Defoe and the Anxieties of Autobiography." *Genre* 6 (1973): 76–97.

Brown, Homer. "The Displaced Self in the Novels of Daniel Defoe." *ELH* 38 (1971): 562–90.

Burke, John J., Jr. "Observing the Observer in Historical Fictions by Defoe." *Philological Quarterly* 61 (1982): 13–32.

Butler, Mary. "The Effect of the Narrator's Rhetorical Uncertainty on the Fiction of *Robinson Crusoe.*" *Studies in the Novel* 15 (1983): 77–90.

Castle, Terry. " 'Any, Who Knew My Disease': A Psychosexual Pattern in Defoe's *Roxana.*" *ELH* 46 (1979): 81–96.

Damrosch, Leopold, Jr. "Defoe as Ambiguous Impersonator." *Modern Philology* 71 (1972–73): 153–59.

Durant, David. "Roxana's Fictions." *Studies in the Novel* 13 (1981): 225–36.

Flanders, W. Austin. "Defoe's *Journal of the Plague Year* and the Modern Urban Experience." *The Centennial Review* 16 (1972): 328–48.

Hunter, J. Paul. *The Reluctant Pilgrim: Defoe's Emblematic Method and Quest for Form in* Robinson Crusoe. Baltimore: The Johns Hopkins University Press, 1966.

James, E. Anthony. *Daniel Defoe's Many Voices: A Rhetorical Study of Prose Style and Literary Method.* Amsterdam: Rodopi, 1972.

Joyce, James. "Daniel Defoe." *Buffalo Studies* 1, no. 1 (1964): 7–25.

Koonce, Howard L. "Moll's Muddle: Defoe's Use of Irony in *Moll Flanders.*" *ELH* 30 (1963): 377–94.

Lannert, Gustav. "An Investigation of the Language of *Robinson Crusoe.*" Uppsala, Sweden: Uppsala University, 1910.

McNeil, David. "*A Journal of the Plague Year*: Defoe and Claustrophobia." *The Southern Review* 16 (1983): 374–85.

Maddox, James H., Jr. "Interpreter Crusoe." *ELH* 51 (1984): 33–52.

———. "On Defoe's *Roxana.*" *ELH* 51 (1984): 669–91.

Mason, Shirlene. *Daniel Defoe and the Status of Women.* St. Alban's, Vt.: Eden Press Women's Publications, 1978.

Novak, Maximillian. "Defoe and the Disordered City." *PMLA* 92 (1977): 241–52.

———. *Defoe and the Nature of Man.* New York: Oxford University Press, 1963.

———. *The Economics and the Fiction of Daniel Defoe.* Berkeley and Los Angeles: University of California Press, 1962.

Peck, H. Daniel. *"Robinson Crusoe:* The Moral Geography of Limitation.*" The Journal of Narrative Technique* 3 (1973): 20–31.

Richetti, John J. *Defoe's Narratives: Situations and Strategies.* Oxford: Oxford University Press, 1975.

Rogers, Pat. "Literary Art in Defoe's *Tour:* The Rhetoric of Growth and Decay." *Eighteenth-Century Studies* 6 (1972–73): 153–85.

———. *Robinson Crusoe.* London: Allen & Unwin, 1979.

Schonhorn, Manuel. "Defoe's *Journal of the Plague Year:* Topography and Intention." *The Review of English Studies* 19 (1968): 387–402.

Spacks, Patricia Meyer. "The Soul's Imaginings: Daniel Defoe, William Cowper." *PMLA* 91 (1976): 420–35.

Starr, George A. *Defoe and Casuistry.* Princeton: Princeton University Press, 1971.

———. *Defoe and Spiritual Autobiography.* Princeton: Princeton University Press, 1965.

———. "Defoe's Prose Style: 1. The Language of Interpretation." *Modern Philology* 71 (1974): 277–94.

Sutherland, James R. *Daniel Defoe: A Critical Study.* New York: Houghton Mifflin, 1971.

Swados, Harvey. *"Robinson Crusoe:* The Man Alone." In *Twelve Original Essays on Great English Novels,* edited by Charles Shapiro. Detroit: Wayne State University Press, 1960.

Tillyard, E. M. W. *The Epic Strain in the English Novel.* Fair Lawn, N. J.: Essential Books, 1958.

Weinstein, Arnold. *The Fictions of the Self: 1500–1800.* Princeton: Princeton University Press, 1981.

Zimmerman, Everett. *Defoe and the Novel.* Berkeley and Los Angeles: University of California Press, 1975.

JONATHAN SWIFT

Bentman, Raymond. "Satiric Structure and Tone in the Conclusion of *Gulliver's Travels." Studies in English Literature 1500–1900* 11 (1971): 535–48.

Bogel, Fredric V. "Irony, Inference, and Critical Uncertainty." *Yale Review* 69 (1980): 503–19.

Champion, Larry S. "Gulliver's Voyages: The Framing Events as a Guide to Interpretation." *Texas Studies in Literature and Language* 10 (1969): 529–36.

Clifford, Gay. *The Transformations of Allegory.* London: Routledge & Kegan Paul, 1974.

Gill, James E. "Beast over Man: Theriophilic Paradox in Gulliver's 'Voyage to the Country of the Houyhnhnms.' " *Studies in Philology* 67 (1970): 532–49.

Greenacre, Phyllis. *Swift and Carroll: A Psychoanalytic Study of Two Lives.* New York: International Universities Press, 1955.

Gubar, Susan. "The Female Monster in Augustan Satire." *Signs: Journal of Women in Culture and Society* 3, no. 2 (1977): 380–94.

Jeffares, A. Norman, ed. *Swift: Modern Judgements.* London: Macmillan, 1969.

McManmon, John J. "The Problem of a Religious Interpretation of Gulliver's Fourth Voyage." *Journal of the History of Ideas* 27 (1966): 59–72.

Mezciems, Jenny. "The Unity of Swift's 'Voyage to Laputa': Structure as Meaning in Utopian Fiction." *The Modern Language Review* 72 (1977): 1–21.

Murry, John Middleton. *Jonathan Swift: A Critical Biography.* New York: Noonday Press, 1955.

Orwell, George. "Politics vs. Literature: An Examination of *Gulliver's Travels."* In

The Collected Essays, Journalism, and Letters of George Orwell. London: Secker & Warburg, 1968.

Paulson, Ronald. *The Fictions of Satire*. Baltimore: The Johns Hopkins University Press, 1967.

Pollak, Ellen. "Comment on Susan Gubar's 'The Female Monster in Augustan Satire' (vol. 3, no. 2)." *Signs: Journal of Women in Culture and Society* 3, no. 3 (1978): 729–32.

Probyn, Clive T., ed. *The Art of Jonathan Swift*. New York: Barnes & Noble; London: Vision Press, 1978.

———, ed. *Jonathan Swift: The Contemporary Background*. Manchester: Manchester University Press, 1978.

Quilligan, Maureen. *The Language of Allegory*. Ithaca: Cornell University Press, 1979.

Quinlan, Maurice. "Swift's Use of Literalization as a Rhetorical Device." *PMLA* 82 (1967): 516–21.

Quintana, Ricardo. *The Mind and Art of Jonathan Swift*. New York: Oxford University Press, 1936.

Rawson, Claude, ed. *The Character of Swift's Satire: A Revised Focus*. Newark: University of Delaware Press, 1983.

Reed, Gail S. "Dr. Greenacre and Captain Gulliver: Notes on Conventions of Interpretation and Reading." *Literature and Psychology* 26 (1976): 185–90.

Reilly, Patrick. *Jonathan Swift: The Brave Desponder*. Carbondale: Southern Illinois University Press, 1982.

Steele, Peter. *Jonathan Swift: Preacher and Jester*. Oxford: Oxford University Press, 1978.

Williams, Kathleen. *Jonathan Swift and the Age of Compromise*. Lawrence: University of Kansas Press, 1958.

SAMUEL RICHARDSON

Brophy, Elizabeth Bergen. *Samuel Richardson: The Triumph of Craft*. Knoxville: University of Tennessee Press, 1974.

Brownstein, Rachel. *Becoming a Heroine: Reading about Women in Novels*. New York: Viking-Penguin, 1982.

Castle, Terry. "P/B: *Pamela* as Sexual Fiction." *Studies in English Literature 1500–1900* 22 (1982): 469–89.

Cohan, Steven M. "*Clarissa* and the Individualization of Character." *ELH* 43 (1976): 163–83.

Copeland, Edward W. "Allegory and Analogy in *Clarisssa*: The 'Plan' and 'No-Plan.' " *ELH* 39 (1972): 254–65.

———. "Samuel Richardson and Naive Allegory: Some Beauties of the Mixed Metaphor." *Novel* 4 (1971): 231–39.

Donaldson, Ian. "Fielding, Richardson, and the Ends of the Novel." *Essays in Criticism* 32 (1982): 26–47.

Doody, Margaret Anne. *A Natural Passion: A Study of the Novels of Samuel Richardson*. Oxford: Oxford University Press, 1974.

Downs, B. W. *Richardson*. London: G. Routledge & Sons, 1928.

Dussinger, John A. "Conscience and the Pattern of Christian Perfection in *Clarissa*." *PMLA* 81 (1966): 236–45.

———. "Richardson's Tragic Muse." *Philological Quarterly* 46 (1967): 18–33.

Eagleton, Terry. *The Rape of Clarissa: Writing, Sexuality, and Class Struggle in Richardson*. Minneapolis: University of Minnesota Press, 1983.

Erickson, Robert A. "Mother Jewkes, Pamela, and the Midwives." *ELH* 43 (1976): 500–516.

Flynn, Carol Houlihan. *Samuel Richardson: A Man of Letters*. Princeton: Princeton University Press, 1982.

Folkenflik, Robert. "A Room of Pamela's Own." *ELH* 39 (1972): 585–96.

Goldknopf, David. *The Life of the Novel*. Chicago: University of Chicago Press, 1972.

Indyk, Ivor. "Interpretative Relevance, and Richardson's *Pamela*." *The Southern Review* 16 (1983): 31–43.

Kinkead-Weekes, Mark. *Samuel Richardson: Dramatic Novelist*. London: Methuen, 1973.

Larson, Kerry. " 'Naming the Writer': Exposure, Authority, and Desire in *Pamela*." *Criticism* 23 (1981): 126–40.

MacAndrew, Elizabeth. "Courtly-Genteel or Moral-Didactic?—A Response to Carey McIntosh." In *Studies in Eighteenth-Century Culture*, vol. 4, edited by Harold E. Paglianro. Madison: University of Wisconsin Press, 1975.

McKillop, Alan D. *Samuel Richardson: Printer and Novelist*. Hamden, Conn.: Shoestring Press, 1960.

Maddox, James, Jr. "Lovelace and the World of Ressentiment in *Clarissa*." *Texas Studies in Literature and Language* 24 (1982): 271–92.

Park, William. "*Clarissa* as Tragedy." *Studies in English Literature 1500–1900* 16 (1976): 461–71.

———. "Fielding and Richardson." *PMLA* 81 (1966): 381–88.

Paulson, Ronald, ed. *Fielding: A Collection of Critical Essays*. Englewood Cliffs, N. J.: Prentice-Hall, 1962.

Roussel, Roy. "Reflections on the Letter: The Reconciliation of Distance and Presence in *Pamela*." *ELH* 41 (1974): 375–99.

Schmitz, Robert M. "Death and Colonel Morden in *Clarissa*." *The South Atlantic Quarterly* 69 (1970): 346–53.

Traugott, John. "*Clarissa*'s Richardson: An Essay to Find the Reader." In *English Literature in the Age of Disguise*, edited by Maximillian Novak. Berkeley and Los Angeles: University of California Press, 1977.

Warner, William Beatty. *Reading* Clarissa: *The Struggle of Interpretation*. New Haven: Yale University Press, 1979.

HENRY FIELDING

Alkon, Paul K. *Defoe and Fictional Time*. Athens: University of Georgia Press, 1979.

Alter, Robert. *Fielding and the Nature of the Novel*. Cambridge: Harvard University Press, 1968.

Anderson, Howard. "Answers to the Author of *Clarissa*: Theme and Narrative Technique in *Tom Jones* and *Tristram Shandy*." *Philological Quarterly* 51 (1972): 859–73.

Baker, Sheridan. "Henry Fielding and the Cliché." *Criticism* 1 (1959): 354–61.

Battestin, Martin C. "Fielding, *Amelia*, and the 'Constitution' of England." In *Literature and Society: The Lawrence Henry Gipson Symposium 1978*, edited by Jan Fergus. Bethlehem, Pa.: The Lawrence Henry Gipson Institute, 1981.

———. "Fielding and 'Master Punch' in Panton Street." *Philological Quarterly* 45 (1966): 191–208.

———. "Fielding's Definition of Wisdom: Some Functions of Ambiguity and Emblem in *Tom Jones*. *ELH* 35 (1968): 188–217.

———. "*Tom Jones* and 'His Egyptian Majesty': Fielding's Parable of Good." *PMLA* 82 (1967): 68–79.

———, ed. *Twentieth Century Interpretations of* Tom Jones: *A Collection of Critical Essays*. Englewood Cliffs, N. J.: Prentice-Hall, 1968.

Bloch, Tuvia. "*Amelia* and Booth's Doctrine of the Passions." *Studies in English Literature 1500–1900* 13 (1973): 461–73.

Booth, Wayne C. *The Rhetoric of Fiction*. Chicago: University of Chicago Press, 1961.

Coley, William. "The Background of Fielding's Laughter." *ELH* 26 (1959): 229–52.

Coolidge, John. "Fielding and the 'Conservation of Character.' " *Modern Philology* 57 (1960): 245–59.

Crane, R. S. "The Plot of *Tom Jones*." *Journal of General Education* 4 (1950): 112–30.

Digeon, Aurelien. *The Novels of Fielding*. London: George Routledge & Sons, 1925.

Ehrenpreis, Irvin. *Fielding: Tom Jones*. London: Edward Arnold, 1964.

———. "Fielding's Use of Fiction: The Autonomy of *Joseph Andrews*." In *Twelve Original Essays on Great English Novels*, edited by Charles Shapiro. Detroit: Wayne State University Press, 1960.

Ek, Grete. "Glory, Jest, and Riddle: The Masque of Tom Jones in London." *English Studies* 60 (1979): 113–58.

Empson, William. "Tom Jones." *The Kenyon Review* 20 (1958): 217–49.

Evans, James E. "Fielding, *The Whole Duty of Man*, *Shamela*, and *Joseph Andrews*." *Philological Quarterly* 6 (1982): 212–19.

———. "The World According to Paul: Comedy and Theology in *Joseph Andrews*." *Ariel* 15, no. 1 (January 1984): 45–56.

Goldberg, Homer. *The Art of* Joseph Andrews. Chicago: University of Chicago Press, 1969.

———. "The Interpolated Stories in *Joseph Andrews* or 'The History of the World in General' Satirically Revised." *Modern Philology* 63 (1966): 295–310.

Golden, Morris. *Fielding's Moral Psychology*. Amherst: University of Massachussetts Press, 1966.

Goldknopf, David. "The Failure of Plot in *Tom Jones*." *Criticism* 11 (1969): 262–74.

Harrison, Bernard. *Henry Fielding's* Tom Jones: *The Novelist as Moral Philosopher*. London: Sussex University Press, 1975.

Hassall, Anthony. "Fielding and the Novel as Parody." *The Southern Review* 13 (1980): 30–40.

Hatfield, Glenn W. *Henry Fielding and the Language of Irony*. Chicago: University of Chicago Press, 1968.

Hunter, J. Paul. *Occasional Form: Henry Fielding and the Chain of Circumstance*. Baltimore: The Johns Hopkins University Press, 1975.

Hutchens, Eleanor Newman. *Irony in* Tom Jones. University: University of Alabama Press, 1965.

Kermode, Frank. "Richardson and Fielding." *Cambridge Journal* 4 (1950): 106–14.

LePage, Peter. "The Prison and the Dark Beauty of *Amelia*." *Criticism* 9 (1967): 337–54.

McCrea, Brian. *Henry Fielding and the Politics of Mid-Eighteenth-Century England*. Athens: University of Georgia Press, 1981.

———. "Rewriting *Pamela*: Social Change and Religious Faith in *Joseph Andrews*." *Studies in the Novel* 16 (1984): 137–49.

———. "Romances, Newspapers, and the Style of Fielding's True History." *Studies in English Literature 1500–1900* 21 (1981): 471–80.

Mandel, Jerome. "The Man of the Hill and Mrs. Fitzpatrick: Character and Narrative Technique in *Tom Jones*." *Papers on Language and Literature* 5 (1969): 26–38.

Mendilow, A. A. *Time and the Novel*. New York: Humanities Press, 1972.

Miller, Henry Knight. "The 'Digressive' Tales in Fielding's *Tom Jones* and the Perspective of Romance." *Philological Quarterly* 54 (1975): 258–74.

———. *Essays on Fielding's "Miscellanies": A Commentary on Vol. I*. Princeton: Princeton University Press, 1961.

———. *Henry Fielding's* Tom Jones *and the Romance Tradition*. Victoria, B. C.: English Literary Studies, 1976.

Miller, Henry Knight, Eric Rothstein, and G. S. Rousseau, eds. *The Augustan Milieu: Essays Presented to Louis A. Landa*. Oxford: Oxford University Press, 1970.

Mulford, Carla. "Booth's Progress and the Resolution of *Amelia.*" *Studies in the Novel* 16 (1984): 20–31.

Murry, John Middleton. *Unprofessional Essays.* London: Jonathan Cape, 1956.

Oakman, Robert L. "The Character of the Hero: A Key to Fielding's *Amelia.*" *Studies in English Literature 1500–1900* 16 (1976): 473–90.

Park, William. "Fielding and Richardson." *PMLA* 81 (1966): 381–88.

———. "Models and Paradigms: *Joseph Andrews,* Hogarth's *Good Samaritan,* and Fenelon's *Telemaque.*" *MLN* 91 (1976): 1186–1207.

———. "The Pilgrimage and the Family: Structures in the Novels of Fielding and Smollett." In *Tobias Smollett: Bicentennial Essays Presented to Lewis M. Knapp,* edited by G. S. Rousseau and P.-G. Bouce. New York: Oxford University Press, 1971.

Paulson, Ronald, ed. *Fielding: A Collection of Critical Essays.* Englewood Cliffs, N. J.: Prentice-Hall, 1962.

Perl, Jeffrey. "Anagogic Surfaces: How to Read *Joseph Andrews.*" *Eighteenth Century* 22, no. 3 (1981): 249–70.

Rawson, C. J. *Fielding and the Augustan Ideal under Stress.* London: Routledge & Kegan Paul, 1972.

Ribble, Frederick G. "Aristotle and the 'Prudence' Theme of *Tom Jones.*" *Eighteenth-Century Studies* 15 (1981): 26–47.

———. "The Constitution of the Mind and the Concept of Emotion in Fielding's *Amelia.*" *Philological Quarterly* 56 (1977): 104–22.

Rogers, Pat. *Fielding: A Biography.* London: Paul Elek, 1979.

Sacks, Sheldon. *Fiction and the Shape of Belief: A Study of Henry Fielding, with Glances at Swift, Johnson, and Richardson.* Berkeley and Los Angeles: University of California Press, 1966.

Schonhorn, Manuel. "Fielding's Digressive-Parodic Artistry: *Tom Jones* and The Man of the Hill." *Texas Studies in Literature and Language* 10 (1968): 207–14.

———. "Fielding's Ecphrastic Moment: Tom Jones and His Egyptian Majesty." *Studies in Philology* 78 (1981): 305–23.

Spilka, Mark. "Fielding and the Epic Impulse." *Criticism* 11 (1969): 68–77.

Stevick, Philip. "On Fielding Talking." *College Literature* 1 (1974): 19–33.

Vopat, James B. "Narrative Technique in *Tom Jones:* The Balance of Art and Nature." *The Journal of Narrative Technique* 4 (1974): 144–54.

Weinbrot, Howard. "Chastity and Interpolation: Two Aspects of *Joseph Andrews.*" *Journal of English and Germanic Philology* 69 (1970): 14–31.

Wendt, Allan. "The Moral Allegory of *Jonathan Wild.*" *ELH* 24 (1957): 306–20.

———. "The Naked Virtue of *Amelia.*" *ELH* 27 (1960): 131–48.

Williams, Murial Brittain. *Marriage: Fielding's Mirror of Morality.* University: University of Alabama Press, 1973.

Wood, Carl. "*Shamela's* Subtle Satire: Fielding's Characterization of Mrs. Jewkes and Mrs. Jervis." *English Language Notes* 13, no. 4 (1976): 266–70.

Zirker, Marvin R., Jr. *Fielding's Social Pamphlets: A Study of "An Enquiry into the Causes of the Late Increase of Robbers" and "A Proposal for Making an Effectual Provision for the Poor."* Berkeley and Los Angeles: University of California Press, 1966.

SAMUEL JOHNSON

Alkon, Paul. *Samuel Johnson and Moral Discipline.* Evanston, Ill.: Northwestern University Press, 1967.

Bailey, John. *Dr. Johnson and His Circle.* Revised by L. F. Powell. Oxford: Oxford University Press, 1944.

Baker, Sheridan. "*Rasselas:* Psychological Irony and Romance." *Philological Quarterly* 45 (1966): 249–61.

Bate, Walter Jackson. *The Achievement of Samuel Johnson.* Oxford: Oxford University Press, 1955.

Bloom, Edward A. *Samuel Johnson in Grub Street.* Providence, R. I.: Brown University Press, 1957.

Bronson, Bertrand H. *Johnson Agonistes and Other Essays.* Cambridge: Cambridge University Press, 1946.

Chapin, Chester. *The Religious Thought of Samuel Johnson.* Ann Arbor: University of Michigan Press, 1968.

Clifford, James L. *Young Samuel Johnson.* New York: McGraw-Hill, 1955.

Damrosch, Leopold, Jr. *Samuel Johnson and the Tragic Sense.* Princeton: Princeton University Press, 1979.

Davis, Bertram. *Johnson before Boswell.* New Haven: Yale University Press, 1960.

Fussell, Paul. *Samuel Johnson and the Life of Writing.* New York: Harcourt Brace Jovanovich, 1971.

Greene, Donald J. *The Politics of Samuel Johnson.* New Haven: Yale University Press, 1957.

Hilles, Frederick W. "*Rasselas,* an 'Uninstructive Tale.' " In *Johnson, Boswell, and Their Circle: Essays Presented to Lawrence Fitzroy Powell,* edited by Mary Lascelles et al. Oxford: Oxford University Press, 1965.

————, ed. *New Light on Johnson.* New Haven: Yale University Press, 1959.

Hodgart, M. J. C. *Samuel Johnson.* London: Batsford, 1962.

Kenney, William. "Johnson's *Rasselas* after Two Centuries." *Boston University Studies in English* 3 (1957): 88–96.

Kolb, Gwin J. "The 'Paradise' in *Abyssinia* and the 'Happy Valley' in *Rasselas.*" *Modern Philology* 56 (1958): 10–16.

————. "The Structure of *Rasselas.*" *PMLA* 66 (1951): 698–717.

Leavis, F. R. *The Common Pursuit.* London: Chatto & Windus, 1952.

Leyburn, Ellen Douglas. " 'No Romantick Absurdities or Incredible Fictions': The Relation of Johnson's *Rasselas* to Lobo's *Voyage to Abyssinia.*" *PMLA* 70 (1955): 1059–67.

Lockhart, Donald M. " 'The Fourth Son of the Mighty Emperor': The Ethiopian Background of Johnson's *Rasselas.*" *PMLA* 78 (1963): 516–28.

Quinlan, Maurice. *Samuel Johnson: A Layman's Religion.* Madison: University of Wisconsin Press, 1963.

Sachs, Ariel. *Passionate Intelligence: Imagination and Reason in the Work of Samuel Johnson.* Baltimore: The Johns Hopkins University Press, 1967.

Tracy, Clarence F. " 'Democritus Arise!' A Study of Dr. Johnson's Humor." *Yale Review* 39 (1949): 305–10.

Turberville, A. S. *Johnson's England.* Oxford: Oxford University Press, 1933.

Vesterman, William. *The Stylistic Life of Samuel Johnson.* New Brunswick, N. J.: Rutgers University Press, 1977.

Voitle, Robert. *Samuel Johnson the Moralist.* Cambridge: Harvard University Press, 1961.

Wahba, Magdi, ed. *Bicentenary Essays on* Rasselas. Cairo: Cairo Studies in English (supplement), 1959.

Whitley, Alvin. "The Comedy of *Rasselas.*" *ELH* 23 (1956): 63–65.

Wimsatt, W. K. *The Prose Style of Samuel Johnson.* New Haven: Yale University Press, 1941.

LAURENCE STERNE

Alter, Robert. "*Tristram Shandy* and the Game of Love." *American Scholar* 37 (1968): 316–22.

Anderson, Howard. "Associationism and Wit in *Tristram Shandy.*" *Philological Quarterly* 48 (1969): 27–41.
———. "*Tristram Shandy* and the Reader's Imagination." *PMLA* 86 (1971): 966–73.
———. "A Version of Pastoral: Class and Society in *Tristram Shandy.*" *Studies in English Literature 1500–1900* 7 (1967): 509–29.
Baird, Theodore. "The Time-Scheme of *Tristram Shandy* and a Source." *PMLA* 51 (1936): 803–20.
Bakhtin, M. M. *The Dialogic Imagination.* Austin: University of Texas Press, 1981.
Banerjee, Chinmoy. "*Tristram Shandy* and the Association of Ideas." *Texas Studies in Literature and Language* 15 (1974): 693–706.
Booth, Wayne C. *The Rhetoric of Fiction.* Chicago: University of Chicago Press, 1961.
———. "The Self-Conscious Narrator in Comic Fiction before *Tristram Shandy.*" *PMLA* 67 (1952): 163–85.
Brissenden, R. F. *Virtue in Distress: Studies in the Novel of Sentiment from Richardson to Sade.* London: Macmillan, 1974.
Burckhardt, Sigurd. "*Tristram Shandy*'s Law of Gravity." *ELH* 28 (1961): 70–88.
Byrd, Max. *Tristram Shandy.* London: Allen & Unwin, 1985.
Cash, Arthur H., and John M. Stedmont, eds. *The Winged Skull: Papers from the Laurence Sterne Bicentenary Conference.* Kent, Ohio: Kent State University Press, 1971.
Clifford, James L., ed. *Eighteenth-Century English Literature: Modern Essays in Criticism.* New York: Oxford University Press, 1959.
Conrad, Peter. *Shandyism: The Character of Romantic Irony.* Oxford: Basil Blackwell, 1978.
Cruttwell, Patrick. "Makers and Persons." *The Hudson Review* 12 (1959–60): 487–507.
Davies, Richard A. "*Tristram Shandy*'s Eccentric Public Orator." *English Studies in Canada* 5 (1979): 154–66.
Dobrée, Bonamy, ed. *From Anne to Victoria: Essays by Various Hands.* London: Cassell, 1937.
Donaldson, Ian. "The Clockwork Novel: Three Notes on an Eighteenth-Century Analogy. *The Review of English Studies* 21 (February 1970): 14–22.
Donovan, Robert Alan. *The Shaping Vision: Imagination in the English Novel from Defoe to Dickens.* Ithaca: Cornell University Press, 1966.
Dowling, William C. "*Tristram Shandy*'s Phantom Audience." *Novel* 13 (1980): 284–95.
Dyson, A. E. *The Crazy Fabric: Essays in Irony.* 1965. Reprint. Salem, N.H.: Ayer, 1973.
———. "Sterne: The Novelist as Jester." *Critical Quarterly* 4 (1962): 309–20.
Farrell, William J. "Nature Versus Art as a Comic Pattern in *Tristram Shandy.*" *ELH* 30 (1963): 16–35.
Faurot, Ruth Marie. "Mrs. Shandy Observed." *Studies in English Literature 1500–1900* 10 (1970): 579–89.
Fluchère, Henri. *Laurence Sterne. From Tristram to Yorick: An Interpretation of* Tristram Shandy, translated by Barbara Bray. London: Oxford University Press, 1965.
Hartley, Lodwick. " ' 'Tis a Picture of Myself': The Author in *Tristram Shandy.*" *Southern Humanities Review* 4 (1970): 301–13.
Hunter, J. Paul. "Response as Reformation: *Tristram Shandy* and the Art of Interruption." *Novel* 4 (1971): 132–46.
Lamb, Jonathan. "The Comic Sublime and Sterne's Fiction." *ELH* 48 (1981): 110–43.
Lanham, Richard A. Tristram Shandy: *The Games of Pleasure.* Berkeley: University of California Press, 1973.
Macksey, Richard. " 'Alas, Poor Yorick': Sterne Thoughts." *MLN* 98 (1983): 1006–20.

McMaster, Juliet. "Experience to Expression: Thematic Character Contracts in *Tristram Shandy*." *Modern Language Quarterly* 32 (1971): 42–57.

Maskell, Duke. "Locke and Sterne, or Can Philosophy Influence Literature?" *Essays in Criticism* 23 (1973): 22–40.

Moglen, Helene. *The Philosophical Irony of Laurence Sterne*. Gainesville: University Presses of Florida, 1975.

Myer, Valerie Grosvenor, ed. *Laurence Sterne: Riddles and Mysteries*. New York: Barnes & Noble, 1984.

Nänny, Max. "Similarity and Continuity in *Tristram Shandy*." *English Studies* 60 (1979): 422–35.

New, Melvyn. *Laurence Sterne as Satirist: A Reading of* Tristram Shandy. Gainesville: University Presses of Florida, 1969.

Parish, Charles. "A Table of Contents for *Tristram Shandy*." *College English* 22 (1960): 143–50.

Park, William. "*Tristram Shandy* and the New 'Novel of Sensibility.' " *Studies in the Novel* 6 (1974): 268–79.

Piper, William Bowman. *Laurence Sterne*. New York: Twayne, 1965.

Rosenblum, Michael. "The Sermon, the King of Bohemia, and the Art of Interpolation in *Tristram Shandy*." *Studies in Philology* 75 (1978): 472–91.

———. "Shandean Geometry and the Challenge of Contingency." *Novel* 10 (1977): 237–47.

Sherbo, Arthur. *Studies in the Eighteenth-Century English Novel*. East Lansing: Michigan State University Press, 1969.

Stedmont, John M. *The Comic Art of Laurence Sterne*. Toronto: University of Toronto Press, 1967.

Swearingen, James E. *Reflexivity in* Tristram Shandy: *An Essay in Phenomenological Criticism*. New Haven: Yale University Press, 1977.

Traugott, John. *Tristram Shandy's World: Sterne's Philosophical Rhetoric*. Berkeley: University of California Press, 1954.

———, ed. *Laurence Sterne: A Collection of Critical Essays*. Englewood Cliffs, N. J.: Prentice-Hall, 1968.

Weales, Gerald. "Tristram Shandy's Anti-Book." In *Twelve Original Essays on Great English Novels*, edited by Charles Shapiro, 43–68. Detroit: Wayne State University Press, 1960.

Woolf, Virginia. *The Second Common Reader*. London: Hogarth Press, 1932.

Wright, Andrew. "The Artifice of Failure in *Tristram Shandy*." *Novel* 2 (1969): 213–20.

TOBIAS SMOLLETT

Batten, Charles, Jr. "*Humphry Clinker* and Eighteenth-Century Travel Literature." *Genre* 7 (1974): 392–408.

Beasley, Jerry C. *Novels of the 1740s*. Athens: University of Georgia Press, 1982.

———. "Smollett's Novels: *Ferdinand Count Fathom* for the Defense." *Papers on Language and Literature* 20 (1984): 165–84.

Bloch, Tuvia. "Smollett's Quest for Form." *Modern Philology* 65 (1967): 103–13.

Bold, Alan, ed. *Smollett: Author of the First Distinction*. London: Vision, 1982.

Bouce, Paul-Gabriel. *The Novels of Tobias Smollett*. London: Longman, 1976.

———. " 'Snakes in Iceland': The 'Picaresque' in Smollett's *Roderick Random* (1748)." *Caliban* 22 (1983): 29–39.

Bourgeois, Susan. "The Domestication of the Launcelot Legend in Smollett's *Sir Launcelot Greaves*." *Publications of the Missouri Philological Association* 8 (1983): 45–50.

Bunn, James. "Signs of Randomness in *Roderick Random.*" *Eighteenth-Century Studies* 14 (1981): 452–69.

Campbell Ross, Ian. "Language, Structure, and Vision in Smollett's *Roderick Random.*" *Etudes Anglaises* 31 (1978): 52–63.

Day, Robert Adams. "Sex, Scatology, Smollett." In *Sexuality in Eighteenth-Century Britain*, edited by Paul-Gabriel Bouce. Manchester: Manchester University Press, 1982.

———. "*Ut Pictura Poesis:* Smollett, Satire, and the Graphic Arts." *Studies in Eighteenth-Century Culture* 10 (1981): 297–312.

Evans, David. "*Humphry Clinker:* Smollett's Tempered Augustanism." *Criticism* 9 (1967): 257–74.

Folkenflik, Robert. "Self and Society: Comic Union in *Humphry Clinker.*" *Philological Quarterly* 53 (1974): 195–204.

Goldberg, M. A. *Smollett and the Scottish School.* Albuquerque: University of New Mexico Press, 1959.

Grant, Damian. *Tobias Smollett: A Study in Style.* Manchester: Manchester University Press, 1977.

Knapp, Lewis. *Tobias Smollett: Doctor of Men and Manners.* Princeton: Princeton University Press, 1949.

Miles, Peter. "Platonic Topography and the Locations of *Humphry Clinker.*" *Trivium* 16 (1981): 81–98.

———. "A Semi-Mental Journey: Structure and Illusion in Smollett's *Travels.*" *Prose Studies* 5, no. 1 (1982): 43–60.

New, Melvyn. " 'The Grease of God': The Form of Eighteenth-Century English Fiction." *PMLA* 91 (1976): 235–44.

Orwell, George. "Smollett." In *Collected Essays, Journalism, and Letters III.* Harmondsworth, England: Penguin, 1970.

Park, William. "Fathers and Sons—*Humphry Clinker.*" *Literature and Psychology* 16, nos. 3–4 (1966): 166–74.

Paulson, Ronald. "Satire in the Early Novels of Smollett." *Journal of English and Germanic Philology* 59 (1960): 381–402.

Preston, Thomas. "Smollett and the Benevolent Misanthrope Type." *PMLA* 79 (1964): 51–57.

Price, John Vladimir. *Tobias Smollett: The Expedition of Humphry Clinker.* London: E. Arnold, 1973.

Pritchett, V. S. *The Living Novel.* 1947. New York: Random House, 1964.

Punter, David. "Smollett and the Logic of Domination." *Literature and History* 1 (1975): 60–83.

Reid, B. L. "Smollett's Healing Journey." *Virginia Quarterly Review* 41 (1965): 549–70.

Rogers, Pat. *The Augustan Vision.* New York: Barnes & Noble, 1974.

Ross, Angus. "The Show of Violence in Smollett's Novels." *Yearbook of English Studies* 77 (1972): 118–29.

Rothstein, Eric. "Scotophilia and *Humphry Clinker:* The Politics of Beggary, Bugs, and Buttocks." *University of Toronto Quarterly* 52 (1982): 63–78.

Rousseau, G. S. *Tobias Smollet: Essays of Two Decades.* Edinburgh: T. & T. Clark, 1982.

Rousseau, G. S., and P.-G. Bouce, eds. *Tobias Smollett: Bicentennial Essays Presented to Lewis M. Knapp.* New York: Oxford University Press, 1971.

Sekora, John. *Luxury: The Concept in Western Thought, Eden to Smollett.* Baltimore: The Johns Hopkins University Press, 1977.

Spector, Robert Donald. *Tobias George Smollett.* New York: Twayne, 1968.

Stevick, Philip. "Stylistic Energy in the Early Smollett." *Studies in Philology* 64 (1967): 712–19.

Strauss, Albrecht P. "On Smollett's Language: A Paragraph in *Ferdinand Count Fathom.*" In *Style in Prose Fiction: English Institute Essays 1958,* edited by Harold C. Martin. New York: Columbia University Press, 1959.

Warner, John. "The Interpolated Narrations in the Fiction of Fielding and Smollett: An Epistemological View." *Studies in the Novel* 5 (1973): 271–83.

OLIVER GOLDSMITH

Backman, Sven. *This Singular Tale: A Study of* The Vicar of Wakefield *and Its Literary Background.* Lund, Sweden: CWK Gleerup, 1971.

Bligh, John. "Neglected Aspects of *The Vicar of Wakefield.*" *Dalhousie Review* 56 (1976): 103–11.

Dahl, Curtis. "Patterns of Disguise in *The Vicar of Wakefield.*" *ELH* 25 (1958): 90–104.

Duncan, Jeffrey. "The Rural Ideal in Eighteenth-Century Fiction." *Studies in English Literature 1500–1900* 8 (1968): 517–35.

Durant, David. *"The Vicar of Wakefield* and the Sentimental Novel." *Studies in English Literature 1500–1900* 17 (1977): 477–91.

Emslie, Macdonald. *Goldsmith:* The Vicar of Wakefield. London: Edward Arnold, 1963.

Ferguson, O. W. "Dr. Primrose and Goldsmith's Clerical Ideal." *Philological Quarterly* 54 (1975): 322–32.

———. "Goldsmith." *The South Atlantic Quarterly* 66 (1967): 465–72.

———. "Goldsmith as Ironist." *Studies in Philology* 81 (1984): 212–28.

Friedman, Arthur. "Aspects of Sentimentalism in Eighteenth-Century Literature." In *The Augustan Age: Essays Presented to Louis A. Landa,* edited by Henry Miller, Eric Rothstein, and G. S. Rousseau. Oxford: Oxford University Press, 1970.

Ginger, John. *The Notable Man: The Life and Times of Oliver Goldsmith.* London: Hamish Hamilton, 1977.

Golden, Morris. "Goldsmith, *The Vicar of Wakefield,* and the Periodicals." *Journal of English and Germanic Philology* 76 (1977): 525–36.

Green, Mary Elizabeth. "Oliver Goldsmith and the Wisdom of the World." *Studies in Philology* 77 (1980): 202–12.

Helgerson, Richard. "The Two Worlds of Oliver Goldsmith." *Studies in English Literature 1500–1900* 13 (1973): 516–34.

Hopkins, Robert H. *The True Genius of Oliver Goldsmith.* Baltimore: The Johns Hopkins University Press, 1969.

Kirk, Clara. *Oliver Goldsmith.* New York: Twayne, 1967.

McCracken, David. "Goldsmith and the 'Natural Revolution of Things.' " *Journal of English and Germanic Philology* 78 (1979): 33–48.

May, James. "Goldsmith's Theory of Composition: 'My heart dictates the whole.' " *Papers on Language and Literature* 15 (1979): 418–21.

Orwell, George. *"The Vicar of Wakefield."* In *Collected Essays, Journalism, and Letters of George Orwell.* New York: Harcourt, Brace & World, 1968.

Quintana, Ricardo. *Oliver Goldsmith: A Georgian Study.* New York: Macmillan, 1967.

———. *"The Vicar of Wakefield:* The Problem of the Critical Approach." *Modern Philology* 71 (1973): 59–65.

Rousseau, G. S., ed. *Goldsmith: The Critical Heritage.* London: Routledge & Kegan Paul, 1974.

Swarbrick, Andrew, ed. *The Art of Oliver Goldsmith.* London: Vision, 1984.

Wibberly, Leonard. *The Good-Natured Man: A Portrait of Oliver Goldsmith.* New York: William Morrow, 1979.

Woolf, Virginia. "Oliver Goldsmith." In *The Captain's Death Bed and Other Essays.* New York: Harcourt Brace Jovanovich, 1973.

Yearling, Elizabeth. "The Good-Natured Heroes of Cumberland, Goldsmith, and Sheridan." *The Modern Language Review* 67 (1972): 490–500.

FANNY BURNEY

Bloom, Lillian, and Edward Bloom. "Fanny Burney's Novels: The Retreat from Wonder." *Novel* 12 (1979): 215–35.
Cutting, Rose Marie. "A Wreath for Fanny Burney's Last Novel: *The Wanderer's* Contribution to Women's Studies." *CLA Journal* 20 (1976): 57–67.
Hemlow, Joyce. *The History of Fanny Burney.* Oxford: Oxford University Press, 1958.
Mews, Hazel. *Frail Vessels: Woman's Role in Women's Novels from Fanny Burney to George Eliot.* London: Athlone, 1969.
Olshin, Toby. " 'To Whom I Most Belong': The Role of Family in *Evelina.*" *Eighteenth-Century Life* 6, no. 1 (1980): 29–42.
Parke, Catherine. "Vision and Revision: A Model for Reading the Eighteenth-Century Novel of Education." *Eighteenth-Century Studies* 16 (1982–83): 162–74.
Rogers, Katharine M. "Fanny Burney: The Private Self and the Published Self." *International Journal of Women's Studies* 7 (1984): 110–17.
Spacks, Patricia Meyer. "Women and the City." In *Johnson and His Age*, edited by James Engell. Cambridge: Harvard University Press, 1984.

JANE AUSTEN

Babb, Howard. *Jane Austen's Novels: The Fabric of Dialogue.* Columbus: Ohio State University Press, 1962.
Bradbrook, Frank. *Jane Austen and Her Predecessors.* Cambridge: Cambridge University Press, 1967.
Brown, Julia Prewitt. *Jane Austen's Novels: Social Change and Literary Form.* Cambridge: Harvard University Press, 1979.
Brown, Lloyd. *Bits of Ivory: Narrative Techniques in Jane Austen's Fiction.* Baton Rouge: Louisiana State University Press, 1973.
Bush, Douglas. *Jane Austen.* New York: Macmillan, 1975.
Butler, Marilyn. *Jane Austen and the War of Ideas.* Oxford: Oxford University Press, 1975.
Chapman, R. W. *Jane Austen: Facts and Problems.* Oxford: Oxford University Press, 1948.
Devlin, David. *Jane Austen and Education.* New York: Barnes & Noble, 1975.
Duckworth, Alistair. *The Improvement of the Estate: A Study of Jane Austen's Novels.* Baltimore: The Johns Hopkins University Press, 1971.
Fergus, Jan. *Jane Austen and the Didactic Novel:* Northanger Abbey, Sense and Sensibility, *and* Pride and Prejudice. Totowa, N. J.: Barnes & Noble, 1983.
Gilbert, Sandra M., and Susan Gubar. *The Madwoman in the Attic: The Woman Writer and the Nineteenth-Century Literary Imagination.* New Haven: Yale University Press, 1979.
Halperin, John. *The Life of Jane Austen.* Sussex: Harvester, 1984.
———, ed. *Jane Austen: Bicentenary Essays.* Cambridge: Cambridge University Press, 1975.
Hardy, Barbara. *A Reading of Jane Austen.* New York: New York University Press, 1976.
Lascelles, Mary. *Jane Austen and Her Art.* Oxford: Oxford University Press, 1939.

Litz, A. Walton. *Jane Austen: A Study of Her Artistic Development.* New York: Oxford University Press, 1965.

McMaster, Juliet. *Jane Austen on Love.* Victoria, B. C.: University of Victoria Press, 1978.

———, ed. *Jane Austen's Achievement.* London: Macmillan, 1976.

Monaghan, David. *Jane Austen: Structure and Social Vision.* London: Macmillan, 1980.

———, ed. *Jane Austen in a Social Context.* London: Macmillan, 1981.

Morgan, Susan. *In the Meantime: Character and Perception in Jane Austen's Fiction.* Chicago: University of Chicago Press, 1980.

Nardin, Jane. *Those Elegant Decorums: The Concept of Propriety in Jane Austen's Novels.* Albany: State University of New York Press, 1973.

Newton, Judith Lowder. *Women, Power, and Subversion: Social Strategies in British Fiction, 1778–1860.* Athens: University of Georgia Press, 1981.

Odmark, John. *An Understanding of Jane Austen's Novels.* Oxford: Basil Blackwell, 1981.

Poovey, Mary. *The Proper Lady and the Woman Writer: Ideology as Style in the Works of Mary Wollstonecraft, Mary Shelley, and Jane Austen.* Chicago: University of Chicago Press, 1984.

Rees, Joan. *Jane Austen: Woman and Writer.* New York: St. Martin's, 1976.

Roberts, Warren. *Jane Austen and the French Revolution.* New York: St. Martin's, 1979.

Roth, Barry, and Joel Weinsheimer, eds. *An Annotated Bibliography of Jane Austen Studies, 1952–1972.* Charlottesville: University Press of Virginia, 1973.

Southam, B. C. *Jane Austen.* Essex: Longman Group, 1975.

———, ed. *Critical Essays on Jane Austen.* London: Routledge & Kegan Paul, 1968.

———, ed. *Jane Austen: The Critical Heritage.* London: Routledge & Kegan Paul, 1968.

Steeves, Harrison. *Before Jane Austen.* New York: Holt, Rinehart & Winston, 1965.

Tave, Stuart M. *Some Words of Jane Austen.* Chicago: University of Chicago Press, 1973.

Todd, Janet, ed. *Jane Austen: New Perspectives* (Women and Literature, n.s., vol. 3). New York: Holmes & Meier, 1983.

Acknowledgments

"The Divided Heart: Defoe's Novels" (originally entitled "The Divided Heart") by Martin Price from *To the Palace of Wisdom: Studies in Order and Energy from Dryden to Blake* by Martin Price, © 1964 by Martin Price. Reprinted by permission of the author and Southern Illinois University Press.

"*Gulliver's Travels*: The Displaced Person" (originally entitled "The Displaced Person") by Patrick Reilly from *Jonathan Swift: The Brave Desponder* by Patrick Reilly, © 1982 by Patrick Reilly. Reprinted by permission of the author and Manchester University Press.

"Defoe, Richardson, and the Concept of Form in the Novel" (originally entitled "Defoe, Richardson, Joyce, and the Concept of Form in the Novel") by Ralph W. Rader from *Autobiography, Biography, and the Novel: Papers Read at a Clark Library Seminar* (13 May 1972), coauthored by William Matthews, © 1973 by the William Andrews Clark Memorial Library. Reprinted by permission of the author and the William Andrews Clark Library, UCLA, Los Angeles, California.

"Richardson's Dramatic Art in *Clarissa*" by John J. Richetti from *British Theatre and the Other Arts, 1660–1800*, edited by Shirley Strum Kenny, © 1984 by Associated University Presses, Inc. Reprinted by permission of the publisher, Associated University Presses, Inc.

"Journeys from this World to the Next: The Providential Promise in *Clarissa* and *Tom Jones*" by Mary Poovey from *ELH* 43, no. 3 (Fall 1976), © 1976 by The Johns Hopkins University Press, Baltimore/London. Reprinted by permission of the Johns Hopkins University Press.

"Comic Resolution in Fielding's *Joseph Andrews*" by Mark Spilka from *College English* 15, no. 1 (October 1953), © 1953 by the National Council of Teachers of English. Reprinted by permission of the publisher.

"Fielding as Novelist: *Tom Jones*" by Ian Watt from *The Rise of the Novel: Studies in Defoe, Richardson and Fielding* by Ian Watt, © 1957 by Ian Watt. Reprinted by permission of the University of California Press and Chatto & Windus Ltd.

"In Praise of *Rasselas*: Four Notes (Converging)" by W. K. Wimsatt from *Imagined Worlds: Essays on Some English Novels and Novelists in Honour of John Butt*, edited by Maynard Mack and Ian Gregor, © 1968 by Methuen & Co., Ltd. Reprinted by permission.

"Fictions of Romantic Irony: *Tristram Shandy*" (originally entitled "Laurence Sterne: *Tristram Shandy, 1760–67*") by Lilian R. Furst from *Fictions of Romantic Irony* by Lilian R. Furst, © 1984 by Lilian R. Furst. Reprinted by permission of Harvard University Press, Cambridge, Massachusetts, and Macmillan Press Ltd., London and Basingstoke.

"A Digression on *Tristram Shandy*" (originally entitled "*Tom Jones* and the Farewell to Providential Fiction") by Leopold Damrosch, Jr., from *God's Plot and Man's Stories: Studies in the Fictional Imagination from Milton to Fielding* by Leopold Damrosch, Jr., © 1985 by the University of Chicago. Reprinted by permission of the University of Chicago Press.

"Smollett's Picaresque Games" by Philip Stevick from *Tobias Smollett: Bicentennial Essays Presented to Lewis M. Knapp*, edited by G. S. Rousseau and P.-G. Bouce, © 1971 by Oxford University Press. Reprinted by permission.

"Richardson, Fielding, and Smollett: Private Experience as Public History" (originally entitled "Fiction as Contemporary History") by Jerry C. Beasley from *Novels of the 1740s* by Jerry C. Beasley, © 1982 by the University of Georgia Press. Reprinted by permission of the University of Georgia Press.

"*The Vicar of Wakefield*: Goldsmith's Sublime, Oriental Job" by James H. Lehmann from *ELH* 46, no. 1 (Spring 1979), © 1979 by The Johns Hopkins University Press, Baltimore/London. Reprinted by permission of the Johns Hopkins University Press.

"Money in the Novels of Fanny Burney" by Edward W. Copeland from *Studies in the Novel* 8, no. 1 (Spring 1976), © 1976 by North Texas State University. Reprinted by permission.

"Gothic Heroes in the Novels of Walpole, Lewis, and Radcliffe" (originally entitled "Gothic Heroes") by Howard Anderson from *The English Hero, 1660–1800*, edited by Robert Folkenflik, © 1982 by Associated University Presses, Inc. Reprinted by permission.

"Feminist Irony and the Priceless Heroine of *Mansfield Park*" by Margaret

Kirkham from *Jane Austen: New Perspectives* (Women and Literature, n.s., vol. 3), edited by Janet Todd, © 1983 by Holmes & Meier Publishers, Inc. Reprinted by permission of the publisher, Holmes & Meier Publishers, Inc., 30 Irving Place, New York, New York.

Index